DISCOVERING CHEMISTRY YOU NEED TO KNOW

KENDALL/HUNT

CHEMISTRY

$C_3H_6O_5 + 3 NaOH$

DISCOVERING CHEMISTRY YOU NEED TO KNOW

Kendall Hunt
publishing company

Kelly Deters

X80038027

CONTENTS

Preface xvi

To the Student xviii

Chapter 1   Scientists' Tools 1

Section 1.1: Doing Science 6
There's more to science than experimentation 7
Two types of experiments..7
Variables and constants 8
Predictions and hypotheses...8
Designing procedures 9
Gathering data 9
Drawing conclusions—Theories and laws 11
Communicating findings 11
You as a scientist..11

Section 1.2: Observations and Measurements 13
Taking observations 14
Gathering data 14
Uncertainty in measurement and choosing the right tool.............15
Relative error..15
Number of decimal places to record 16

Section 1.3: Designing Your Own Labs 18
Identifying the purpose, problem, or question.............................18
Gathering background information..18
Designing the results, calculations, and data table 19
Writing the procedure 19
Determining the materials needed and writing safety concerns ...19
Making changes to prewritten procedures...................................20
Discussing results 20

Section 1.4: Converting Units 23
Dimensional analysis 23
Dimensional analysis steps...24
Metric conversions 25
Help with metric prefixes 25
Volume units 25
Converting with multiple steps 25

Section 1.5: Significant Digits 27
Rules for counting significant digits 27

CONTENTS

Performing calculations with significant digits 28
Rules for math with significant digits 29
Section 1.6: Scientific Notation 30
Rules for using scientific notation 30
Summary 32
Review 33

Chapter 2   Antacids

Antacids 34

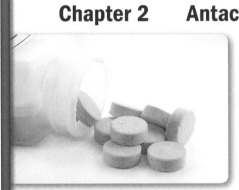

Section 2.1: Types of Matter 38
Classifying pure substances...38
Classifying mixtures 38
Section 2.2: Naming Chemicals 41
Writing the names of ionic compounds 41
Writing molecular compound names..46
Molecules with common names...47
Writing element names...47
Section 2.3: Writing Chemical Formulas 48
Writing ionic compound formulas 48
Molecular compounds 50
Writing diatomic element formulas 51
**Section 2.4: Defining, Naming, and Writing Acids
and Bases** 51
Naming acids 52
Writing acid formulas 52
Bases...54
Section 2.5: Characteristics of Acids and Bases 56
Strength versus concentration of acids and bases..............................57
pH scale 58
Measuring pH 59
Section 2.6: Chemical Reactions 59
Examples of chemical equations..59
Parts of a chemical equation 60
Double replacement and neutralization reactions...............................61
Section 2.7: Balancing Chemical Reactions 63
Law of conservation of mass/matter..64
Balancing chemical equations 64
Section 2.8: Speeding Up Chemical Reactions 67
Collision theory..68

CONTENTS

Catalysts speed up reactions 71

Summary 74

Review 75

Chapter 3   Airbags 78

Section 3.1: States of Matter 82

Properties of three states of matter 82

Changes in state 83

What's between the molecules? 84

Section 3.2: Properties of Matter 85

Physical and chemical properties 85

Intensive and extensive properties 85

Section 3.3: Density 87

Density units 88

Density graphs 88

Floating and layers 89

Section 3.4: Changes in Matter 92

Physical changes 94

Chemical changes 94

Common misconceptions concerning changes 94

Section 3.5: Gas Behavior 95

Gases exert pressure 95

Changes in gases result in changes in pressure 96

Kinetic molecular theory 97

Real versus ideal gases 97

Diffusion and effusion 98

Section 3.6: Counting Molecules 100

The mole 100

Atomic and molecular masses 102

Molecular mass is used to convert between moles and grams 103

Section 3.7: Gas Laws 105

Converting units of pressure 107

Temperature units used when working with gas laws 108

Avogadro's gas law 108

Charles' gas law 108

Boyle's gas law 109

Combined gas law 109

Ideal gas law 110

CONTENTS

Choosing the appropriate law.. 110

Standard temperature and pressure (STP)............................. 110

Summary 116

Review 117

Chapter 4   Glowing Things 120

Section 4.1: Development of Atomic Theory 124

Dalton's atomic theory 124

Discovering the fundamental particles of the atom................ 125

Refining the atomic theory further 126

Modern atomic theory.. 127

Section 4.2: Atomic Structure 128

Protons in the atom.. 128

Mass number and neutrons in the atom 128

Isotopes—Atoms of the same element can be different 131

Section 4.3: Electron Structure 134

Electron levels, subshells, and orbitals.................................. 135

Showing electron configurations... 137

Section 4.4: Periodic Table 139

The modern periodic table.. 140

Electron configurations and the periodic table 141

Periodic table as a map for electron configurations............... 142

Section 4.5: Periodicity 144

Atomic radius... 145

Ionization energy.. 146

Electron affinity 146

Ion radius... 147

Section 4.6: Light 148

Wave properties 148

Energies and colors of visible light.. 149

Section 4.7: Light and Matter 150

Light interaction with matter.. 151

Quantization of photons and absorption by electrons 152

Step-wise relaxation 153

Measuring light's interaction with matter 154

Ways of producing light.. 155

Summary 158

Review 159

Chapter 5   Soap

Chapter 5   Soap 160

Section 5.1: Types of Bonds 164
Bonding between metals and nonmetals 164
Bonding between nonmetals 165
Bonding between metals 165
Characteristics of different types of bonds 166
Melting and boiling points 166
Solubility in water 166
Conduction of electricity 166

Section 5.2: Drawing Molecules 170
Determining valence electrons 170
Placing the electrons around the symbol 170
Lewis dot structures for ionic compounds 171
Lewis structures for covalent compounds 173
Lone pairs 174
Lewis structures that can be written more than one way 176
Lewis dot structures for polyatomic ions 178
Exceptions to the octet rule 179

Section 5.3: Molecules in 3D 181
Geometry of covalent bonding 182
Distortion of angles with lone pairs 182
Ionic compound structures 182

Section 5.4: Polarity of Molecules 183
Electronegativity and the periodic table 183
Electronegativity and polarity of bonds 184
Polarity of bonds and polarity of molecules 185

Section 5.5: Intermolecular Forces 186
Intramolecular versus intermolecular forces 186
London dispersion forces 186
Dipole–dipole interactions 187
Hydrogen bonding 187

Section 5.6: Intermolecular Forces and Properties 188
Melting, evaporating, and boiling 189
Importance of water's intermolecular forces to life 190
Viscosity 190
Solubility 190
Oil and water 191
How soap affects solubility 191
Surface tension 192

CONTENTS

Effect of soap on surface tension 193

Summary 198

Review 199

Chapter 6   Sports Drinks 202

Section 6.1: Solutions and Electrolytes 207
How ionic compounds dissolve in water 207
A misconception about dissolving 208
Forming electrolytes in water 208
Clarification of terms 209
Making a solution 210

Section 6.2: Concentrations of Solutions 212
Percent concentration 212
Molarity concentration 213
Converting between %(W/V) and molarity 213
Concentration of electrolytes 214

Section 6.3: Acidity and pH 216
Calculating pH from concentration of hydronium 216
Solving for concentration of hydronium 218
Strength of acids and pH 218
Bases 219
Acids and bases are electrolytes 220
Autoionization of water 220

Section 6.4: Solubility and Precipitation 221
Precipitation reactions 223
Solubility of ionic compounds 223
Solubility rules 223

Section 6.5: Stoichiometry 225
Mole ratio in a balanced chemical equation 226
Molecular mass and finding moles for stoichiometry 227
Molarity and finding moles for stoichiometry 228
Combining molecular mass and molarity in
    stoichiometry problems 229
Stoichiometry with gases 229
Keeping equalities straight 230
Titration 230
Percent yield 231

Section 6.6: Limiting Reactants 236
Limiting and excess reactants 237

Section 6.7: Properties of Solutions 239

Vapor pressure 240

Vapor pressure of a solution.. 241

Effects of electrolyte versus non-electrolyte solutes.................... 241

Boiling point of a solution.. 242

Calculating boiling point of an aqueous solution 242

Freezing point of a solution 243

Calculating freezing point of an aqueous solution 244

Summary 247

Review 248

Chapter 7   Hot and Cold Packs 250

Section 7.1: Endothermic and Exothermic 254

System versus surroundings... 254

Endothermic processes.. 255

Exothermic processes 255

Section 7.2: Calorimetry and Heat Capacity 256

Heat, energy, and enthalpy.. 256

Units for measuring energy... 257

Heat capacity... 257

Using heat capacity in calculations 258

Calorimetry... 261

Section 7.3: Changes in State 263

Temperature does not change during change in state 263

Enthalpy changes during change in state 264

Heating curves—adding energy to a substance......................... 265

Cooling curves—removing energy from a substance.................... 266

Section 7.4: Enthalpy of a Chemical Reaction 269

Enthalpy of formation.. 269

Enthalpy of reaction.. 270

Taking into account the number of moles of the compound
    in the reaction 271

Enthalpy and stoichiometry.. 272

Section 7.5: Hess's Law 275

Steps for completing a Hess's law problem............................ 275

Summary 280

Review 281

CONTENTS

Chapter 8   **Chemistry in Industry** 282

    Section 8.1: Equilibrium 286

    Reversible reactions.. 286

    Establishing equilibrium 287

    Dynamic equilibrium.. 288

    Determining whether a system is at equilibrium........................ 289

    Section 8.2: Equilibrium Constants 289

    Writing equilibrium constant expressions 290

    Not all reactants and products are included in the
        equilibrium constant expression..................................... 290

    Using equilibrium constant expressions in calculations 291

    Units of equilibrium constants 292

    Meaning of an equilibrium constant.. 292

    Equilibrium constants and temperature.. 293

    Section 8.3: Reaction Quotients 297

    Reaction quotient 298

    Which way to go to get to equilibrium................................... 298

    Section 8.4: Le Chatelier's Principle 299

    Le Chatelier's principle 301

    Effect of changing concentrations... 301

    Effect of changes in volume (changes in pressure) 302

    Effect of changing temperature... 303

    When changes do not disturb the equilibrium............................ 304

    Speeding up the time it takes to reach equilibrium 304

    Section 8.5: Environmental Concerns 305

    Earth... 305

    Air.. 309

    Ozone.. 310

    Greenhouse gases and global warming 311

    Your job... 312

    Summary 314

    Review 315

Chapter 9   **Forensic Chemistry** 316

    Section 9.1: Analysis Using Solubility 320

    What substances will dissolve in water?....................................... 320

    Dissolving a substance and equilibrium.. 321

CONTENTS

Writing equations and equilibrium constant expressions for
  dissolving a substance 322
Determining whether a substance will precipitate out 324
Precipitation reactions 326
Using solubility information for analysis of a sample 327
Qualitative and quantitative analysis 327

Section 9.2: Analysis Using Chromatography 330
Paper chromatography 330
Thin layer chromatography 332
Liquid chromatography 332
Gas chromatography 333

Section 9.3: Analysis of a Chemical Formula 337
Percent composition 337
Empirical formulas 339
Molecular formulas 340
Hydrates 344
Hydrate formulas 344
Summary 348
Review 349

Chapter 10   Batteries

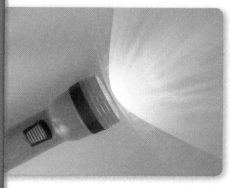

Batteries 350

Section 10.1: Reduction and Oxidation 354
Defining reduction and oxidation 354
Reduction and oxidation happen simultaneously 355
Determining oxidation number 355
Identifying what element is being reduced or oxidized in
  a reaction 356
Oxidizing agent and reducing agent 357

Section 10.2: Redox Reactions 358
Single replacement reactions 358
Activity series 360
Balancing redox reactions 362
Balancing redox reactions in an acidic solution 362
Balancing redox reactions in a basic solution 364

Section 10.3: Batteries and Redox Reactions 366
Voltaic cells 366
Line notation 367
Calculating cell potential 370
Standard reduction potentials 370

CONTENTS

Cell potential 370

Standard reduction potential is an intensive property 371

Nonstandard cells 371

Concentration cells 372

Electrolytic cells 373

Summary 376

Review 377

Chapter 11   Polymers 378

Section 11.1: Hydrocarbons 382

Alkanes 383

Alkenes 384

Isomers 384

Alkynes 385

Alkene/alkyne isomers 386

Saturation of hydrocarbons 386

Hydrocarbon side branches 387

Section 11.2: Organic Functional Groups 389

Haloalkanes 389

Alcohols 390

Ethers 391

Amines 392

Carbonyl-containing compounds 392

Aromatic compounds 395

Section 11.3: Polymers 398

Thermoplastic versus thermoset polymers 399

Reactions forming polymers 399

Properties of polymers 401

Polymers in biological settings 402

Summary 407

Review 408

Chapter 12   Nuclear Radiation 410

Section 12.1: Nuclear Reactions 414

Discovery of nuclear radioactivity 414

What is nuclear radioactivity? 414

Types of radioactive decay 416

Nuclear reactions and equations 417

Half-lives 419

CONTENTS

Section 12.2: Nuclear Radiation: Harmful or Helpful? . 422

Effects of radiation on the body 422

Nuclear dating.. 425

Energy—fission versus fusion.. 426

Summary 428

Review 429

Appendices 430

A. Units & Measurement 430

Quantities Commonly Measured in Chemistry 430

Common Equivalents 430

Unit Abbreviations 430

Metric Prefixes 430

Symbols 431

State Symbols 431

B. Writing and Naming Formulas 432

Common Polyatomic Ions 432

Common Multivalent Metals and Their Charges 433

Prefixes Used in Molecular Compounds 433

Diatomic Elements and Formulas 433

Organic Nomenclature Prefixes 433

C. Solubility 434

Solubility Rules 434

Solubility Product Constants (25°C) 434

Compound Solubility 435

D. Useful Constants 436

Equilibrium 436

E. Electrochemistry 437

Activity Series 437

Reduction 437

F. Enthalpies of Formation (H_f) kJ/mole 438

G. The Elements 440

Name, Symbol, Atomic Number, Atomic Mass............................ 440

Element Properties 443

Periodic Table 444

Glossary 445

Index 451

Photo Credits 461

PREFACE

Why I Wrote This Textbook, and How It's Different from Other Textbooks

I wrote this textbook for my students! I wanted my students to see how chemistry applies to their lives and to see it as concepts that are interconnected. They have loved it and I hope you will, too.

Other chemistry textbooks have each "concept" as a separate chapter. The problems with these textbooks include: (1) students see chemistry as a group of separate concepts rather than seeing the interconnections between the different ideas; (2) students don't see the application to their lives (the "application" is often placed in sidebars that students don't read); and (3) students don't feel like they're "doing science."

This textbook is different. It presents the information as scientists learn it. Scientists presented with a new problem or challenge would seek out the information they need in order to study or solve a problem and apply it to that situation. This textbook is centered around twelve real-life themes and the chemistry needed to understand each theme. Concepts are not artificially introduced—only those that are needed to understand the theme are covered in that chapter. This allows you to see the relevance of every concept you study.

Additionally, this textbook includes "inquiry" labs—which is the science-education term used when students design their own procedures. Inquiry labs are included at least once in every chapter. They include lots of instruction in the beginning, but by the end students are so competent at lab design that I provide a mere list of things to include in the write-up. This will help you develop scientific process skills and allow you to "do science" yourself.

Why I Chose This Title

The title *Discovering Chemistry You Need to Know* has two meanings. First, the content is introduced in a need-to-know format. This means that you learn the chemistry concepts that you "need to know" in order to understand each theme. Second, since I've been using this way of teaching with my students, I've never once been asked, "When are we ever going to need to know this?" Instead, students have eagerly asked what the next theme will be and gone home to share with their family how an airbag, or some other theme, works.

Acknowledgments

I'd like to thank the many people who have helped me along the way. First, my chemistry teacher and mentor, Sue Rusco (now retired), was a wonderful influence, and my mom, Dr. Frances Morgan (a chemist herself) both opened up an exciting world of color and reactions, and supported my every leap over the years. Thanks to my dad, Roger Morgan, who always lets me know how proud he is. Dr. Howard Drossman first introduced me to thematic teaching and gave me my start in curriculum development. He told me he believed that one day I'd change the way chemistry is taught. I hope I'm reaching that day! Thank you, Dr. Paul Kuerbis, for introducing me to inquiry.

My publisher, Kendall/Hunt, and their former science editor, Troy Jacobsen, supported my efforts financially with field testing and guided this project through publication. Thanks also to Lynn Molony, Victoria Noel, Beth Trowbridge, Kelly Heinrichs, Charmayne McMurray, Dennis Jaeger, and many others who helped bring this project to print.

I'd like to thank the students who acted as guinea pigs for this book over the last few years. They cheerfully went with the flow and were a constant source of support and motivation. All my colleagues (some of whom I've never met face-to-face) have provided tremendous support and encouragement.

This text wouldn't be what it is without the invaluable help of the field test and pilot teachers (listed below) and their students. They were willing to try this innovative project and have had wonderful responses from it. I thank them for their time, effort, and attention to detail, especially Craig Pierson, who went above and beyond the call of duty to support this project.

Field Test Teachers

Steve Freers, Temescal Canyon High School, Lake Elsinore, CA

Pat Hoffman, East High School, Sioux City, IA

Melissa Nielsen, Olathe East High School, Olathe, KS

Craig Pierson, Ph.D., Billings Central Catholic High School, Billings, MT

Paula Roberts, Hillsboro High School, Hillsboro, OR

Jeff Venable, Northwestern High School, Rock Hill, SC

Pilot Teachers

Karen Ahrens, Immaculate Heart High School, Tucson, AZ

Ryan Bleth, Bismarck High School, Bismarck, ND

Judy Hom Cheng, Riverdale Country School, Riverdale, NY

Adela J. Dziekanowski, Montville Township High School, Montville, NJ

Sheri Furby, Monsignor Kelly Catholic High School, Beaumont, TX

Catherine Gammage, Melvindale High School, Melvindale, MI

Lisa Glass, New Garden Friends School, Greensboro, NC

Leigh Grass, Central Aroostook High School, Mars Hill, ME

Valerie Smallbeck, Bismarck High School, Bismarck, ND

Richard Smith, Buena High School, Ventura, CA

Carolyn Stonecipher, Monsignor Kelly Catholic High School, Beaumont, TX

Andrew Wood, East Butler Public School, Brainard, NE

TO THE STUDENT

Tips for Using This Text

How to Use the Examples

The examples in this text fall directly after concepts and calculations are introduced and explain how to do that type of problem. Please don't skip those boxes! There's valuable information in them.

Here's how to make the best use of an example:

- Read the paragraphs once all the way through.
- Go through the example and connect it to what was explained in the paragraphs to make more sense of the concepts.
- Look at the example again, if you need to, when working on practice problems.

KENDALL/HUNT

CHEMISTRY

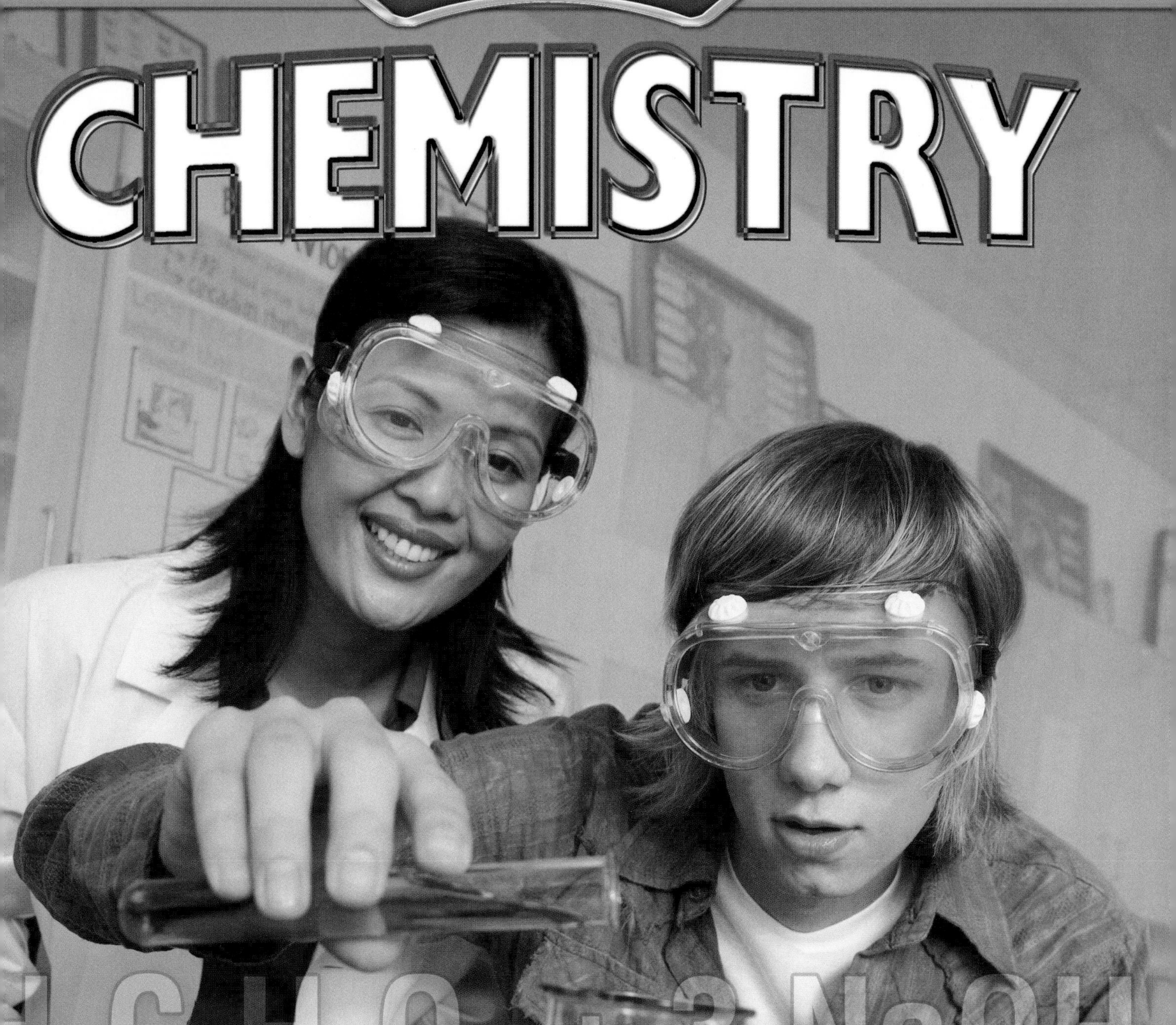

DISCOVERING CHEMISTRY YOU NEED TO KNOW

Kelly Deters

CHAPTER 1

Scientists' Tools
Everyone Is a Scientist

IN THIS CHAPTER

- Doing science
- Observations and measurements
- Designing your own labs
- Converting units
- Significant digits
- Scientific notation

INTRODUCTORY
ACTIVITY

What does "doing science" mean to you? Who "does science"? What do scientists do? What do you think of when you hear about science or scientists? What comes to mind when you hear about chemistry or chemists?

Do you think science plays an important role in your life? If yes, where do you see science in your world? If no, explain why not.

Think about these questions; share your answers with a partner and then with the class.

This chapter has the

CHEMISTRY YOU NEED TO KNOW

to be able to design and carry out scientific investigations, analyze data, and reach conclusions.

Introduction

Science, including chemistry, is often thought of as complicated, abstract, and for "smart" people. However, we were all born to be scientists! Watch a toddler perform experiments to learn about his or her environment: What happens if I fill this with water? What happens if I dump it out? Does dirt dissolve in water? Oh, it makes mud! Will it do the same thing next time? Although these "experiments" may be simple, they are experiments nonetheless. Humans have an innate desire to know how things work. That's all science is—figuring out how things work.

Although science contains many difficult or abstract concepts, science as a subject is far from abstract; it's absolutely everywhere in our world. Science describes our body, our food, our clothes, our cars, our buildings, our environment, and, literally, everything we touch. The traditional disciplines of physics, chemistry, and biology are so intermingled in the real world that it's difficult to separate them. In order for you to walk across the room, you need the chemistry involved in building every molecule in your body and in sending impulses to your brain telling you to walk; you need the biology of the cells, muscles, tendons, and all the other aspects of your body; you also need the physics of the friction between your foot and the ground to be able to move forward. However, there is also chemistry involved in the biology of the cells and muscles, and there is physics in those chemical impulses sent to your brain. The sciences are connected in endless ways.

Chemistry is defined as the study of matter and its interactions and changes. **Matter** is anything that takes up space and has mass. By this point in your life, you've heard of atoms. You may not have a great understanding of what exactly they are, but you've probably heard that they are the "building blocks of matter." Everything you see, and even what you don't see (such as the air around you), is made of atoms. Atoms have mass and take up space; therefore they are matter, and everything made from them is also matter. Chemistry is the study of how matter behaves, interacts, reacts, and mixes.

Chemistry—An Experimental Science

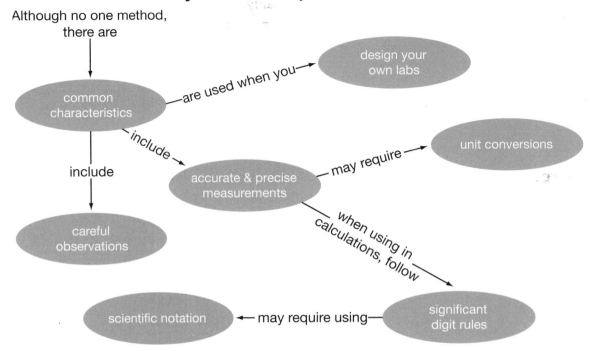

Although no one method, there are

common characteristics —are used when you→ design your own labs

common characteristics —include→ accurate & precise measurements —may require→ unit conversions

common characteristics —include→ careful observations

accurate & precise measurements —when using in calculations, follow→ significant digit rules

significant digit rules —may require using→ scientific notation

SECTION 1.1

Doing Science

Science is not just something done by old men in white coats surrounded by strange-looking glassware with bubbling, colorful solutions. You will do science, too. Sometimes that will mean that you follow a written procedure to learn techniques used in chemistry or to confirm the findings of previous work. Sometimes you will design a lab to solve a problem or come to a conclusion on your own. Both are part of a scientist's education and work.

There is no one scientific method. Rather, there are infinite ways in which to conduct scientific investigations and research. (See Figure 1–1.) Science is not linear—you don't pose a question, perform an experiment, find a conclusion, and that's the end. Instead, science is circular. The findings of one investigation often lead to other questions that need investigating. Sometimes a scientist will spend an entire career researching different aspects of the same question. Many scientists begin their work where others have left off. It is a continual search to understand more, and each time we discover something, it leads to even more questions. Also, not all science is meant to test a hypothesis or form a theory or model. Some scientists are trying to create better products, processes, or technologies.

Often, discoveries about one topic come as a complete surprise while scientists are working on something else—they must keep their eyes and mind open in order to make use of all the available evidence. This is how such products as synthetic rubber, penicillin, Post-It® notes, and many other things were discovered or invented. Science takes a great amount of creativity!

Within scientific investigations, there are common components or processes. There must be a focused question, problem, or purpose that can be investigated in a reasonable amount of time. These questions can come from observations about our world, the results of other scientists' work, or a need in our society, such as medicine or technology. Questions that are too broad leave a scientist with no logical place to begin. Scientists use data-gathering techniques, observation, and logic to draw conclusions.

There's more to science than experimentation

Data-gathering techniques can involve experimentation, but they can also include field studies, long-term observation, surveys, literature review, and more. Different science disciplines use different techniques. It's common for a biologist or geologist to use field studies and long-term observation, whereas chemists and physicists more often use experimentation. But it's likely that all scientists will use a variety of techniques in their careers.

This text will focus on experimentation, because that will make up the majority of your investigations throughout your first-year chemistry course. (You will, however, use literature review as you write research papers.)

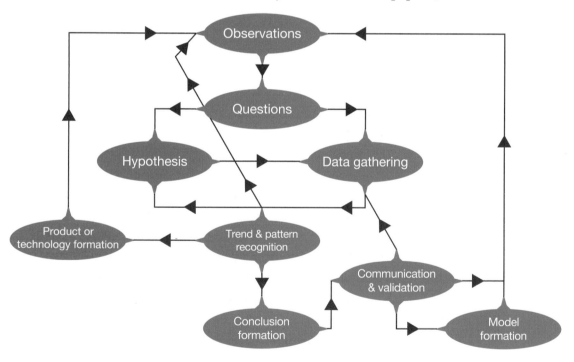

Figure 1–1. There are many pathways through common processes that scientists can take— even more than are shown here.

Two types of experiments

You will be doing two types of labs in this course. In one type, you will investigate relationships or the effect that a change of one variable has on another variable. An example of this type would be determining the speed of a reaction with sunlight versus without sunlight. In this experiment, you

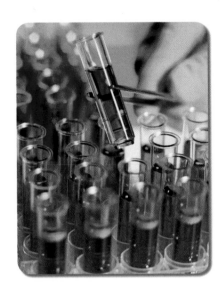

would determine the relationship between exposure to sunlight and speed of reaction. The next section will give details on variables and constants used in this type of investigation.

The second type of lab is to determine a specific quantity or fact. An example of this type of investigation would be determining the concentration of an unknown solution. There is no relationship or effect to be studied; therefore, variables and constants are not appropriate and do not need to be included in the investigation planning.

Variables and constants

When it's appropriate (as discussed above), the question should define the variables. Variables are manipulated or measured in an experiment. An **independent variable** is one that is manipulated by the scientist, whereas a **dependent variable** is measured or observed. A change in a dependent variable will show that the independent variable had an effect. For example, if someone were investigating whether exposure to sunlight had an effect on the speed of a reaction, the scientist would control whether the reaction is exposed to sunlight. The experiment manipulates (or changes) exposure to sunlight, and therefore it is the independent variable. The scientist will then measure the speed of the reaction, perhaps by timing it until a color appears. The speed of reaction is the dependent variable, the one the investigator is measuring. If times are different for the reaction in the sun versus the reaction not exposed to sunlight, then it can be said that the speed of reaction depends on exposure to sunlight. The dependent variable was influenced by the independent variable.

All variables other than the independent variable must be controlled in order to draw valid conclusions. For example, if the researcher in the above example allowed the experiment in the sunlight to be done at a higher temperature than the one not exposed to sunlight, we could not be sure that the reaction speed was dependent on exposure to sunlight. Perhaps the real cause of the faster reaction involved the difference in temperature and not the sunlight at all. All aspects of the experiment that are not the variables being tested are called **constants.**

Sometimes it is appropriate to have a **control setup.** Imagine that the investigator now wants to study the effect of temperature on the speed of the reaction. The control setup would be the reaction at room temperature. The **experimental setups** could be one reaction run at a higher temperature and one at a lower temperature. Temperature would be the independent variable, with speed of reaction remaining the dependent variable in this example.

Predictions and hypotheses

Another aspect of scientific investigations is forming a hypothesis or prediction. However, as with variables and constants, it is not always appropriate. An investigation to determine relationships or effects would involve predictions and hypotheses. They would not be appropriate for an experiment to determine a specific quantity. For example, when planning an experiment to determine the concentration of a solution, it would not be appropriate to make a prediction—you'd just be guessing a random number.

Although the terms *hypothesis* and *prediction* mean different things, they are often confused or used interchangeably. A **prediction** is simply a statement of what you believe will happen. An example of a prediction would be, "The reaction at a higher temperature will be the fastest, followed by the control, and the reaction at the cool temperature will be the slowest."

A **hypothesis,** however, attempts to explain why behavior happens and how phenomena relate to one another. An example would be, "The reaction will be faster at a higher temperature because the molecules will have more kinetic energy, resulting in more frequent collisions with the minimum energy to cause the reaction to happen." This hypothesis attempts to explain a relationship between kinetic energy and what it takes for a reaction to happen, rather than just predicting that one will be faster than the other.

Hypotheses may be formed before performing the experiment, or they may be formed afterward—after gathering evidence, making observations, and formulating a possible explanation for those observations. Hypotheses formed as the result of an experiment often serve as a starting point for further experimentation to confirm or adjust the possible explanation.

Designing procedures

Scientific investigations also have well-written, repeatable procedures. Procedures must follow a logical order and be able to be performed by others and lead to similar results. **Multiple trials** are also important in order to show that a result wasn't just a one-time fluke but rather that the same result will happen each time. (This can be seen with toddler scientists as well: how many times will they repeat the same experiment before they are satisfied that they can predict the results and move on?)

Also, multiple trials give a chance to average data together. Careful observations and data are collected and recorded with the most appropriate tools. However, all measurements have an element of error to them—things can't be measured to infinite precision. Therefore, multiple trials may have slightly different results. But the scientist must decide if these differences are "within acceptable experimental error." If they are really the same results, taking into account tiny errors of each measurement, then they are averaged together and used. If the amount of error in results is too great, then the experiment must be redesigned to minimize errors and produce more consistent results.

Gathering data

Results can also be described in terms of precision and accuracy. **Precision** describes measurements or results that are consistent (within acceptable experimental error)—similar results are found over and over again. A dart

thrower is precise when he or she lands a dart in roughly the same area of the dartboard with each throw.

Accuracy means "correct" data, meaning that they match the theoretical values or accepted results from other investigations. This is similar to when the darts land on the bull's eye over and over again. Note that the thrower does not need to land in exactly the same spot each time—just within the bull's eye. This shows what "within acceptable experimental error" means. You don't have to get exactly the same number for each trial you perform. If your results are close enough that the small errors related to reading instruments and taking measurements can explain the differences, then you can consider yourself accurate. (There are statistical tests that scientists use to determine if their variance is within experimental error, but we won't worry about that in this course.)

In order for data to be accurate, it must also be precise—just getting the bull's eye one time doesn't mean that you're the best dart thrower; you must get the bull's eye every time. Sometimes scientists don't know whether their results are accurate until many other people evaluate them. If other scientists separately agree and obtain similar results with their own experiments, then the results begin to be accepted.

Although **precision** is used to describe consistent data, the word **precise** is also used to say how carefully a measurement was taken. Measurements that are precise have less uncertainty.

Drawing conclusions—Theories and laws

Scientists look for patterns in their data and attempt to state generalizations. These results are written in a conclusion that addresses the original question, purpose, or problem of the lab. The conclusion will also address an earlier hypothesis, if one was made—either supporting or not supporting the stated hypothesis. But often results or findings can lead to new hypotheses, which lead to new questions, which lead to new investigations, and the process begins again.

Repeated investigations and cooperative work among scientists lead to theories and laws. **Theories** explain how or why behavior happens. What about the way that molecules move and interact is causing them to behave in the way observed in the experiments? Theories can be revised over time as new evidence is presented. A theory can never be completely proven as 100% true and complete.

Laws simply describe what happens; they do not attempt to explain why. A law is usually a mathematical equation that can be used to describe or predict a situation. A law can be proven as true—a mathematical relationship can be measured and proven.

Many people believe that, if it's proven enough times, a theory will become a law. However, these definitions show that a theory cannot "grow up and become a law," because they address two different things.

Communicating findings

A very important aspect of scientific investigations is the communication of findings. Scientists share what they do and what they find in an effort to add to the pool of scientific knowledge. The work done by one person or group may be along the same lines as that of another person or group. By sharing their results (even about different aspects of similar questions), they may help to support the findings of the groups or help them go in a new or different direction. It's also important that work be repeatable, and communicating findings allows others to compare work done by several scientists to ensure that results are valid and reliable. Scientists use many different methods of communicating results, including presentations at conferences, poster presentations, professional journal articles, and online collaboration.

You as a scientist

In this course, you will make observations, ask questions, design experiments, gather data, evaluate the data, and share your results with classmates. You'll use evidence and logic to critically evaluate and solve discrepancies and to form theories and conclusions. And don't forget that it's OK to change your understanding of your data. You were not necessarily "wrong" before, but you had formed conclusions and theories based on the evidence you had. When scientists (including you) evaluate more data and evidence, they often change their understanding of how something works. You will be an open-minded chemist in this course!

Go Online
Check your understanding
http://webcom4.grtxle.com/khk12Chemistry

PRACTICE 1.1

Doing Science

1. A scientist is trying to find how changing the thickness of a paper towel affects the volume of water that it will hold.

   a. Identify the independent variable.

   b. Identify the dependent variable.

   c. Identify as many constants as you can think of.

   d. Write a prediction for this experiment.

   e. Write a hypothesis for this experiment.

2. For each of the following experiment problems/purposes, if it is appropriate, define the independent and dependent variables and write a prediction. If it is not appropriate to do these things, say so.

   a. To determine the solubility of sugar in room-temperature water

   b. To determine the effect of temperature on solubility of sugar

   c. To find the effect of volume on pressure

   d. To find the gas law constant

   e. To examine how surface area affects rate of reaction

   f. To find the concentration of citric acid in sports drinks

3. Contrast the following pairs of words—explain how they are different:

   a. Prediction and hypothesis

   b. Independent and dependent variables

   c. Variable and constant

   d. Control setup and experimental setup

   e. Precision and accuracy

   f. Theory and law

SECTION 1.2

Observations and Measurements

LAB 1.2A

Taking Observations
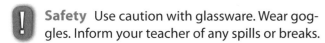 Procedure printed with permission of Russ Thiel, Andover High School, Andover, KS.

Purpose To take observations in several ways

Materials Tea bag, paper clip, 250 mL beaker

! **Safety** Use caution with glassware. Wear goggles. Inform your teacher of any spills or breaks.

Procedure

1. Read the observation requirements (below) *first* so that you know what you'll be asked to do before you begin.

2. Fill the beaker about three-quarters full with tap water.

3. Place the Tea bag in the beaker. Use the unfolded paper clip to hang the bag over the side of the beaker.

4. Record observations as instructed below for 10–15 minutes until you're satisfied you've recorded everything.

Observations Use only the left two-thirds of the paper for this.

1. In words, write what you see before you put the tea bag in the water (describe both the tea bag and the water) and each change you see after putting the bag in the water.

2. Visually show the molecules and particles for each of your word observations above. Make sure to label each type of particle you draw (or use a "key"). Be sure that each of your written observations is represented by a different picture. If your teacher provides whiteboards, do this on the whiteboard.

Discussion

1. Use the right one-third of your paper from the "words" observations, and classify each thing you wrote down as an Observation or an Inference. (Use your own working definitions of these words for this; don't ask the teacher or look up the definitions.)

2. Share your "words" observations and their classifications (observation versus inference) with the class.

3. What did other groups have that you didn't?

4. What did you have that other groups didn't?

5. Were there any discrepancies in the classifications? How were discrepancies resolved?

6. Write the difference between an observation and an inference after discussion as a class.

7. Should inferences be included in the "observations" section of labs? Why or why not? If not, where should they go?

8. Is it important that your observations be able to be read and visualized by other people? Why?

9. Was it easier to do the word observations or the pictures? Why?

10. What pros and cons do you see for both the word and the picture observations?

11. What did you learn about how different people/groups visualized the molecules/particles?

12. What's between each of the particles you drew in the pictures?

13. Why is it important to take observations before you begin doing anything (as you did for the tea bag and water before you put the bag in the water)?

When scientists do science, one of the most important aspects is taking careful observations and measurements. It is important to make complete notes about occurrences during an experiment for analysis and confirmation by other trials and experiments.

Taking observations

Observations are **qualitative** records, meaning they do not include numbers and measurements. They include notes about color; texture; formation of solids, liquids, or gases; heat flow, and anything else that happens throughout an experiment. It is important to observe things before, during, and after the experiment to note changes.

Two common ways of describing material involve the words *clear* and *colorless,* which are often confused. **Clear** means that you can see through something, whereas **colorless** means that it has no color. Something can be clear and colored, such as pink lemonade or water with food coloring in it. You can also have clear and colorless objects, such as water or plain glass.

If an object is not clear, then it is **opaque** (solid and not see-through, such as a book) or **cloudy** (some parts are see-through, but there are solid or liquid particles floating around to make a "cloud"). If an object is cloudy, you must describe the material of the "cloud" as well as the liquid that it is in. For example, you could have a blue solid in a colorless liquid or a white solid in a blue liquid.

Gathering data

Data are often **quantitative,** consisting of measurements with numbers; however, data can be qualitative. Common quantities that are measured are in Table 1–1.

Scientists use a system of measurement based on the metric system called the **International System of Measurement.** The units in this system are called **SI units.** Ways of converting between units will be discussed later in this chapter.

In December 1998, the NASA Mars Climate Orbiter was launched. However, programmers failed to convert units from English to metric in one of the software programs. The closest the satellite could come to

Go Online
Topic: accurate measurements
Go to: www.scilinks.org
Code: Chem1e14

SC INKS
NSTA

Table 1–1 Quantities in Chemistry		
Quantity	SI Unit	What Is Used to Measure It?
Mass—the amount of matter in a sample	Kilograms (kg)	Balance (not a "scale")
Volume—the amount of space an object takes up	Milliliter (mL)	Graduated cylinder
Temperature—related to the speed with which molecules move	Celsius (°C) or Kelvin (K)	Thermometer
Length	Meters (m)	Ruler, meter stick
Time	Seconds (s or sec)	Stopwatch, clock
Energy	Joule (J)	Measured indirectly

Problems with the NASA Mars Climate Orbiter occurred due to a failure of those people involved to use the same units of measurement.

the surface of Mars was about 93 km. NASA officials, assuming that the programmers had used proper units of measurement, thought the orbiter was a safe distance of 110 km above the surface; however, it was actually only about 57 km above the planet when the correct unit was used in the calculations. The satellite did not survive—$327.6 million dollars spent on development, production, launch, and mission costs wasted, all because two groups didn't use the same units, and they didn't specify which units they were using! It is important that all units are reported with each measurement so that everyone understands what that measurement is really saying.

Uncertainty in measurement and choosing the right tool

It is important to choose the right-sized tool to measure a quantity so that the error is as small as possible. For example, you wouldn't use a large meter stick to measure the thickness of one piece of paper. You would use something with smaller markings on it so that the measurement is as precise as possible. If you want to measure out a volume of 5 mL, it is better to use a graduated cylinder that goes up to only 10 mL with a mark every 0.1 mL, than one for holding volumes up to 100 mL, with a mark every 2 mL. You won't have to estimate as much with the smaller instrument, so you have a better chance of getting closer to exactly 5.0 mL. (See Figure 1–2 about choosing the right instrument.)

Relative error

The smaller the quantity that you are measuring, the more important it is that you are precise. If you're off by 1 mL when you measure out 5 mL, it

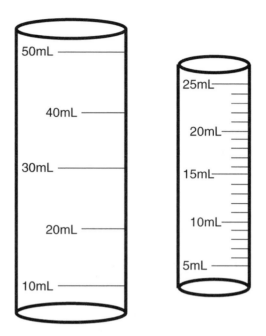

Figure 1–2. Choosing the right instrument. Measurements will be more precise if the most appropriate tool is chosen. Which graduated cylinder would you choose to measure approximately 15 mL of a liquid? The large cylinder on the left with few markings would give a much greater error than the smaller one on the right with more frequent markings.

is a 20% error. However, if you are off by 1 mL when measuring 100 mL, that's only a 1% error. Therefore, use even more care when measuring smaller amounts.

Number of decimal places to record

When taking a measurement, you can estimate *one decimal place*. For example, if there are lines on the graduated cylinder at 4.3 mL and at 4.4 mL, and the liquid level is between those two lines, you know for sure that it's more than 4.3 mL and less than 4.4 mL (see Figure 1–3). However, it is probably hard to tell if it's 4.325 mL versus 4.345 mL—human eyes are not that precise. Therefore, we write down the 4.3 that we know for sure and then a 5 at the end, which means that it's in between lines. Our reading would be 4.35 mL. You can estimate only one decimal place—no more!

We use "0" at the end of a reading to indicate that it's on a line. For example, if it were right on the 4.3 mL line, we'd write 4.30 mL as our reading.

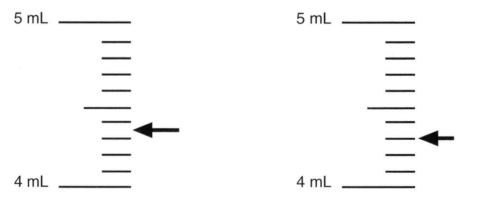

Figure 1–3. Recording decimal places. The drawing on the left shows a reading of 4.35 mL—it's in between the 4.3 line and the 4.4 line. The drawing on the right shows a reading of 4.30 mL—it's right on the line, so we write the "0."

LAB 1.2ʙ

Taking Measurements

Purpose To practice taking accurate measurements

⚠ **Safety** Wear goggles. Handle glassware carefully. Report any incidents to your instructor.

Procedure Each station will have a task for you to perform that includes taking measurements. Be as precise as possible with your work. Remember always to bend to read measurements at eye level—do not lift the containers or tools to your eyes. At each station, **undo your work and return everything to its original position for the next group.** Do not move on to the next station until your instructor tells you to do so.

1. Record the mass of the object. Be sure to check that the balance is zeroed before beginning (by pressing the "tare" button on an electronic balance, or by sliding all the weights to zero and making sure it's balanced for a beam-balance).

2. Add the liquid from one sample container to the graduated cylinder. Record the volume of the liquid. Be sure to record volumes from the bottom of the meniscus (the curve the liquid forms in the cylinder because its molecules are attracted to the glass). Empty the liquid into the sink when finished.

3. Fill the beaker half-full with tap water. Add two ice cubes. Stir gently with the thermometer and watch until the thermometer reading stays steady for about 10 seconds. Record the temperature of the water. Empty the beaker into the sink.

4. Measure the volume of a rubber stopper by water displacement. To do this, add some water to the graduated cylinder and record the volume. Add the rubber stopper and record the new volume. In the calculations section (not the data section),

you'll find the volume of the stopper by subtraction.

5. Record the mass of the chemical sample. You cannot put chemicals directly on a balance. Therefore, find the mass of the empty beaker or weighing dish and then the mass of the beaker/weighing dish with one of the samples. In the calculations section, you'll subtract the readings to find the mass of the sample. Empty the sample into the trash.

6. To find the mass of 30.0 mL of water, first find the mass of the empty beaker. Then use the graduated cylinder to measure out exactly 30.0 mL of water. Add the water to the beaker and find the new mass. In the calculations section, you'll find the mass of the water by subtraction.

Data

Station 1: Mass of object _____

Station 2: Volume of liquid _____

Station 3: Temperature of ice water _____

Station 4: Volume of water _____

    Volume of water and rubber stopper _____

Station 5: Mass of beaker/weighing dish _____

    Mass of beaker/weighing dish and sample _____

Station 6: Mass of beaker _____

    Mass of beaker and water _____

Calculations

Station 4: Find the volume of the rubber stopper.

Station 5: Find the mass of the sample.

Station 6: Find the mass of the water.

Discussion

1. Which station(s) used the most precise tool to measure? How did you decide?

2. Which station(s) had the highest possibility for error? How did you decide?

3. Why is it important to be consistent in measurements?

This system of estimating one and only one decimal place allows everyone to understand approximately what degree of error is in a measurement—a nonzero number at the end of a recording indicates it's between lines, a 0 indicates that it's on a line.

Designing Your Own Labs

Designing a lab procedure on your own can be a challenging experience, especially if you are accustomed to being given a procedure with carefully outlined steps to follow. However, it can be a rewarding experience that provides you with increased skills in logic, communication, and writing, as well as understanding of scientific principles.

Although a lab traditionally follows the order "purpose, materials, safety, procedure, data table, calculations, results," sometimes that is not the most efficient way to design a lab from scratch. Often, it is easier to go almost in reverse order.

This section serves as a guide that will help you design your own labs. It is not a definitive scientific method, but rather a way to help you focus on the purpose of the investigation and enable you to design a lab more efficiently.

Identifying the purpose, problem, or question

Sometimes you will have a specific problem or purpose that you must try to answer; other times you will have a broader question that you will have to focus by selecting a variable yourself. If so, make sure that you have only one variable. Hold all conditions constant except for the variable that you wish to test. The purpose, problem, or question should be clear and complete and include the independent and dependent variables, if appropriate (see Section 1.1 for a discussion of when they are and are not appropriate).

Gathering background information

Many students want to skip this step because they think it is redundant; however, the Background Information section is very important. It is where you gather different concepts, equations, and knowledge so you can integrate and apply them to the specific problem at hand. It's the step of gathering your thoughts (and knowledge) between defining the problem and planning the actual lab. Taking the time to write a good background information section can save you time on the lab-designing process later.

Designing the results, calculations, and data table

From the purpose or question, you can define what variables or quantities you are trying to find. You should then identify any equations or calculations, comparisons, or relationship statements that need to be done to reach those quantities. These will set up the results/calculations section of your lab.

From the results setup or from the variable definitions, if there are any, you can make a data table. The data table should include any quantities that you need to measure in the lab (based on the results section you just set up), but no calculations. All calculations should appear in the results section of the report. Make sure that everything you think you will need to measure in the lab is included in the data table (using the results section as your guide), but try not to waste time measuring quantities that won't be needed. Remember that you can go back and adjust your results section if you discover something is missing or not needed while creating your data table.

Writing the procedure

From the data, you can usually write a procedure fairly efficiently. If the data table has "mass of beaker," then write a step in the procedure to "Find and record the mass of the beaker." If the data table has "temperature of water," write a step to find that temperature. Often, there are steps in between the data table measurements. For example, if the data table says "Mass of beaker and sodium chloride," then your procedure will have to include something like: "Add approximately 2 g of sodium chloride to the beaker and find exact mass of beaker and sodium chloride." You must tell approximately how much of the substance the experimenters should put into the container before you have them find its mass.

Procedures should have clear and concise steps, numbered and complete enough so that someone else could repeat the experiment in the same manner that you originally performed it.

Determining the materials needed and writing safety concerns

From the procedure, you can write a materials list. Go through each step of the procedure and make a list of everything that will be needed. If your instructor gave you a list of possible materials, make sure to check with him or her about anything you'd like to use that isn't on that list before you finalize your plans (to check for availability and safety).

From your materials list and procedure, you can then list any safety concerns. Your instructor can probably tell you the safety concerns for any chemicals that you propose to work with, but you should always include that goggles are to be worn and that any incident/spill/breakage should be reported to the teacher. When appropriate, include the following as well: wearing aprons or gloves, always using caution around glassware—especially when heated—and careful handling of fire and hot liquids (even water).

Professor Marcus Lindström, pictured here next to his lab equipment, is a pioneer in a new type of environmentally friendly chemistry.

Making changes to prewritten procedures

Suppose you begin performing your procedure and realize that you left out a step, don't need a step that you had written, or that you've written a couple of steps in the wrong order. Don't worry—scientists run into that problem often; they call it optimization. When they design a lab, the procedure often has to be revised and refined several times to obtain the optimal results with the least amount of error. However, if you do decide to change something, you must do it in writing—change the written procedure, materials list, or data table on your report. When you finish the lab, the final report should say exactly what you actually did in the lab.

Discussing results

You will often be asked to share your findings with the class. For several labs in this course, there is no single right way to perform the lab, and no single right answer.

When scientists share and discuss results, they always try to eliminate personal bias and opinions (including preconceptions about what *should* have happened) and rely on the collective evidence to come to a consensus (agreement). Sometimes they decide more evidence is needed to come to a valid conclusion; that's part of the fluid nature of "doing science."

LAB 1.3

The Most Absorbent Paper Towel

You are being given fairly detailed instructions on how to design your own labs—instructions will be given to you stating exactly what goes in each section of a lab report. As you progress through the book, less information will be given as you become more accustomed to designing your own labs.

Purpose To determine which paper towel is most absorbent for its price

Possible materials water, various paper towel samples, graduated cylinder, beakers, balance, ruler

! Safety No chemicals other than water are being used, and there is no heating of any chemicals. Use caution with glassware.

Instructions You need to further define your purpose/problem. You know you're going to compare differently priced paper towels, but how will you define "absorbent"—by mass of water absorbed or by volume? (Don't write this down now, just decide—you'll write it in a minute.)

Begin writing your lab report:

- Restate the purpose/problem. Remember to clearly state your variables in the purpose/problem—don't use the generic statement above.

- Write background information—what information do you already know about your variables and how paper towels absorb water?

- Next, write a hypothesis. Which sample do you believe will perform best based on your variables? Remember to write a hypothesis and not a prediction!

- List your variables (specify dependent and independent) and as many constants as you can.

Although the next sections typically appear in the order "materials, safety, procedure, data table, calculations," it is often most effective to write them in the order "calculations, data table, procedure, materials, safety."

- For the calculations/results, you will need to compare your dependent and independent variables in some way. For this lab, the most appropriate way is to find a ratio of dependent to independent measurement (amount of water absorbed/price of paper towel). Be sure to specify how you're going to measure "amount of water"—either "mass of water" or "volume of water." You'll also need to average multiple trials for each paper towel. Set these calculations up (you'll plug in the numbers after performing the experiment, but get them set up first).

- Once you determine what you need for your calculations, you can then determine what you need to put in your data table. Make sure everything needed in your calculations is included in your data table. You will need to take into account how you plan to measure the water: volumes are measured in graduated cylinders, and masses on balances. Keep in mind when making your data table and procedure that you should not put wet paper towels directly on the balance—if you want to find the mass of a wet paper towel, you will have to put it in a beaker to use the balance, so then you would also have to know the mass of the empty beaker to find the mass of the paper towel. This type of calculation (finding the mass of the wet paper towel from subtraction) would also need to be added to your calculations section that you made above—not in the data table.

- Next, write the procedure. For each quantity that you need to measure in the data table, write a procedure step to either set it up or to measure it. Include steps specifying how you will know when to stop adding water to the paper towel. There are many ways to do this—just pick one and be consistent. Use clear, concise language, and number your steps. Include three trials of each type of paper towel.

- From your procedure, make a detailed materials list. Write down each item you need in your procedure, and exactly how much you need of it. The only exception to this is water—you have access to an unlimited supply of water in most situations, and therefore you do not need to write down the amount you will use in the materials list. A list of possible materials is

(continues)

The Most Absorbent Paper Towel (*cont'd.*)

provided above. You may not need all the materials listed, and you may think of something not on the list. If you do, be sure to ask your instructor before you finalize your plans to make sure that it will be available for you.

 Safety

- Go through the materials list and write down any safety concerns about materials. Your instructor will probably give you safety information about any chemicals that you are using. You should also consider the safety of using glass (especially hot glass), hot plates, burners, open flames near flammable chemicals, and anything else you see in your procedure that could cause a problem. You should always use goggles if you are using any chemical other than water and if you are heating any chemical (including water).

Only after your lab is planned and written up, perform your experiment. If you need to make adjustments to any section of your report, do so in writing. For example, if you realize you forgot a step in the procedure, write it in as you do it. When you are finished with the experiment, the report should accurately state exactly what you did.

- Complete your calculations/results section by performing the calculations you set up earlier. You should show each of the equations for these calculations, as well as the numbers plugged into the equation for the first trial. For the second and third trials, you may just write the answer to the calculations; it is assumed that you did it the same way as the first trial. After your calculations, write a general statement of any trends or patterns in your results (such as "X brand absorbed a higher volume of water per mass

The Most Absorbent Paper Towel (*cont'd.*)

of paper towel than Y brand"). Do not attempt to explain why you got these results, just state them in sentence form.

- Write your conclusion. It should restate the purpose/problem and completely answer it. Was your original hypothesis supported or not? Explain why you think you got these results based on the chemistry you understand up to this point. Give at least two possible sources of error (remember, "human error" is too broad, and "calculations" won't count). "Possible sources of error" does not mean that you did things wrong, but points to places in the lab where error could occur in data gathering to throw off the results. Also write one additional investigation or one question that you now wonder about.

- Compare your results and conclusions as a class. Do this on whiteboards if your teacher provides them. Discuss as a class the different ways that were used to determine when to stop adding water. Include your answers to these questions in your conclusion as well.

- What are the pros and cons of these different methods?

- Did the different methods give similar or different results for the most absorbent paper towel for the price? Explain why.

SECTION 1.4

Converting Units

Often, more than one unit is available to describe the same thing. For example, 1 ft is the same as 12 in, which is the same as 30.5 cm or 0.305 m. Sometimes a quantity has been measured in a unit that is not the one we need for calculations or comparisons. Scientists use a method of converting units called **dimensional analysis** (discussed next). Although there are other ways to convert units that you may have learned in math class or other science classes, this same method also helps solve many other types of problems in chemistry, as you will see later in this book. It is best to get comfortable with it now, so when you need to use it for more difficult problems later on, you'll already know how.

Dimensional analysis

The method of **dimensional analysis** is based on the idea that you can multiply anything by 1 as many times as you want and not change the value of the measurement. To do this, scientists use equivalents. For example, 1 foot = 12 inches; they mean the same thing. If you write those units as a fraction, they equal 1 because the quantities on top and bottom are the same and therefore cancel out to equal 1. So when you multiply another number by this fraction, you don't actually change the measurement—just the unit or label with which it is reported.

Go Online
Topic: dimensional analysis
Go to: www.scilinks.org
Code: Chem1e23

SC INKS
NSTA

Dimensional analysis steps

Go Online
Animated examples
http://webcom4.grtxle.com/
khk12Chemistry

1. Write down your "given" information.

2. Identify the unit that you want at the far right side of the problem, where the answer will go. (This helps you keep your eye on where you're headed throughout multistep problems.)

3. Multiply the given information by equivalents so that the "given" unit cancels and the "wanted" unit is left. A unit will cancel out when it appears on the top and the bottom of the expression.

4. Calculate the answer by multiplying across the top of the expression and dividing across the bottom. Remember that if there is more than one number on the bottom of the expression, hit the "divide" key before each number to let your calculator know that the number is on the bottom!

Example 1.4A

Converting Units

How many inches are there in 13.5 feet?

- Inches are the "wanted" unit, so set up the expression so that "foot" cancels.

$$13.5 \text{ feet} \times \frac{12 \text{ inches}}{1 \text{ foot}} = 162 \text{ inches}$$

Tables 1–2 and 1–3 show some common equivalent measurements, and metric prefixes that are often used by chemists, respectively.

Table 1–2	Common Equivalents
1 ft = 12 in	1 quart = 0.946 L
1 in = 2.54 cm	2 pints = 1 quart
1 min = 60 s	1 pound = 454 g
1 hr = 3600 s	

Table 1–3	Metric Prefixes Used in Chemistry		
Prefix	Symbol	Equivalent	Example
kilo-	k	1 kilo = 1000 base units	1 kg = 1000 g
deka-	da	1 deka = 10 base units	1 dag = 10 g
deci-	d	1 deci = 0.1 base unit	1 dg = 0.1 g
centi-	c	1 cent = 0.01 base unit	1 cg = 0.01 g
milli-	m	1 milli = 0.001 base unit	1 mg = 0.001 g
micro-	μ	1 micro = 1×10^{-6} base unit	1 μg = 1×10^{-6} g
nano-	n	1 nano = 1×10^{-9} base unit	1 ng = 1×10^{-9} g

Metric conversions

Converting within metric units follows the same principles of dimensional analysis. Metric units use prefixes to describe the equalities involved, such as milli- and kilo-. These prefixes are used with a base unit, such as grams or liters. There are 1000 liters in a kiloliter, just as there are 1000 grams in a kilogram. The prefixes work the same no matter which base unit they are combined with.

Help with metric prefixes

Many students make mistakes putting the number with the wrong part of the equivalent. Use these numbers with the base unit only! For example, write 1 mg = 0.001 g. The metric equivalent number went with the g, not the mg.

You can think of the metric equivalent number as "reading" the same as the prefix. For example, read "0.001" as "milli." Thus, 1 mg = 0.001 g would read "1 milligram = milli gram." Writing it as 0.001 mg = 1 g would read "milli milli gram = gram," which isn't correct.

Volume units

Volume is measured for a cube by multiplying length × width × height. If each of these distance measurements is in centimeters, then the volume unit would be in centimeters × centimeters × centimeters, or cm^3. However, not all objects are cubes, and volume can't always be found by multiplying three distance measurements. Volume is often given in milliliters in chemistry: $1 \ cm^3 = 1 \ mL$.

Example 1.4B

Converting Metric Units

1. How many meters are in 125 cm?

$$125 \ cm \times \frac{0.01 \ m}{1 \ cm} = 1.25 \ m$$

2. How many milliliters are in 1.5 L?

$$1.5 \ L \times \frac{1 \ mL}{0.001 \ L} = 1500 \ mL$$

Converting with multiple steps

Sometimes it's easier to convert in multiple steps rather than trying to figure out a new equivalency that goes straight from the "given" unit to the "wanted" unit. This way, you need to remember only a few equivalencies—the rest can be done in multiple steps.

Example 1.4C

Multistep Conversions

1. How many milligrams are in 0.546 kg?

   - There is no equivalent in Table 1-3 that goes directly from milligrams to kilograms. Therefore, it will take more than one step.

   - All metric prefixes are related to the base unit, so the base unit can be thought of as a bridge between other metric prefixes.

   - For multistep conversions, it is often easier to begin by filling in the units for each step that will produce the cancellations that you need:

   $$\frac{0.546 \text{ kg}}{} \times \frac{\text{g}}{\text{kg}} \times \frac{\text{mg}}{\text{g}} = \underline{\hspace{1cm}} \text{ mg}$$

   - Then, go back and fill in the numbers for the equivalencies afterward.

   $$\frac{0.546 \text{ kg}}{} \times \frac{1000 \text{ g}}{1 \text{ kg}} \times \frac{1 \text{ mg}}{0.001 \text{ g}} = \underline{\hspace{1cm}} \text{ mg}$$

   - Remember, when calculating the answer, multiply across the top and divide across the bottom. In your calculator, you'd enter: $0.546 \times 1000 \times 1/1/0.001$. (If you recognize that multiplying and dividing by 1 won't change the answer, you may skip those and enter: $0.546 \times 1000/.001$. Both methods will give the same answer.)

   $$\frac{0.546 \text{ kg}}{} \times \frac{1000 \text{ g}}{1 \text{ kg}} \times \frac{1 \text{ mg}}{0.001 \text{ g}} = 546,000 \text{ mg}$$

2. How many mL are in 3.50 pints?

   - Equivalents that you know: 2 pints = 1 quart, 1 quart = 0.946 L, 1 mL = 0.001 L

   $$\frac{3.50 \text{ pt}}{} \times \frac{1 \text{ qt}}{2 \text{ pt}} \times \frac{0.946 \text{ L}}{1 \text{ qt}} \times \frac{1 \text{ mL}}{0.001 \text{ L}} = 414 \text{ mL}$$

   - In the calculator, enter: $3.50 \times 1 \times 0.946 \times 1/2/1/0.001$

Go Online
Check your understanding
http://webcom4.grtxle.com/
khk12Chemistry

PRACTICE 1.4

Converting Units

Complete the following conversions:

1. 84 grams to milligrams

2. 177 millimeters to meters

3. 56 meters to centimeters

4. 9.3 kilograms to grams

5. 2.2 liters to mL

6. 500 cm^3 to mL

7. 4.0 liters to dm^3

8. 844 milligrams to grams

9. 742 milligrams to kilograms

10. 0.75 L to mL

11. 9.2 km to cm

Significant Digits

When taking measurements, scientists are careful to write down only those decimal places that they know for certain, plus one estimated place. The estimated decimal place is a 5 if the measurement is between two markings on the tool or a 0 if the measurement is exactly on a line (see Section 1.2). Therefore, if a zero is written at the end of the number, it is important. Zeros cannot just be added or left off—they have meaning and show the precision with which a measurement was taken. Therefore, scientists have devised a set of rules for working with numbers called "significant digits." **Significant digits** allow everyone looking at data and results to see how precisely measurements were taken and which decimal place is estimated or uncertain.

Rules for counting significant digits

1. Numbers that were measured are significant.

2. All nonzero numbers are significant.

3. Zeros:

   a. Are always significant when between two nonzero numbers.

   b. Are significant after a nonzero number (called a trailing zero) if a decimal place is present.

   c. Are never significant when coming before the first nonzero number (called a leading zero), no matter whether there is a decimal place present or not.

Go Online
Animated examples
http://webcom4.grtxle.com/
khk12Chemistry

These significant-digit rules can be summarized by two shorter rules: (1) if you see a decimal place anywhere in the number, start with the first nonzero number and count to the end, and (2) if there is no decimal point, count the numbers beginning with the first nonzero number and ending with the last nonzero number.

Example 1.5A

Counting Significant Digits

How many significant digits are in the following numbers?

1. 0.004550 L
   Four significant digits: 0.004550 L. All nonzero numbers are significant, and trailing zeros are significant if there is a decimal point present. Leading zeros are never significant.

2. 250 m
   Two significant digits: 250 m. All nonzero numbers are significant. The trailing zero is significant only if there is a decimal point present, and this number doesn't have a decimal point.

3. 250. m
   Three significant digits: 250. m. All nonzero numbers are significant. The trailing zero does count in this example because there is a decimal point.

Go Online
Check your understanding
http://webcom4.grtxle.com/
khk12Chemistry

PRACTICE 1.5A

Counting Significant Digits

How many significant digits are in each of the following?

1. 34.4 g
2. 90.50 g
3. 2700 lb
4. 903.2 m
5. 5.10 ft
6. 800.0 km
7. 0.023 m
8. 0.0030 mL
9. 70200 kg
10. 0.00250 s
11. 0.04010 s
12. 0.088 L
13. 2.700 mg
14. 0.02 mm
15. 0.0304 oz
16. 0.049 g
17. 5.10 mile
18. 70°C

Go Online
Animated examples
http://webcom4.grtxle.com/
khk12Chemistry

Performing calculations with significant digits

Scientists are careful to write the correct number of decimal places for the tool they are using, but raw data often have to be used in calculations in order to obtain results. Sometimes, when numbers are punched into a calculator, a long list of decimal places results. For example, if you divide 1.0 by 3.00, your calculator will give you 0.3333333 and continue on until the end of the screen. How can those pieces of data that could be read to a precision of only one or two decimal places suddenly become precise enough to give seven or eight decimal places, simply by being used in a calculation? They can't.

Results of calculations can be only as precise as the least precise number in the equation. Therefore, scientists have a set of rules to determine how many significant digits an answer contains.

Rules for math with significant digits

For multiplication and division:

1. Count the number of significant digits in each piece of given information.

2. The answer to the calculation will have the same number of significant digits as the smallest number of significant digits in the given information.

For addition and subtraction:

1. Count the number of decimal places in each piece of given information.

2. The answer to the calculation will have the same number of decimal places as the smallest number of decimal places in the given information.

Rounding should not take place until the final calculation is complete—this prevents error from rounding at each point along the way.

Example 1.5B

Calculations with Significant Digits

Write the answer with the correct number of significant digits.

1. 21.55 mL – 20.4 mL = ?

    - When typed into a calculator, the answer is 1.15 mL. However, when adding and subtracting, the answer can only have the least number of decimal places as in the problem.
    - The first number has two decimal places, and the second number has one. Therefore the answer can have only one decimal place, so we round the calculator answer to 1.2 mL.

2. $\dfrac{1.15 \text{ g}}{3.0 \text{ g/L}} = ?$

    - The calculator will give you an answer of 0.3833333 and continue with the 3s until the end of the screen.
    - When multiplying and dividing, the answer can have the same number of significant digits as the least number in the problem.
    - The top number has three, and the bottom number has two. Therefore, the answer can have two significant digits, and so we round it to 0.38 L.

Go Online
Check your understanding
http://webcom4.grtxle.com/
khk12Chemistry

PRACTICE 1.5B

Calculating with Significant Digits

Write the answers to the following problems with the correct number of significant digits.

1. 12.45 g – 9.501 g = ?

2. 1.200 g ÷ 0.49 L = ?

3. 150 mL × 1.25 g/mL = ?

4. 23.456 mL + 125.8 mL = ?

5. 0.00250 L × 120 g/L = ?

6. 105.0 g – 94.9 g = ?

7. 24.38 g/mole × 0.012 mole = ?

SECTION 1.6

Scientific Notation

You've probably used scientific notation in math class, but it will have more meaning and purpose now that you understand significant digits. It is true that scientific notation is used as shorthand to keep you from having to write out very large or very small numbers, but it also has another purpose. Scientific notation allows numbers to be written with the correct number of significant digits when they otherwise could not.

For example, say that the calculator gives you an answer of: 125002.2398, and you need to record that answer using exactly four significant digits. If you write the number as 125000, without a decimal point, there are only three significant digits, and if you write the number as 125002 or 125000, then there are six significant digits. If the number is written as 1.250×10^5, there are four significant digits. Numbers in scientific notation can have any number of significant digits that you need.

Go Online
Animated examples
http://webcom4.grtxle.com/
khk12Chemistry

Rules for using scientific notation

1. The decimal place must always be moved to a position after the first nonzero number. It cannot be any other place.

2. The value of the power of 10 is equal to how many places the decimal point was moved to get it to the new location, after the first nonzero number.

3. The sign of the power of 10 will be positive if the original number was large (greater than 1), and negative if the original number was small (less than 1).

Example 1.6

Scientific Notation

1. Write 0.004567 g in scientific notation with three significant digits.

   - The decimal point needs to go behind the first nonzero number, so 4.567.
   - It needs to be rounded to three significant digits, so round to 4.57.
   - The power of 10 is the number of places you moved the decimal point, so 10^3.
   - The sign of the power of 10 is positive for a large original number and negative for a small original number, so 10^{-3}.
   - 4.57×10^{-3} g

2. Write 327,209 L in scientific notation with four significant digits.

   - The decimal point needs to go behind the first nonzero number, so 3.27209.
   - It needs to be rounded to four significant digits, so 3.272.

- The power of 10 is the number of places you moved the decimal point, so 10^5.
- The sign of the power of 10 is positive for a large original number and negative for a small original number, so 10^5.
- 3.272×10^5 L

3. Write out 2.509×10^6 m in decimal notation.

   - The power of 10 is positive, so the answer will be a large number.
   - Move the decimal six places—the power of 10.
   - 2509000 m

4. Write out 3.76×10^{-5} L in decimal notation.

   - The power of 10 is negative, so the answer will be a small number.
   - Move the decimal five places—the power of 10.
   - 0.0000376 L

PRACTICE 1.6

Scientific Notation

1. Write the following numbers in scientific notation, with the specified number of significant digits.

   a. 102000 (with four significant digits)

   b. 0.02670 (with three significant digits)

   c. 3670.2 (with two significant digits)

   d. 0.00000009625 (with three significant digits)

   e. 12570000000 (with five significant digits)

   f. 1927000.008 (with three significant digits)

   g. 0.000000198 (with three significant digits)

2. Write out the following numbers.

   a. 1.267×10^6

   b. 2.608×10^8

   c. 3.70235×10^{-5}

   d. 1.2×10^{-8}

   e. 9.897×10^6

   f. 5.2470×10^3

   g. 2.786×10^{-7}

   h. 3.004×10^{-4}

Go Online
Check your understanding
http://webcom4.grtxle.com/khk12Chemistry

Science is a process in which scientists form questions, purposes, or problems through a societal need, observations, or continuation of others' work. Scientists gather data and analyze patterns and relationships to form laws and theories.

Measurements and observations must be taken with care to obtain results as accurate and precise as possible. Data are recorded in metric units, specifically the SI units (international system). Data can be changed from one unit to another using dimensional analysis. Significant digits are used to communicate which numbers are known for certain and which are estimated. Rules exist as to how many digits are written when calculating results. Scientific notation is the method of writing the correct number of digits, as well as shorthand for very large or small numbers.

A chemist in the 1930s, Dr. F. E. Allison is performing nitrogen fixation by bacteria. In this process, he uses the bacteria to change the nitrogen from its natural form from the atmosphere into nitrogen compounds such as ammonia, nitrate, and nitrogen dioxide. Such research aided farmers.

CHAPTER 1 Review

1. Explain the difference between each set of terms.

   a. Independent variable and dependent variable

   b. Variable and constant

   c. Control setup and experimental setup

   d. Hypothesis and prediction

   e. Theory and law

   f. Accuracy and precision

   g. Clear and colorless

2. Draw a picture of a dartboard with darts showing:

   a. Poor precision

   b. Good precision but not accurate

   c. Good precision and accuracy

3. What is the SI unit for each? And what is used to measure it?

   a. Time   c. Volume

   b. Length   d. Mass

4. Convert 125 mL to L.

5. Convert 0.8256 cm to mm.

6. Convert 2.54 km to m.

7. Convert 125 cm^3 to L.

8. Convert 89.54 cm to m.

9. Convert 25,000,000 nm to km.

10. Convert 7.85 mg to dg.

11. How many significant digits are in each of the following?

    a. 0.0012 g   c. 1.950 cm

    b. 1200 g   d. 20010 m

    e. 0.000130 km   i. 20 M

    f. 0.123 s   j. 200.0 g

    g. 20.0 m   k. 0.0045700 L

    h. 20 m

12. Write each of the following in scientific notation with three significant digits.

    a. 0.0012 g   e. 0.000130 km

    b. 1200 g   f. 0.123 s

    c. 1.950 cm   g. 200.0 g

    d. 20010 m   h. 0.0045700 L

13. Write each of the following with the correct number of significant digits (you can use scientific notation if you want, but you don't have to).

    a. 1.52648 g with two significant digits

    b. 0.00124563 m with three significant digits

    c. 125621.0 km with three significant digits

    d. 0.012000 g with four significant digits

14. Write the answers to the following math problems with the correct number of significant digits.

    a. 12.521 m + 1.29 m

    b. 82.1 g – 19.02 g

    c. 1925 L + 1.034 L

    d. 20.1 g/L × 1.2 L

    e. 15.75 L × 20.021 g/L

    f. 12.2 g ÷ 1.9 g/L

CHAPTER 2

Antacids
Chemistry Brings Relief

IN THIS CHAPTER

- Types of matter
- Naming chemicals
- Writing chemical formulas
- Defining, naming, and writing acids and bases
- Characteristics of acids and bases
- Chemical reactions
- Balancing chemical reactions
- Speeding up chemical reactions

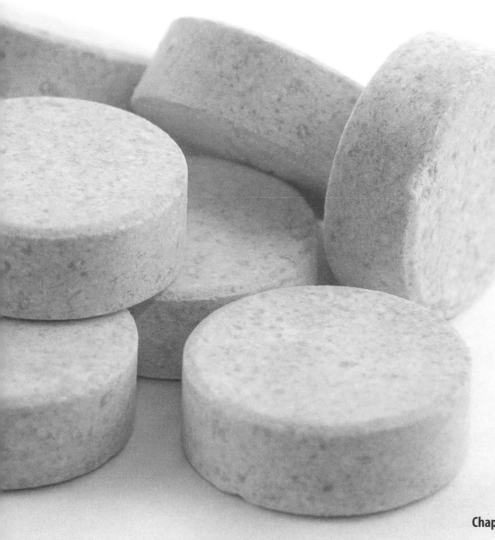

INTRODUCTORY ACTIVITY — Alka-Seltzer® Cannon

Part 1: Fill a film canister about half-full with room temperature water. Place about a quarter of a tablet of Alka-Seltzer® in the canister and quickly push the top on. Stand back and observe. This is called an "Alka-Seltzer® cannon."

In your lab group, brainstorm the chemistry involved in this process. What chemistry would you need to learn about to understand what's happening? Share your brainstorming with the class.

Part 2: List everything you know about acids and bases. Where have you used them or come in contact with them in your life? Explain what you understand about antacids. Share your ideas with the class.

CHEMISTRY YOU NEED TO KNOW

to make decisions about which medications to purchase as an informed consumer.

Introduction

Heartburn wakes you up in the middle of the night. You get up and find a bottle of antacids in the bathroom. What caused the heartburn? How do antacids work?

Gastric juices are excreted by the lining of the digestive system. Those juices contain hydrochloric acid, which is needed by enzymes that break down food. If too much acid is produced (hyperacidity), heartburn or ulcers (holes in the stomach lining) can occur. Medicine can help in two ways: (1) antacids neutralize the extra acid in the stomach and (2) acid inhibitors slow down the production of more acid. TV commercials for antacids often criticize competing medicines by saying that they don't work fast enough, and that you have to take them for an extended period of time. This is misleading—the antacids are meant to work quickly, but for a limited time. They are comparing themselves to acid inhibitors, which are not meant to work in the same way but instead provide a longer-term solution by shutting down acid production. These commercials are comparing apples and oranges! Common antacids include Alka-Seltzer®, Rolaids®, Tums®, Maalox®, and Mylanta®. Medicines such as Tagamet®, Zantac®, and Pepcid AC® are acid inhibitors.

Untreated heartburn can lead to bacterial infection and esophageal cancer, due to chronic inflammation.

Antacids are a . . .

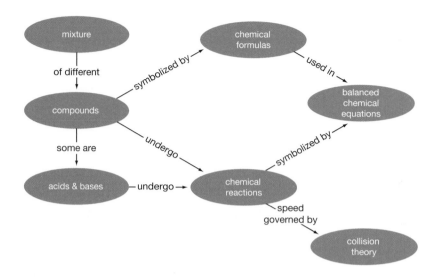

Types of Matter

In the last chapter, you learned that **matter** is anything that has mass and takes up space. Matter can be categorized into different types. There are **pure substances,** when every piece of the matter is exactly the same, and **mixtures,** with more than one type of substance mixed together.

Classifying pure substances

There are two types of pure substances—elements and compounds. **Elements** can be found on the periodic table. Some are found naturally, and some are manufactured. An element is a pure substance because every atom of the sample is the same element. The top picture in Figure 2–1 is an element. Elements cannot be broken down physically or chemically to form anything else. They are the basis for forming molecules or compounds. The aluminum foil that seals your new medicine bottle is an element.

Compounds are formed when more than one element combines with a chemical bond (see the middle image in Figure 2–1). A compound is also a pure substance, because every single molecule in that sample is identical. A compound can be broken down into its elements through a chemical reaction, but it cannot be separated by physical processes. Pure water is a compound—two hydrogen atoms and one oxygen atom are chemically bonded together to form H_2O.

Classifying mixtures

Mixtures have more than one pure substance mixed together (see the bottom picture in Figure 2–1). Mixtures can be any combination of solids,

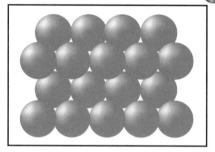

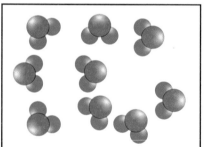

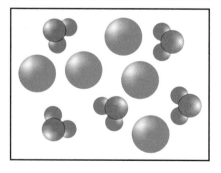

Figure 2–1. Types of matter. The substance on top is pure (an element). The substance in the middle is pure (a compound). The substance on the bottom is a mixture.

liquids, and gases. They can be separated into their pure substance components through physical means—a chemical reaction is not necessary. Mixtures are divided into two categories: homogeneous mixtures and heterogeneous mixtures.

Homogeneous mixtures, also called **solutions,** are present when a mixture looks the same throughout. These solutions will not settle out over time. Tap water is such a mixture; hopefully, it won't separate out all the things that are dissolved in it, such as chloride to kill bacteria and fluoride to strengthen teeth. It does have these things dissolved in it; however, simply looking at it won't tell us that—therefore, it's a homogeneous mixture. A **heterogeneous mixture** clearly shows more than one component—it can have layers, chunks, floating items, bubbles, or some other indication that there is more than one substance present. Lake water often has visible particles floating in it—therefore, it's a heterogeneous mixture.

Medicines, including antacids, are mixtures. Not only are there active ingredients listed (the medicines), but there are also fillers, substances that help the medicine compress into a pill, taste good, or be a certain color. Fillers are also needed to make many medicines large enough to handle. Taking a few milligrams of medicine would be difficult to do—a pill would be too tiny, and a liquid sample would be too small to measure accurately—so fillers are added to make it a manageable size that we can take consistently.

Young children are given liquid medicines before they are able to swallow pills. Those liquids are often colloids or suspensions. **Colloids** (such as milk) are solutions that have particles large enough to scatter light but small enough that they don't settle out over time. A colloid that scatters light is demonstrating the Tyndall effect. A flashlight beam shone through a colloid can be seen traveling through the mixture and spreading out as it is deflected off the particles (see Figure 2–2). A true solution will not exhibit the **Tyndall effect**—the particles dissolved in a solution are too small to scatter light. A **suspension** has particles large enough that they will settle out over time—that's why you should always shake a liquid antibiotic before giving it to a child or have new paint shaken at the store before taking it home.

Sunlight and clouds illustrate the Tyndall Effect.

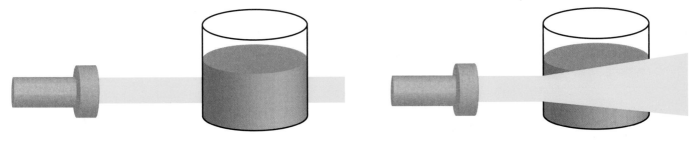

Figure 2–2. Types of matter. The Tyndall effect. The homogeneous mixture (solution) on the left does not scatter light because the dissolved particles are too small. However the colloid on the right does scatter light as the light runs into the dissolved particles

Types of Matter

1. Are medicines elements, compounds, or mixtures? Explain how you know this.

2. Explain why medicine needs to be a mixture of substances instead of just the active ingredients. What purpose do fillers have in medicine?

3. How could you determine whether a child's liquid medicine was a solution or a colloid?

4. How can you tell if a liquid medicine is a colloid or a suspension, since both will exhibit the Tyndall effect?

5. Classify each of the following images as element, compound, or mixture.

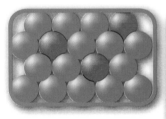   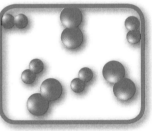

6. Draw a particle visualization (question 5 shows particle visualizations) of a mixture with two different elements and one compound.

7. Indicate whether each is an element (E), compound (C), or mixture (M).

a. Iron nail	h. Bronze (alloy of copper and tin)	o. Liquid mercury
b. Diamond	i. Gasoline	p. Sea water
c. Glass	j. Cola can	q. Lead shot
d. Salt water	k. Steel	r. Tap water
e. Distilled water	l. Tea	s. Air
f. "Flat" cola	m. Oxygen gas	t. Pure salt
g. Lead weight	n. Potassium	u. Motor oil

8. Indicate whether each mixture is a heterogeneous mixture (HE) or a homogeneous mixture (HO).

a. Tap water	f. River water	k. Carbonated cola
b. Granite	g. "Flat" cola	l. Ice water
c. Candle wax	h. Orange juice with pulp	m. Salad
d. White toothpaste	i. Ranch dressing	n. Chunky peanut butter
e. Gasoline	j. Glass	

Go Online
Check your understanding
http://webcom4.grtxle.com/
khk12Chemistry

Naming Chemicals

In order to talk about chemicals in medicines such as antacids, you must learn how to read and write their formulas. The rules for doing this are called **nomenclature**. Chemicals are named with standard sets of rules based on what type of compound they are.

Each element has a **symbol** that has one or two letters. Each element's symbol begins with a capital letter, so every time you see a capital letter in a chemical formula you know that it's a different element. For example, "Co" is the symbol for the element cobalt, whereas "CO" contains two element symbols, for carbon and oxygen.

The **subscripts** (numbers written below the text line) tell how many atoms of each element are in the chemical. The absence of a subscript means there is 1 atom. For example, H_2SO_4 contains 2 hydrogen atoms, 1 sulfur atom, and 4 oxygen atoms.

Writing the names of ionic compounds

Ionic compounds are made when metal atoms bond with nonmetal atoms. (There are a few exceptions where metals and nonmetals bond covalently, but we are not concerned with those for now.) You can tell whether an atom is a metal or a nonmetal based on which side of the periodic table it is on. A "stairstep" line near the right side of the periodic table separates them—metals on the left, nonmetals on the right (see Figure 2–3). If you have

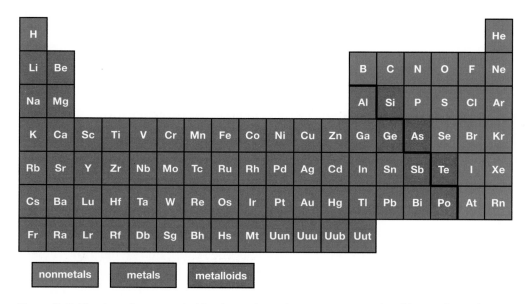

Figure 2–3. Metals and nonmetals. Metals are shown in green, nonmetals in blue, and metalloids in pink. Metalloids act like metals in some respects and nonmetals in others. Note that, although hydrogen is on the metal side, it often bonds in the same manner as nonmetals.

Gold and silicon atoms as an artist views them, used commonly together in most electronic devices.

trouble remembering which side is which, find something you know for sure. For example, you probably know that copper is a metal, and because it's located to the left of the stairstep, all elements on the left are metals.

Atoms that gain or lose electrons (which have a negative charge) are no longer neutral; they now have an electrical charge and are called **ions.** (How atoms gain or lose electrons will be discussed in Chapters 4 and 5.) When a metal and a nonmetal bond, the nonmetal takes the metal's bonding electrons. A metal that has given up its electrons is called a **cation.** A nonmetal that has taken on extra electrons is called an **anion.** Because electrons have a negative charge, giving away negative electrons produces cations that have a positive charge, whereas taking on extra negative electrons causes anions to have a negative charge. These positive and negative charges attract and form a bond. As a standard for all chemical names, the most metallic element is written first in a chemical formula, so the metal element (cation) will be first, followed by the nonmetal (anion).

Go Online
Animated examples
http://webcom4.grtxle.com/
khk12Chemistry

Binary ionic compounds   "Bi" means two, and "ionic compound" means a bond between metals and nonmetals. Therefore, a binary ionic compound is a bond between two elements—one being a metal and one a nonmetal. Rules for naming this type of molecule are:

1. Look up the name of the metal, the cation, on the periodic table and spell it normally.

2. Look up the name of the nonmetal, the anion, on the periodic table and write its name without the last syllable. Replace the last syllable with "-ide" instead.

3. The subscripts don't matter in naming this type of compound. (You'll learn why they're there in Section 2.3.)

Example 2.2A

Naming Binary Ionic Compounds

1. Write the name for NaCl.

   It's binary ionic, because it's two elements together—a metal and a nonmetal.

   The cation's symbol is Na, which is sodium.

   The anion's symbol is Cl, which is chlorine, which gets changed to chloride.

   Sodium chloride

2. Write the name for $CaBr_2$.

   It's binary ionic, because it's two elements together—a metal and a nonmetal.

   The cation's symbol is Ca, which is calcium.

   The anion's symbol is Br, which is bromine, which gets changed to bromide (the subscript 2 after the Br is not important in naming this kind of compound).

   Calcium bromide

Polyatomic ion compounds "Poly" means many, so a polyatomic ion is an ion composed of many atoms. Table 2–1 lists the names of common polyatomic ions. Sometimes many atoms bond, and together they become an ion. Most of the polyatomic ions you will use are anions (they took on extra electrons), but ammonium, NH_4^{+1}, is a cation (it gave away its extra electron). You will be able to identify this type of compound because it will have more than two elements, with metals and nonmetals included. Rules for naming this type of compound are:

Go Online
Animated examples
http://webcom4.grtxle.com/khk12Chemistry

1. Look up the name of the cation; it will either be an element on the periodic table or it will be NH_4 (which is ammonium). Write the element's name, or "ammonium."

2. Look up the anion. If it is more than one element, look it up on a polyatomic ion chart (see Table 2–1). It must match exactly. For example, SO_4^{-2} is sulfate, whereas SO_3^{-2} is sulfite. For now, ignore the superscripts (numbers up high), which give the charge of the ion. If you see parentheses in a chemical formula, look up what's inside the parentheses. (The reason for the parentheses is explained in Section 2.3.)

   a. If the anion is a polyatomic ion, write the name exactly as it appears on the polyatomic ion chart.

   b. If the anion is made up of just one element (one capital letter), write the anion name with "-ide" substituted for the last syllable, as in the binary ionic compounds.

3. The subscripts *within* the polyatomic ion do matter when looking up polyatomic ions—they must match exactly with the chart in order to name it. However, subscripts after a single element or outside a set of parentheses don't matter when naming this type of compound.

Table 2–1   Common Polyatomic Ions

Acetate, CH_3COO^{-1} or $C_2H_3O_2^{-1}$	Hypochlorite, ClO^{-1}
Ammonium, NH_4^{+1}	Iodate, IO_3^{-1}
Bromate, BrO_3^{-1}	Iodite, IO_2^{-1}
Bromite, BrO_2^{-1}	Nitrate, NO_3^{-1}
Carbonate, CO_3^{-2}	Nitrite, NO_2^{-1}
Chlorate, ClO_3^{-1}	Oxalate, $C_2O_4^{-2}$
Chlorite, ClO_2^{-1}	Perchlorate, ClO_4^{-1}
Chromate, CrO_4^{-2}	Permanganate, MnO_4^{-1}
Cyanide, CN^{-1}	Peroxide, O_2^{-2}
Dichromate, $Cr_2O_7^{-2}$	Phosphate, PO_4^{-3}
Dihydrogen phosphate, $H_2PO_4^{-1}$	Phosphite, PO_3^{-3}
Hydrogen carbonate (or bicarbonate*), HCO_3^{-1}	Silicate, SiO_3^{-1}
Hydrogen phosphate (or biphosphate*), HPO_4^{-2}	Sulfate, SO_4^{-2}
Hydrogen sulfate (or bisulfate*), HSO_4^{-1}	Sulfite, SO_3^{-2}
Hydroxide, OH^{-1}	

*For these polyatomic ions, either name is acceptable. Note that the bi- prefix does not indicate "2," but rather "hydrogen." The number "2" is indicated in chemical names with the prefix di-.

Example 2.2B

Naming Polyatomic Ionic Compounds

1. Write the name for $LiNO_3$.
   - It's a polyatomic ion compound, because there are more than two elements consisting of metals and nonmetals.
   - The cation is not NH_4, therefore it's not a polyatomic ion—just one element, with the symbol Li, or lithium.
   - The anion is therefore a polyatomic ion with the symbol NO_3, which is nitrate in Table 2–1.

   Lithium nitrate

2. Write the name for $Ba(OH)_2$.
   - It's a polyatomic ion compound, because there are more than two elements consisting of metals and nonmetals.
   - The cation is not NH_4, therefore it's not a polyatomic ion—just one element, with the symbol Ba, or barium.
   - The anion is a polyatomic ion that is in parentheses. Look up the symbol inside the parentheses in Table 2–1, and find OH, or hydroxide.

   Barium hydroxide

3. Write the name for $(NH_4)_2S$.
   - It's a polyatomic ion compound, because there are more than two elements consisting of metals and nonmetals.
   - The cation is NH_4, which is ammonium.
   - The anion's symbol is S, which is sulfur; it gets changed to sulfide.

   Ammonium sulfide

Ionic compounds with multivalent metals. Multivalent metals are metals that can give away different numbers of electrons to become a cation: they have more than one possible charge. The most common multivalent metals are shown in Table 2–2. When compounds form, the number of electrons given away by the cations equals the number of electrons taken by the anions. Therefore, the overall charge of the compound is neutral. This helps us determine which of the possible charges the multivalent metal has in a specific compound. You will be able to identify this type because it starts with one of the common multivalent metals. The rules for naming these compounds are:

Table 2–2 Common Multivalent Metals and Their Charges		
Cobalt	Co^{+2}	Co^{+3}
Copper	Cu^{+1}	Cu^{+2}
Iron	Fe^{+2}	Fe^{+3}
Lead	Pb^{+2}	Pb^{+4}
Manganese	Mn^{+2}	Mn^{+3}
Mercury	Hg_2^{+2}	Hg^{+2}
Tin	Sn^{+2}	Sn^{+4}

1. Write the compound's name based on the rules above for a binary ionic compound or a polyatomic ion compound, whichever is appropriate.

2. Look up the charge of the anion. If it's a polyatomic ion, the table you found the name in will tell you the charge. If it's an element, look at which column of the periodic table it's in (see Figure 2–4).

3. Add up the total negative charge in the compound by multiplying the anion's charge by their number in the chemical (the subscript number).

   a. If it's an element, multiply the charge by the subscript.

   b. If it's a polyatomic anion, multiply the charge by the subscript only if the subscript is outside of the parentheses—otherwise, the subscripts are already taken into account when looking up the ion in the table.

4. The total negative charge must be equal to the total positive charge, because all compounds are neutral.

Go Online
Animated examples
http://webcom4.grtxle.com/khk12Chemistry

Charges of Common Ions

H⁺¹																	
Li^{+1}	Be^{+2}												N^{-3}	O^{-2}	F^{-1}	
Na^{+1}	Mg^{+2}											Al^{+3}	P^{-3}	S^{-2}	Cl^{-1}	
K^{+1}	Ca^{+2}										Zn^{+2}	Ga^{+3}		Se^{-2}	Br^{-1}	
Rb^{+1}	Sr^{+2}									Ag^{+1}	Cd^{+2}				I^{-1}	
Cs^{+1}	Ba^{+2}															
Fr^{+1}	Ra^{+2}															

Figure 2–4. Common charges formed. As metals lose electrons and nonmetals gain electrons to form ions (atoms with a charge), there are patterns seen on the periodic table. Notice that elements in the same column often form the same charge. Elements not shown either don't readily form ions or they have more than one possibility.

Example 2.2C

Writing Names with Multivalent Metals

1. Write the name for SnO_2.
   - The cation is on the multivalent metals list.
   - The cation's symbol is Sn, for tin.
   - The anion's symbol is O, for oxygen, which is changed to "oxide." Oxygen has a –2 charge. There are two oxygen anions, as shown by the subscript 2 after the O. This gives a total negative charge of –4.
   - The total positive charge must be +4 to create a neutral compound. There is only one tin cation, therefore it must be a +4 charge; this will be written as a roman numeral in the compound's name.

   Tin(IV) oxide

2. Write the name for Fe_2S_3.
   - The cation is on the multivalent metals list.
   - The cation's symbol is Fe, for iron.
   - The anion's symbol is S, for sulfur, which is changed to sulfide. Sulfur's charge is –2. There are three sulfur anions, therefore the total negative charge is –6.
   - The total positive charge must be +6 to create a neutral compound. There are two iron cations available to create this total +6 charge. Therefore, each is +3, which is written as a roman numeral in the compound's name.

   Iron(III) sulfide

5. Divide the total positive charge by the number of cations available to make that total (the subscript number) to get the charge on each cation.

6. This charge is then written in roman numerals in parentheses after the cation's name.

Writing molecular compound names

Molecular compounds form when nonmetals bond with other nonmetals. Nonmetals share electrons with one another rather than giving and taking them like ions; therefore, there are no charges to worry about when naming this type. Molecular compounds that you name will consist of two nonmetals.

Nonmetals can combine in multiple ways with the same two elements. Therefore, we will need to specify how many of each element are in that specific chemical. (We did not need to do this with ionic compounds because they can come together in only one way to form neutral compounds.) You will be able to identify this type because it contains two nonmetals. Rules for naming this type are:

1. Write the name of the first element. Use a prefix to indicate how many atoms are in the molecule (the subscript gives this information). The only exception is that "mono-" is not used as a prefix for the first element when there's only one atom. Table 2–3 lists the prefixes used in naming molecular compounds.

2. Write the name of the second element. Use a prefix to indicate how many atoms are in the molecule, as told by the subscript. Remove the last syllable and use the ending -ide.

Go Online
Animated examples
http://webcom4.grtxle.com/
khk12Chemistry

Table 2–3 Prefixes Used on Molecular Compounds	
1. Mono-	6. Hexa-
2. Di-	7. Hepta-
3. Tri-	8. Octa-
4. Tetra-	9. Nona-
5. Penta-	10. Deca-

Example 2.2D

Naming Molecular Compounds

1. Write the name for N_2O_4.
   - It is a molecular compound because there are two elements—both nonmetals.
   - The first element's symbol is N, which is nitrogen. The subscript shows there are two atoms (di-), so write "dinitrogen."
   - The second element's symbol is O, which is oxygen, which is changed to oxide. The subscript shows there are 4 (tetra-), so write "tetraoxide."

   Dinitrogen tetraoxide (also known as *dinitrogen tetroxide*)

2. Write the name for CO_2.
   - It is a molecular compound, because there are two elements—both nonmetals.
   - The first element's symbol is C, which is carbon. There is no subscript written, so it is an implied 1 (mono-, but do not write "mono" with the first element's name).
   - The second element's symbol is O, which is oxygen, and that gets changed to oxide. The subscript is a 2 (di-), so write "dioxide."

   Carbon dioxide

Molecules with common names

A few common molecules are not named with this system but rather are just given names. For example, H_2O could be called "dihydrogen monoxide," but instead it's just called **water**. **Ammonia** is the name for NH_3 (note this is different from ammonium, the cation NH_4^{+1}).

Writing element names

Elements that are by themselves are simply called by their element name. For example, Cu without another element bonded to itself is simply copper.

PRACTICE 2.2

Naming Compounds

1. Name these compounds commonly found in antacids.

   a. $Al(OH)_3$

   b. $CaCO_3$

   c. $MgCO_3$

   d. $Mg(OH)_2$

   e. $NaHCO_3$

2. Name the following compounds.

   a. CuO

   b. ClF_3

   c. MgS

   d. Na_3P

   e. $Fe(OH)_2$

   f. Ga_2O_3

   g. Ba_3As_2

   h. N_2O_4

   i. $Ca(CH_3COO)_2$

   j. $AlCl_3$

   k. SnO_2

   l. K_2CrO_4

   m. CO_2

   n. NH_4NO_2

   o. K_2HPO_4

   p. $Fe_2(CO_3)_3$

   q. $KMnO_4$

   r. AgCN

   s. $Ca(ClO)_2$

   t. PbS

Go Online
Check your understanding
http://webcom4.grtxle.com/
khk12Chemistry

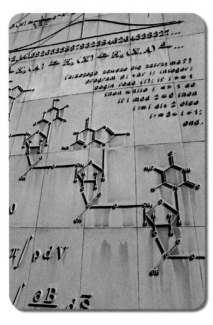

Go Online
Animated examples
http://webcom4.grtxle.com/
khk12Chemistry

SECTION 2.3

Writing Chemical Formulas

It is also important to be able to write chemical formulas from their names. We can place chemicals into categories based on their type and follow rules for writing formulas just as we did for naming. The key to writing formulas for all ionic compounds is that they are always neutral— the positive charge of the cation(s) always exactly balances the negative charge of the anion(s). Learning how to write formulas from their names may clear up any confusion you still have about when to look at the subscripts and when to ignore them for naming.

Writing ionic compound formulas

Binary ionic compounds   You can recognize this type of molecule because it will have no prefix (unlike the molecular compound) and the second name will end with -ide.

1. The first name will be the metal, the cation. Write the element's symbol and find the charge.

    a. If it is one of the multivalent metals discussed in the last section (cobalt, copper, iron, lead, manganese, mercury, or tin), then the roman numerals give you the charge. For example, copper(II) would be Cu^{+2}.

    b. For all other metals, see Figure 2–4 in the previous section for the charges of common elements.

2. Write the name of the second element (remember that "-ide" was used in place of the last syllable of the element's name). Find the charge of the element, again using Figure 2–4 for the charges of common elements.

3. The charges must balance to zero. Add subscripts to the cation and the anion to make the charges balance. The subscript is multiplied by the charge. For example, Ca_3^{+2} is the same as $Ca^{+2}Ca^{+2}Ca^{+2}$, and there would be a total positive charge of +6—the same as taking the subscript "3" and multiplying it by "+2." Subscripts of 1 are not written—1 is assumed if there is no subscript.

It was a Swedish chemist, Jons Jakob Berzelius, who in the 19th century developed the concept of writing chemical formulas. Formulas explain how reactions occur.

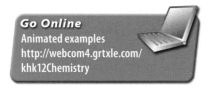

Go Online
Animated examples
http://webcom4.grtxle.com/
khk12Chemistry

Example 2.3A

Writing Binary Ionic Formulas

Write the formula for strontium bromide.
- It is binary ionic, because it has a metal and a non-metal and ends with -ide.
- The cation is strontium, whose symbol and charge is Sr^{+2}.
- The anion is bromide, which comes from bromine, and it has a symbol and charge of Br^{-1}.

- $Sr^{+2}Br^{-1}$: There are charges of +2 and –1. These don't add up to zero, so we need a total negative charge of –2 to cancel out the positive charge. Therefore, we need two Br^{-1} ions: $Sr^{+2}Br^{-1}Br^{-1}$.

  $SrBr_2$

Polyatomic ion compounds   You will recognize this type because it will have no prefixes and the second word will end with -ate, -ite cyanide, hydroxide, or peroxide. Molecules beginning with ammonium are also of this type.

Go Online
Animated examples
http://webcom4.grtxle.com/
khk12Chemistry

1. Find the symbol and charge for the cation. It will either be an element, in which case you follow the same instructions as for binary ionic compounds above, or it will be ammonium (the only polyatomic cation you will deal with), which is NH_4^{+1}.

2. Look up the symbol and charge of the anion. It will be in Table 2–1, polyatomic ions. (Note that an ammonium compound might have a single element as the anion, in which case you'd look it up in Figure 2–4.)

3. Balance the charges by adding subscripts until they total zero. If you add a subscript to a polyatomic ion, then you must put parentheses around the polyatomic ion. For example, if you want two nitrates, you must write $(NO_3)_2$ rather than NO_{32}—which looks like one nitrogen and 32 oxygens. The subscript on the *outside* of the parentheses is the only one you need to worry about when finding the total negative charge. For example, the entire NO_3 "chunk" has a charge of –1; you would not multiply the –1 charge that's written on the ion chart by the oxygen's subscript of 3 in the NO_3. Subscripts of "1" are not written—they are assumed if nothing else is there.

Example 2.3B

Writing Polyatomic Ionic Formulas

1. Write the formula for calcium phosphate.
   - It is a polyatomic ion compound, because it ends with -ate.
   - The cation is calcium, which is Ca^{+2}.
   - The anion is phosphate, which is PO_4^{-3}.
   - $Ca^{+2}PO_4^{-3}$: There are charges of +2 and –3. They do not add up to zero, but both can be multiplied for a +6 or –6 total charge. Then they would add up to zero. Therefore, three calcium cations are needed (3 × +2) with two phosphate anions (2 × –3).
   - Ca_3PO_{42}: But this is incorrect—it shows that 42 oxygen atoms are present, when what needs to be shown is that two of the entire phosphate anion are present. A polyatomic ion needs to be placed in parentheses to be multiplied by a subscript.

   $Ca_3(PO_4)_2$

2. Write the formula for ammonium chloride.
   - This is a polyatomic ion compound, because it begins with ammonium.
   - The cation is ammonium, which is NH_4^{+1}.
   - The anion is chloride, which came from chlorine, and is Cl^{-1}.
   - $NH_4^{+1}Cl^{-1}$: There are charges of +1 and –1. They add up to zero, so no subscripts are needed.

   NH_4Cl

Go Online
Animated examples
http://webcom4.grtxle.com/
khk12Chemistry

Molecular compounds

You will recognize this type by the use of prefixes in the name. Because molecular compounds do not form charges (they do not give and take electrons, but instead share them), you don't have to worry about balancing the charges.

1. Write the first element's name. Use the prefix to write the subscript (note that no prefix on the first element means 1, so write nothing).

2. Write the second element's name. Use the prefix to write the subscript.

Example 2.3C

Writing Molecular Compound Formulas

1. Write the formula for boron trifluoride.
   - This is a molecular compound, because prefixes are used.
   - The first element is boron, and there is no prefix. No prefix on the first element implies mono-.
   - The second element is trifluoride, which comes from fluorine, with the "tri" meaning 3.

   BF_3

2. Write the formula for tetraphosphorus decaoxide.
   - This is a molecular compound, because prefixes are used.
   - The first element is tetraphosphorus, which means four phosphorus atoms.
   - The second element is decaoxide, which comes from oxygen, with the "deca-" meaning 10.

   P_4O_{10}

Writing diatomic element formulas

There is one more type of formula that you will need now—**diatomic elements.** Some elements are so chemically reactive that, when they are not bonded to any other elements, they find another atom of their same kind and bond. Whenever you see such an element's name written by itself, the atoms always come in twos. Table 2–4 lists these elements.

Table 2–4 Diatomic Elements	
Hydrogen, H_2	Iodine, I_2
Oxygen, O_2	Nitrogen, N_2
Fluorine, F_2	Chlorine, Cl_2
Bromine, Br_2	

*Symbols can be placed in a "word" to remember: HOFBrINCl

PRACTICE 2.3

Writing Chemical Formulas

1. Write the following chemical formulas commonly found in antacids.

   a. Magnesium carbonate   d. Magnesium hydroxide

   b. Sodium bicarbonate   e. Calcium carbonate

   c. Aluminum hydroxide

2. Write the following chemical formulas.

   a. Magnesium fluoride   k. Ammonium acetate

   b. Cesium bromide   l. Cobalt(III) nitrate

   c. Copper(II) nitrate   m. Sodium sulfite

   d. Potassium chlorate   n. Silicon tetrachloride

   e. Phosphorus trichloride   o. Sodium oxide

   f. Chromium(III) carbonate p. Potassium cyanide

   g. Sodium bisulfate   q. Barium sulfate

   h. Silicon dioxide   r. Silver nitrate

   i. Lead(IV) sulfide   s. Barium hydroxide

   j. Lithium nitride   t. Iron(III) carbonate

Go Online
Check your understanding
http://webcom4.grtxle.com/khk12Chemistry

SECTION 2.4

Defining, Naming, and Writing Acids and Bases

You've undoubtedly heard of acids and bases, for example, in heartburn and the antacids that this chapter is investigating. However, do you know what those terms really mean?

Go Online
Animated examples
http://webcom4.grtxle.com/khk12Chemistry

According to the **Arrhenius** definition of an **acid,** it is a compound that has a hydrogen cation (H^{+1}) to donate to water (H_2O), forming the **hydronium ion** (H_3O^{+1}). As shown in Figure 2–5, the hydronium ion is formed

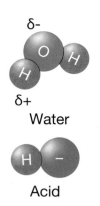

δ-

Water

δ+

Acid

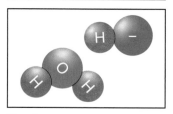

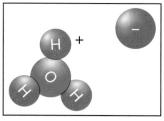

Figure 2–5. Acids in water. The key on top shows the water and acid molecules. The second frame shows the water and acid molecules coming toward each other. The third frame shows them in contact, and the last shows the hydronium ion and resulting anion from the acid transferring the hydrogen ion to the water molecule.

when the two hydrogen atoms and the one oxygen atom from water bond with the hydrogen cation (it has a +1 charge in the cation form). Therefore, the hydronium ion has three hydrogen atoms, one oxygen atom, and a +1 charge. If we use this definition of an acid, then all acids must have a hydrogen ion that they can donate. Therefore, for now all acid formulas will begin with H.

Naming acids

You will recognize an acid because it will begin with hydrogen. There are two types of acids: those that do not contain oxygen atoms and those that do. To name the **nonoxygen acids**:

1. The prefix hydro- is used to indicate that it is an acid without oxygen.

2. Look up the name of the anion after the hydrogen. Remove the last syllable of the anion name, and add the ending -ic.

3. End the name with the word *acid*.

To name oxygen-containing acids (**oxyacids**):

1. The prefix hydro- is not used for oxygen-containing acids.

2. Look up the anion name; it will be a polyatomic ion. If the polyatomic ion name ends with -ate, remove it and end the acid name with -ic. If the polyatomic ion name ends with -ite, remove it and end the acid name with -ous.

3. Complete the name with the word *acid*.

Writing acid formulas

To write acids, we use the same principle of balancing charges that we discussed in the last section, along with the rules for naming acids above. For acids *containing* hydro- as a prefix:

1. Begin the formula with the hydrogen cation (H^{+1}).

2. Because the prefix hydro- is used, we know that the anion does not contain oxygen. Write the anion's formula and charge.

3. Balance the charges by adding any necessary subscripts.

For acids *without* the hydro- prefix:

1. Begin the formula with the hydrogen cation (H^{+1}).

2. If the acid ends with -ic, look up the polyatomic ion ending with -ate. If the acid ends with -ous, look up the polyatomic ion ending with -ite.

3. Balance the charges by adding any necessary subscripts.

Example 2.4A

Naming Acids

1. Write the name for H_2S.
   - This is a non-oxygen-containing acid, because it begins with H and has no O.
   - Use the prefix hydro-.
   - It doesn't matter, for naming purposes, that there are two hydrogen atoms—that's how many are needed to balance the negative charge of the anion to create a neutral molecule. It still begins with H, regardless of the number of atoms.
   - The anion element is sulfur, which is changed to sulfuric (sulfur is an exception to dropping the last syllable; you just add the -ic ending to the whole word).
   - Finish with the word *acid*.

   Hydrosulfuric acid

2. Write the name for HCH_3COO.
   - This is an oxygen-containing acid, because it starts with H and does have O.

   - Do *not* use the prefix hydro- for oxygen-containing acids!
   - The anion is a polyatomic ion, acetate. The -ate ending is changed to -ic, acetic.
   - Use the ending word *acid*.

   Acetic acid

3. Write the name for H_2SO_3.
   - This is an oxygen-containing acid, because it starts with H and does have O.
   - Do not use the prefix hydro- (oxygen-containing acid).
   - The anion is a polyatomic ion, sulfite. The -ite ending is changed to -ous to make sulfurous acid (again, the last syllable is left on for sulfur).
   - Use the ending word *acid*.

   Sulfurous acid

Example 2.4B

Writing Acid Formulas

1. Write the formula for hydrobromic acid.
   - It is a non-oxygen-containing acid, because of the prefix hydro-.
   - The cation will be H^{+1}, because it's an acid.
   - Bromic came from the anion of bromine, or Br^{-1}.
   - $H^{+1}Br^{-1}$: There are +1 and –1 charges. They add up to zero, so no subscripts are needed.

   HBr

2. Write the formula for carbonic acid.
   - It is an oxygen-containing acid, because there is no prefix hydro-.
   - The cation will be H^{+1}, because it's an acid.
   - Carbonic comes from the anion carbonate, which is CO_3^{-2}.

   - $H^{+1}CO_3^{-2}$: There are +1 and –2 charges. The +1 charge can be multiplied by 2 to cancel out the –2 charge.

   H_2CO_3

3. Write the formula for nitrous acid.
   - It is an oxygen-containing acid, because there is no prefix hydro-.
   - The cation will be H^{+1}, because it's an acid.
   - Nitrous comes from nitrite, which is NO_2^{-1}.
   - $H^{+1}NO_2^{-1}$: There are +1 and –1 charges. They add up to zero, so no subscripts are needed.

   HNO_2

Bases

If acids donate a hydrogen cation to water, what do bases do?

According to the Arrhenius definition, **bases** produce the hydroxide ion in water. The **hydroxide ion** is OH^{-1}. Most bases in this book will be ionic compounds with the hydroxide ion as their anion. One common exception to this is ammonia, NH_3, which does not contain the hydroxide ion in its formula, but does still produce the hydroxide ion upon reacting with water. Naming and writing bases is just like the process for polyatomic ion compounds—except that the anion will be the hydroxide ion. The most commonly used base in chemistry labs is sodium hydroxide (NaOH).

Example 2.4C

Naming and Writing Bases

1. Write the name for the base $Sr(OH)_2$.
   - Bases with OH as the anion follow the polyatomic ionic rules above.
   - Write the name of the cation, strontium.
   - Write the name of the anion, hydroxide.

   Strontium hydroxide

2. Write the formula for the base calcium hydroxide.
   - Bases with hydroxide follow the polyatomic ionic rules above.
   - Calcium is Ca^{+2}.
   - Hydroxide is OH^{-1}.
   - $Ca^{+2}OH^{-1}$: More hydroxides are needed to balance the charges. Use parentheses, because it's a polyatomic ion.

   Ca(OH)₂

Naming and Writing Acids and Bases

1. Write the formula for hydrochloric acid—the acid produced by cells in your stomach that antacids work to neutralize.

2. Name the following acids.

   a. HNO_3 **f.** HIO_3 **k.** H_3PO_4

   b. $HClO_4$ **g.** H_3P **l.** HBr

   c. H_3PO_3 **h.** HC **m.** H_2CO_3

   d. HF **i.** H_2SO_3

   e. HI **j.** HCH_3COO

3. Write the formulas for the following acids.

   a. Phosphoric acid   **f.** Hydrobromic acid   **k.** Hydroiodic acid

   b. Sulfurous acid   **g.** Hypochlorous acid   **l.** Perchloric acid

   c. Hydrosulfuric acid   **h.** Nitric acid   **m.** Acetic acid

   d. Nitrous acid   **i.** Sulfuric acid

   e. Phosphorous acid   **j.** Chlorous acid

4. Write the names of the following bases.

   a. NH_4OH **c.** $Fe(OH)_3$

   b. KOH **d.** $Cu(OH)_2$

5. Write the formulas for the following bases.

   a. Cesium hydroxide

   b. Aluminum hydroxide

   c. Barium hydroxide

   d. Ammonia (the most common non-hydroxide-containing base you'll encounter in beginning chemistry)

Go Online
Check your understanding
http://webcom4.grtxle.com/
khk12Chemistry

Characteristics of Acids and Bases

LAB 2.5

Acids and Bases

Purpose To identify common substances as acids or bases using a variety of techniques

Materials Various indicators and household substances, well-plate, droppers, watchglass, stir-rod

Safety Use caution with all acids and bases—they can be caustic and cause burns. Never touch or taste chemicals in the lab. Wear goggles. Report any skin or clothing exposure to your teacher.

Procedure

1. Create a data table with all of the household substances' names along the top, and the indicator names down the left side.

2. Test each substance with each indicator. The following three steps give the proper technique for using a liquid indicator, a paper indicator, or a pH meter. Follow the appropriate steps for each indicator you have been supplied.

3. To test substances with a **liquid indicator:**

   a. Use a clean dropper to add a few drops of the solution to be tested into a clean well in the well-plate.

   b. Add one drop of the indicator and stir with a clean stir-rod.

   c. Record the color of the indicator in the test solution.

   d. Use the color guide in Figure 2–6 to record the pH of the substance.

4. To test substances with a **paper indicator:**

   a. Place a small piece of the test paper (pH paper or litmus paper) on a clean, dry watchglass.

   b. Dip a clean stir-rod into the substance to be tested.

   c. Touch the stir-rod to the paper on the watchglass.

   d. Record the color of the paper.

   e. For litmus paper, blue indicates base and red indicates acid—record "acid" or "base." For pH paper, match the test strip with the color guide on the pH paper container, and record the pH.

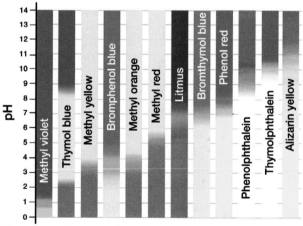

Figure 2-6. Common indicator colors. (© 1998 David Dice).

Acids and Bases (*cont'd.*)

5. To test a substance with a pH meter:

   a. Rinse the pH meter with distilled water.

   b. Stir the substance to be tested with the pH meter.

   c. Wait for the meter to settle on a reading, and record the reading.

   d. Rinse the pH meter with distilled water before putting it back in the buffer solution.

6. Clean up the lab area and place all equipment as found.

Discussion

1. Make a list of all the substances that are acids, all that are neutral, and all that are basic. If you do not know which pH's are considered acidic and which are basic, find a substance that you think is acidic, one that you think is basic, or one that you think is neutral. Use the pH of those substances to determine what other substances might be acidic or basic.

2. What are the pros and cons of each of the three types of indicators: liquid, paper, and meter?

3. In what situation might a liquid indicator be most appropriate or efficient? What about paper indicators? How about pH meters?

4. Were your readings consistent for each substance? (Did all of the indicators give the same pH reading for the same substance?) If not, what are some reasons that readings would be inconsistent with different indicators?

5. Share your lists of acids, neutrals, and bases with the class. Use whiteboards if your teacher provides them. What discrepancies do you find between the different lists? What are some possible reasons for the discrepancies, if there were any? Do you need to make any changes to your lists?

Table 2–5	Characteristics of Acids and Bases	
	Acids	**Bases**
Produce in water	Hydronium, H_3O^{+1}	Hydroxide ion, OH^{-1}
Taste	Sour	Bitter
Other	React with active metals to form hydrogen gas	Feel slippery

 Never touch or taste any chemicals in this course. These sensory characteristics are found in safe acids and bases, such as citrus fruits or bitter foods. Consider anything in a science classroom to be contaminated and never to be tasted or touched!)

Now you have learned the definitions of acids and bases, but what do these chemicals really do? How do they act? Table 2–5 gives some common characteristics of acids and bases.

Many people think of acids as being dangerous and bases as less dangerous, or even fairly safe. Both acids and bases can be extremely dangerous to people—for example, battery acid or bleach (a base). However, there are also acids and bases that are safe for people to use, such as vinegar (an acid) and hand soap (a base).

Go Online
Molecular animations
http://webcom4.grtxle.com/khk12Chemistry

Go Online
SC*INKS*
NSTA
Topic: Acids and bases
Go to: www.scilinks.org
Code: Chem1e57

Strength versus concentration of acids and bases

What causes some acids and bases to be more harmful than others? Acids and bases are characterized as strong or weak. A **strong acid** is one that

Figure 2-7. Strong versus weak acids. The image on the left shows a strong acid—more of the acid molecules donated their hydrogen ion than not. The image on the right shows a weak acid. Most of the acid molecules are still intact.

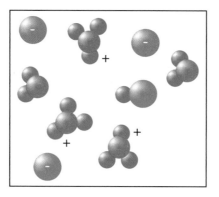

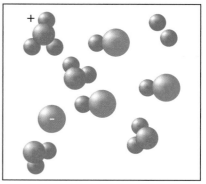

Go Online
Molecular animations
http://webcom4.grtxle.com/
khk12Chemistry

Solute   Solvent

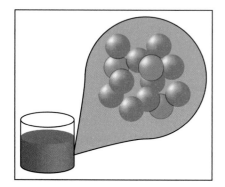

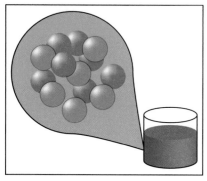

Figure 2–8. Concentration. The beaker on top has a lower concentration than the one on the bottom. The lower concentration has less dissolved substance (solute—the lighter spheres) and more water (solvent—the darker spheres).

has almost every molecule in the sample donating its hydrogen ion to the water. A **weak acid** has only a few molecules that donate their hydrogen ion—the rest hang on to it (see Figure 2–7). Bases are similar—a **strong base** is one that produces almost as many hydroxide ions as possible for the number of base molecules that are in the water, and a **weak base** produces only a few.

Strength of an acid or base has nothing to do with the concentration of the solution. **Concentration** is how many molecules of the acid or base are in the sample to begin with—it doesn't matter how many have produced hydronium or hydroxide ions, just how many acid or base molecules were added to the solution (see Figure 2–8).

Varieties of combinations of strength and concentration are described in Table 2–6. The descriptions can also apply to bases if the words "base" and "hydroxide ion" are substituted for "acid" and "hydronium ion."

Table 2–6. Descriptions of Acid Solutions	
Type of Solution	**Description**
Concentrated and strong	Many acid molecules are added to the water (concentrated), and almost every molecule that is added donates its hydrogen to the water (strong)
Dilute and strong	Only a few acid molecules are added to the water (dilute), but almost every one that is added donates its hydrogen to water (strong)
Concentrated and weak	Many acid molecules are added to the water (concentrated), but only a few of them donate their hydrogen to the water (weak)
Dilute and weak	Only a few acid molecules are added to the water (dilute), and only a few of those actually donate their hydrogen to the water (weak)

pH scale

How can the number of hydronium or hydroxide ions be measured? The **pH scale** measures the level of acidity (or basicity) of a sample. It measures how many hydronium ions are in the sample and how this number compares to the overall number of particles in the sample. The scale goes from 1 to 14. Samples with pH between 1 and 7 are considered acidic, a sample with a pH of 7.0 is neutral, and samples with pH between 7 and 14 are basic. (More about how pH is calculated based on hydronium concentration will be discussed in Chapter 6.)

Measuring pH

pH can be measured in several ways: with a meter that gives a readout of the pH level, with an indicator added to solution that changes color and can be matched to a "key" to read the pH, and with papers that have indicators on them which change color in the same way to indicate the pH of the sample.

Liquid indicators turn a color at a certain pH—you can match the color to the key to determine the pH level. Figure 2–6 in Lab 2.5 shows several indicators and the pH at which they change color. **Universal indicators** are mixtures of several different color—change indicators that produce a variety of colors at many different pH's.

pH paper contains a universal indicator—it changes color many times over the pH range, and the color is matched to a key. Another type of paper used for this is **litmus paper**—it turns red in an acid and blue in a base. Litmus paper is a quick and easy way to tell if something is acidic or basic, but it doesn't tell the specific pH.

pH meters or **pH probes** are placed in a sample to give a digital readout of the pH. They come in different levels of precision—some can read a pH level to many decimal places. Scientists can select among all these methods to choose the one that works best for their needs.

SECTION 2.6

Chemical Reactions

Chemical reactions rearrange atoms to produce chemicals different from those that were originally present. Chemical equations describe what occurs during a chemical reaction. Equations can be written in word form or using chemical formulas.

Examples of chemical equations

Word equation: magnesium metal is reacted with aqueous hydrochloric acid to produce aqueous magnesium chloride and hydrogen gas

Formula equation: $Mg(s) + 2\ HCl(aq) \rightarrow MgCl_2(aq) + H_2(g)$

Visualization:

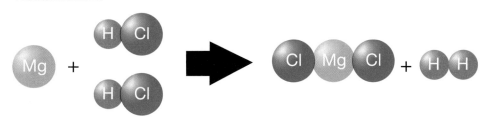

Go Online
Molecular animations
http://webcom4.grtxle.com/
khk12Chemistry

Parts of a chemical equation

The left side of the equation gives the reactants. **Reactants** are the original chemicals that are reacting together. The reactants then produce different chemicals, **products,** which are on the right side of the reaction. The arrow (→) indicates reaction direction, and is sometimes read as "yields" or "produces." A chemical reaction uses the format "reactants yield products." Chemical equations can also give information about the form the matter is in (solid, liquid, gas, aqueous—dissolved in water) as well as information about energy gained or released in the reaction. These ideas will be discussed in future chapters.

When writing chemical equations, write each chemical's formula separately, as you learned earlier in this chapter. Each formula needs to be written correctly—with the charges balanced for ionic compounds. The reactants are separated by + signs. The reactants and products are then separated by the →. The products are also separated by + signs. At this point, we will not balance the chemical equations—that will come in the next section—but rather just practice writing formulas in the equation format.

Example 2.6A

Writing Formula Equations

1. Silver nitrate and calcium chloride produce calcium nitrate and silver chloride.

   $AgNO_3 + CaCl_2 \rightarrow Ca(NO_3)_2 + AgCl$

2. Hydrogen gas and oxygen gas react to produce water.
   Hydrogen and oxygen are diatommic molecules, so because they are by themselves, they need to come in pairs.

   $H_2 + O_2 \rightarrow H_2O$

Writing Formula Equations

Change the following word equations into formula equations.

1. Hydrochloric acid (stomach acid) reacts with calcium carbonate (a compound found in antacids) to produce calcium chloride, carbon dioxide, and water.

2. In the above antacid reaction, carbon dioxide is produced. What effect might this have on you when you take this antacid?

3. Chlorine gas reacts with potassium bromide to form potassium chloride and bromine gas.

4. Methane (CH_4) reacts with oxygen gas to form carbon dioxide and water.

5. Hydrogen gas and nitrogen gas react to form ammonia.

6. Potassium chlorate decomposes into potassium chloride and oxygen gas.

7. Hydrochloric acid and aluminum oxide form aluminum chloride and water.

Go Online
Check your understanding
http://webcom4.grtxle.com/khk12Chemistry

Double replacement and neutralization reactions

You will learn about many types of chemical reactions throughout this book. One type of chemical reaction is a neutralization reaction. Neutralization reactions occur between an acid and base and produce a salt and water. These reactions are one type of double replacement reaction.

The generic form for **double replacement reactions** is AX + BZ → AZ + BX (see Figure 2–9). Two ionic compounds react together, and their cations and anions trade partners to produce two new ionic compounds. When the ions are trading places, two cations cannot join together, and neither can two anions, so the cation of the first reactant must join with the anion of the second reactant and vice versa.

Go Online
Molecular animations
http://webcom4.grtxle.com/khk12Chemistry

Figure 2–9. Double replacement reaction. The cation of the first compound combines with the anion of the second compound and vice versa.

The generic form of a **neutralization reaction** is HX + BOH → HOH + BX (see Figure 2–10). The first reactant is an acid (containing a hydrogen cation and an anion X), and the second reactant is a base (containing a cation B and the hydroxide anion). They form two products: water (H_2O

can also be written as HOH to show that the hydrogen cation from the first reactant joined the hydroxide anion from the second reactant), and a salt from the leftover cation and anion. **Salt** is another name for an ionic compound.

Figure 2–10. Neutalization reaction. A neutralization reaction is a double replacement where the cation of the acid (H^{+1}) and the anion of the base (OH^{-1}) form water, and the other ions form a salt.

Example 2.6B

Writing Neutralization Reactions

1. Finish the reaction: hydrochloric acid and sodium hydroxide react to form _____.

   • $HCl + NaOH \rightarrow$?
   • An acid and a base will form water and a salt. The water (HOH) will take the hydrogen from the acid and the OH from the base.
   • Whatever is left over forms the salt. There is a chloride left over from the acid, and a sodium is left over from the base. The cation (made from the metal) always goes first, so it will be sodium chloride.

   $HCl + NaOH \rightarrow HOH + NaCl$

2. Finish the reaction: hydrobromic acid and calcium hydroxide react to form _____.

   • $HBr + Ca(OH)_2 \rightarrow$?
   • The water (HOH) takes the hydrogen from the acid and the hydroxide from the base. It's OK that there are two hydroxides in the base—that will get worked out when you learn to balance equations. Just think of all the hydroxides being used to make water molecules.
   • The salt is formed from the remaining ions. The bromide is left from the acid, and the calcium from the base. The cation (made from the metal) is always written first, thus, calcium bromide.

   $HBr + Ca(OH)_2 \rightarrow HOH + CaBr_2$

PRACTICE 2.6B

Writing Neutralization Reactions

Write the following word equations into formula equations, and add the products.

1. Ammonium hydroxide and nitric acid react to form _____.

2. Calcium hydroxide and nitric acid react to form _____.

3. Hydroiodic acid and sodium hydroxide react to form _____.

4. Strontium hydroxide and sulfuric acid react to form _____.

Go Online
Check your understanding
http://webcom4.grtxle.com/
khk12Chemistry

SECTION 2.7

Balancing Chemical Reactions

LAB 2.7

Conservation of Matter

Purpose To find a relationship between the mass of reactants and the mass of products in a chemical reaction

Materials Snack-size plastic bag, baking soda (sodium bicarbonate), vinegar (acetic acid), balance, rubber band

! **Safety** Wear goggles. Report any chemical exposure to skin or clothing to your teacher.

Procedure

1. Place 1.0 g of baking soda (sodium bicarbonate) in the small plastic bag. Shake into one bottom corner of the bag, and use a rubber band to seal off this corner from the rest of the bag.

2. Put 10 mL of vinegar (acetic acid) into the rest of the bag.

3. Squeeze as much air as possible out of the bag and seal it. Carefully find the mass so that the two chemicals do not yet begin mixing.

4. Take observations on the reactants (see below).

5. Remove the rubber band from the corner and allow the two chemicals to mix. Record observations.

6. When the reaction has completed, find the mass of the bag (don't forget the rubber band, too, because it was in your earlier reading).

7. Take observations on the products (see below).

8. Dispose of the contents as indicated by your teacher.

Data

Mass of bag, rubber band, and reactants _____

Mass of bag, rubber band, and products _____

Observations Record all observations during the reaction. What did the reactants look and smell like? What happened during the reaction? What did the products look and smell like? (Do not open your bag to smell the products until you've found the mass.)

Results/Calculations Find the difference in mass between the bag with the reactants and the bag with the products.

Discussion

1. What evidence do you have that the products are not the same as the reactants? How do you know that a chemical reaction took place?

2. The reaction between sodium bicarbonate and acetic acid produces sodium acetate, carbon dioxide gas, and water. Write the formula equation for this reaction.

3. Describe the relationship between the mass of the reactants in the chemical reaction and the mass of the products.

4. The law of conservation of mass says that mass cannot be created or destroyed in a chemical reaction. Therefore, the mass of the contents of the bag after the reaction should be the same as the mass of the contents of the bag before the reaction. If yours was not the same, give a possible reason why not.

5. Make a class histogram of the results. (a) Determine the largest change (either gain or loss). (b) Make a number line from the largest change with a negative sign, through zero, to the largest change with a positive sign. Make a mark every 0.1 g along this number line. This will be your x axis. (c) Start the y axis at 0 and mark 1, 2, 3.... (d) Each group will color in a bar (similar to making a bar graph) above the x axis value for their change.

6. This will give a visual representation of how often each value was obtained as a result. What value was the most common (the mode)? Did it follow the law of conservation of mass? Give possible reasons if it did not.

Law of conservation of mass/matter

When a chemical reaction takes place, the atoms that make up the reactants are rearranged to form the products. Atoms cannot be created or destroyed in a chemical reaction—they are just rearranged. This idea is stated in the **law of conservation of matter.** Because all matter has mass, this law is sometimes also called the **law of conservation of mass.** Either way, it says the same thing: the atoms that make up the reactants are still there in the products—they are just in different arrangements. If the matter itself is not being created or destroyed, then the mass is not changing, either. The total mass of the reactants must equal the total mass of the products.

Balancing chemical equations

Go Online
Molecular animations
http://webcom4.grtxle.com/
khk12Chemistry

If atoms in a chemical reaction cannot be created or destroyed, then the atoms on the reactant side of the chemical equation must be identical to the atoms on the products side. They can be in different compounds, rearranged, but they must be the same atoms. Therefore, we must balance chemical equations. **Balancing chemical equations** is a sort of accounting—making sure the numbers of atoms are the same on both sides.

When balancing, we *cannot change the subscripts of the chemical formula* in order to make the reactant atoms equal to the product atoms. This would change the very identity of the chemicals—to an entirely different chemical. For example, for the reaction $CH_4 + O_2 \rightarrow CO_2 + H_2O$, the reactant side has four hydrogen atoms and the products side has only two, in a molecule of water. We cannot change the water to read "H_4O" so that it will have four hydrogen atoms, because then it's not water anymore. Instead, if we had two water molecules (one H_2O and another H_2O), then there would be four hydrogen atoms—two in each water molecule. We can write that as "$2\ H_2O$." The 2 in front of the water chemical formula is called a coefficient. **Coefficients** are used to balance equations by telling how many of each molecule are involved in the chemical reaction. The balanced reaction and visualization would be:

$$1\ CH_4 + 2\ O_2 \rightarrow 1\ CO_2 + 2\ H_2O$$

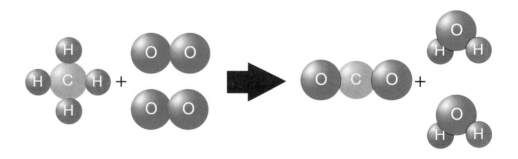

Example 2.7

Balancing Equations

1. Balance the equation $H_2 + O_2 \rightarrow H_2O$.
   - Count the atoms on each side using the subscripts.

Element	Reactants side	Products side
H	2	2
O	2	1

   - Any elements that are uneven need coefficients to balance them. Although hydrogen is balanced (two on each side), oxygen is unbalanced—two on the reactants side and one on the products side.
   - Coefficients are applied to the entire molecule that has unbalanced elements. Place a 2 in front of the water molecule: $H_2 + O_2 \rightarrow 2\,H_2O$
     The count is now:

Element	Reactants side	Products side
H	2	2̶ 4
O	2	1̶ 2

   - The oxygen is now balanced, but the hydrogen became unbalanced. Use a 2 as a coefficient on the reactant side for the hydrogen:
     $2\,H_2 + O_2 \rightarrow 2\,H_2O$.
   - The reaction is now balanced.

Element	Reactants side	Products side
H	2̶ 4	2̶ 4
O	2	1̶ 2

2. Balance the equation $Pb(NO_3)_2 + NaCl \rightarrow PbCl_2 + NaNO_3$
   - If there are polyatomic ions that appear exactly the same on both sides, you may treat them as a "chunk" for balancing. You can use this method only if the polyatomic is exactly the same on both sides (for example, CO_3 and CO_2 are *not* the same).

Element	Reactants side	Products side
Pb	1	1
NO_3	2	1
Na	1	1
Cl	1	2

   - Remember that the subscript on the outside of the parentheses applies to everything within the parentheses.
   - The nitrate "chunks" are unbalanced. Use a coefficient of 2 on the products side to balance them: $Pb(NO_3)_2 + NaCl \rightarrow PbCl_2 + 2\,NaNO_3$

Element	Reactants side	Products side
Pb	1	1
NO_3	2	1̶ 2
Na	1	1̶ 2
Cl	1	2

   - That coefficient also affects the sodium atoms.
   - Balance the now-unbalanced sodium atoms with a coefficient of 2 on the reactants side: $Pb(NO_3)_2 + 2\,NaCl \rightarrow PbCl_2 + 2\,NaNO_3$

Element	Reactants side	Products side
Pb	1	1
NO_3	2	1̶ 2
Na	1̶ 2	1̶ 2
Cl	1̶ 2	2

   - This also affects the chlorine atoms, which are now balanced as well.

Balancing Chemical Equations

Go Online
Check your understanding
http://webcom4.grtxle.com/
khk12Chemistry

1. A 2.0 g antacid tablet is added to 45.0 g HCl solution. The reaction results in a salt and water. What is the mass of the salt and the water?

2. Rust is formed from the combination of iron with oxygen from the air around it. If a 4.0 g sample of iron is completely rusted, would the mass of the resulting rust be more than 4.0 g, equal to 4.0 g, or less than 4.0 g? Explain how you know.

3. Explain how mass is still conserved when a log is burned, even though the resulting ashes have less mass than the original log. Where did the other mass go?

4. Balance the following equations visually (add more particle drawings to increase numbers of atoms; do not use coefficients):

   a.

   b.

Balance the following reactions that occur between antacids and stomach acid:

5. $Al(OH)_3 + HCl \rightarrow AlCl_3 + HOH$

6. $CaCO_3 + HCl \rightarrow CaCl_2 + HOH + CO_2$

7. $MgCO_3 + HCl \rightarrow MgCl_2 + HOH + CO_2$

8. $Mg(OH)_2 + HCl \rightarrow MgCl_2 + HOH$

9. $Ca(OH)_2 + HCl \rightarrow CaCl_2 + HOH$

10. $NaHCO_3 + HCl \rightarrow NaCl + HOH + CO_2$

11. Balance the equation from Lab 2.7.

12. Balance all the equations written in Practices 2.6A and 2.6B. You will need to make sure that your answers to those practice questions are correct before you balance the equations.

Speeding Up Chemical Reactions

LAB 2.8

Speeding Up a Reaction

Purpose To identify ways to speed up the reaction in the "Alka-Seltzer® cannon"

Instructions

- Brainstorm things that you could change about the way you set up the cannon at the beginning of the chapter that might make a difference in how quickly the cannon goes off. Share lists as a class to form a master list.

- Your dependent variable will be the time it takes for the cannon to go off. Choose an independent variable from the class master list.

- Write the beginning of the lab report:
  - Title
  - Purpose/problem
  - Background information about the Alka-Seltzer® cannon and how/why it works
  - Hypothesis
  - Variables and constants—list the dependent and independent variables and as many constants as you can think of.
  - Remember that it is more efficient to write the next sections in reverse order than in the order that they typically appear. Write:
    - Results/calculations—set up calculations, remembering to average multiple trials together.
    - Data table
    - Procedure—step by step, numbered procedure. Be clear and concise. Use multiple trials.
    - Materials—list exact amounts of every material used (except water). A list of possible materials is below—you may not need all those listed, or you may need additional materials (always check with your teacher before planning for additional materials to ensure that they are available).
    - Safety—a partial list of safety concerns follows.

- Have your teacher check to make sure your procedure is safe.

- Perform your lab. Fill in the data table as you go. Be sure to note in writing if you make any changes to your procedure as you go.

- Finish your lab write-up:
  - Complete your calculations/results and include a sentence summary of your data—don't attempt to explain why it happened, just write what happened.
  - Conclusion—restate purpose/problem and hypothesis. Give results. Do the results support the hypothesis? If not, do you have a new hypothesis? Give at least two possible sources of error. (Remember, "calculations" doesn't count, and "human error" is too vague!) What other questions would you like to investigate, or what other types of experiments could be done with Alka-Seltzer® or the cannon?

- Share the results for your variables with the class. Do this on whiteboards if your teacher provides them. Discuss the effects of the different variables, and as a class determine common themes and ideas about how to speed up a reaction. Write these in your conclusion.

Possible materials Water, beaker, graduated cylinder, balance, mortar and pestle (for crushing), hot plate/Bunsen burner setup, ice, stopwatch, film canister, Alka-Seltzer® (a maximum of two tablets per group, unless your variable is the amount of Alka-Seltzer® used and you require more)

 Safety Always use caution with glassware and any hot liquids. Stand back when cannon goes off, and be careful to point it away from people. Wear goggles. If working with liquids other than water, ask your instructor for specific safety information for that liquid.

What is a common formula found in antacids?

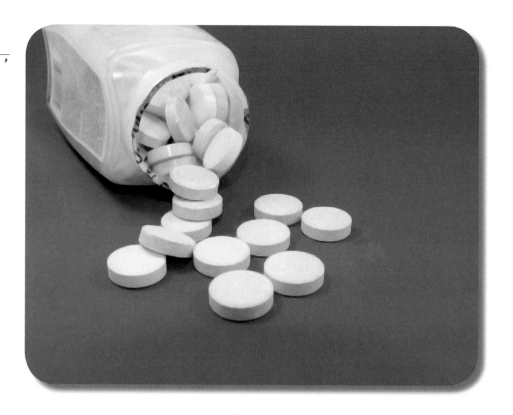

Go Online
Molecular animations
http://webcom4.grtxle.com/
khk12Chemistry

Collision theory

What does it take for a chemical reaction to take place? First, the reactant molecules have to run into each other (**collisions**). Once they come in contact, they can react to rearrange their atoms. If they do not come into contact, they cannot react.

Test tubes showing Liesegang rings, a phenomenon in chemicals during a reaction. You can see the bands of precipitate formed.

One way of increasing the chance that the molecules will collide is by increasing the number of molecules. Adding more molecules of the reactants means that there are more of them to run into each other, increasing the chances of collisions. Another way is to stir or shake them. Moving the molecules around will increase the chances that they'll run into a molecule of the other reactant. Crushing a solid also increases contacts by providing a larger surface area. Adding a larger piece of a solid will also provide more surface area. This means that there are more molecules of the solid available for contact with the other reactants—they can't come into contact if they are trapped inside a chunk of solid. Raising the temperature often works (but not always, as will be discussed in Chapter 8). Molecules at a higher temperature move faster—and this increased speed raises the chance that they will find and react with the other reactant molecules.

The molecules must also run into each other with the **correct orientation.** They have to hit in a certain way in order for the reaction to occur. Only a fraction of collisions that occur will happen with the correct orientation (see Figure 2–11). Therefore, increasing the overall number of collisions (as described above) will increase the number that have the correct orientation.

Molecules also need to have enough energy, known as the **activation energy** (Figure 2–12), to make the transition from their original reactant molecular arrangement to the products of the reaction.

If only a fraction of the collisions have the correct orientation, then an even smaller fraction will have both the correct orientation *and* enough energy. The temperature of the molecules is related to the speed with which they move around. Their speed is related to the kinetic energy of the molecules, which is directly related to temperature. Therefore, higher-temperature molecules have more energy. Raising the temperature will increase the chance that a

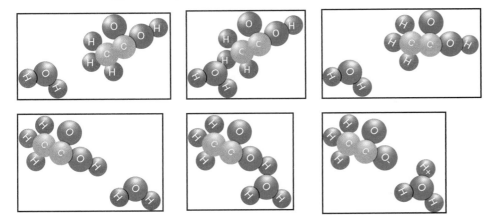

Figure 2–11. Collisions with the correct orientation. (Top panels) The collision occurs between the water and acetic acid molecules, but the reactive (acidic) hydrogen of the acid is not the one that is colliding with the water. No change occurs—the molecules are the same after the collision as they were before it. (Bottom panels) This time the collision occurs with the acidic hydrogen (the one that dissociates in water), and therefore the dissociation does occur, resulting in hydronium and acetate ions.

Reaction Coordinate Diagram

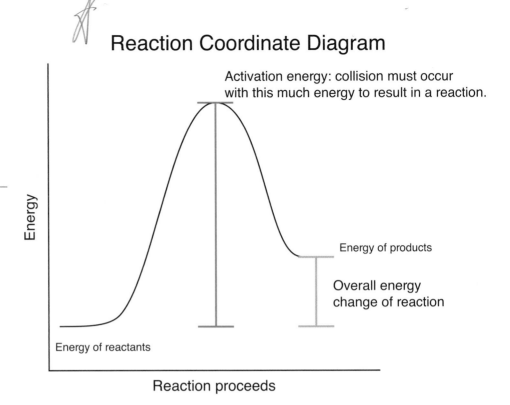

Activation energy: collision must occur with this much energy to result in a reaction.

Energy of products

Overall energy change of reaction

Energy of reactants

Reaction proceeds

Figure 2–12. Reaction coordinate diagram. A reaction coordinate diagram shows the energy of the reactants and the products and the activation energy (the minimum energy needed in a collision to cause a reaction). The higher this hill, the less likely that a collision will occur with the minimum energy necessary for reaction.

collision will occur with the needed energy to make the transition. Stirring or shaking can also increase this probability, because energy is put into the system by stirring, which causes the molecules to move faster.

In order for a reaction to be successful, the reactant molecules must first collide, but they must do so with the correct orientation and the minimum

Reaction Coordinate Diagram

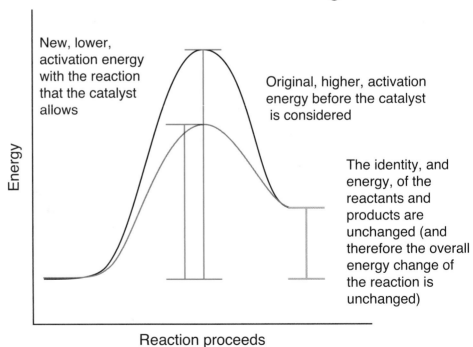

New, lower, activation energy with the reaction that the catalyst allows

Original, higher, activation energy before the catalyst is considered

The identity, and energy, of the reactants and products are unchanged (and therefore the overall energy change of the reaction is unchanged)

Reaction proceeds

Figure 2–13. Reaction coordinate diagram with a catalyst. This reaction coordinate diagram shows the original reaction pathway with the higher activation energy, as well as the new reaction pathway with the lower activation energy. The starting and ending points (reactants and products) are unchanged—just the way that they change from one to the other.

activation energy to make the transition to the product molecules. Many collisions happen, but most don't result in a reaction because they don't fulfill the other two requirements. The study of these ideas and how to change the speed of a reaction is called **kinetics.**

Catalysts speed up reactions

Catalysts are substances that speed up a reaction without being used up in that reaction. Catalysts can work in many ways, but they basically provide an environment where it is easier for reactants to form products. They often hold the reacting molecules in position so that collisions occur in the correct orientation.

Catalysts can also change the pathway of the reaction, lowering the activation energy (Figure 2–13). Therefore, it is more likely that a collision will result in a reaction, because more collisions will have the new, lower, activation energy.

Once the collision and reaction occur, the catalyst releases the molecules and can then be used again with another reactant. In other words, the catalyst itself does not get used—it is recycled and ready to help another set of reactants. Catalysts perform their duty over and over again until all the reactants have been reacted. They don't change the reactants or the products themselves; they just change how fast reactants form the products. Catalysts do this by providing an environment where collisions are more likely to be successful. The more likely they are to be successful, the faster the reactants are transformed into products.

There are many catalysts that work in biological functions, such as in our body. They are called **enzymes.**

PRACTICE 2.8

Collision Theory

1. Crushing an antacid tablet will allow it to react more quickly with an acid. Draw a storyboard (like a cartoon strip) of a solid antacid tablet versus a crushed tablet reacting with acid. Make sure that your storyboards show why the crushed tablet reacts more quickly.

2. Increasing the temperature will, in general, increase the rate of reaction. Draw another set of storyboards showing how an antacid tablet will react with acid at a higher temperature more quickly than at a lower temperature.

Go Online
Check your understanding
http://webcom4.grtxle.com/
khk12Chemistry

Here's your chance to use the chemistry you know to make decisions about which medications to purchase, as an informed consumer.

The most effective antacid

Purpose To determine which antacid more effectively neutralizes 25.0 mL of hydrochloric acid

Possible materials 0.1 M hydrochloric acid, graduated cylinder, balance, beakers, materials for testing pH (see Lab 2.5 for specifics for each method of testing), mortar and pestle, stir-rods

Safety Use caution with hydrochloric acid—it will cause burns. Wear goggles. Report any incident to your teacher.

Instructions
Write the beginning of the lab

- **Title**

- **Purpose/problem**

- **Variables and constants**—list the dependent and independent variables and as many constants as you can think of. For the dependent variable, you will need to decide between two methods: (1) add antacid until you reach a designated pH and see how much antacid is needed to reach it, or (2) add a designated amount of antacid and see how much the pH changes. Both are acceptable—make a choice about which you think is the better way to determine the most effective antacid.

- **Background information** about antacids, acids, neutralization reactions, indicators, etc. Include the chemical name and formula for the active ingredients of each antacid and the balanced chemical equation for the reaction of the active ingredient in the antacid with the hydrochloric acid.

- **Hypothesis** (Remember, not a prediction!)

- Write the following in the reverse order from how they typically appear:

  - **Results/calculations**—set these up to find change in mass of antacid added if following

method 1 from "Variables" above or to find change in pH if following method 2. (Remember to average multiple trials together.)

  - **Data table**—make it appropriate to what you'll need for your results/calculations.

  - **Procedure**—step by step, numbered procedure. Be clear and concise. Use multiple trials. You must choose how you will measure pH before, during, and after the neutralization with the antacid and include the procedure for using that method (see Lab 2.5 for explanations). Remember the ideas of kinetics you learned in order to produce a more efficient reaction (taking less time to neutralize).

  - **Materials**—exact amounts of every material used (except water) in a list. A possible list is given above.

  - **Safety**—safety information is given above.

Have your instructor check your procedure for safety.

Perform the lab and fill in the data table as you go. Be sure to note changes in your written procedure if you make any adjustments to your plan as you go.

Finish your write-up.

- **Results**—write a sentence summary of your results (just what, not why).

- **Conclusion**—restate purpose/problem and hypothesis. Give results. Do the results support the hypothesis? If not, do you have a new hypothesis? Give at least two possible sources of error. What other questions would you like to investigate, or what other types of experiments could be done about antacids?

Discuss the results as a class. Use whiteboards if your teacher provides them. Do the two different methods of determining the best antacid give the same results? Why or why not? Include the answers to these questions in your conclusion as well.

READ

There are two types of matter: pure substances and mixtures. Elements and compounds are pure substances. Elements cannot be separated physically or chemically, and compounds cannot be separated physically. Mixtures can be separated physically, and are divided into two categories: homogeneous (also called solutions) and heterogeneous. Homogenous mixtures look the same throughout, whereas heterogeneous mixtures have different "parts" that can be seen. Colloids are mixtures that have particles large enough to deflect light (the Tyndall effect), and suspensions have particles large enough to settle out. Chemicals are written and named based on what type they are: binary ionic, polyatomic ionic, multivalent metal ionic, molecular compounds, or acids. Subscripts are used to write chemical formulas to show how many of each kind of atom are in the compound. Formulas for ionic compounds must balance the charges to form a neutral compound. Molecular compounds use prefixes to describe the number of atoms in the compound.

Chemical equations can be in word form or formula form to show the reactants and products involved in a chemical reaction. Those chemical equations are balanced with coefficients to comply with the law of conservation of matter. This law states that the atoms involved in a chemical reaction cannot be created or destroyed—only rearranged. Therefore, the total mass of the reactants must equal the total mass of the products. Equations cannot be balanced with subscripts, because that would change the molecules themselves—coefficients tell how many of each kind of molecule is involved in the reaction.

Acids are molecules that form the hydronium ion in water, whereas bases form the hydroxide ion in water. The acidity or basicity of a solution is measured on the pH scale. A number below 7 indicates an acid, 7 is neutral, and numbers above 7 indicate bases. Indicators are used to determine pH. The terms *strong* and *weak* refer to how many of the acid or base molecules perform their "duty," but the words *concentrated* and *dilute* refer to how many acid or base molecules were in the container to begin with. Acids and bases react together in a neutralization reaction—a type of double replacement reaction—where the cation of the base and the anion of the acid form a salt, while the hydrogen ion from the acid and the hydroxide ion from the base form water.

Kinetics is the study of the speed of reactions. In order for a chemical reaction to occur, the molecules must collide in the correct orientation, and with enough energy to make the transition to the products. In order to increase the chances of this happening, we can increase the number of reactant molecules, increase the surface area of a solid reactant, stir or shake the molecules, or raise the temperature. Catalysts are substances that speed up a reaction by enabling more successful collisions without themselves being consumed in the reaction.

1. Compare and contrast elements and compounds.

2. Compare and contrast pure substance and mixture.

3. Compare and contrast heterogeneous mixture, homogeneous mixture and solution.

4. What cannot be separated by physical or chemical means?

5. What can be separated by physical means?

6. What can be separated by chemical means but not by physical means?

7. How can you tell the difference between a solution, a colloid, and a suspension?

8. Mark each of the following as compounds (C), elements (E), or mixtures (M).

   a. Air

   b. Aluminum foil

   c. Steel

   d. Tap water

   e. Pure water

   f. Salt (sodium chloride)

   g. Iron filings

   h. Carbon dioxide gas

   i. Lead weights

   j. Pool water

   k. Pop (soda)

   l. Tin foil

   m. Sodium bicarbonate

9. For each of the following, is it homogeneous (HO) or heterogeneous (HE)?

   a. Tap water

   b. Air

   c. Ice water

   d. "Flat" cola

   e. Oil

   f. River water

   g. Orange juice with pulp

   h. Chocolate chip cookies

   i. Salt water

10. Name the following compounds.

    a. $MgCl_2$

    b. Cu_2O

    c. CsF

    d. S_4N_3

    e. NH_4NO_3

    f. $KMnO_4$

    g. $Ca_3(PO_4)_2$

    h. SF_2

    i. F_6

    j. CF_4

    k. HNO_3

    l. HNO_2

    m. $NaClO$

    n. H_3PO_4

    o. HBr

    p. HCl

    q. P_2O_5

    r. $FeBr_2$

11. Write formulas for the following compounds.

    a. Mercury(I) sulfide

    b. Sodium sulfite

    c. Aluminum hydrogen sulfate

    d. Lead(II) oxide

    e. Lead(IV) oxide

    f. Silicon dioxide

    g. Magnesium fluoride

    h. Magnesium hydroxide

    i. Barium sulfate

    j. Ammonium acetate

    k. Sodium peroxide

    l. Acetic acid

    m. Sulfurous acid

    n. Phosphorous acid

    o. Aluminum hydroxide

    p. Hydroiodic acid

    q. Nitrogen trichloride

12. In your own words, explain the difference between a strong acid and a weak acid. What about strong bases and weak bases?

13. How does the strength of an acid or base relate to the concentration? Explain.

14. Explain in your own words what pH indicators do.

15. For each of the following, would the pH be below 7, at 7, or above 7?

   a. Lemon juice

   b. Soap

   c. Pure water

16. Define the law of conservation of matter in your own words, and describe how it is important in chemistry.

17. Balance the following equations.

   a. $Fe + H_2O \rightarrow Fe_3O_4 + H_2$

   b. $C_8H_{18} + O_2 \rightarrow CO_2 + H_2O$

   c. $MnO_2 + HCl \rightarrow MnCl_2 + H_2O + Cl_2$

   d. $Na_2CO_3 + HCH_3COO \rightarrow NaCH_3COO + CO_2 + H_2O$

   e. $C_2H_2 + O_2 \rightarrow CO_2 + H_2O$

   f. $AgNO_3 + H_2S \rightarrow Ag_2S + HNO_3$

   g. $P_2S_5 + O_2 \rightarrow P_4O_{10} + SO_2$

   h. $O_3 \rightarrow O_2$

   i. $SO_3 + H_2O \rightarrow H_2SO_4$

   j. $K + H_2O \rightarrow KOH + H_2$

   k. $BaCl_2 + Na_2SO_4 \rightarrow NaCl + BaSO_4$

   l. $Ca + HCl \rightarrow CaCl_2 + H_2$

   m. $FeS + HCl \rightarrow H_2S + FeCl_2$

   n. $Pb(NO_3)_2 + H_2SO_4 \rightarrow PbSO_4 + HNO_3$

   o. $ZnCl_2 + (NH_4)_2S \rightarrow ZnS + NH_4Cl$

   p. $Mg + HNO_3 \rightarrow Mg(NO_3)_2 + H_2$

18. For the following, write the equation in formula form and then balance it.

   a. Aluminum plus copper(II) chloride yields copper plus aluminum chloride

   b. Sodium plus water yields sodium hydroxide plus hydrogen gas

   c. Silver nitrate plus copper yields copper(II) nitrate plus silver

   d. Lead plus chlorine yields lead(IV) chloride

   e. Ammonia plus nitric acid yields ammonium nitrate

   f. Iron(II) sulfate plus cobalt(III) bromide yields iron(III) bromide and cobalt(II) sulfate

   g. Sulfur dioxide plus oxygen plus water yields sulfuric acid

19. What do you use to balance charges when writing a molecule's formula?

20. What do you use to balance the number of atoms on each side of the reaction?

21. What are the chemicals on the left side of the arrow called?

22. What are the chemicals on the right side of the arrow called?

23. According to kinetics, what events/situations are necessary for a chemical reaction to occur?

24. Name several ways to increase the chances that a chemical reaction will occur.

CHAPTER 3

Airbags
Chemistry Making Car Rides Safer

IN THIS CHAPTER

- States of matter
- Properties of matter
- Density
- Changes in matter
- Gas behavior
- Counting molecules
- Gas laws

INTRODUCTORY ACTIVITY

What makes an effective airbag?

List criteria necessary for an airbag, considering characteristics that would be good and those you'd want to avoid.

Make your own list, and then share as a class.

Save this list to use in the final chapter project.

A crash test dummy, not seat-belted, tries out an airbag.

This chapter has the

CHEMISTRY YOU NEED TO KNOW

to weigh, as an automotive engineer, the benefits and risks of several methods of producing a gas for automobile airbags.

Introduction

Have you ever been in a car accident where an airbag deployed? Airbags are one of those advances in technology that we all hope we don't ever need to use, but we're glad to have just in case.

Airbags are nylon bags inside a car's steering wheel, dashboard, or side panel, for passenger seats. They contain a solid chemical that, when ignited with electricity, will decompose into nitrogen gas very rapidly—expanding the airbag. The nylon bag has holes in it to allow the gas to escape as the person's body collides into it—thereby cushioning the person (rather than the person hitting a "hard" airbag filled with gas). A trigger system tells the airbag when to ignite the solid chemical and deploy, based on the speed at which a car crash occurs. The chemical reaction that is commonly used in airbags is: $2\ NaN_3\ (s) \rightarrow 2\ Na\ (s) + 3\ N_2\ (g)$. This process occurs in 1/25 of a second. Figure 3–1 and the concept map will give you a visual and chemical idea of an airbag deployment, respectively.

There are some concerns with this reaction: (1) it produces sodium metal, which—when reacting with water—produces hydrogen gas and so much energy (heat) that the hydrogen gas could catch fire, causing an

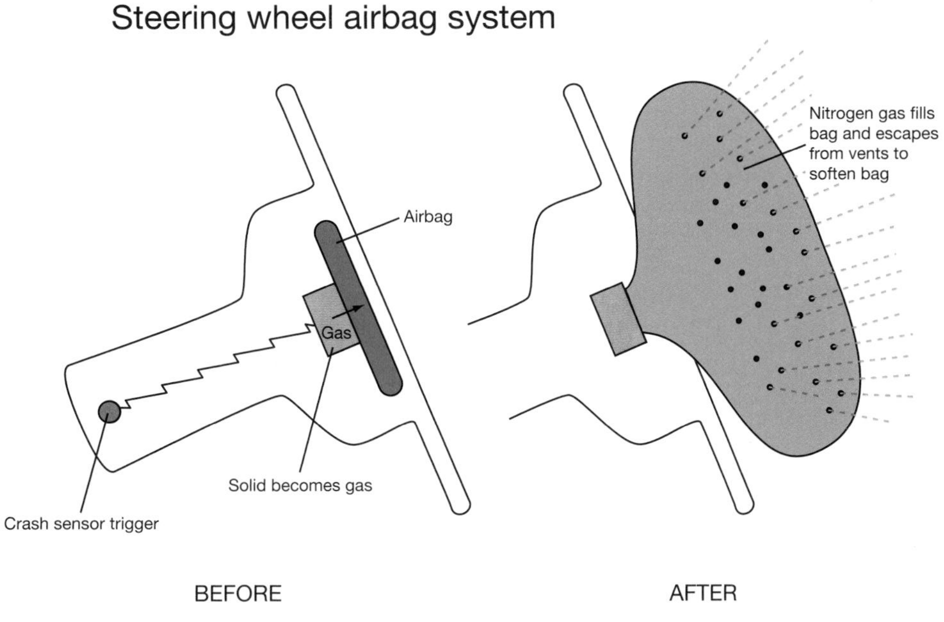

Steering wheel airbag system
Airbag
Gas
Solid becomes gas
Crash sensor trigger
Nitrogen gas fills bag and escapes from vents to soften bag
BEFORE
AFTER

Figure 3–1. How airbags work.

Airbags

explosion; (2) it produces heat during the reaction, so the gas could be warm or even hot as it fills the airbag; and (3) the reactant, sodium azide (NaN_3), is highly toxic—if some of the solid reactant chemical escaped and was ingested or inhaled by people in the car, it could be lethal. The reason this chemical is used in airbags is that (1) the reaction is quick enough for rapid deployment of the airbag, but not so quick that people are injured more by the presence of the airbag; (2) the space needed to store the reactants in the airbag is small and therefore cheap; (3) the amount of sodium azide used in airbags is small enough that people are highly unlikely to ingest enough to kill them; and (4) the heat that the reaction produces is not as great as some alternative chemical reactions. Most of the heat is absorbed by the reaction chamber, the steering column, and the air; the nylon bag itself is an insulator. When the risks and benefits are weighed, sodium azide is currently the best option for use in airbags.

SECTION 3.1

States of Matter

There are three states of matter that you will work with in chemistry class: solid, liquid, or gas.

Properties of three states of matter

The atoms or molecules making up a **solid** are closely packed together, and although they don't appear to be moving, they are vibrating in place. Solid material is not compressible because the particles are already as

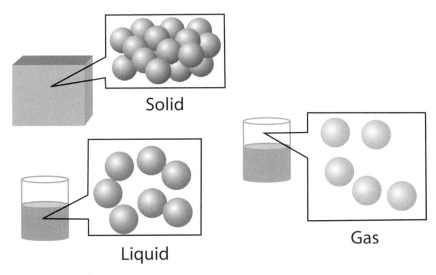

Figure 3–2. Images of solid cube (top), liquid (left), and gas (right), with close-ups of particle spacing.

close together as they can be. Solids have a definite shape—you can put a solid in any shape container you want, but the shape of the actual solid will not change. Solids also have a definite volume, so they won't change how much space they take up regardless of their container.

The atoms or molecules in **liquid** have more energy, are farther apart, and are free to flow around each other. Liquids are compressible because there is distance between the molecules, but for most liquids the amount they can be compressed while remaining a liquid is very small. Liquids have no definite shape. If you put a liquid into a spherical container (like a ball), the liquid will take on that shape. If you put a liquid into a cubic container, the liquid will take the shape of a cube. They do, however, have a definite volume. Pouring a 12-ounce can of soda pop into a 24-ounce cup will not produce more pop—you'll still have only 12 ounces.

Gas atoms or molecules have even higher energy, are spaced as far apart as their container will allow, and move randomly and rapidly throughout the entire container. Gases are highly compressible, because there are large spaces between molecules. Gases have no definite shape or volume. You can fill any size or shape with the same number of gas particles. The gas molecules move everywhere they can, and therefore expand or compact with the volume and shape of their container.

The temperature of a sample is directly related to how fast the particles are moving. Gases exist at higher temperatures than liquids at the same pressure, and liquids are at higher temperatures than solids. The relative speed of their particles follows the same pattern.

Changes in state

Matter can change states. A solid that **melts** becomes a liquid. If that liquid **freezes,** it turns back into a solid. The temperature at which a solid melts or a liquid freezes is the same (the **melting point** or **freezing point**). For

Figure 3–3. Diagram showing changes in state.

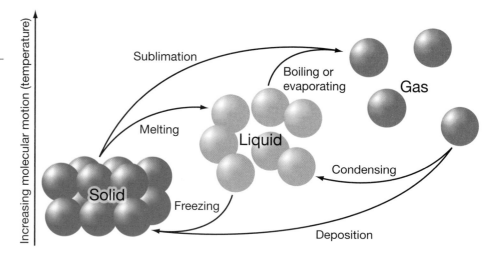

example, ice melts into water at 0°C, and water freezes into ice at 0°C. Similarly, a liquid can turn into a gas when it is boiled, and a gas can become a liquid by condensing. These two processes happen at the same temperature as well (referred to as the **boiling point** or **condensation point**). Water **boils** to steam at 100°C, which is the same temperature at which steam **condenses** to water. When a solid undergoes a change directly to a gas, it's called **sublimation.** The opposite process, from gas directly to solid, is called **deposition.** Some solids, such as carbon dioxide (dry ice), sublime at normal Earth temperatures and pressures.

As a sample changes states from solid to liquid to gas, the particles move faster and faster (they have more **kinetic energy**—the energy of motion) and spread apart. Likewise, as state changes from gas to liquid to solid, the particles move more and more slowly and get closer together. The energy input and changes during these processes will be discussed more in Chapter 7.

What's between the molecules?

Speaking of how far apart the molecules are in each of the three states of matter, what's between those molecules? People commonly answer, "Air." But "air" is the gas molecules themselves; what's between those air molecules? The answer is nothing—absolutely nothing! Not air, not any particle, nothing. For solids, liquids, and gases, there are spaces between the molecules that are completely and totally empty. See Figure 3–4.

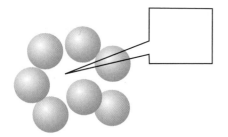

Figure 3–4. Close-up of what's "in between."

States of Matter

1. List reasons that gases are used to fill airbags rather than solids or liquids.

2. All three states of matter have potential for use in airbags. Solids could react chemically or sublime to produce a gas to fill the bag; liquids could boil or react chemically to make a gas; and gases could be compressed and then released to fill the bag. What would be some advantages and disadvantages of each state of matter as a starting reactant for an air-bag?

3. List common examples of changes of state in your daily life.

4. Make a table comparing the characteristics of solids, liquids, and gases. Include information about the packing of the particles, movement of the particles, compressibility, shapes, and volumes.

5. Draw the following using particle visualizations. Include a key to show the differences between the types of particles.

   a. A mixture of a solid in a liquid

   b. A mixture of two gases

Go Online
Check your understanding
http://webcom4.grtxle.com/
khk12Chemistry

SECTION 3.2

Properties of Matter

Physical and chemical properties

Physical properties are those that you can observe without changing the atoms or molecules that make up the matter. Examples of physical properties include color, texture, size (mass and volume), density, boiling point, melting point, solubility (ability to dissolve), malleability (ability to be hammered into a thin sheet), and ductility (ability to be pulled into a wire).

Chemical properties describe how something reacts with other elements or molecules. Once you observe a chemical property, the original element or molecule has now been chemically changed and will have new chemical and physical properties. Examples of chemical properties include flammability, ability to form rust, and reactivity with water, oxygen, acid, base, or any other type of chemical.

Intensive and extensive properties

Properties can also be described as being intensive properties or extensive properties. An **intensive property** is one that does not change, no matter what size sample you have. For example, a small piece of construction

paper would be the same color as a large piece of the same paper. Therefore, color is an intensive property. An **extensive property** is one that will change as the size of the sample changes. For example, the mass of a large piece of rock is greater than the mass of a small piece of the same rock. This makes mass an extensive property.

Properties can be used to identify substances. If you know the properties of a known or reference substance, you can observe the properties of your unknown or test substance and compare them to identify your unknown.

Go Online
Check your understanding
http://webcom4.grtxle.com/
khk12Chemistry

PRACTICE 3.2

Properties of Matter

1. What properties would be desirable in a gas that fills an airbag? What properties would be desirable in the beginning reactants that are stored in an airbag system?

2. One of the products of the reaction in an airbag is sodium metal. Sodium metal reacts explosively with water. Is this a chemical or physical property? How might this property affect the airbag and how it is constructed?

3. Classify each as a chemical property (CP) or physical property (PP).

   a. Mass

   b. Ease of rusting

   c. Volume

   d. Ductility (ability to be pulled into a wire)

   e. Malleability (ability to be hammered into a sheet)

   f. Color

   g. Taste

   h. Reactivity with water

   i. Flammability

4. Classify each as an intensive property (IP) or extensive property (EP).

   a. Mass

   b. Ease of rusting

   c. Volume

   d. Ductility

   e. Malleability

   f. Color

   g. Taste

   h. Reactivity with water

   i. Flammability

Density

LAB 3.3

Density

Purpose (1) To find the ratio of mass to volume of a type of matter using graphical analysis, and (2) to determine whether the ratio of mass to volume is an intensive or extensive property. Graphical analysis means that a graph will be used to find the ratio; don't use an equation to calculate density in this lab.

Possible materials Various-sized samples of unknown material, graduated cylinder, balance, water, beaker(s), list of known metal densities. If you need additional materials for your procedure, check with your instructor for availability before finalizing your plans.

! **Safety** Use caution with glassware. Report any breakage to your instructor.

Instructions Design a lab to find the ratio of mass to volume of your unknown material. Remember that it is often more efficient to set up the results section followed by the data table and procedure and then the materials and safety sections. Remember to have your write-up checked for safety by your teacher before carrying out the procedure. Include the following in your write-up:

- **Title**

- **Purpose/problem**

- **Background information** Information you know about density and graphing mass and volume to find density

- **Materials**

- **Procedure** Be sure to include multiple trials with various-sized samples.

- **Data table** No calculations, just data you record from the lab.

- **Graph** Make a scatter-plot of your data, with volume on the x axis and mass on the y axis. Draw a best-fit line.

- **Results/calculations** All calculations go here. Use your graph to find the ratio of mass to volume of your substance (**graphical analysis**); the slope of a mass–volume graph will be "mass ÷ volume," which is equal to this ratio. To find the slope, pick two points where your best-fit line crosses an intersection on your graph paper (these two places do *not* need to be original data points; pick places on your best-fit line where the line you drew crosses neatly). Find the slope of this line using the slope equation: $(y_2 - y_1) \div (x_2 - x_1)$. Be sure to pay attention to significant digits and units.

- **Conclusion** In complete sentences, restate purpose/problem and give results that answer the purpose/problem completely. Suggest at least two possible sources of error (be specific; "calculations" would not count as a source of error in the lab itself). Give an application of this type of lab to your life.

Discuss the results as a class. Make a histogram of the density results (see Lab 2.2, Discussion question 5, for instructions on how to do this). How would you describe the distribution of results? Is there a clear statistical mode? Does the class agree whether density is an intensive or extensive property? If there's disagreement, discuss the evidence to determine the correct property.

Density is a property that is often used to identify a substance. **Density** is the expression for the mass per unit volume. It takes into account how much matter an object has (the mass) and the space that it takes up (the volume). An object with a high density would have a large mass compared to its volume. A low-density object would have a relatively low mass compared to how much space it takes up, seeming light for its size. Lead is more dense than aluminum. A bowling ball is more dense than a soccer ball.

$$\text{Density} = \frac{\text{Mass}}{\text{Volume}}$$

Density units

There will be a mass unit on top of the ratio and a volume unit on the bottom. Mass and volume measure different properties of an object, and therefore their units cannot be converted to allow them to cancel one another out. Therefore, there must be two different units. Density is commonly expressed with the units g/mL or g/cm^3.

Density graphs

A graph with mass on the y axis and volume on the x axis can be used to find density. If the

$$\text{slope} = \frac{\text{rise}}{\text{run}}$$

and the "rise" is the mass (y axis) and the "run" is the volume (x axis), then the slope is the density. Figure 3–5 shows how density causes layering.

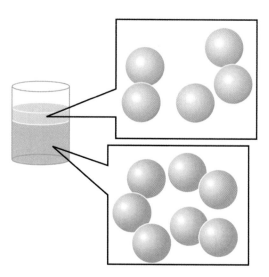

Figure 3-5. The less-dense layer (less mass in the same volume) floats above the more-dense layer.

Gas balloons are inflated with a gas which is of a lower molecular weight than the ambient atmosphere.

Floating and layers

Density is responsible for the phenomenon of floating. Less-dense materials will float on top of more-dense items. Water has a density of 1.0 g/mL. Anything with a density greater than this will sink, whereas any object with a density lower than water's will float. The same principle is also true for air. A helium balloon floats because helium is less dense than air, whereas a balloon filled with carbon dioxide would sink, because it is more dense than air. Table 3–1 shows the densities of many everyday substances.

Table 3–1 Densities of Common Materials (in g/mL at 0°C and 1 atm)			
Air	0.0013	Rubber	1.34
Balsa wood	0.16	Corn syrup	1.38
Oak wood	0.710	Table salt	2.16
Ice	0.917	Aluminum	2.70
Corn oil	0.925	Iron	7.86
Water, liquid	1.00	Copper	8.92
Plastic	1.17	Gold	19.3
Glycerol	1.26		

Example 3.3

Density Problems

1. A rock has a mass of 5.47 g. What is the density if the volume is 7.85 mL?

$m = 5.47$ $V = 7.85$ mL $D = ?$

$$D = \frac{m}{V}$$

$$D = \frac{5.47 \text{ g}}{7.85 \text{ mL}}$$

$$D = 0.697 \text{ g/mL}$$

2. A sample of liquid has a density of 1.75 g/cm³. What is the mass of a 35.5 cm³ sample?

$m = ?$ $V = 35.5$ cm³ $D = 1.75$ g/cm³

$$D = \frac{m}{V}$$

$$1.75 \text{ g/mL} = \frac{m}{35.5 \text{ cm}^3}$$

$$(35.5 \text{ cm}^3) \times (1.75 \text{ g/mL}) = m$$

$$m = 62.1 \text{ g}$$

3. What is the volume of a piece of metal with a mass of 45.25 g and a density of 3.50 g/mL?

$m = 45.25$ $V = ?$ $D = 3.50$ g/m

$$D = \frac{m}{V}$$

$$3.50 \text{ g/mL} = \frac{45.25 \text{ g}}{V}$$

$$V = \frac{45.25 \text{ g}}{3.50 \text{ g/mL}}$$

$$V = 12.9 \text{ mL}$$

It's harder to fly in the thin air of a hot day. Pilots also have a problem with that when taking off from high-altitude airports. Why does a plane fly sluggish when the air's density decreases? Because decreased air density reduces the amount of lift that a wing creates. So pilots must calculate safety by looking at the factors of air pressure, temperature, altitude, and humidity (because humid air is less dense than dry air).

Density

1. How does the density of gases compare to that of liquids and solids? Why is this another reason to use gases in airbags?

2. Would you want the starting reactants in an airbag system to have a higher density or a lower density? Why?

3. Liquid nitrogen has a density of 0.8081 g/mL. In order to have enough gaseous nitrogen to fill an airbag, you would need a mass of 68.5 g of liquid nitrogen. What volume would be needed for a holding tank for the liquid nitrogen?

4. Calculate the density of the 68.5 g of nitrogen once it is gaseous and has a volume of 60.0 L in the airbag. (Hint: Change L to mL before computing density.)

5. How does the density of the gaseous nitrogen in question 4 compare to the liquid nitrogen in question 3? Is this what you expected? Why or why not?

6. What is the density of a piece of concrete that has a mass of 8.765 g and a volume of 3.07 cm^3?

7. Limestone has a density of 2.72 g/cm^3. What is the mass of 24 cm^3 of limestone?

8. Calcium chloride is used as a deicer on roads in winter. It has a density of 2.50 g/cm^3. What is the volume of 7.91 g of this deicer?

9. Ammonium magnesium chromate has a density of 1.845 g/cm^3. What is the mass of 7.6212 cm^3 of this substance?

10. Bismuth has a density of 9.80 g/cm^3. What is the mass of 3.74 cm^3 of Bi?

11. Iron has a density of 7.872 g/cm^3. What volume would 26.3341 g of iron occupy?

Go Online
Check your understanding
http://webcom4.grtxle.com/
khk12Chemistry

Changes in Matter

LAB 3.4

Chemical Changes

Purpose (1) To observe chemical changes and (2) to identify common indicators that a chemical change has taken place

Materials 0.5 M $Cu(NO_3)_2$, 1.0 M HCl, 1.0 M NaOH, 2 beakers, zinc metal, Bunsen burner/ring stand/ring/wire gauze or hot plate, stir-rod, test tube, test tube rack, and test tube holder

! **Safety** Use caution with glassware (especially hot glassware), flames or hot plates, boiling liquids, and heated test tubes. Wear goggles. Hydrochloric acid and sodium hydroxide are corrosive; IMMEDIATELY flush with soap and water and inform your instructor if any chemical comes in contact with skin or eyes.

Procedure

1. Fill one of the beakers about one-third full with water, and put it over the Bunsen burner or on the hot plate to boil. You will use it in step 5. Fill the second beaker half full with cool tap water.

2. Use a marker to make three lines on the test tube. Mark the first line 1 cm from the bottom, and then two more spaced 1 cm apart up the test tube.

3. Add the copper(II) nitrate to the first mark on the test tube.

Chemical Changes (*cont'd.*)

NOTE—After each step from now until the end, record observations about what each chemical looks like before, during, and after the reaction. Also, feel the test tube for any heat changes and record your observations.

4. Add the sodium hydroxide to the second mark on the test tube. Mix with a stir-rod. The reaction is: copper(II) nitrate and sodium hydroxide produce copper(II) hydroxide and sodium nitrate.

5. Put the test tube in the hot water from step 1. Heat the test tube for a few minutes, and then add a small amount of NaOH. Stir the test tube. Add more NaOH (in small amounts) until the entire test tube has undergone the change. The reaction is: copper(II) hydroxide, when heated, produces copper(II) oxide and water.

6. Take the test tube out of the hot water bath and cool it in the room temperature water. Add the hydrochloric acid to the third line (you may need to go above the third line if you had to add much extra NaOH in step 5). Mix with a stir-rod. If there is still some black precipitate in the test tube, add more hydrochloric acid and stir. Repeat until the entire black solid is gone. The reaction is: copper(II) oxide and hydrochloric acid produce copper(II) chloride and water.

7. Put a piece of zinc in the test tube. Wait a few minutes for the reaction to begin. Watch until you see no more changes. Two reactions are occurring: (1) copper(II) chloride and zinc form copper solid and zinc chloride, and (2) zinc and leftover hydrochloric acid form hydrogen and zinc chloride.

Observations Record your observations for steps 4–7 as indicated in the procedure.

Discussion

1. Draw a particle visualization of the observations you made from steps 4–7. Draw the test tube after each change, showing the particles and giving a key to the different types of particles.

2. If your teacher provides whiteboards, put these drawings on the whiteboard and share and discuss them as a class. What differences did you see? Do you want to make any adjustments to the way you drew them?

3. Write the chemical formula equations for steps 4–7.

4. You studied double replacement reactions in Section 2.6. Use your understanding of these reactions (and your general knowledge) to determine definitions for the following types of reactions: single replacement, decomposition, composition (or synthesis).

5. Classify each reaction you wrote in question 2 as: double replacement, single replacement, decomposition, or composition. Hints: You may or may not use all the types in this question, and it may help to write water as "HOH" to see replacement reactions containing OH in a reactant.

6. What things did you do to cause a chemical reaction?

7. If you want to separate two chemicals—one that is soluble in water and one that is not—what would you do? Are these steps a chemical or physical change? What does that tell you about how mixtures can be separated?

8. What does "forming a precipitate" mean?

9. On the basis of your observations, what are some common indicators of a chemical change?

10. Do any of these indicators also occur in some physical changes? If so, which ones?

11. If some indicators occur in both chemical and physical changes, how can you determine which it was?

12. Discuss the answers to questions 8–10 as a class. Use whiteboards if your teacher provides them. Are there any differences among the class? Discuss the differences. Do you end up changing any of your answers?

Physical changes

Chemistry is the study of matter and its interactions or changes. What changes occur? **Physical changes** are those which do not affect the chemical structure of the molecules or elements. They change only a physical property of the sample. All changes in state (melting, freezing, boiling, condensing, etc.) are physical changes. For example, when you melt ice to form liquid water, it's still chemically the same as the ice—it's still H_2O—the molecules are just more spread out and move faster than before. Another physical change that is often confusing is dissolving. Even though salt seems to disappear when you dissolve it in water, what happens when you let the water evaporate or boil away? The salt is left on the bottom of the container, just as it was before. Because evaporating and boiling are both physical changes that undo the dissolving, dissolving must be physical as well. Other examples of physical changes include breaking, tearing, cutting, crushing, filtering, drying, and distilling (separating mixtures by using their different boiling points). Physical changes that produce a gas, such as boiling or sublimation, would be possibilities for use in airbags.

Chemical changes

Chemical changes are those that change how the elements or molecules are chemically arranged. You cannot get your beginning materials back by a physical change (such as when salt is dissolved in water and then separated back out again). You wrote chemical equations and saw examples of chemical changes in the last chapter. Those chemical equations described what occurred in the chemical changes. Examples of chemical changes include burning, rusting, and reacting with water, acid, or any other chemical. There are many chemical changes that produce a gas, and they all would be possibilities for use in airbags.

Common misconceptions concerning changes

Some changes, such as burning and drying, are often confused by students. One is a chemical change, and the other is a physical change. When something is burned it is chemically combined with the oxygen in air, and produces different chemicals. Wood, for example, produces carbon dioxide and water. When something is heated or dried, it simply means that the water is boiled away or evaporated. Drying wood begins as damp wood (water molecules are in and around the wood fibers, but not chemically attached) and ends as wood with no water molecules (it's just wood fibers). When you burn wood, you're left with ash, carbon dioxide, and water (which was in gas form, and dissipated), but when you heat it (or dry it), you still have wood.

Another common mix-up concerns dissolving and melting. Melting is a change in state—when a solid becomes a liquid (think of setting an ice cube on a stove). Dissolving occurs when two different substances blend together; the molecules intermingle but do not chemically combine (think of stirring salt into water).

PRACTICE 3.4

Changes in Matter

1. What indicators of a chemical reaction would you want in a reaction used in airbags? What indicators would you want to avoid?

2. Do you think a chemical change or a physical change would be better in an airbag? Why?

3. What is inside the bubbles in boiling water? Explain why you answered as you did.

4. Label each as a chemical change (CC) or physical change (PC).

   a. Burning match

   b. Melting ice

   c. Boiling water

   d. Tearing a piece of paper

   e. Digestion of food

   f. Rusting of iron

   g. Dissolving salt in water

   h. Evaporating water from sugar water

   i. Adding food coloring to water

   j. Reacting sodium metal with water

   k. Breaking glass

   l. Melting glass

   m. Weathering copper (forms a green patina)

   n. Forming a precipitate

   o. Crystallizing rock candy

Go Online
Check your understanding
http://webcom4.grtxle.com/
khk12Chemistry

Gas Behavior

Gases exert pressure

Pressure is the force of the gas atoms or molecules running into the wall of their container. A balloon stays inflated because the molecules inside run into the balloon skin and push it out. So why doesn't it just keep inflating

Go Online
Molecular animations
http://webcom4.grtxle.com/
khk12Chemistry

forever? What keeps it from getting bigger as more particles run into the skin? Pressure from molecules in the air outside the balloon, also running into the skin, balance the pressure from inside. The balloon inflates until the inside pressure and the outside pressure are the same; then it remains at that size until something changes.

The pressure on the balloon from the air outside is called atmospheric pressure. **Atmospheric pressure** is the result of layers of air molecules above us in the atmosphere causing pressure. As you climb in altitude, there are fewer layers of air over you, and the pressure decreases. Therefore, there is much less atmospheric pressure at the top of a mountain than at its base (often referred to as "thinner air").

Changes in gases result in changes in pressure

If molecules running into the wall of a container cause pressure, then an increase in those collisions would increase the pressure. How could we increase the number of collisions? Imagine the molecules in the container as people in a room. As people walk around the room, they occasionally

Geysers erupt because of changes of state and buildup of pressure.

run into walls, causing "pressure." What would happen if you added a lot more people to the room? Would there be a greater number of collisions? Yes. *An increase in the number of particles will increase the pressure.*

The temperature of a substance is related to how fast the particles move. So if you increase the temperature of a gas, the gas particles move faster. What would happen if the people in the room began moving around even faster? Would there be more collisions? Yes. *An increase in temperature will increase the pressure.*

Now imagine that instead of people walking around in a classroom, you put them in a storage closet. How will the number of collisions change with a smaller container? There will be more collisions with the walls. *As the container's volume decreases, the pressure will increase.*

In the balloon explanation at the beginning of this section, you learned that the balloon expands until the pressure caused by the particles inside equals the pressure caused by the particles outside. This is true of any container that can expand and contract (such as a balloon, syringe, or soft plastic bottle). If a container cannot expand or contract, uneven pressures on the outside and inside can cause the container to explode (the pressure inside is greater) or implode (the pressure outside is greater). Explosions and implosions can also happen with expandable containers, if they are pushed too far. A balloon pops if you add too much air.

Kinetic molecular theory

The theory that helps explain these behaviors of gases is called the **kinetic molecular theory** (KMT). The assumptions of the KMT are:

- Matter (including gases) consists of small particles, which all have mass.

- The distances separating gas molecules are so large that the volume of the molecules themselves is insignificant.

- Gas particles move constantly, randomly, and rapidly.

- Collisions with the container or other gas particles are perfectly elastic (meaning no kinetic energy is lost to other types of energy, such as heat, sound, or light).

- The temperature of the gas particles is directly related to their kinetic energy.

- Gas particles exert no force on each other—they neither attract nor repel other gas particles.

Real versus ideal gases

KMT describes how an ideal gas behaves. **Real gases** sometimes behave slightly differently than this theory assumes. Still, the assumptions in the theory make predicting gas behavior simpler. When we use these assumptions to predict how real gases behave, the predictions can be slightly off, since real gases do not necessarily fulfill all the points of the theory. Unlike the second point in the KMT, real gases' volumes are sometimes significant. They also do not have perfectly elastic collisions as in point 4 of the theory—some energy is lost to other forms. Finally, real gas particles do exert forces on each other, contrary to point 6 of the KMT. But even with these deviations from the ideal, predictions based on the KMT are still fairly accurate.

Diffusion and effusion

Go Online
Molecular animations
http://webcom4.grtxle.com/khk12Chemistry

Two other properties of gases are diffusion and effusion.

Diffusion is the speed with which gas particles move across a space. How quickly do you smell perfume sprayed on the other side of the room?

Effusion is the speed with which gas particles escape through a tiny hole in the container. How quickly will a balloon with a tiny pinhole deflate?

Both of these properties are inversely related to the size of a gas particle. The larger (and therefore heavier) a particle is, the more slowly it moves at any given temperature. The more slowly it moves, the more time it will take to move across a space (diffusion), and the more time it will take to move around the container and locate the tiny hole to escape (effusion).

Example 3.5

Gas Behavior

1. A balloon is removed from a warm store to a cold car. What happens to the balloon?

    -   As the temperature of the gas inside the balloon decreases, the pressure inside the balloon will also decrease. The pressure outside the balloon does not change; the store has the same pressure as outside (you know this is true because the store is not totally sealed off from the outside—it shares air with the outside through cracks and doors). This produces a difference in pressures—the air inside the balloon is now less than the atmospheric pressure. The pressures want to be the same. Therefore, the balloon needs to increase its pressure again. A decrease in volume of the balloon would increase the pressure again. Therefore, the balloon shrinks.

2. A bag of chips is filled and sealed at low altitude (say, in Kansas) and is transported to a high altitude (such as Colorado). What happens to the bag of chips?

    -   The bag of chips has an inside pressure that is equal to the outside pressure in the place that it was made. In Kansas (at lower altitude), the atmospheric pressure is higher and the bag of chips has the same pressure. As the chips are brought to a higher altitude (Colorado), the atmospheric pressure decreases. The chips bag wants to decrease its own pressure in order for the outside and inside to be the same. In order to decrease its own pressure, it increases its volume. The bag will expand. (It might even pop if the difference in pressures is too great for the bag to handle—it will keep expanding until the bag breaks.)

Converting between Particles and Moles

1. How many moles are equal to 5.97×10^{21} sulfur atoms?

$$5.97 \times 10^{21} \text{ atoms sulfur} \times \frac{1 \text{ mole}}{6.02 \times 10^{23} \text{ atoms}}$$

$$= .00992 \text{ moles sulfur}$$

2. How many molecules of water are in 1.25 moles of water?

$$1.25 \text{ moles water} \times \frac{6.02 \times 10^{23} \text{ molecules}}{1 \text{ mole}}$$

$$= 7.53 \times 10^{23} \text{ molecules water}$$

LAB 3.6

Moles

Purpose To find how much a mole of common things is.

Materials Paper, basketball, pen, ruler, string

Procedure

1. Find the thickness of a piece of paper. In order to do this, find the thickness of 20 pieces of paper, and then divide that thickness by 20.

2. Find the volume of a basketball. In order to do this, use string to find the circumference of the ball by wrapping the string around the largest part of the ball, marking where the string ends meet and then finding the length of that string. You'll use that circumference to find the volume of the basketball.

3. Find the length of a pen.

Data

Thickness of 20 pieces of paper (cm) _____

Circumference of basketball (cm) _____

Length of pen (cm) _____

Results

1. Find the thickness of 1 piece of paper and convert it to meters.

2. Convert the circumference of the basketball to meters and then find the volume of the basketball if $V = \dfrac{c^3}{8\pi^2}$, where c is circumference.

3. Convert the length of your pen to meters.

Discussion

1. What is the thickness of a mole of pieces of paper?

2. If the distance from the Earth to the moon is 3.82×10^8 m, how many times could the paper stack reach to the moon and back?

3. What is the volume of a mole of basketballs?

4. If the volume of the Earth is approximately 1.17×10^{21} m^3, how does the volume of a mole of basketballs compare?

5. What is the length of a mole of pens laid end to end?

6. If the circumference of the Earth is approximately 4.00×10^8 m, how many times could the line of pens circle the planet?

Go Online
Check your understanding
http://webcom4.grtxle.com/
khk12Chemistry

Converting between Particles and Moles

1. You need 2.45 moles of nitrogen gas to fill a 60-L airbag. Find the number of nitrogen molecules needed.

2. How many moles of oxygen are 7.58×10^{20} molecules?

3. How many molecules of water are in 0.578 moles of water?

4. How many moles are 5.98×10^{18} atoms?

Go Online
Animated exampless
http://webcom4.grtxle.com/
khk12Chemistry

Atomic and molecular masses

Each element on the periodic table has an **atomic mass.** That atomic mass is equal to the number of grams for one mole of that atom. For example, carbon's atomic mass is 12.01; this means that one mole of carbon atoms (or 6.02×10^{23} carbon atoms) has a mass of 12.01 g.

A compound contains atoms from different elements. If a compound contains 1 carbon atom (atomic mass of 12.01 g/mole) and two oxygen atoms (atomic mass of 16.00 g/mole), then the mass of the entire compound (CO_2) would be 12.01 g/mole + 16.00 g/mole + 16.00 g/mole = 44.01 g/mole. This could also be figured as 12.01 g/mole + 2 × (16.00 g/mole) = 44.01 g/mole. This means that one mole of carbon dioxide molecules (6.02×10^{23} molecules) would have a mass of 44.01 g/mole. This is called the **formula** or **molecular mass.** It is the sum of all the atomic masses in a compound, and is equal to the mass for one mole of molecules. (Many people also use the term formula or molecular weight, even though it is mass, not weight.)

In just 18 mL of water, there are 602,000,000,000,000,000,000,000 water molecules.

Example 3.6B

Molecular Mass

1. Find the molecular mass for $CaCl_2$.

Ca	1×40.08 g/mole
Cl	2×35.45 g/mole
	110.98 g/mole

2. Find the molecular mass for $Ba(NO_3)_2$.

Ba	1×137.33 g/mole
N	2×14.01 g/mole
O	6×16.00 g/mole
	261.35 g/mole

PRACTICE 3.6B

Molecular Mass

Find the molecular mass for the following chemicals that decompose to produce gases and could be used in an airbag.

1. NaN_3, $CaCO_3$, $KClO_3$
2. $Pb(OH)_2$
3. $SnSO_4$
4. $Fe_2(SO_4)_3$
5. CH_3OH
6. C_2H_6
7. $C_{12}H_{22}O_{11}$
8. C_3H_8O
9. $Zn(CH_3COO)_2$
10. HCl

11. NH_4NO_3
12. $CuBr_2$
13. Iron(III) sulfate
14. Copper(II) hydroxide
15. Tin(IV) sulfate
16. Iron(III) hydroxide
17. Calcium nitrate
18. Barium hydroxide
19. Chromium(III) chloride
20. Lead(II) phosphate

Go Online
Check your understanding
http://webcom4.grtxle.com/
khk12Chemistry

Molecular mass is used to convert between moles and grams

Now that we can use moles to count particles, and we can figure out how many grams are in a mole, we are ready to count the molecules in our gas samples using dimensional analysis (see Section 1.4).

Go Online
Animated examples
http://webcom4.grtxle.com/
khk12Chemistry

Example 3.6C

Converting with Molecular Mass

1. How many grams are in 1.55 moles of water molecules?

Molecular mass of water:
H   2 ×   1.01 g/mole
O   1 × 16.00 g/mole
       18.02 g/mole

$$1.55 \text{ mole water} \times \frac{18.02 \text{ g water}}{1 \text{ mole water}} = 27.9 \text{ g water}$$

2. How many moles are in 10.0 g of sodium chloride?

Molecular mass of sodium Chloride (NaCl):
Na   1 × 22.99 g/mole
Cl   1 × 35.45 g/mole
        58.44 g/mole

$$10.0 \text{ g NaCl} \times \frac{1 \text{ mole NaCl}}{58.44 \text{ g NaCl}} = 0.171 \text{ mole NaCl}$$

3. How many molecules are in 12.5 g calcium nitrate?

Molecular mass of calcium nitrate $Ca(NO_3)_2$:
Ca   1 ×   40.08 g/mole
N   2 ×   14.01 g/mole
O   6 ×   16.00 g/mole
         164.10 g/mole

$$12.5 \text{ g Ca(NO}_3)_2 \times \frac{1 \text{ mole Ca(NO}_3)_2}{164.10 \text{ g Ca(NO}_3)_2}$$

$$\times \frac{6.02 \times 10^{23} \text{ molecules Ca(NO}_3)_2}{1 \text{ mole Ca(NO}_3)_2}$$

$$= 4.59 \times 10^{22} \text{ molecules Ca(NO}_3)_2$$

PRACTICE 3.6C

Converting with Molecular Mass

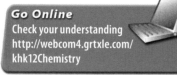

Go Online
Check your understanding
http://webcom4.grtxle.com/
khk12Chemistry

1. If you need 1.63 moles of solid NaN_3 to decompose to fill an airbag with nitrogen gas, how many grams of NaN_3 are needed?

2. Find the mass of 0.89 mole of $CaCl_2$.

3. Find the number of molecules in 158.1 g of $PbSO_4$.

4. Find the mass of 1.112×10^{22} molecules of HF.

5. Find the moles in 362.0 g of pentane, C_5H_{12}.

6. Find the mass of 0.159 mole of SiO_2.

7. Find the moles in 12.35 g of $C_4H_8O_2$.

8. Find the mass of 3.66 moles of N_2.

9. Find the number of molecules in 66.38 g of $KMnO_4$.

10. Find the mass of 0.58 mole of Se.

11. Find the mass of 1.25×10^{20} molecules of O_2.

12. Find the mass of 0.688 mole of $AgNO_3$.

Gas Laws

LAB 3.7

Gas Laws

Purpose To investigate the relationship between (1) pressure and volume and (2) temperature and volume of gases

Materials Part 1— syringe, pressure sensor, and data collection device; **Part 2—**syringe, 600 mL beaker, Bunsen burner/ring stand/ring/wire gauze, or hot plate, thermometer

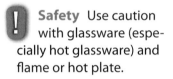
Safety Use caution with glassware (especially hot glassware) and flame or hot plate.

Procedure

Part 1 Pressure and volume

NOTE—In order to investigate the relationship between pressure and volume, the temperature must be held constant. By completing the whole procedure at the same time in the open air of the room, we will make sure that the temperature is the same the entire time.

1. Connect your pressure sensor to the data collection device (calculator or computer). Set the data collection device up to give a live readout of pressure.

2. Pull the syringe plunger out to halfway on your syringe. Connect the syringe to the pressure sensor. Record the pressure and the volume of the syringe.

3. Move the plunger to various positions on the syringe (use trials where you push in and trials where you pull out on the plunger). Record the pressure and the volume at each position. Record a total of 5 pressure–volume data sets.

Part 2 Temperature and volume

NOTE—When working with gases, the temperature must always be in the kelvin scale, with the symbol K (the reason why you must use kelvin will be discussed in this section of the text). In order to convert to kelvin, add 273 to your Celsius reading.

NOTE—In order to investigate the relationship between temperature and volume, we must hold the pressure constant for each reading that is taken. In order to do this, the same person each time will press down as hard as he or she can on the plunger of the syringe and hold it while the second person takes the reading. People are very consistent in how hard they push on the plunger for each trial, and therefore the pressure inside the syringe will be consistent for each trial, too.

1. Place a 600-mL beaker 3/4 full of water on the burner/hot plate to heat. (You will use it in a later step.) Mount a thermometer on the stand to monitor the temperature.

2. Pull the syringe plunger out as far as it will go on your syringe. Place the cap on the end of the syringe.

3. Remove the beaker with hot water from the heat source when it approaches 60°C.

4. Hold the syringe in the beaker so that the air inside the syringe is completely covered by the water. Place the thermometer in the beaker as well. Wait for the reading on the thermometer to hold steady, and record the temperature of the water in Celsius and in kelvin.

5. With the syringe still in the water, have one person push down on the plunger as hard as possible and hold it. The second person reads the volume of the syringe through the beaker and water. Record the volume.

(continues)

Gas Laws (cont'd.)

6. Remove the thermometer and the syringe from the beaker. Pour out less than one-fourth of the water in the beaker into the sink, and add about the same amount of tap water. Stir the beaker with the thermometer to mix the cool and hot water.

7. Repeat steps 4–6 for a total of 5 trials.

Data table

Trial	Part 1		Part 2	
	Pressure (kPa)	Volume (mL)	Temperature (mL)	Volume (mL)
1				
2				
3				
4				
5				

Results

1. As pressure increases, volume _____. Is this a direct or inverse relationship?

2. As temperature increases, volume _____. Is this a direct or inverse relationship?

3. For your data in Part 1,

   a. Find the product of each pressure–volume pair (pressure times volume).

   b. Find the range of these products (the maximum minus the minimum).

   c. Find the average of these products.

   d. Find the percentage of the range to the average (range/average × 100). This will give some idea of how wide the variance in the products is; the larger the percentage, the more different the products are from each other.

   e. Find the ratio of the pressure-to-volume pairs (pressure divided by volume).

   f. Find the range of these ratios.

   g. Find the average of these ratios.

   h. Find the percentage of the range of ratios to the average (range/average × 100).

   i. Which method was more consistent—the products of pressure times volume or the ratios of pressure to volume?

   j. For a direct relationship, the ratio of the two variables will always remain the same (with some variance due to experimental error). For an inverse relationship, the product of the two variables will always remain the same. What does your answer to question 3i say about the relationship between pressure and volume? Does this support your answer to question 1?

4. Repeat all of question 3 for the temperature–volume data in Part 2.

Discussion

1. Which statement is correct based on your data: $\frac{P_1}{V_1} = \frac{P_2}{V_2}$ or $P_1V_1 = P_2V_2$? Explain why you made your choice.

2. Which statement is correct based on your data: $\frac{V_1}{T_1} = \frac{V_2}{T_2}$ or $V_1T_1 = V_2T_2$? Explain why you made your choice.

3. What are three possible sources of error that could cause your ratios or products to be slightly different rather than exactly the same?

4. Share your results for questions 1 and 2 with the class. Is there agreement? If not, discuss possible reasons for the differences.

Converting units of pressure

Now that we can count molecules, we can put numbers to the behaviors of gases. First, pressure can be measured in several different units: atmospheres (atm), millimeters of mercury (mm Hg), pounds per square inch (psi or lb/in^2), torr, and kilopascals (kPa). The unit of "atmospheres" is calibrated with atmospheric pressure; 1 atm is the atmospheric pressure at sea level. The millimeters of mercury unit describes how tall a column of mercury the pressure could hold up in a barometer. You may hear on the weather report of the barometric pressure in inches—that means inches of mercury, which can be converted back to millimeters of mercury to reach the metric unit used in this text. Pounds per square inch is the unit commonly used for tire pressure. The last two units, torr and kilopascals, are named for famous scientists working in the area of pressures (Evangelista Torricelli and Blaise Pascal, respectively; both lived in the 1600s). All pressure units can be converted to other pressure units.

$$1 \text{ atm} = 760 \text{ mm Hg} = 14.7 \text{ psi} = 760 \text{ Torr} = 101.3 \text{ kPa}$$

Example 3.7A

Converting Pressure Units

How many kPa are equal to 1.57 atm?

$$1.57 \text{ atm} \times \frac{101.3 \text{ kPa}}{1 \text{ atm}} = 159 \text{ kPa}$$

Within a tornado, there is a spinning air column called a vortex. As more air is drawn into the vortex, the air pressure in the vortex's center drops. With more air drawn in, the tornado starts to stretch. Because it is hard for scientists to put instruments inside a live tornado, no one knows just how low the air pressure gets. It is a misconception that opening your windows to relieve this pressure would keep your house intact. Just use the time to seek shelter!

Go Online
Check your understanding
http://webcom4.grtxle.com/
khk12Chemistry

PRACTICE 3.7A

Converting Pressure Units

1. The air pressure for a tire is 109 kPa. What is the pressure in atm?

2. The air pressure inside a submarine is 0.62 atm. What would be the mm of mercury balanced by this pressure?

3. The weather news gives the atmospheric pressure as 1.07 atm. What is this pressure in mm Hg?

4. An experiment at Sandia National Labs in New Mexico is performed at an atmospheric pressure of 758.7 mm Hg. What is this pressure in atm?

5. A bag of potato chips is sealed in a factory near sea level. The atmospheric pressure at the factory is 761.3 mm Hg. The pressure inside the bag is the same. What is the pressure inside the bag of chips in kPa?

6. The same bag of chips is shipped to a town in Colorado, where the atmospheric pressure is 99.82 kPa. What is the difference (in kPa) between the bag of chips at the factory and in the town in Colorado?

7. The pressure on a compressed air tank reads 43.2 psi. What is the pressure in atm?

8. The pressure in the tire of a car is 34.8 psi. What is the pressure in atm?

Temperature units used when working with gas laws

$$K = °C + 273$$

When using gas laws, the temperature must be in kelvin (K). The kelvin scale has an absolute zero (the temperature at which all particle motion stops); temperatures do not go below this value. Therefore, there are no negative temperatures in the kelvin scale. If we used Celsius instead, the gas laws would give answers of negative pressures or negative volumes, which do not exist.

Avogadro's gas law

Several laws are used to predict the behavior of gases. In Section 3.5, you learned that, as the number of particles increases, the pressure also increases. This is a direct relationship that is expressed by **Avogadro's law,**

$$\frac{P_1}{T_1} = \frac{P_2}{T_2}$$

where P is pressure and n is number of moles. Both pressure units must be the same. This law assumes that the volume and temperature are not changing.

Charles' gas law

The second relationship discussed earlier was between the temperature of the particles and the volume. As the temperature increases, the pressure increases. As the pressure inside increases, it wants to equal the outside pressure again. In order to do this, it increases its volume. Therefore, when temperature increases, volume also increases. This is a direct relationship expressed by **Charles' law,**

$$\frac{V_1}{T_1} = \frac{V_2}{T_2}$$

where V is volume and T is temperature. Both volume units and both temperature units must be the same. This law assumes that the pressure and number of moles remain constant. (Remember to use kelvin with this law!)

Go Online
Topic: gas behavior/ gas laws
Go to: www.scilinks.org
Code: Chem1e137

SC*LINKS*
NSTA

Boyle's gas law

The last relationship in Section 3.5 was between the volume and the pressure. As volume increases, pressure decreases. This is an inverse relationship, expressed by **Boyle's law,**

$$P_1 V_1 = P_2 V_2$$

where P is pressure and V is volume. The pressure units must match, as must the volume units. This law assumes that temperature and number of moles are not changing.

Go Online
Animated examples
http://webcom4.grtxle.com/ khk12Chemistry

Combined gas law

All three of these laws can be written together in the **combined law,**

$$\frac{P_1 V_1}{n_1 T_1} = \frac{P_2 V_2}{n_2 T_2}$$

This law needs nothing to be held constant—all four variables can be changing at once. All units must match with their counterpart (both volume units must be the same, etc.).

Robert Boyle devised much that is the basis for today's chemistry. He lived in the 1600s. A philosopher, chemist, physicist, and inventor, he is best known for devising Boyle's law. This chemical rule is about gas pressure and volume.

Ideal gas law

The last four gas laws have had an initial situation (the 1's in the equation, such as P_1) and a final situation (the 2's, such as P_2)—something was changing, and you were predicting the new information. The final gas law does not have a change occurring; it is just predicting information about a current situation. The **ideal gas law** is

$$PV = nRT$$

where P is pressure, V is volume, n is number of moles, and T is temperature, just as before. However, this time a new letter, R, stands for the gas law constant. You choose the value for R based on the pressure unit that is used. The volume unit must be in liters for the ideal gas law for either R value.

Choosing the appropriate law

How do you know which of these gas laws to use? The combined gas law has Avogadro's, Boyle's, and Charles' laws within it. Whichever quantities are being held constant can just be deleted from the equation; this way you need to remember only one law. You will know to use the ideal gas law because there won't be a change—for example, you won't have an initial volume and a final volume—just a volume.

Pressure Unit	R
atm	$0.0821 \dfrac{L \times atm}{mole \times K}$
kPa	$8.31 \dfrac{L \times kPa}{mole \times K}$

Standard temperature and pressure (STP)

Scientists use a standard value for temperature and pressure so that they can compare their results. Standard temperature is 0.0°C (or 273K), and standard pressure is 1 atm (or 101.3 kPa, or 760 mm Hg, or any of the other units that are equal to 1 atm).

Now that you're learning about the Ideal Gas Law, you will be able to understand the universe better. Whew, Venus is a hot place! It is a toasty 890°F. There's so much CO_2 that the planet has a huge greenhouse effect; the atmosphere is 97% CO_2. You know from your chemistry study that when you increase a gas's pressure, its temperature can rise or its density goes down. By lowering the density, the pressure will go down or the temperature will go up.

Example 3.7B

Gas Laws

1. A gas occupies 15.7 L at 1.25 atm. What is the volume at standard pressure?

   - The problem gives a volume and a pressure and then asks for a new volume at a new pressure. This is a change in conditions, so the combined law will be used.

   $$\frac{P_1V_1}{n_1T_1} = \frac{P_2V_2}{n_2T_2}$$

   - There is no mention of temperature or number of moles or particles. Therefore, these are assumed to be held constant and don't need to be considered: $P_1V_1 = P_2V_2$ (which is also Boyle's law).

     $P_1 = 1.25$ atm $\quad V_1 = 15.7$ L

     $P_2 = 1$ atm $\quad\quad V_2 = ?$

   - The second pressure is "standard pressure"—it was chosen to be 1 atm because the first pressure reading is given in atm.

     $(1.25 \text{ atm}) \times (15.7 \text{ L}) = (1 \text{ atm}) \times V_2$

     $$\frac{(1.25 \text{ atm}) \times (15.7 \text{ L})}{1 \text{ atm}} = V_2$$

     $V_2 = 19.6$ L

2. What is the volume of a gas at 30°C if it is 10.5 L at 22°C?

   - This problem gives a temperature and a volume, and asks for a new volume at a new temperature. This is a change in conditions, so the combined law will be used.

     $$\frac{P_1V_1}{n_1T_1} = \frac{P_2V_2}{n_2T_2}$$

   - There is no mention of temperature or number of moles or particles. Therefore, these are assumed to be held constant and don't need to be considered:

     $$\frac{V_1}{T_1} = \frac{V_2}{T_2}$$

   - (which is also Charles' law).

     $V_1 = 10.5$ L $\quad T_1 = 22°C = 295$ K

     $V_2 = ?$ $\quad\quad T_2 = 30°C = 303$ K

   - Temperature needs to be in kelvin for gas laws, so 273 was added to the Celsius reading:

     $$\frac{10.5 \text{ L}}{295 \text{ K}} = \frac{V_2}{303 \text{ K}} \quad (303 \text{ K}) \times \frac{10.5 \text{ L}}{295 \text{ K}} = V_2$$

     $V_2 = 10.8$ L

3. How many moles are needed to create 25.0 L at 105 kPa and 20°C?

   - This problem gives only one situation—there is no changing. Therefore, the ideal gas law will be used, $PV = nRT$

     $P = 105$ kPa $\quad V = 25.0$ L

     $n = ?$ $\quad\quad T = 20°C = 293$ K

     $$R = 8.31 \frac{\text{L} \cdot \text{KPa}}{\text{M} \quad 06 \cdot K}$$

   - The R value was chosen with the kPa units because the pressure was given in the problem in kPa.

     $(105 \text{ kPa}) \times (25.0 \text{ L})$
     $= n \times (8.31 \text{ L} \times \text{kPa/mole} \times \text{K}) \times (293 \text{ K})$

     $$\frac{(105 \text{ kPa}) \times (25.0 \text{ L})}{(8.31 \text{ L} \times \text{kPa/mole} \times \text{K}) \times (293 \text{ K})} = n$$

     $n = 1.08$ mole

Gas Laws

Go Online
Check your understanding
http://webcom4.grtxle.com/
khk12Chemistry

1. A 60.0-L airbag needs to be filled with nitrogen gas. If the gas is going to be at 25°C and at a pressure of 1.00 atm, how many moles of nitrogen gas are needed? How many grams of nitrogen gas (N_2) are needed?

2. What if the airbag is now being used on top of a mountain and the pressure will be only 0.70 atm? How many moles of nitrogen gas are needed? How many grams of nitrogen gas are needed?

3. A 1.0-L tank of compressed gas is released to fill a 60.0-L airbag at 0.95 atm. What was the original pressure of the gas? Is this a safe way to store gas in the car before the airbag is needed? Why or why not?

4. Given 7.91 L of a gas at 52°C that is changed to 538 K, find the new volume.

5. Given 338 mL of a gas at 86.1 kPa that is changed to 104.0 kPa, find the new volume.

6. Given 31.5 mL of a gas at 97.8 kPa that is changed to 82.3 kPa, find the new volume.

7. Given 2.90 L of a gas at 226 K that is changed to 23°C, find the new volume.

8. Given 7.51 L of a gas at 5.0°C and 59.9 kPa, find the new volume at standard temperature and pressure.

9. How many moles of gas occupy a 486-mL flask at 11°C and 66.7 kPa?

10. Given 0.873 L of a gas at 94.3 kPa that is changed to 102.3 kPa, find the new volume.

(continues)

PRACTICE 3.7B

Gas Laws (*cont'd*)

11. Given 351 mL of a gas at 19°C and 82.5 kPa, find the new volume at 36°C and 94.5 kPa.

12. Given 7.03 L of a gas at 31°C and 111 kPa, find the new volume at standard temperature and pressure.

13. Given 955 mL of a gas at 58°C and 108.0 kPa, find the new volume at 76°C and 123.0 kPa.

14. Given 2.13 L of a gas at 95°C and 103 kPa, find the new volume at standard temperature and pressure.

15. Given 376 mL of a gas at 379 K that is changed to 51°C, find the new volume.

16. Given 61.4 mL of a gas at 67°C and 96.8 kPa, find the new volume at 0°C and 52.2 kPa.

17. What pressure is exerted by 0.622 mole of gas contained in a 9.22-L vessel at 16°C?

18. Given 4.76 L of a gas at 6.0°C and 124.5 kPa, find the new volume at 25°C and 99.4 kPa.

19. What volume is occupied by 0.684 mole of gas at 99.1 kPa and 9.0°C?

Here is your chance to use the chemistry you know to weigh, as an automotive engineer, the benefits and risks of several methods of producing a gas.

Different ways to make a gas in an airbag

Purpose To observe three methods of inflating an airbag and determine which is best

Materials Three test tubes, three rubber stoppers (with holes) that fit the test tube (one must have two holes), three balloons, test tube rack, test tube holder, two plastic pipettes, small beaker, weighing boats, balance, Bunsen burner, sodium bicarbonate, vinegar, copper(II) carbonate (basic), dry ice

! **Safety** Use caution with the Bunsen burner; while heating the test tube, always point it away from people. Use caution with the hot glass and with dry ice—it can burn the skin.

Procedure

Part 1 Chemical reaction between sodium bicarbonate and acetic acid producing a gas

1. Pour a small amount of vinegar (acetic acid) into the beaker.

2. Fill the two pipettes with vinegar. In order to get them completely full (no air inside), use the following method.

3. Squeeze the bulb as much as you can to fill it with vinegar.

4. Turn the pipette upside down. The air will now rise to the stem. Squeeze the pipette bulb until all the air is squeezed out through the stem and vinegar begins to come out. DO NOT RELEASE THE BULB.

5. Put the pipette back in the beaker of vinegar and release the bulb. The pipette should be completely full of vinegar—no air.

6. Place the pipettes inside the balloon with the stems sticking out through the end of the balloon.

7. Thread the stems of the pipettes through the holes in a rubber stopper with two holes (put the wider end of the stopper closer to the balloon).

8. Fit the end of the balloon onto the rubber stopper so that it seals the balloon and the two pipette stems are sticking out the bottom of the rubber stopper.

9. Carefully squeeze out any air from the balloon without squeezing the pipette bulbs that are inside.

10. Use a weighing boat to weigh out approximately 1.0 gram of sodium bicarbonate.

11. Transfer the sodium bicarbonate to a test tube.

12. Put the rubber stopper into the test tube and seal tightly. Pull the end of the balloon over the test tube so that it completely covers the stopper and is now sealing the test tube itself.

13. Squeeze the pipette bulbs to release the vinegar into the test tube. It will react with the sodium bicarbonate and form a gas; the gas will go back through the holes in the stopper and inflate the balloon. Be careful, though, not to squeeze the balloon and cause it to unseal from the rubber stopper—just squeeze the pipette bulbs inside of it.

14. Make observations on the reactants involved, what happened during the reaction, and how quickly the balloon filled.

15. Place the test tube, rubber stopper, and balloon in the test tube rack. Do not disassemble it yet, and leave the balloon inflated.

Part 2 Decomposing copper(II) carbonate to form a gas

1. Place another rubber stopper in the end of another balloon (wide end of the stopper in the balloon).

2. Use a weighing boat to measure out about 1 gram of copper(II) carbonate.

3. Transfer the chemical to a test tube.

4. Seal the test tube with the rubber stopper with the balloon attached.

5. Hold the test tube with test tube tongs and heat it over the Bunsen burner. Point the test tube away from all people. Move it around in the flame to evenly heat the solid. You may also want to shake the test tube every so often to allow even heating. The reaction produces a gas, which will fill the balloon, as well as a black solid (copper(II) oxide). When the entire solid is black, the reaction is complete.

6. Make observations on the reactants involved, what happened during the reaction, and how quickly the balloon filled.

7. Place the test tube, rubber stopper, and balloon in the test tube rack. Do not disassemble it yet, and leave the balloon inflated.

Part 3 Sublimation of dry ice to produce a gas

1. Place another rubber stopper in the end of another balloon (wide end of the stopper in the balloon).

2. Carefully transfer a few pieces of dry ice (approximately equivalent to the amount of solids you used in Parts 1 and 2; it's impossible to find the mass of the solid dry ice because it continually sublimes and turns into a gas, so its mass is always changing). Use caution, and do not directly touch the dry ice because it will burn your skin.

3. Quickly place the rubber stopper with the balloon in the test tube. The dry ice will sublime (turn from a solid directly to a gas), and the gas will fill the balloon.

4. Make observations on the reactants involved, what happened during the reaction, and how quickly the balloon filled.

5. Place the test tube, rubber stopper, and balloon in the test tube rack. Do not disassemble it yet, and leave the balloon inflated.

Final observations

1. Record observations on the size and pressure of the three balloons—which reaction produced the most gas? Which produced the least?

2. Clean up and leave all equipment as you found it.

Observations

Part 1:

Part 2:

Part 3:

Final observations.

Discussion

1. Which parts were chemical reactions and which were physical processes?

2. Part 1 is the following reaction: sodium bicarbonate and acetic acid produce sodium acetate, carbon dioxide gas, and water. Write and balance this equation.

3. Part 2 is the following reaction: copper(II) carbonate ($CuCO_3 \cdot Cu(OH)_2$) is decomposed to form carbon dioxide gas, copper(II) oxide, and water. Write and balance this equation.

4. Part 3 is the following reaction: solid carbon dioxide sublimes to gaseous carbon dioxide. Write and balance this equation.

5. Make a chart with the different ways of producing a gas in this lab across the top, and the criteria for a good airbag that you developed at the beginning of the chapter down the side. For each criterion, rank the three different processes on how well they meet that criterion (1 being the best, 3 being the worst). Your observations from the lab will help in this process.

6. Add up all the rankings for each process. The lower the total score, the better overall it met the criteria. Which process is the best for an airbag?

7. List advantages of the best process for use in airbags.

8. List disadvantages of the best process for use in airbags.

9. Describe one other way (different from the methods used in this lab) that you could fill an airbag.

10. Describe why this other method would be better than the best method from the lab. Describe how this other method would be worse than the best method from the lab.

CHAPTER 3 Summary

There are three states of matter: solids, liquids, and gases. The states differ in their particle packing and mobility, compressibility, and whether they maintain a definite shape or volume.

All matter has properties that can be used to identify it. Physical properties can be measured or observed without changing the chemical composition of the matter. When chemical properties are measured or observed, the chemical structure of the matter changes. A physical change alters the physical properties of a sample, without changing the chemical structure. A chemical change rearranges the atoms to form new chemical structures.

Density is a common physical property used to identify a substance. Density is an intensive property, meaning that a small sample and a large sample of the same substance will have the same density. An extensive property would be different for a large and a small sample, such as mass or volume. Density is the mass/volume of a sample. A graph of mass on the y axis and volume on the x axis will have a slope equal to the density of the substance.

Atoms or molecules cannot be counted individually; therefore, we use the counting unit mole. One mole of anything is equal to Avogadro's number (6.02×10^{23}). The atomic mass on the periodic table is the number of grams for one mole of that element's atoms. Adding the atomic masses for a compound will give you the molecular mass—the grams per mole for a molecule of that chemical.

Gas particles behave according to kinetic molecular theory. They are in constant, rapid motion that fills the entire container. Pressure is caused by the particles running into the walls of the container. Atmospheric pressure is due to the layers of gas particles in the atmosphere pushing down on the Earth. The higher the altitude, the lower the atmospheric pressure. Flexible containers adjust so that the inside pressure (caused by the gases inside) is equal to the outside pressure (the atmospheric pressure).

The gas laws can predict the effect of changes in a gas's environment. Pressure and volume are inversely related. Volume and temperature are directly related. The number of particles (moles) and pressure are directly related. These relationships can be summed up in the combined gas law,

$$\frac{P_1 V_1}{n_1 T_1} = \frac{P_2 V_2}{n_2 T_2}$$

The ideal gas law relates quantities when there are no changes, $PV = nRT$. The temperature unit of kelvin (which has an absolute zero; °C + 273 = K) is used in the gas laws in order to avoid having negative values for volume and moles, which isn't physically possible.

1. What is matter?

2. Compare and contrast solid, liquid and gas.

3. Give an example of a physical property and a chemical property.

4. Give an example of a physical change and a chemical change.

5. Which of the following are chemical properties (CP) or physical properties (PP)?

   a. Mass
   b. Volume
   c. Density
   d. Reactivity with water
   e. Ability to be oxidized
   f. Color
   g. Taste
   h. Malleability
   i. Ductility
   j. Flammability

6. Which of the following are intensive properties (IP) or extensive properties (EP)?

   a. Mass
   b. Volume
   c. Density
   d. Reactivity with water
   e. Ability to be oxidized
   f. Color
   g. Taste
   h. Malleability
   i. Ductility
   j. Flammability

7. Which of the following are chemical changes (CC) or physical changes (PC)?

   a. Rusting
   b. Melting
   c. Boiling
   d. Evaporating
   e. Filtering
   f. Crystallizing
   g. Dissolving
   h. Burning
   i. Forming a precipitate
   j. Breaking
   k. Electrolysis
   l. Metabolizing food

8. A sample of a substance has a mass of 3.5 g and a volume of 2.1 mL. What is the density of that substance?

9. A sample has a density of 1.025 g/mL and a volume of 18.2 cm^3. What is the sample's mass?

10. If a rock has a mass of 19.25 g and a volume of 3.5 mL, what is its density?

11. A piece of metal has a density of 12.3 g/mL and a mass of 18.97 g. What is the volume of the piece?

12. Find the density of the rock with the following data:

Mass of rock	19.5 g
Initial volume of water	25.0 mL
Final volume of water	34.5 mL

13. Graph the tabulated data below. Draw a best-fit line.

Volume (mL)	Mass (g)	Volume (mL)	Mass (g)
22	85	10	26
20	73	8	24
25	97	1	1
23	88	8	28
8	27	10	41
16	57	14	55
16	59	14	50
17	68	11	39
19	71	20	74
23	87	15	55
17	61	19	72

14. Use the graph to find the volume of a piece of metal that is 12.5 g. Circle the point on the line that you used to find this information.

15. Use the graph to find the mass of a piece of metal that has a volume of 9.0 mL. Circle the point on the line that you used to find this information.

16. What will the slope of the line on your graph give you?

17. Find the slope of the best-fit line. Show your work, and circle the two points that you used to find your slope.

18. Use the slope to find the volume of a piece of metal that is 12.5 g. How does this calculated answer compare to your graphical one from question 11?

19. Use the slope to find the mass of a piece of metal that has a volume of 9.0 mL. How does this calculated answer compare to your graphical one from question 12?

20. Find the molecular mass of

    a. $Ca(NO_3)_2$

    b. Lead(II) phosphate

    c. Ammonium bromide

    d. $Zn(CH_3COO)_2$

    e. HCl

    f. $Mg(OH)_2$

21. How many moles are in 10.96 g of K_3PO_4? How many molecules are there?

22. Find the mass of 0.0324 moles of NH_4NO_3. How many molecules are there?

23. How many moles are in 7.5×10^{22} atoms of aluminum?

24. How many grams are 9.87×10^{21} molecules of water?

25. How many kPa are equal to 1.23 atm?

26. 16.2 psi are equal to how many mm Hg?

27. How does atmospheric pressure change as you climb a mountain? Why?

28. Why do sealed cans with gases in them explode when they get too hot?

29. Why do balloons shrink when you take them from the warm store to your cold car?

30. Why does your shampoo bottle expand when you travel to Colorado from San Francisco?

31. A gas is 1.25 L at 107.8 kPa. Find the volume at standard pressure.

32. A gas is 8.77 L at 145.2 kPa. What is the volume at 115.4 kPa?

33. A gas is 475 mL at 282 K and 108.5 kPa. Find the volume at STP.

34. How many moles are in 1.98 L of a gas at STP?

35. A gas is 257 mL at 255 K. Find the volume at standard temperature.

36. What is the pressure of a gas if there are 0.125 moles of it in 12.25 L at 18°C?

37. A gas is 148.2 mL at 229 K and 125.0 kPa. Find the new volume at 315 K and 104.5 kPa.

38. What is the volume of a gas that has 0.752 moles at STP?

39. A gas is 12.54 L at 35°C. What is the volume at 15°C?

Research chemists use computers and lab equipment to study the structure of matter with the aim of creating new products or processes or making existing products even better.

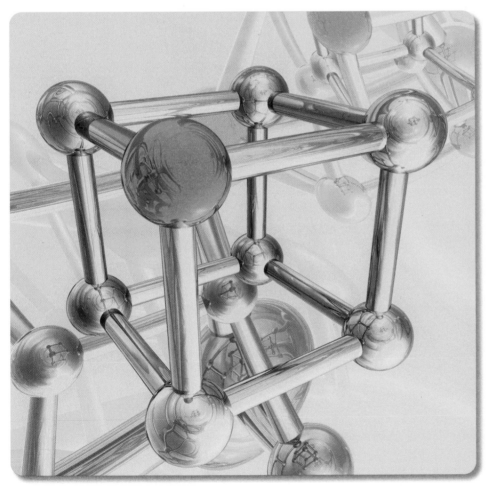

CHAPTER
4

Glowing Things
Chemistry Sheds Light on Our Lives

IN THIS CHAPTER

- Development of atomic theory
- Atomic structure
- Electron structure
- Periodic table
- Periodicity
- Light
- Light and matter

Jellyfish use bioluminescence to lure their prey.

INTRODUCTORY
ACTIVITY

List as many things as you can that you've ever heard about glowing or seen glow.

What do these glowing things need to work?

to make a presentation on a glowing object of your choice.

Introduction

You've probably seen glow-in-the-dark stickers or clothing, black lights, glowsticks, lightning bugs, and various other "glowing" things in your life. You may even have seen TV shows or movies that show the use of Luminol (a substance that glows in the dark when it comes in contact with blood) but did you know that even algae can glow?

Jim Lovell, the astronaut who commanded the Apollo mission portrayed in the movie *Apollo 13,* was an Air Force pilot before joining the space program. Returning one night from a combat patrol to an aircraft carrier near Japan, he encountered trouble. Rather than picking up the signal from the aircraft carrier, as the two other American planes had, Lovell's instruments were picking up a signal being broadcast from Japan. Circling in the air, unable to locate the correct signal or the ship, he attempted to use a device that he had designed to search the radio frequencies. But when he plugged it in, it created a short circuit, and the entire cockpit went pitch black. Now he could not rely on technology to guide him back to the aircraft carrier. Lovell looked at the dark ocean below and saw a faint green glow. Several types of algae can glow green—they produce light as a part of their biological processes (similar to lightning bugs). The propellers of an aircraft carrier can churn these organisms into releasing their light, forming a trail of glowing green behind the ship. Although this is the least reliable way a pilot can guide himself in for a landing, it could be used as a last resort. Desperate to try anything, Lovell followed the glow and landed safely on the ship. He would not have been able to see the faint glow below had he not shorted out the cockpit and been surrounded by total darkness—what could have been disastrous was actually a stroke of luck.[1]

In order to understand how light and glowing things work, you need to understand atomic structure, including the arrangement of electrons in an atom, what light is, and how it interacts with matter.

---

[1] This story can be found in *Lost Moon: The Perilous Voyage of Apollo 13,* by Jim Lovell and Jeffrey Kluger, published by Houghton Mifflin, 1994.

Glow in the dark

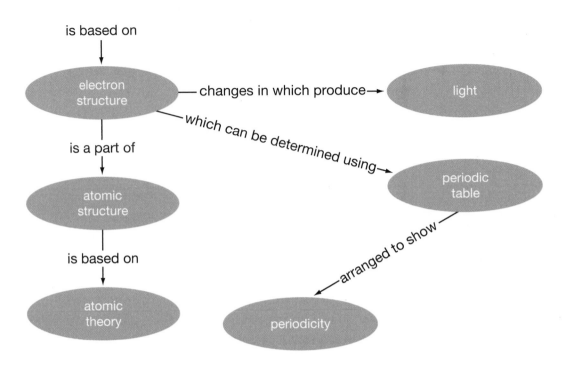

SECTION 4.1

Development of Atomic Theory

Dalton's atomic theory

John Dalton presented the first atomic theory based on experiments in the early 1800s. (Remember—theories attempt to explain why observed phenomena occur, and can be changed as new information is discovered.) **Dalton's atomic theory** had several points:

- All matter is made of tiny particles, called atoms.
- An atom cannot be created, divided, destroyed, or changed into any other type of atom.
- Atoms of the same element are identical in their properties.
- Atoms of different elements are different in their properties.
- Atoms of different elements combine in whole-number ratios to form compounds.
- Chemical changes join, separate, or rearrange atoms in compounds.

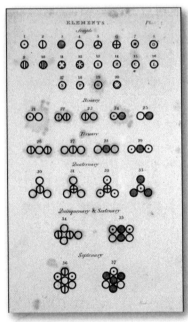

John Dalton's artwork for his early 1800s text, *A New System of Chemical Philosophy*. His idea was to show the structure of atoms in a molecule.

It's amazing that so many of Dalton's ideas from so long ago are still considered to be true today. Only the second and third points are no longer valid—the reasons why will be explained later in this chapter.

Discovering the fundamental particles of the atom

Dalton had envisioned atoms as being round, solid, BB-like spheres that could not be separated into smaller pieces. In 1897 J. J. Thomson used cathode rays to change this understanding of the atom. A **cathode ray** is a ray of electrons that travels in a vacuum tube (which has been emptied of all atoms and molecules, even "air," which consists of various gas molecules) from a negative electrode to a positive electrode (electrodes are metal disks that have electricity connected to them). Thomson placed a positive plate outside the tube, and the cathode ray turned toward the positive plate (see Figure 4–1). A negative plate placed outside the tube pushed the cathode ray away from the plate. Because opposites attract and like charges repel, Thomson concluded that the cathode ray was composed of negatively charged particles. It didn't matter what material the electrodes were made out of—all types of material seemed to produce these streams of negatively charged particles. Thomson announced that the ray was made of negatively charged particles called **electrons**, and that all matter had them.

Go Online
Topic: history of atomic theory
Go to: www.scilinks.org
Code: Chem1e125

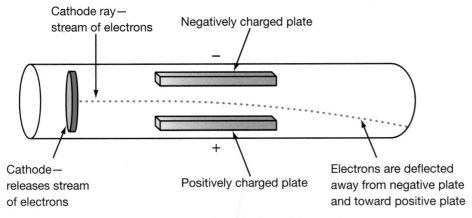

Figure 4–1. Cathode ray experiment. As the cathode ray (electrons) travels through the tube, it is deflected away from the negative charge in the middle of the tube. Thus, electrons are negatively charged.

Cathode ray—stream of electrons

Negatively charged plate

−

Cathode—releases stream of electrons

Positively charged plate

+

Electrons are deflected away from negative plate and toward positive plate

Old vacuum tube

If atoms were neutral overall but contained negative electrons, there must be something positive in the atom. Eugene Goldstein conducted experiments in the 1870s that led to the discovery of the **proton,** which had the same charge as the electron but with the opposite sign, and was 1837 times heavier than the electron.

By the early 1900s, scientists no longer believed that the atom was the solid, indivisible sphere that Dalton had suggested. Now they thought that it was a uniform mixture of positive and negative. This version of atomic theory, presented by Thomson, is often called the **plum pudding model.**

(Most Americans are not familiar with plum pudding, so you can think of chocolate chip cookie dough instead!) The dough is the positive portion of the atom, and the electrons are mixed throughout like chocolate chips.

Hans Geiger performed an experiment in 1908 in which he bombarded a thin layer of gold atoms with radioactive material, alpha particles. This is known as the **gold foil experiment** (radioactive material will be discussed in Chapter 12). The alpha particles should have been like a bowling ball flying at a thin piece of paper, because they were thought to be so much denser than the atoms of the foil. They were expected to travel through with only a small amount of deflection. Most of the alpha particles did fly straight through the foil without being deflected at all; however, some of them were reflected back to where they came from, and some traveled through with slight deflection (see Figure 4-2). Ernest Rutherford interpreted this experiment in 1911. He stated that most of the atom was empty space—large sections of empty space where the alpha particles flew through with absolutely no deflection. However, there must be a small section of the atom that contains most of the mass, since it was dense enough to reflect the alpha particles back to where they came from. He called this dense area the **nucleus**. The alpha particles that traveled through with a slight deflection must have hit a particle of smaller mass than the nucleus—enough mass to deflect the alpha particle slightly, but not so much as to reflect it back completely. These particles of smaller mass were the electrons. So now the atom was thought to have a dense, positively charged nucleus with negatively charged electrons distributed within a large area of empty space outside the nucleus. How the electrons were arranged was not known at this time—they were just known to be outside the nucleus.

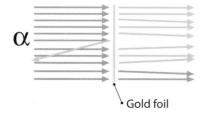

Figure 4-2. Gold foil experiment. Alpha particles were shot at a thin foil of gold atoms.

Refining the atomic theory further

The positive charge on the proton explained how the electron could be negative, and the overall atom neutral. However, the masses of the protons and electrons did not explain the total mass of an atom—there was something else in atoms with mass. A neutral particle was first proposed in the early 1920s, but it was 1932 before James Chadwick found experimental evidence of a neutral particle with a mass similar to a proton's; he called it a **neutron**. The neutron was also located in the nucleus.

Niels Bohr performed experiments in 1913 with atoms of hydrogen and light to discover that electrons are in levels. They were not free floating around a nucleus, but rather had specific places and energy amounts that were possible. **Bohr's atomic model** (see Figure 4-3) shows the nucleus in the center (containing protons and neutrons) with concentric rings surrounding it. Electrons resided in the rings—the lowest energy being closest to the nucleus, and Bohr thought that since protons and electrons are attracted to one another, it would take more energy for an electron to

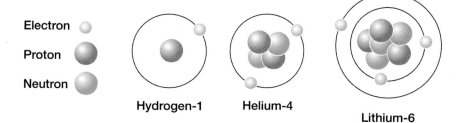

Figure 4–3. Examples of Bohr models.

reside farther from the nucleus. Although modern atomic theory no longer believes that electrons reside in concentric rings of energy levels, it is the easiest way to draw these "levels" on two-dimensional paper. Therefore, the Bohr model is the most commonly drawn visualization of an atom.

Modern atomic theory

Although Bohr's model was limited in what it could explain, its use of energy levels for electrons led the way for scientists in the late 1920s to propose **quantum mechanics**—the study of very tiny particles and how they behave. Modern atomic theory uses complicated calculus equations to describe how these tiny protons, neutrons, and electrons act as both particles and waves. The equations give regions of probability that an electron could be found in—rather than drawing a circle that shows the orbit path of an electron, as in the Bohr model. These regions of probability of finding an electron are called **atomic orbitals**.

PRACTICE 4.1

Developing Atomic Theory

1. Explain how Dalton's atomic theory changed after J. J. Thomson's experiments. What was the experimental proof that warranted these theory changes?

2. Explain how J. J. Thomson's atomic theory changed after the gold foil experiments. What was the experimental proof that brought about these changes?

3. According to Rutherford, why is most of the atom's mass located in its nucleus? In other words, what experimental evidence did he have to say this?

4. How did Bohr change atomic theory? What experimental proof justified these changes?

5. What changed in Bohr's atomic theory to produce the modern atomic theory?

6. Do you think that the modern atomic theory is complete and correct? Explain why or why not.

7. What role did light play in changing atomic theory?

Go Online
Check your understanding
http://webcom4.grtxle.com/
khk12Chemistry

Atomic Structure

From the previous section, you know that atoms are made of electrons surrounding a nucleus, which contains protons and neutrons. Protons are positively charged, neutrons are neutral, and electrons are negatively charged. What makes an atom the element that it is? Why does carbon behave differently than fluorine? The difference is in the number and organization of the protons and electrons.

Protons in the atom

Every element has a different number of protons; that fact is what defines each atom. Every atom with six protons is carbon, and every atom with nine protons is fluorine—that's what makes these two elements different. The number of protons in an atom is its **atomic number** on the periodic table. It is the whole number near the element's symbol (different versions of the periodic table have the atomic number in slightly different places). The periodic table is organized by the atomic number—elements are in order from left to right, increasing by one for each next element. The atomic number can also be written as a subscript on the left side of the element's symbol: $_6$C.

Atomic number = number of protons

A periodic table is organized by atomic number, shown here under the names of the elements.

Mass number and neutrons in the atom

Because it would be impractical to discuss such tiny particles as protons, neutrons, and electrons in terms of grams, a new unit was defined: **atomic mass unit (amu)**. The proton has a mass of 1.00 amu, the neutron has a mass of 1.00 amu, and the electron has a mass of 0.00054 amu. This means that the mass of an electron is only 0.054% the mass of a proton or neutron. This percentage is so small that the mass of an electron is estimated to be 0 amu relative to the proton and neutron. The **mass number** of an atom is equal to the number of protons plus the number of neutrons (since the electrons have no relative mass, they are not included in the mass number). The mass number is *not* found on the periodic table—you will be given either the mass number or the number of neutrons. (You'll find out later in this section what the "mass" on the periodic table is telling you.) The mass number can be written as a superscript to the left of an element's symbol or as a number after the element's name: ^{13}C or carbon-13.

Mass number = number of protons + number of neutrons

Charges on atoms and electrons   Because neutrons have a neutral charge, protons and electrons are the only things that matter when talking about the total charge on an atom. Actually, an atom is always neutral. If it has a charge (meaning the numbers of negative electrons and positive protons are not equal), then it's called an ion. The charge of an ion is equal to the number of positives (protons) minus the number of negatives (electrons). If there is a greater number of electrons than protons (the atom has gained extra electrons), then it will have an overall negative charge and be called an **anion.** If the ion has fewer electrons than protons (the atom has lost electrons), then it will have an overall positive charge and be called a **cation.** You cannot find the charge on the periodic table, either—you need to be given either the charge or the number of electrons. The charge is written as a superscript on the right side of the element's symbol: F^{-1}.

$$\text{Charge} = \text{number of protons} - \text{number of electrons}$$

Example 4.2A

Atomic Structure

Fill in the following table.

Symbol	Name	Atomic number	Mass number	Charge	Protons	Neutrons	Electrons
$^{36}_{17}Cl^{-1}$				−1			

- The symbol gives not only the element's letter symbol, but also the mass number (the superscript) and the atomic number (the subscript).

- The name is Chlorine-36 (the element name, known from the element's letter symbol and mass number from the superscript).

- The atomic number is given by the subscript—17.

- The mass number is given by the superscript—36.

- The protons are always the same as the atomic number—17.

- The neutrons are found by mass number = protons + neutrons; $36 = 17 + n$. This gives 19 neutrons.

Symbol	Name	Atomic number	Mass number	Charge	Protons	Neutrons	Electrons
$^{36}_{17}Cl^{-1}$	Chloride ion	17	36	−1	17	19	18

Fireflies (also known as lightning bugs) attract mates with biolumi-nescence produced at a wavelength of 510 to 670 nanometers. What causes this beetle to glow? A body enzyme stimulates luciferin in their lower abdomen. Perhaps someday you will travel to the Malaysian jungle, where many fireflies throng at the riverbanks at night. That certain species flashes in unison, a spectacular sight. Young larvae of fireflies also glow, and in this case they do so to scare away predators. Predators have learned that these glowing youngsters taste terrible due to the chemicals in the larvae.

Go Online
Check your understanding
http://webcom4.grtxle.com/
khk12Chemistry

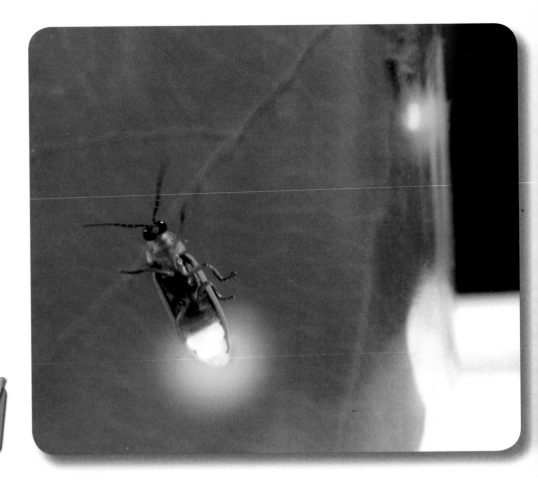

PRACTICE 4.2A

Atomic Structure

Fill in the following table.

	Symbol	Name	Atomic number	Mass number	Charge	Protons	Neutrons	Electrons
1	$^{29}_{14}Si$				0			
2		Cobalt-58			+2			
3			28	58	+2			
4			48		0		63	
5					0	33	40	
6					0		125	85
7			88	226				88
8	$^{197}_{79}Au$							76
9		Rhodium-103			0			
10			80	201	0			
11			78		+4		117	
12					+2	82	125	

Isotopes—Atoms of the same element can be different

Dalton's atomic theory stated that all atoms of the same element are identical. Scientists now know that this is not exactly true. Some atoms have a different number of neutrons, but they are the same element because the number of protons has not changed. They have the same charge because the neutrons are neutral, and adding or removing them does not affect the charge. But the neutrons do affect the mass (they have a mass of 1.00 amu). Atoms of the same element with a different number of neutrons are called **isotopes**. Because isotopes are of the same element but they have differences in neutrons and mass, they are not identical, as Dalton had first thought. Some isotopes are radioactive, and some are not. The fact that some isotopes are radioactive disproves the part of Dalton's atomic theory that stated an atom could not be changed into another type of atom; radioactive isotopes decay until they form a stable atom of a different element (more about this in Chapter 12).

The mass number tells you which isotope is being discussed. The mass number can be written either as a part of the element's symbol (a superscript to the left of the symbol) or as a part of its name; for example, hydrogen always has 1 proton. The isotope of hydrogen with 0 neutrons (which would have a mass number of 1) is hydrogen-1 (or ^{1}H); the isotope with 1 neutron (mass number 2) is hydrogen-2 (or ^{2}H). Figure 4–4 shows these different possibilities.

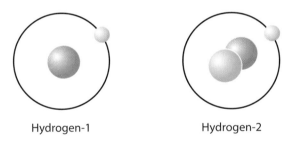

Hydrogen-1   Hydrogen-2

Figure 4–4. Hydrogen isotopes.

LAB 4.2

Average Atomic Mass

Purpose   To find the average mass of isotopes by several methods and determine which formula is used for average atomic mass

Background information   The composition of United States pennies has changed over the years, from solid copper to a zinc core with a copper cover in order to save on the cost of production (when they were made of solid copper, they cost more than a penny to make). The two types of pennies are the same size, but pennies before the change have a larger mass than the more recent ones (though they have the same volume, they are more dense).

(continues)

Average Atomic Mass (*cont'd.*)

Materials 20 pennies of various dates; balance

Procedure Find the mass of each individual penny, and record the year and mass in the data table.

Data Make a data table that includes the year and mass for each penny.

Results There should be two different types of pennies in your data. Small variances in the mass are due to wear and tear on the coin, but the same type should be in the same general ballpark for mass. Look at your data and make two new lists of years and masses—separating the two types.

1. Method 1 for averaging the data—average of entire data set

   a. Average the complete set of data—add all 20 masses and divide by 20.

2. Method 2 for averaging the data—average of the averages

   a. Find the average mass of each type.

   b. Then find the average mass of the two types; add the two type averages and divide by 2.

3. Method 3 for averaging the data—weighted average

   a. Find the percentage of pennies of each type.

   b. Multiply the average mass of the first type (you found it in method 2) by the percentage (in decimal form) that it occurs. Multiply the average mass of the second type (method 2) by the percentage (in decimal form) that it occurs. Add the two together.

Discussion

1. Look at your two lists of types of pennies from question 1 in the results. According to your data, what was the newest old type of penny, and what was the oldest new type? Depending on the sample that you had, you may be able to give a specific year that it changed, or you may be able to give only a range of years in which it changed types. Give the year or range in which the switch was made.

2. Method 1 is the most common method of averaging data—finding the average taking into account the entire data set. Which method, 2 or 3, was closer to the answer from method 1?

3. Method 2 does not take into account how many times each type was present; it treats the two types as equal by averaging the averages. Explain why this is not as accurate.

4. Which method would you like your teacher to use to figure your grade if you received nine A's and one C? Explain why.

5. How are the pennies similar to isotopes of atoms?

6. Which method do you suppose is used to find the average atomic mass from the isotope masses?

Some isotopes occur frequently in nature, and others are less frequent. The **average atomic mass**, which is found on the periodic table, is the average of all the isotope masses. It is a weighted average—meaning it takes into account how often that particular isotope occurs. For example, if you received an A on nine of your tests and then scored a C on one test, would it be fair to give you an average grade of B? Of course not! You'd take into account the nine A's and the one C and end up with a lower A average. The result of a weighted average should always be closest to the value that occurs most frequently (the mode), rather than directly in the middle (the mean), which is what we usually associate with "average."

You may notice in the example and practice problems that the masses of the isotopes are not whole numbers. The *mass number* of an atom is equal to the number of protons + number of neutrons. Because you can't have a fraction or decimal of a proton or neutron, the mass number is always a whole number. The actual mass of an atom is not a whole number, due to the mass of the electrons and the unusual things that occur with energy and mass when a nucleus is formed.

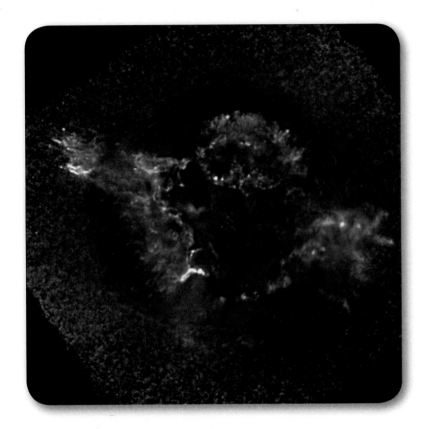

There's lots to see in the universe, but some of it takes an X-ray telescope to show up. Here's a supernova remnant in the Milky Way. The X-ray telescope shows intense X-radiation, which is from silicon ions with two orbital electrons.

Example 4.2B

Average Atomic Mass

1. Find the average atomic mass of an atom that has one isotope with a mass of 27.9768 amu and is present 92.2% of the time, another isotope with a mass of 28.9765 amu that is present 4.67% of the time, and a third isotope with a mass of 29.9754 amu that occurs 3.10% of the time.

   • The percents are changed to their fractional form to find a weighted average.

   • (27.9768 amu)(0.922) + (28.9765 amu)(0.0467) + (29.9754)(0.0310) = *28.0770 amu*

2. What element is described in problem 1?

   • By looking at the periodic table, you find that silicon has a mass of 28.08; the problem is talking about *Silicon*.

Go Online
Check your understanding
http://webcom4.grtxle.com/
khk12Chemistry

PRACTICE 4.2B

Average Atomic Mass

1. Define isotope.

2. Magnesium has three stable isotopes with the following masses and abundances:

   Mg-24 has a mass of 23.9850 amu and an abundance of 78.99%;

   Mg-25 has a mass of 24.9858 amu and an abundance of 10.0%;

   Mg-26 has a mass of 25.9826 amu and an abundance of 11.01%.

   Find the average atomic mass of Mg.

3. How many protons and neutrons does Mg-24 have?

4. How many protons and neutrons does Mg-25 have?

5. How many protons and neutrons does Mg-26 have?

6. An element is a mixture of two isotopes: one has a mass of 34.96885 amu and an abundance of 75.53%; the other has a mass of 36.96590 amu. Find the average atomic mass.

7. What element is described in question 6?

8. An element has the following isotopes. Find its average atomic mass.

Mass (amu)	Abundance (%)
203.973	1.40
205.9745	24.10
206.9759	22.10
207.9766	52.40

9. What element is described in question 8?

10. The element Re has two naturally occurring isotopes, Re-185 and Re-187, with an average mass of 186.207. Re is 62.60% Re-187 (which has a mass of 186.956 amu). Find the mass of Re-185.

11. The element europium exists in nature as two isotopes: Eu-151 and Eu-153. Eu-151 has a mass of 150.9196 amu, and Eu-153 has a mass of 152.9209 amu. The average atomic mass of europium is 151.96 amu. Find the abundances of the two isotopes.

SECTION 4.3

Go Online
Topic: electron structure
Go to: www.scilinks.org
Code: Chem1e134

Electron Structure

Electrons exist outside the nucleus in an atom. They are arranged in energy levels, subshells, and orbitals. It is important to understand how electrons are arranged in an atom because they define how that atom bonds with other atoms to form compounds, as well as how the atom interacts with energy, including light—as in glowing!

Electron levels, subshells, and orbitals

The **principal energy level** is what is shown in the rings around the nucleus in the Bohr model. Because electrons are negative and protons are positive, they attract each other. It takes energy for an electron to pull away from this attraction and move further away from the nucleus. Therefore, the lower energy levels are closest to the nucleus, and the higher energy levels are farther away. Principal energy levels are described by a number, with 1 being closest to the nucleus (and lowest energy).

Each principal energy level has subshells. **Subshells** show the shape of the area that a particular electron is most likely moving around. There are four types of subshell that electrons ordinarily occupy. Subshells are given letters: s, p, d, and f. Each type of subshell requires a different amount of energy in order for an electron to remain there. The lowest energy subshell type is s, and the highest, f.

Principal energy level 1 (the ring closest to the nucleus) is so low in energy that its electrons can only occupy the lowest possible subshell, type s. Principal energy level 2 has enough energy that electrons can occupy s or p subshells. Principal energy level 3 has more energy, and can therefore have electrons in s, p, or d subshells. Subshell type f can be occupied with electrons in the principal energy level 4. Subshells are described by their energy level number and their subshell type level. For example, the s orbital in energy level 2 would be called 2s.

Each subshell type has orbitals. An **orbital** is the specific orientation of the shape of the subshell. An orbital shows *an area of high probability where the electron is located*—it is not an exact location, just a likely area. The s subshells have only one orientation (orbital), because they are spherical. The p subshells have three orientations (orbitals), d subshells have five, and f subshells have seven. Each orbital can hold two electrons, no matter what subshell type it is.

Electron "addresses" are like our addresses, in a way (see Figure 4–5). The number of subshells in an energy level depends on the size (energy) of that level, just as the number of streets in a city depends on the size of the city. The number of orbitals in a subshell depends on the size (energy) of that subshell, just as the number of houses on a street depends on the size (length) of the street.

When electrons are assigned a principal energy level and subshell type to occupy, they go to the one that has the lowest possible energy level that is available, which is known as the **Aufbau principle**. The order of possibilities (see Figure 4–6) from lowest energy to highest energy is as

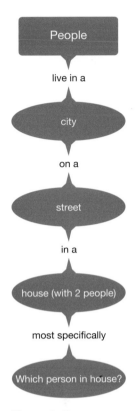

Figure 4–5a.
"Addresses" for people.

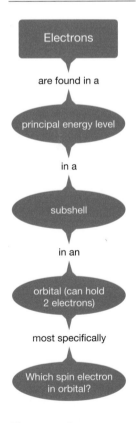

Figure 4–5b.
"Addresses" for electrons.

Go Online
Animated analogy
http://webcom4.grtxle.com/
khk12Chemistry

follows: 1s 2s 2p 3s 3p 4s 3d 4p 5s 4d 5p 6s 4f 5d 6p 7s 5f 6d 7p. (You do not need to memorize this order, because Section 4.4 will show you how to use the periodic table as a key.)

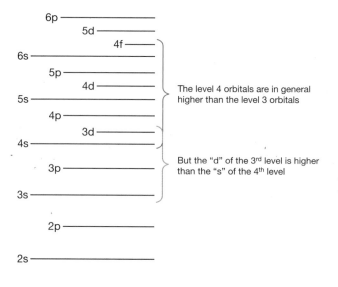

6p
5d
4f
6s
5p
4d
5s   The level 4 orbitals are in general higher than the level 3 orbitals
4p
3d
4s
            But the "d" of the 3rd level is higher than the "s" of the 4th level
3p
3s
2p
2s
1s

Figure 4–6. Electron energy levels.

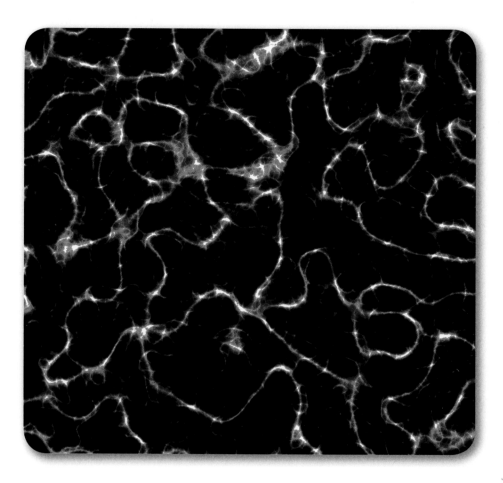

Light is quantized and comes in "packets" called photons that must have the exact energy, a form of electromagnetic radiation, to match an electron jump so that the electron can absorb it.

Showing electron configurations

There are several methods of showing electron configurations: orbital diagrams (or "boxes and arrows"), spectroscopic notation, and noble gas notation. For the first, **orbital diagrams,** a box is drawn for each orbital, and electrons are placed in these orbitals with arrows. Each orbital (box) can hold two electrons (arrows).

There are two important things to remember when placing electrons in their orbitals. The first is the Aufbau principle mentioned above—always place electrons (arrows) in the lowest energy orbitals first before moving to higher energy level placements. This means not only that electrons fill subshells in the order given above, but also that when subshells contain more than one orbital (orientation), the electrons are placed in their own orbital before they are doubled up. This is known as **Hund's rule.** Because electrons are negatively charged, having two negatively charged electrons in the same orbital takes more energy than having them in their own separate orbitals—similar to people sharing rooms—most people would like their own room before having to share!

The second key idea is the **Pauli exclusion principle**. This rule says that in order for two electrons to share an orbital, they must be different in some way. The way in which electrons are described as being different is called their *spin,* although electrons do not really spin. This is shown in the boxes and arrows method by having one arrow in an orbital point up and the other one point down.

Go Online
Animated examples
http://webcom4.grtxle.com/
khk12Chemistry

Example 4.3A

Orbital Diagrams

1. Draw an orbital diagram for a phosphorus atom.

   - Phosphorus has an atomic number of 15. This means that there are 15 protons. A neutral atom contains 15 electrons. Begin filling orbitals following the rules above until 15 electrons are placed.

   1s ↑↓ 2s ↑↓ 2p ↑↓ ↑↓ ↑↓ 3s ↑↓ 3p ↑ | ↑ | ↑

   - The orbitals were filled in the order from lowest energy to highest energy, as stated by the Aufbau principle.

   - Notice that for the 3p subshell, an electron was placed in each of the three equal energy orbitals before doubling up would become necessary. This is Hund's rule.

   - Also, each orbital (if it contained two electrons) contained an electron with an "up spin" and an electron with a "down spin." This fulfills the Pauli exclusion principle.

2. Draw an orbital diagram for a nickel atom.

   - Nickel atoms have 28 protons (the atomic number is 28), and therefore 28 electrons.

   1s ↑↓ 2s ↑↓ 2p ↑↓ ↑↓ ↑↓ 3s ↑↓ 3p ↑↓ ↑↓ ↑↓

   4s ↑↓ 3d ↑↓ ↑↓ ↑↓ ↑ | ↑

Spectroscopic notation is a shorthand version for representing electron configurations. It uses superscripts following the subshell name to show how many electrons are occupying the subshell. Although it is a shorter method, it doesn't show how electrons occupy the orbitals—whether they are in pairs or alone.

Example 4.3B

Spectroscopic Notation

Write the spectroscopic electron configuration for a phosphorus atom.

- The phosphorus atom has 15 electrons (see previous example for explanation).

- $1s^2 \, 2s^2 \, 2p^6 \, 3s^2 \, 3p^3$ This notation matches the orbital diagram in the previous example.

- It is not necessary to do an orbital diagram first, however; just add subshells in the order given from the Aufbau principle and then fill in electrons to the maximum number for that subshell before moving on.

There is yet another, even shorter method of showing electron configurations, the **noble gas notation**. The noble gases (the column farthest to the right on the periodic table) all have a full outer energy level. The noble gases can be used to represent the inner full energy levels in other atoms, called the **core electrons**, and then the configuration is written for the outermost level of electrons, the **valence electrons**. This allows us to focus on that outermost level of electrons, which are responsible for bonding and other interactions. Only the noble gases may be used as substitutions, because they are the only elements with full outer levels. The following table shows where you start writing electron configurations after using each noble gas. Section 4.4 will show you how this information can be obtained from the periodic table.

Noble gas	Start notation with ___ after noble gas
He	2s
Ne	3s
Ar	4s
Kr	5s
Xe	6s

Example 4.3C

Noble Gas Notation

Write the noble gas electron configuration for a phosphorus atom.

- The phosphorus atom has 15 electrons (see Example 4.3A for explanation).

- The closest noble gas to 15 without going over is neon (with 10). Therefore, neon will be the core, and only the outermost level needs to be written. Use the table above to determine where to start filling subshells after using neon as a core.

- $[Ne] \, 3s^2 \, 3p^3$

Electron Structure

Go Online
Check your understanding
http://webcom4.grtxle.com/
khk12Chemistry

1. The s subshells have how many orbitals?

2. The p subshells have how many orbitals?

3. The d subshells have how many orbitals?

4. The f subshells have how many orbitals?

5. Each orbital (no matter what subshell it's a part of) can hold how many electrons?

6. Write the following electron configurations in boxes and arrows notation.
   - **a.** Li
   - **b.** Si
   - **c.** F
   - **d.** Cr

7. Write the following electron configurations using spectroscopic notation.
   - **a.** Ca
   - **b.** O
   - **c.** Nb
   - **d.** Br

8. Write the following electron configurations using noble gas notation.
   - **a.** Mg
   - **b.** N
   - **c.** Ni
   - **d.** Pt

SECTION 4.4

Periodic Table

LAB 4.4

Making a Periodic Table

Purpose To organize the elements on the periodic table based on their properties

Materials Cards with the properties of the elements on them

Procedure

1. Examine the cards of the elements and their properties.

2. The cards need to be organized in rows and columns based upon these properties. The table may

(continues)

Making a Periodic Table (*cont'd.*)

not be perfect. You may have an element that matches a group in most properties but has one or two properties that don't seem to match the trend. Do the best you can with what you know.

3. All the cards need to be organized into one table—you can't have some that are totally separated from the rest.

Discussion

1. What was the most difficult part of this task?

2. What might explain any holes that you had in your table of elements?

3. What did you learn about organizing data by completing this task?

4. Share the periodic tables as a class. What other ideas did you see? Would you make any changes in yours now that you've seen how others organized their elements? What changes would you make—you don't have to change it physically; just describe what you would do. Why?

Although some people laughed at him for doing so, Mendeleev speculated about elements yet to be discovered and turned out to be right. He correctly questioned the established atomic weights of his time. In his honor, a crater on the moon is named Mendeleev.

Elements are organized on the **periodic table.** Scientists created many ways to organize elements previous to the modern periodic table; however, most of them were inadequate and flawed. For example, German scientist Johann Dobereiner organized some elements in "triads" (groups of three) in 1829. He grouped three elements with similar chemical properties, and noticed that the atomic mass of the middle atom was the average of the other two. He could arrange only a few triads, so his method was abandoned. In 1864, British scientist John A. R. Newlands arranged the elements in order of increasing atomic mass, and put eight elements in each row. He called this arrangement "octaves," and it worked well for the elements up to calcium. However, the patterns became less convincing as the metals and nonmetals differed in properties, and some elements were undiscovered at the time. In 1869, Dmitri Mendeleev (1834–1907) published a periodic table that organized elements by their atomic mass. This method of arranging the elements showed patterns in their chemical and physical properties that repeated across the rows and down the columns. Rather than complete the periodic table with the known elements of the time, he left holes where no element that was yet known matched the pattern of properties. Those holes were later filled with elements as they were discovered. Mendeleev had been remarkably accurate in his predictions about the properties that those missing elements would have.

The modern periodic table

The modern periodic table is similar to Mendeleev's, only it is arranged by atomic number rather than by mass. The atomic mass generally increases with atomic number, so the two versions are quite similar, but there are a few instances where an increase in atomic number doesn't also show an increase in mass. The result is a few elements that switched places from Mendeleev's version to the modern version. The rows of the periodic table are called **periods,** and the columns are called **groups** or **families.** The names of some common periods or groups are shown in Figure 4–7.

Most periodic tables are shown with two rows below the main table. These rows actually belong within the main periodic table, but are often cut out and moved below to allow the other sections to squeeze together and fit nicely on a piece of paper. They are shown in their proper place in Figure 4–8.

Go Online
Animated information
http://webcom4.grtxle.com/
khk12Chemistry

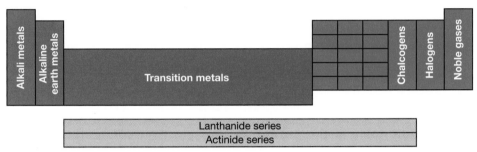

Figure 4–7. Group names on the periodic table.

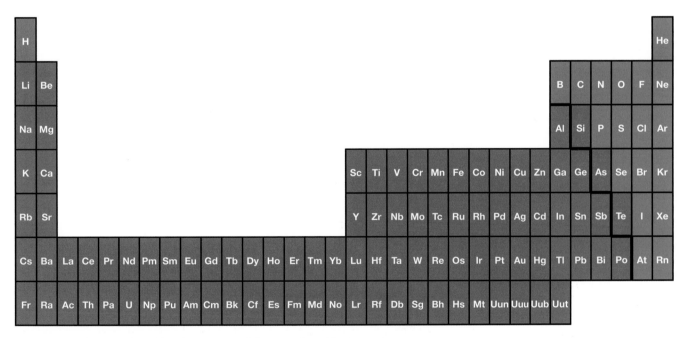

Figure 4–8. The periodic table. This version of the periodic table shows the two rows that are usually separated along the bottom in their proper place.

Electron configurations and the periodic table

One of the patterns revealed in the periodic table is electron configuration. This is a reason why arranging elements by atomic number is better than arranging by atomic mass. The atomic number is equal to the number of

Electron configurations as you move across a period

Li: $1s^2\ 2s^1$

Be: $1s^2\ 2s^2$

B: $1s^2\ 2s^2\ 2p^1$

C: $1s^2\ 2s^2\ 2p^2$

N: $1s^2\ 2s^2\ 2p^3$

O: $1s^2\ 2s^2\ 2p^4$

F: $1s^2\ 2s^2\ 2p^5$

Ne: $1s^2\ 2s^2\ 2p^6$

Electron configurations as you move down a group

F: $1s^2\ 2s^2\ 2p^5$

Cl: $1s^2\ 2s^2\ 2p^6\ 3s^2\ 3p^5$

Br: $1s^2\ 2s^2\ 2p^6\ 3s^2\ 3p^6\ 4s^2$
     $3d^{10}\ 4p^5$

I: $1s^2\ 2s^2\ 2p^6\ 3s^2\ 3p^6\ 4s^2$
     $3d^{10}\ 4p^6\ 5s^2\ 4d^{10}\ 5p^5$

protons. Atoms are neutral, so as the atomic number (and the number of protons) increases by one, the number of electrons also increases by one. As you move from left to right across a row of elements, the atomic number and the number of electrons increase by one until you reach the noble gases and the energy level is full. The next row begins the next energy level.

For example, look at the electron configurations for the elements in the second period. As you move across the row, the number of electrons increases by one until the second level is full (top left).

Now look at the electron configurations for the elements in the halogen family. As you move down the family, the number of full core levels increases (below, left), but the number of electrons in the outside level (the **valence electrons**) remains the same. Each of the halogens has five electrons in the outside p orbital—but they each have one more filled inner level of electrons than the element above it.

Periodic table as a map for electron configurations

The periodic table is the answer key for electron configurations (see Figure 4–9). Each section of the periodic table corresponds to a subshell type. The s section contains two columns (and an s subshell can hold two electrons), the p section contains six columns (and a p subshell can hold six electrons), the d section contains 10 columns (and a d subshell can hold 10 electrons), and the f section contains 14 columns (and an f subshell can hold 14 electrons). The s subshell type begins in level 1, so the s section begins with 1s. The p subshell type begins in level 2, so the p section begins with 2p. The d subshells begin in level 3, and the d section begins with 3d. The f subshells begin in level 4, and the f section begins with 4f. Reading from left to right across the periodic table gives the same order of subshells from lowest to highest energy that was given in Section 4.3.

Figure 4–9. Periodic table with electron subshells.

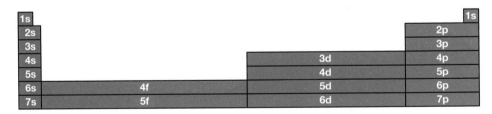

Section 4.3 also gave a chart to show which subshell to start filling in after writing a noble gas in noble gas notation. The periodic table is a better tool for figuring this out. The noble gases are in the farthest column to the right. Each noble gas has a completely full valence level, including the p

subshell. When using noble gas notation to write electron configurations, you always know where to start—you find the noble gas on the periodic table and match it to the chart above. The row that the noble gas is on is full; start writing your valence level configuration with the row below.

Example 4.4

Periodic Table and Electron Configuration

Which element's electron configuration ends with $4p^3$?

- Look at Figure 4–9 with the subshells in the periodic table. Find the 4p subshell on this chart and match it up to the periodic table. On the periodic table, this subshell is from Ga to Kr.

- Once you locate the subshell, count in from the beginning until you reach the number of electrons in that subshell. Ga would be 1, Ge would be 2, and As would be 3.

- *As* ends with $4p^3$.

PRACTICE 4.4

Periodic Table and Electron Configuration

1. Give the name of the group/section on the periodic table that contains each of the following elements.

    a. Na   **e.** Am

    b. Cl   **f.** Ne

    c. Cu   **g.** Ce

    d. Ca   **h.** Se

2. Which element's electron configuration ends with:

    a. $2s^2$ **d.** $3d^4$

    b. $4d^6$ **e.** $5d^8$

    c. $6p^2$

3. Write how the following elements' configurations end (the last subshell).

    a. Na   **e.** Si

    b. As   **f.** Mn

    c. Pb   **g.** Yb

    d. F

Go Online
Check your understanding
http://webcom4.grtxle.com/
khk12Chemistry

Periodicity

LAB 4.5

Periodicity

Purpose To graph properties of elements on the periodic table to see how they relate to the atomic number

Background information Atomic radius is the radius of the atom. Ionization energy is the energy needed to pull away the outermost electron.

Materials Data for physical properties of elements, computer with graphing program or graph paper

Data table

Atomic number	Atomic radius	Ionization energy
1	0.79	13.598
2	0.49	24.587
3	2.05	5.392
4	1.4	9.322
5	1.17	8.298
6	0.91	11.26
7	0.75	14.534
8	0.65	13.618
9	0.57	17.422
10	0.51	21.564
11	2.23	5.139
12	1.72	7.646
13	1.82	5.986
14	1.46	8.151
15	1.23	10.486
16	1.09	10.36
17	0.97	12.967
18	0.88	15.759
19	2.77	4.341
20	2.23	6.113

Procedure

For graph paper

1. Make a graph with the atomic number along the *x* axis and the atomic radius along the *y* axis. Connect the data points in a "connect-the-dots" style. We're using this method instead of a best-fit line method because we want to see the trend of how the variables change, rather than find an average change. Remember to use as much of the paper as possible—stretch out the axis.

2. Make a similar graph with the atomic number along the *x* axis and the ionization energy along the *y* axis.

For computer graphing

1. Open the graphing/spreadsheet program on the computer (Microsoft Excel or other program as designated by your teacher).

2. Spreadsheets are organized with columns labeled with letters and rows labeled with numbers. Each cell is named with the letter and the number (cell 1A is in row 1 and column A).

3. Enter the following labels into cells 1A–1C: atomic number, atomic radius, ionization energy.

4. Fill in the spreadsheet with the data provided.

5. Highlight the block of cells in columns A and B with data (including the labels in row 1).

6. Insert and format the chart. Use the following instructions for Microsoft Excel. If you are using another program, your teacher will provide instructions.

7. From the Insert menu, choose Chart.

8. Select XY (Scatter).

Periodicity (*cont'd.*)

9. Choose the type that has data points marked with straight lines connecting the data points (connect-the-dots style). Again, we're using this type of graphing instead of a best-fit line because we are specifically looking for trends—how the values rise and fall as the atomic number changes, not the overall average of the values.

10. Click Next.

11. Make sure that the "Series in" is set on Columns and click Next.

12. Type "Periodic trends" as the chart title (also put your name in the title so that we know whose printout is whose)—and "Atomic number" as the *x* axis label. Click Next.

13. Place chart "As new sheet" and click Finish.

14. Double click on the gray background of the chart and click None under Area.

15. Print a graph for each member of the group.

16. Repeat steps 5–15 for the cells with data in columns A and C. To highlight columns that are not next to each other, highlight column A, then hold the control button down while highlighting column C.

Discussion

1. Atomic radius:

   a. As you move from left to right across the periodic table (for example, look at elements 11–18), what happens to the atomic radius?

   b. Is the trend fairly smooth, or is it spiky?

   c. As you move down the periodic table (for example, look at elements 3, 11, and 19), what happens to the atomic radius?

   d. Is the trend fairly smooth, or is it spiky?

2. Ionization energy:

   a. As you move from left to right across the periodic table (for example, look at elements 11–18), what happens to the ionization energy?

   b. Is the trend fairly smooth, or is it spiky?

   c. As you move down the periodic table (for example, look at elements 3, 11, and 19), what happens to the ionization energy?

   d. Is the trend fairly smooth, or is it spiky?

3. Both trends:

   a. Put the atomic radius graph on top of the ionization energy graph. Hold them up to the light so that you can see both at the same time. What do you notice about how they compare to each other?

   b. Based on your last question, are atomic radius and ionization energy directly or indirectly related?

   c. Give a reason why you might think that they're related in the way that they are. How might the radius of the atom affect the amount of energy needed to pull off the outermost electron?

The periodic table is named for the periodic trends. A **periodic trend** is something that changes and repeats in a pattern. Many atomic properties are periodic.

Atomic radius

One important periodic trend is atomic radius. As you move from left to right across the periodic table, the atomic number increases by one

Go Online
Molecular animations
http://webcom4.grtxle.com/
khk12Chemistry

(therefore, the number of protons increases by one). The number of electrons in the existing valence level also increases by one. As the positive charge in the nucleus increases and the negative charge outside the nucleus also increases, the attractive force between these two areas increases. Therefore, the electron levels are pulled in more tightly, resulting in a decrease in the radius.

As you move down the periodic table, the atomic number (and number of protons in the nucleus) increases. The number of electrons also increases. However, the new electrons are filling a new principal energy level, or a new level. As shells are added, the new electrons are **shielded** from the increasingly positive nucleus by the core electrons (all the inner shells), and therefore do not feel the full pulling force of the attraction. So as these new shells are added, the radius increases.

Ionization energy

Ionization energy is the amount of energy needed to pull away the outermost electron from an atom (which would result in a cation—a positively charged ion). When an atom is smaller, the outermost electron is closer to the positively charged nucleus and is less shielded from the pull of those protons. Therefore, a smaller atom will need a greater amount of energy to pull away the outermost electron than a larger atom. Because atomic radius decreases as you move from left to right, the ionization energy increases across a period. Likewise, because atomic radius increases from top to bottom of a group, the ionization energy decreases as the electrons become more shielded from the nucleus's pull and are easier to remove. Atomic radius and ionization energy are indirectly related.

The first ionization energy is the energy needed to remove the first electron; the second ionization energy is the energy needed to remove the next electron (after one is already gone), and so forth. When an electron has been removed, there are now more protons in the nucleus than there are electrons outside. This means there is a larger attractive pull on each of those remaining electrons, because there is a higher positive-to-negative ratio. The resulting cation is now smaller than the original "parent" atom. Therefore, it takes even more energy to remove the second electron. The second ionization energy is greater than the first, and so on. If by removing an electron, you would be breaking up a new, full electron level, then the ionization energy is even greater—because the atom is more stable with a full valence level. Disturbing a full level takes more energy than pulling electrons from a partially filled level.

Electron affinity

Electron affinity is the energy released when an electron is added to an atom (forming a negatively charged ion, an anion). The smaller the atom, the more the atom will welcome a new electron. This new electron will feel the pull of the nucleus fairly well and be stable, releasing energy. In a very large atom, with many electron shells, a new electron would be shielded from the nucleus and therefore would not feel the pull from the positive protons as greatly—it would be less stable. Therefore, large atoms have low electron affinities. Atomic radius and electron affinity are indirectly related.

Ion radius

Ions are formed when electrons are gained or lost. If an atom gains an electron, producing an anion, there are now more negative charges than there are positive charges in the nucleus. This lowers the pull the protons have on each electron (because there are now more electrons), so the anion is larger than the parent atom. Cations are formed when an electron is lost, resulting in more positive protons than negative electrons. Therefore, the pull the protons have on each electron is greater than before, pulling the electrons in closer. Cations are smaller than their parent atom.

PRACTICE 4.5

Periodicity

1. As you move from left to right on the periodic table, the atomic radius _____. Why?

2. As you move from top to bottom on the periodic table, the atomic radius _____. Why?

3. What is ionization energy?

4. As you move from left to right on the periodic table, the ionization energy _____. Why?

5. As you move from top to bottom on the periodic table, the ionization energy _____. Why?

6. What is electron affinity?

7. As you move from left to right on the periodic table, the electron affinity _____. Why?

8. As you move from top to bottom on the periodic table, the electron affinity _____. Why?

9. Which has the highest atomic radius? K Rb Si Fr

10. Which has the highest atomic radius? Cl P Al Mg

11. Put the following in order from largest to smallest radius:
Ca O P Rb Zn

12. Which of the following has the highest electron affinity? Na K F Cl Fe

13. Which of the following has the lowest electron affinity? Li K Rb Cs Fr

14. Which of the following has the highest ionization energy?
Cl Si Al Mg Na

15. Which of the following has the highest ionization energy? N P As Sb

Go Online
Check your understanding
http://webcom4.grtxle.com/
khk12Chemistry

Light

Light is a form of electromagnetic radiation. **Electromagnetic radiation** is energy in a wave form that has electric and magnetic fields. There are many types of electromagnetic energy (see Figure 4–10): cosmic rays, gamma rays, X rays, ultraviolet light, visible light, infrared light (heat), microwaves, radio waves, and TV waves.

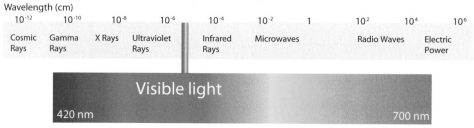

Figure 4–10. Types of electromagnetic radiation.

Wave properties

Waves have properties such as wavelength, frequency, and amplitude. **Wavelength** (λ) is the length that it takes for one full cycle of the wave (see Figure 4–11). For example, if you begin measuring at the peak (the highest point), then wavelength is the distance until the next peak. Wavelength is measured in meters. Visible light—light that our eyes can see—has wavelengths from 420 nm to 700 nm (0.000000420 m to 0.0000007 m).

All electromagnetic radiation travels at the same speed, the **speed of light** (c), which is 3.00×10^8 m/s. If a wave has a shorter wavelength, it can complete more waves in the same amount of time. **Frequency** (ν) is the number of waves completed per second, and it is measured in **hertz** (Hz), which means cycles per second. Waves with a higher frequency, and shorter wavelength, have more energy. Because $c = \lambda \nu$, frequency and wavelength are inversely related.

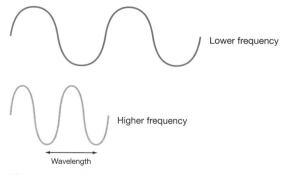

Figure 4–11. Wave properties.

Energies and colors of visible light

The color of light changes as the frequency and wavelength change. Purple light has the shortest wavelength, highest frequency, and highest energy of visible light. The lowest-energy visible light is red, which has a longer wavelength and lower frequency. White light, such as from the sun, combines all the colors of visible light. This is why a prism can separate white light into a rainbow—because all the colors of the rainbow are within the white light. Heat (infrared light) has less energy than visible light, and ultraviolet light (which causes sunburn) has more energy than visible light.

Electromagnetic radiation is said to be quantized. **Quantized** means that it comes in certain values only. Electromagnetic radiation comes in packets called **photons**. You can't have part of a photon—only whole photons. Therefore, the radiation is quantized; it comes in certain amounts only. Mathematically, $E = h\nu$, where E is energy (in joules), h is Planck's constant (6.63×10^{-34} J s), and ν is the frequency in Hz.

PRACTICE 4.6

Light

1. What does "quantized" mean?

2. Draw a picture that shows a wave and indicates the wavelength.

3. What is frequency in terms of waves?

4. How are wavelength and frequency related?

5. Show a wave with a high frequency and one with a low frequency.

6. List the colors of visible light from the highest frequency to the lowest.

7. How are frequency and energy of waves related?

8. List the colors of visible light from the highest energy to the lowest.

9. Name one type of electromagnetic energy with more energy than visible light.

10. Name one type of electromagnetic energy with less energy than visible light.

11. What is the lowest wavelength of light that is visible to humans?

12. Calculate the frequency of the lowest visible wavelength, using $c = \lambda\nu$.

13. Calculate the energy of the lowest visible wavelength, using $E = h\nu$.

14. What is the highest wavelength of light that is visible to humans?

15. Calculate the frequency of the highest visible wavelength, using $c = \lambda\nu$.

16. Calculate the energy of the highest visible wavelength, using $E = h\nu$.

Go Online
Check your understanding
http://webcom4.grtxle.com/khk12Chemistry

This thermal image uses infrared to see a building's heat loss, shown in red. The lake, which is cooler, is aqua. The higher the temperature, the more radiation is being emitted.

 **SECTION 4.7**

Light and Matter

LAB 4.7

Light and Matter

Purpose To determine the effect of temperature on glowsticks

Instructions Design a lab to address the purpose. Your lab write-up should include the following sections:

- **Title**

- **Purpose**

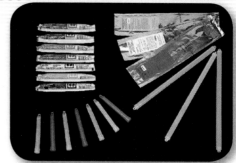

Light and Matter (*cont'd.*)

- **Background information** about how light is produced in a glowstick (what type of light-producing process is it, etc.) and any information from the discussion on kinetics in Section 2.8 that is appropriate.

- **Hypothesis** Be sure to give a thorough explanation as to how the temperature will affect the reaction based on the information you know about kinetics.

- **Variables and constants**

Remember to design the next few components in reverse order for efficiency.

- **Materials**

  ! **Safety** Use caution with hot glassware and hot water. NOTE—Do not heat the glowstick in a microwave oven if you use one!

- **Procedure**

- **Data table**

- **Results** with any calculations necessary

  ! Have your teacher check your procedure for safety; then you can perform your lab, gather the data, and finish the write-up.

- Finish the **Results** section and include a general statement summing up (not explaining) the data.

- Write a **Conclusion** that restates purpose and hypothesis, answers purpose, comments on whether hypothesis was correct, and gives a new possible explanation if hypothesis was not correct. Identify at least two possible sources of error, and another

question or problem that could be investigated. Why do people say that if they put a glowstick in the freezer after using it for awhile they can use it again the next day? What insights does this lab give you about the relationship between energy and glowing?

- **Possible materials** Glowsticks (check with your teacher on the number available for each group), beakers or glasses, way of heating water (hot plate, microwave, Bunsen burner/ring stand/ring/wire gauze)

A Bunsen burner is a small laboratory burner that produces a very hot flame, resulting from a mixture of gas and air.

Light interaction with matter

As photons of light run into an atom, the electrons can absorb the photon. The energy of the photon increases the electron's energy. The electron now has enough energy to hop out to a higher energy level in the atom (remember that being farther from the pull of the nucleus requires more energy). The difference in the energy level that the electron was originally in (the **ground state**) and the energy level that the electron hops out to (the **excited state**) is equal to the energy of the photon—the extra energy the electron absorbed. This process is called **excitation** (see Figure 4–12).

Go Online
Molecular animations
http://webcom4.grtxle.com/
khk12Chemistry

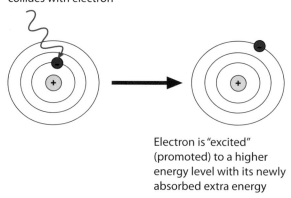

Photon coming into atom collides with electron

Electron is "excited" (promoted) to a higher energy level with its newly absorbed extra energy

Figure 4–12. Electron excitation.

The electron cannot remain at the excited position forever, and must fall back down to the ground state. The ground state, however, doesn't require as much energy. When the electron falls back down, the electron gets rid of the extra energy by releasing a photon of electromagnetic radiation. The amount of energy released is equal to the difference in energy from the excited state and the ground state. This process is called **relaxation** (see Figure 4–13).

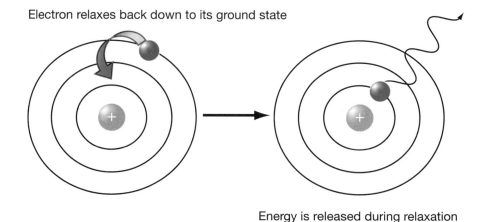

Electron relaxes back down to its ground state

Energy is released during relaxation

Figure 4–13. Electron relaxation.

Quantization of photons and absorption by electrons

An electron can absorb a photon of light only if the energy of the photon is exactly equal to the energy required for a jump in electron levels. If the photon's energy does not match exactly, the photon will pass through the atom without being absorbed. The energy levels of an atom can be displayed in an energy diagram (see Figure 4–14). The difference between the levels decreases as the levels increase—the difference between levels 1 and 2 is greater than the difference between levels 2 and 3.

A photon must have the exact amount of energy to equal a jump from one level to another in order for an electron to absorb it. (This is proof of Bohr's theory that electrons do in fact reside in "levels" of increasing energy, as discussed in Section 4.1.) An electron can jump more than one level at a time if the photon has enough energy.

Every atom and molecule has a different energy level diagram based on its atomic structure—meaning, the energy differences between the levels are not the same for different atoms or molecules. As their ground state electron configurations change, so do the possibilities for excitation and relaxation. This is why every atom and molecule absorb different wavelengths of light.

	Energy Level
	7 (high)
	6
	5
	4
	3
	2
	1 (low)

Figure 4–14. Electron energy level diagrams.

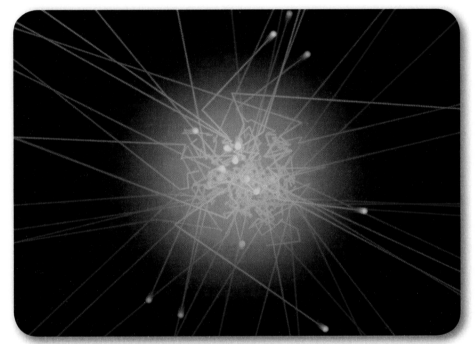

Drawing of the random walk of photons from the sun.

Step-wise relaxation

The relaxation doesn't have to take place all at once. For example, an electron could absorb a photon of purple light, the highest energy of visible light, and be excited to a higher level. That photon provided enough energy to move the electron up more than one energy level. When it relaxes back down and releases energy, it can do so all at once, or step by step until it reaches its ground state. If the energy is released all at once, it will be in the form of a photon of purple light. However, perhaps the electron falls back in two steps—once releasing a photon of red light, and the second time releasing a photon of infrared light (heat). The red light photon and the infrared photon energies must add up to equal the original energy of the purple photon. Finally, the electron can fall back to its ground state in more than one step that produces varying amounts of infrared energy—releasing heat only, no visible light.

Measuring light's interaction with matter

A **spectrometer** is an instrument that measures light. Atoms can be excited, and the spectrometer can measure which wavelengths of light passed through the sample unabsorbed and which were absorbed by the sample. The results are shown as **spectral lines.** A diagram of spectral lines (see Figure 4–15), called a **spectrum,** shows which wavelengths of light were released as electrons relaxed back to their ground state. By knowing the different energy photons that are released, scientists can draw energy diagrams for that atom or molecule. Each atom has a different spectrum that can be used like a fingerprint to identify substances. The spectrum can be measured for an unknown substance and be compared to the spectrum of known substances in order to identify the unknown sample.

Figure 4–15. Spectral lines of hydrogen. The black lines are the wavelengths (colors) of light that are absorbed by hydrogen.

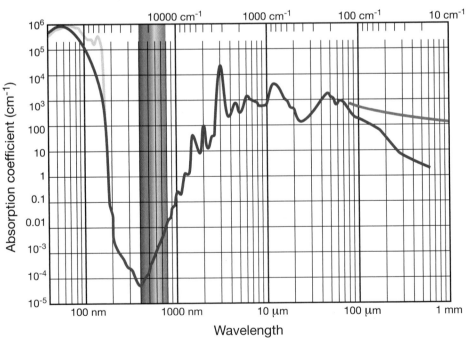

Figure 4–16. Spectrum of a molecule. This curve shows the absorption spectrum of liquid water. Source: http://www.lsbu.ac.uk/water/vibrat.html.

Molecules contain several atoms, each with a different electron configuration. Those atomic electron configurations change when they bond together and form a new, molecular configuration. Because of this complicated molecular electron structure, molecules can absorb regions of wavelengths rather than one specific wavelength. Molecules often absorb in more than one region of the electromagnetic spectrum. Therefore, a molecular absorption spectrum has curves that show how much light is absorbed at each wavelength, rather than lines showing which specific wavelength's light is absorbed (see Figure 4–16).

Ways of producing light

When the excitation of electrons is caused by absorption of light, it is called **fluorescence** (when it absorbs and emits light simultaneously) or **phosphorescence** (when light is absorbed, then, after some time, released again).

The energy that is absorbed by an electron to cause excitation and relaxation does not always come from photons of light. **Incandescence** occurs when atoms are heated. Heat excites the atoms and electrons, which then produce light during relaxation. This can be seen in incandescent lightbulbs or in fire.

A chemical reaction can also produce energy, which then is absorbed by the electrons. When the electrons release that energy, it is in the form of light. This is called **chemiluminescence**. **Bioluminescence** results

Some animals and insects make use of colors that we cannot readily see. Here, under ultraviolet radiation, a scorpion glows green. We can see fluorescence and phosphorescence when we shine such radiation on some things.

when the chemical reaction and light production occurs in a biological organism, such as a firefly. Chemiluminescence and bioluminescence do not require an outside source of light or heat to excite the molecules—the molecules gain energy from the chemical reaction itself.

Another type of reaction is **triboluminescence,** which occurs when physical pressure or torque is applied to a crystal to excite the electrons.

Go Online
Check your understanding
http://webcom4.grtxle.com/
khk12Chemistry

PRACTICE 4.7

Light and Matter

1. Explain why energy levels farther from the nucleus are higher energy levels.

2. What happens when light is absorbed into an atom—where does the energy go? (A picture might help.)

3. What happens when light is emitted from an atom—where does the energy come from? (A picture might help.)

4. Explain why only some colors are absorbed or emitted from hydrogen—why not all colors? Make your answer fairly detailed.

5. Explain how the electron's "fall" compares when it emits a photon of purple light to when it emits a photon of red light. Which fall represents a greater energy difference?

6. Is more energy released when an electron emits a photon of infrared light (heat) or a photon of visible light?

FINAL CHAPTER PROJECT

Here's your chance to use the chemistry you know to make a presentation on a glowing object of your choice.

Writing about glowing things

Choose one of the following topics to research that involves light and chemistry: fireflies, glow-in-the-dark items, black lights, halogen lights, neon lights, television, bacteria, algae, coelenterates, lightning, Luminol, fireworks, glowsticks, jellyfish that glow, or another topic that your teacher approves.

Write a three-page paper, with a fourth page of cited sources. Give the paper 1-inch margins all around, and use double spacing and a font similar to Times New Roman 12.

Find and include information such as: What type of luminescence is present? How does that type of luminescence work? Explain the chemical reaction(s) or processes in detail; specifically, what causes the light? Are there other types of application that could use this way of producing light? If you researched a product or technology, what is the development history of this product? If you chose something not a product, when was it discovered or studied in depth, and who did it?

Information can be found in books, encyclopedias, and other reference materials or on the Internet. Your teacher may have some resources that can be a starting place. You must have three references, including one from the Internet and one from a source other than the Internet.

Create a poster that visually displays the major points of your topic. The poster should not be primarily text—make it easily read and understood, and visually appealing.

Many scientists throughout the history of atomic theory development have changed and refined the atomic theories. Atoms consist of positively charged protons and neutral neutrons in the nucleus, with negatively charged electrons outside the dense nucleus. Atoms of the same element with different numbers of neutrons are called isotopes. The atomic number is equal to the number of protons, the mass number is the number of protons and neutrons, and the atomic mass is the weighted average of the masses of all the isotopes of a specific element. The charge of an ion is found by the number of protons minus the number of electrons.

The electrons reside in energy levels, which consist of subshells containing orbitals. Orbitals are areas of probability where the electron is most likely to be found. The Aufbau principle, Hund's rule, and the Pauli exclusion principle govern how electrons are placed into these orbitals when writing electron configurations. Electron configurations give information about how atoms react and interact with other atoms.

The modern periodic table is organized by atomic number, with groups as columns and periods as rows. Properties of the elements follow trends down the groups and across the periods. Atomic radius increases down a group as new electron levels are shielded from the pull of the nucleus. Atomic radius decreases across a period as increased positive charge in the nucleus and increased negative charge in the electron energy level pull the atom in more tightly. Ionization energy and electron affinity are trends describing the removal of the outermost electron or an addition of a new electron. These trends are

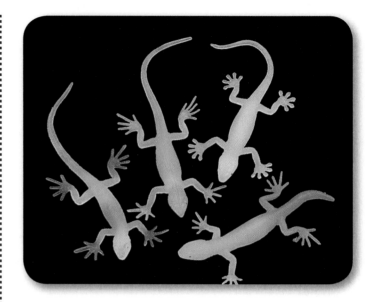

indirectly related to atomic radius. Cations are formed from the removal of an electron and are smaller than the parent atom, whereas anions are larger than the parent atom.

Light is a form of electromagnetic radiation that is absorbed by electrons in atoms and molecules. When electrons absorb this form of energy, they are excited to a higher energy level. When they transition back down to their ground state, the extra energy is released, sometimes in the form of light. Light is quantized and comes in "packets" called photons. A photon must have the exact energy to match an electron jump, or the electron will not absorb it. The electron will release the same amount of energy during relaxation as it absorbed during excitation. Each atom and molecule has a different energy level diagram for the electron energy levels; therefore, each atom and molecule absorbs different wavelengths of light, which are shown in spectra.

1. What are the differences between Dalton's atomic theory and Thomson's plum pudding model?

2. What did the gold foil experiment reveal?

3. How did Rutherford's findings change Thomson's plum pudding model?

4. Compare and contrast isotope, mass number, atomic mass. How do you find each?

5. Fill in the following table.

Element	Symbol	Atomic no.	Mass no.	Charge	Protons	Neutrons	Electron
Carbon			12	0			
		19	39	+1			18
		12		+2		12	
			53		25		23
					35	45	36

6. What is the name of the family that contains potassium?

7. What is the name of the family that contains iodine?

8. What is the name of the family that contains sulfur?

9. What is the name for the d block?

10. What is the name of the family that contains Ne?

11. What is the name of the family that contains beryllium?

12. What is the name of the period that contains Am?

13. What is the name of the period that contains Ce?

14. Atomic radius _____ from left to right and _____ from top to bottom on the periodic table. Explain why.

15. Ionization energy _____ from left to right and _____ from top to bottom on the periodic table. Explain why.

16. Electron affinity _____ from left to right and _____ from top to bottom on the periodic table. Explain why.

17. Which atom in each pair has the higher ionization energy?
    a. Cr   Mo   b. P   Mg

18. Which atom in each pair has the larger atomic radius?
    a. C   F   b. Se   O

19. Which atom in each pair has the higher electron affinity?
    a. Sr   Be   b. In   Te

20. The p subshells have _____ orbitals.

21. The f subshells have _____ orbitals.

22. The s subshells have _____ orbitals.

23. The d subshells have _____ orbitals.

24. Each orbital can hold _____ electrons.

25. Write the following electron configurations using the boxes and arrows method.
    a. Mg   b. S   c. Co

26. Write the following electron configurations using spectroscopic notation.
    a. Na   c. Ru
    b. Cl   d. W

27. Write the following electron configurations using noble gas notation.
    a. Al   c. Y
    b. Br   d. Sm

28. Which element ends with 2 electrons in the 3p subshell?

29. Which element ends with 5 electrons in the 4d subshell?

30. Which element ends with 1 electron in the 5s subshell?

31. Which element ends with 4 electrons in the 4f subshell?

32. Give the ending of the electron configuration for the following elements.
    a. Cr   c. Li
    b. Se   d. Tb

33. Light travels in packets called _____, which are _____, meaning they only come in certain amounts.

34. As wavelength increases, frequency and energy _____.

35. Explain what happens when an atom absorbs a photon. Draw a picture.

36. Explain what happens when an atom emits a photon. Draw a picture.

37. Why are only certain colors of light absorbed by and emitted from an atom?

CHAPTER 5

Soap

Chemistry Making Things Clean

IN THIS CHAPTER

- Types of bonds
- Drawing molecules
- Molecules in 3D
- Polarity of molecules
- Intermolecular forces
- Intermolecular forces and properties

INTRODUCTORY ACTIVITY

Fill a test tube with about an inch of water. Add a pipette squirt of cooking oil to the test tube. Make observations. Stopper the test tube and try to mix the two by inverting the test tube a couple of times, and make observations again. Make particle visualization drawings showing what you think is going on.

Add a few drops of soap to the test tube. Make observations. Try to mix the three (with a stopper in the test tube) and make observations again. Make particle visualization drawings showing these observations as well.

Fill a second test tube with about an inch of water. Add a few drops of soap. Make observations. Mix the two and make observations again. Compare the test tube with soap, oil, and water with the test tube containing soap and water. Make particle visualization drawings showing these observations.

What ideas do you have about how soaps work? What kinds of features do you see in soap advertising and marketing—what do the soap companies want you to know about how soaps work?

**to create and evaluate the effectiveness
of a soap.**

Introduction

If oil and water don't mix, how can water remove oil (and dirt and grime) from dishes, clothes, countertops, and other things? There must be something about soaps and detergents that allows the two to mix together so that the water can wash away oily dirt.

Soaps are alkali salts of fatty acids. *Alkali* means they are basic. *Salts* means they have an ionic bond in them. Fatty acids are long chains of carbon and hydrogen atoms bonded together with a carboxylic acid (COOH) group on one end. They are made from fats or oils (the source of the fatty acid in the soap) that undergo a chemical reaction to add the alkali ionic section.

In this chapter you will learn how molecules bond, how they arrange themselves in 3D, and how those two aspects affect their properties, in order to understand how soap allows oil and water to mix.

Soap

works based on

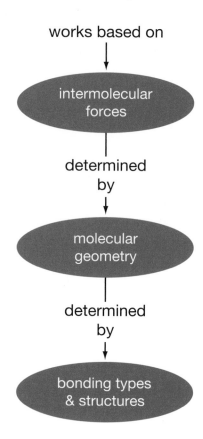

intermolecular
forces

determined
by

molecular
geometry

determined
by

bonding types
& structures

SECTION 5.1

Go Online
Molecular animations
http://webcom4.grtxle.com/
khk12Chemistry

Types of Bonds

Bonding between metals and nonmetals

Atoms are most stable when they have a full valence level. Atoms bond with other atoms in order to get a full valence level. For most elements, eight electrons in the valence level is the most stable arrangement. This idea is called the **octet rule.** The major exceptions are hydrogen and helium, whose valence levels contain only the 1s sublevel that can hold only two electrons. Therefore, hydrogen and helium are most stable with two valence electrons.

Valence levels can become full by adding more electrons to the unfilled level. An atom can also obtain a full outer level by removing electrons in the outermost level to reveal a full level underneath. Metals have less than half-full valence levels (fewer than four valence electrons). It is easier to remove those few electrons (fewer than four) rather than find some (more than four) to fill the level. When electrons are removed from their outer level, a full level is revealed underneath. (The Aufbau principle studied in

Chapter 4 states that each lower energy level must be full before moving on to the next, so we know that all the inner levels are already full.) Nonmetals, however, have levels that are more than half-full (more than four electrons). It is therefore easier to find a few electrons (less than four) to fill their outermost level than to get rid of what they have (more than four).

The concept of ionization energy, which was discussed in Chapter 4, also supports this. Metals have lower ionization energies-they lose their electrons relatively easily. Nonmetals have higher ionization energies, so it is much harder for them to lose their electrons. They tend to add more instead.

These gains and losses of electrons lead to **ionic bonding.** When a metal and a non-metal come together, the metal gives up its valence electrons to reveal a full inner level, and the nonmetal accepts those electrons to fill its valence level. When a neutral metal atom gives up electrons (which are negative), it becomes positively charged, and we call it a **cation.** When electrons are added to a neutral nonmetal atom, it becomes negatively charged, and it is called an **anion.** The positively charged cation and the negatively charged anion are mutually attracted by electrostatic forces (the positive and negative stick together). This attraction becomes the ionic bond. Most metals form ionic bonds with nonmetals; however, there are a few exceptions where they are covalently bonded. This book will use the general rule that metals and nonmetals form ionic bonds.

Bonding between nonmetals

The rules are different when nonmetals bond with other nonmetals. Both have a tendency to keep their own valence electrons and take electrons from others. Because they cannot both take electrons, nonmetals share electrons with other nonmetals so that they have full valence levels. This sharing of electrons is called covalent bonding, and this type of bonding forms **covalent molecules.**

Two atoms can share their electrons evenly, and this sharing is called a **nonpolar covalent bond** (often shortened to **covalent bond**). If one atom pulls on the electrons harder than the other atom, then the bond is called a **polar covalent bond.** Some molecules that contain polar bonds are also **polar covalent molecules.** Polarity of bonds and molecules will be discussed more in Section 5.4.

Bonding between metals

When metals bond with nonmetals, they tend to lose their valence electrons to form cations, and their electrons transfer to the nonmetal. However, when metals bond with other metals, they form a pool of electrons. The electrons are free to move between and among all the metal nuclei in the sample. Because these electrons are free to move about, they conduct electricity.

Metal atoms are not bonded to specific other metal atoms. Rather, they bond in one large group-they are bonded in a network. This arrangement allows the atoms to move around in the network without breaking bonds. Metals therefore can be hammered into a sheet (they are malleable) or pulled into a wire (they are ductile) without the bonds between the individual metal atoms being broken.

Characteristics of different types of bonds

Compounds have properties based on the type of bond that is formed. Of course, these characteristics are generalities-and there are always exceptions—but most compounds with the same bond type have similar properties.

Melting and boiling points

Most ionic compounds have very high melting and boiling points; therefore, they are found as solids at room temperature. One ionic compound, sodium chloride (table salt), has a melting point of 801°C. That is a high melting point-the reason you have probably never seen liquid salt. Polar covalent molecules have medium melting points; and although some are found as gases, most are liquids or solids. Covalent molecules have lower melting points and are often found as liquids or gases. Metallic bonding results in solids, with the exception of mercury, which is liquid at room temperature. Remember, exceptions to these generalities do occur.

Solubility in water

Many ionic compounds dissolve in water. Often, polar covalent molecules are also soluble in water. Few nonpolar covalent molecules dissolve in water. Most metallic solids are insoluble in water. Knowing why things dissolve in one substance but not in another is very important to understanding how soap works, your objective in this chapter. These reasons will be discussed later in this chapter and in Chapter 6.

Conduction of electricity

Electricity is the flow of electrons. Metallic bonding results in electrons that are free to move about throughout a solid-the electrons are in a "pool" that is being shared by all the atoms. Because metallic solids have electrons that are free to move and create that flow of charge, they do conduct electricity. Metallic solids can also conduct energy (**thermal conductance**) very well because the free-moving electrons can transfer kinetic energy around the sample quickly.

When ionic compounds are in their solid form, the ions are not free to move around-they are locked in place. There are charges present, but they are not free to flow. However, when ionic compounds dissolve in water, the ions become free to flow through the water, and they do conduct electricity. (That process will be shown in Chapter 6.) When ionic compounds melt and become liquid (which happens only at very high temperatures), they can conduct electricity because in the liquid state the

Dr. Percy Julian was an American research chemist in the mid 1900s. He pioneered the synthesizing of medicinal drugs from plants. These drugs have helped many people who have arthritis or glaucoma.

particles (ions with charge) are free to move around and provide a flow of charge. Compounds that conduct electricity are called **electrolytes.**

Polar and nonpolar molecules do not have charges. Therefore, they cannot create a flow of charge, and they cannot conduct electricity. Water is a polar molecule. This fact means that pure water does not conduct electricity—it must have ions dissolved in it from ionic compounds in order to conduct.

Water is polar in that its oxygen side is partially charged negatively. Its hydrogen is well bonded, which makes water a good way to store heat. Passive solar homes can use drums of water to gather heat during the day, to warm the house at night.

PRACTICE 5.1

Types of Bonds

1. Make a chart with "ionic bonding," "polar covalent bonding," "non-polar covalent bonding" and "metallic bonding" across the top. Down the side, list different characteristics, including information about what substances make that type of bond, what the electrons do in that type of bond, general statements about melting & boiling points, ability to dissolve in water, and the ability to conduct electricity when dissolved in water or by themselves.

2. Water is a polar covalent compound—which properties from your chart (in the polar covalent column) in the last question apply to water? Oil, grime and grease are non-polar covalent compounds. Which properties from your chart (the non-polar covalent column) apply to them?

3. A solid substance dissolves in water but does not conduct electricity. What type of bond was present?

4. A solid substance does dissolve in water and does conduct electricity when dissolved. What type of bond is it?

5. A liquid substance does not dissolve in water and does not conduct electricity. What type of bond is it?

6. A solid substance does not dissolve in water and conducts electricity by itself. What type of bond is it?

7. For each of the following, state whether it has covalent or ionic bonding: CO_2, CH_3Cl, $CaCl_2$, Fe_2O_3, KBr, SO_2, $NaCl$.

Many dishwashing detergents not only provide cleaning power, but also contain skin conditioners and antimicrobial chemicals to kill bacteria. If you're having trouble with spots left on glassware after they dry, then either the water wasn't hot enough or you put in too much soap, which can leave a filmy residue.

Types of Bonds

Purpose To determine which of three unknown white solid substances is sucrose (table sugar), which is sodium bicarbonate (baking soda), and which is salicylic acid (used on medicated pads for warts).

Instructions Design a lab that answers the purpose. Your write-up should include the following parts:

- **Title**

- **Purpose**

- **Background information** Sucrose is a polar covalent molecule, sodium bicarbonate is an ionic compound, and salicylic acid is a nonpolar covalent molecule. Include information about different properties of the bond types that you will be using as tests in your procedure to identify the three unknown substances.

 Safety Always use extra caution with unknown substances, because you cannot be sure which

ones require safety precautions. Use caution with any glassware (especially hot glassware); wear goggles, and take any other precautions you think appropriate.

- **Materials** Come up with your own list, but you may not use more than 1.00 g of each of the three unknown white solids. Check with your instructor for the availability of all materials.

- **Procedure**

- **Data table**

- **Results:** There are no calculations; just summarize your data in sentence form, but do not draw any conclusions or label the unknowns yet.

- **Conclusion** Restate purpose, label which unknown is which chemical, give two possible sources of error, and tell how this type of logic could be used in a different real-life application.

Drawing Molecules

Atoms and molecules can be represented on paper in drawings called Lewis dot structures (also called Lewis structures). The idea is to draw the element's symbol (representing the nucleus and all the inner, or "core," electron levels) with just the valence electrons around the symbol. Only the valence electrons need to be drawn because they are the ones involved in bonding.

Determining valence electrons

Representative elements are those in the "s" and "p" blocks on the periodic table. In those sections, all elements in the same group have the same number of valence electrons available for bonding. In the transition-metal section, the energy levels of electrons become more complicated, and elements can have more than one possibility for the number of electrons in their valence level. Elements with more than one possible valence level configuration are referred to as multivalent (a word used in Chapter 2 in explaining how to write chemical names and formulas). The periodic table in Figure 5–1 shows the number of valence electrons in commonly used elements.

Placing the electrons around the symbol

Once the number of valence electrons has been determined, the Lewis structure for the element can be drawn. Electrons are placed in four regions around the element's symbol because, for the most part, four orbitals can be used for bonding from the 1 "s" and 3 "p" subshells. In Chapter 4, Hund's rule showed that the lowest possible energy configuration is when elec-

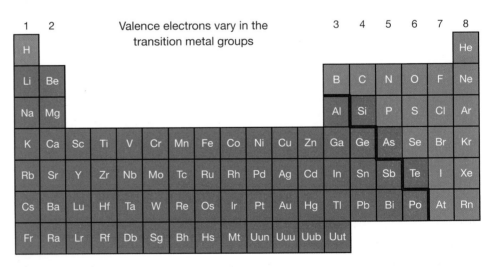

Figure 5–1. Periodic table with valence electrons.

trons are in their own orbital, rather than sharing. Therefore, we put one electron (one dot) in each of the four regions around the symbol before we double up electrons.

Example 5.2A

Drawing an Element's Lewis Dot Structure

1. Draw the Lewis Dot Structure for Carbon.

 • Carbon is in the fourth column of the representative elements, so it has 4 valence electrons.

 • Place one in each region before doubling up.

 $\cdot \overset{\displaystyle \cdot}{\underset{\displaystyle \cdot}{C}} \cdot$

2. Draw the Lewis Dot Structure for Oxygen.

 • Oxygen is in the sixth column of the representative elements, so it has 6 valence electrons.

 • Place one in each region before doubling up.

 $: \overset{\displaystyle \cdot}{O} :$

Lewis dot structures for ionic compounds

When a metal and a nonmetal bond, the metal tends to lose its electrons to the nonmetal (as discussed in Section 5.1). The metal then is a cation, the nonmetal is an anion. . The opposite charges attract, forming the bond.

In order to draw the Lewis dot structure for an ionic compound, begin by drawing the elements' dot structures separately. The metal will "lose" electrons (erase them from around the element's symbol), and the nonmetal will "gain" the electrons (add the metal's erased electrons around the nonmetal's symbol). The total number "lost" and "gained" must be equal. The metal is most stable when there are no dots drawn around the symbol —the outer level has been emptied, so the full level that had been inside the valence level is now the valence level. We do not draw the new outer level—we just assume that if there are no dots drawn in a valence level, then the level beneath is full and is thus the new valence level. The nonmetal is most stable when its valence level contains eight electrons (the octet rule).

Ionic bonds are between ions   When an element loses electrons, it then has more positive protons in the nucleus than negative electrons outside the nucleus. Therefore, it has a positive charge, and that fact needs to be written next to the element's symbol. Likewise, when an element gains electrons, it has more negative electrons than positive protons, and a negative charge needs to be written next to the element's symbol. Drawing these structures explains why ions had the charges introduced in Chapter 2, on naming and writing chemical formulas. Drawing structures also shows why elements in the same group formed ions with the same charge. For example, all the elements in the halogen family (the group beginning with fluorine) have seven valence electrons (they have different numbers of core

Go Online
Topic: moles and mole conversions
Go to: www.scilinks.org
Code: Chem1e171

SCLINKS
NSTA

electron levels, but they all have the same valence electron structure, as shown in Chapter 4). They each need to gain one electron to form a stable octet. Therefore, they all form –1 charged ions. Be sure to show in the Lewis structure the charges that result from removal or addition of electrons. Use brackets when adding a charge to an anion that has electron dots around it.

Ionic bonds are formed by attraction between the ions   When drawing these structures, we draw the cations and anions separated from each other to show clearly that one has given up the electrons and one has taken them on. This separation prevents us from misinterpreting the drawing as the elements sharing electrons in a covalent bond (which will be discussed later in this section). However, in reality, these ions do not stay separated from each other-their positive and negative charges attract and make them stick together (electrostatic attraction) until some force pulls them apart.

Example 5.2B

Ionic Lewis Dot Structures

Draw the Lewis dot structure for sodium chloride.

- Sodium is in the first representative element column, so it has one valence electron. Chlorine is in the seventh representative element column, so it has seven valence electrons.

$$Na\cdot$$

- The sodium (the metal) will give up its electron to become a cation with a full inner level

(that is now the outer level). The chlorine (the nonmetal) will take the electron to have a full outer level.

$$:\overset{\cdot}{\underset{\cdot\cdot}{Cl}}:$$

- Use brackets when writing a charge on an ion with electrons shown (the anion).

$$Na^{+1} \quad \left(:\overset{\cdot\cdot}{\underset{\cdot\cdot}{Cl}}:\right)^{-1}$$

Balancing ion charges   Sometimes the metal and nonmetal do not match up in their needs to lose and gain electrons. Perhaps the metal needs to lose two electrons, whereas the nonmetal only needs to gain one electron. This situation is shown in Example 5.2C. Working out Lewis dot structures like the one in this example shows why charges had to be balanced by adding subscripts when writing chemical formulas in Chapter 2.

Example 5.2C

Balancing Charges in Ionic Structures

Draw the Lewis dot structure for barium fluoride.

- Barium is in the second representative element column, so it has two valence electrons. Fluorine is in the seventh representative element column, so it has seven valence electrons.

$$Ba\cdot \qquad :\overset{\cdot}{\underset{\cdot\cdot}{F}}:$$

- The barium gives up one electron to fill the fluorine valence level, but the barium still has one electron left in its valence level.

$$\left(Ba\cdot\right)^{+1} \qquad \left(:\overset{\cdot\cdot}{\underset{\cdot\cdot}{F}}:\right)^{-1}$$

- The barium gives up the second electron to a second fluorine atom—now both fluorine atoms and the barium atom have full valence levels.

- The chemical formula is BaF_2.

$$Ba^{+2} \qquad \left(:\overset{\cdot\cdot}{\underset{\cdot\cdot}{F}}:\right)^{-1} \qquad \left(:\overset{\cdot\cdot}{\underset{\cdot\cdot}{F}}:\right)^{-1}$$

Lewis structures for covalent compounds

When metals and nonmetals bond, they have such different numbers of valence electrons, ionization energies, and electron affinities that one element gave up electrons and the other element gained them. The resulting ions formed ionic compounds. However, when nonmetals bond together they have similar numbers of valence electrons, ionization energies, and electron affinities. Neither donates electrons as easily as metals do, and neither tends to take on extra electrons. Instead, nonmetals share electrons to form a covalent bond. These structures look different from those drawn for ionic compounds because the elements are connected, sharing their electrons rather than being separate, with a give-and-take relationship.

Go Online
Animated examples
http://webcom4.grtxle.com/
khk12Chemistry

Single bonds   A **single bond** is formed when one pair of electrons is shared —usually an electron from each element (but not always, as we will see later on). Both elements can count shared electrons to make sure they have stable octets.

Arranging atoms and forming bonds   To draw the Lewis dot structure, element symbols are written in relation to each other as they bond together. This relationship is sometimes difficult for beginners to determine. However, the chemical formula often gives clues on how to arrange the atoms in the molecule. If the formula is a relatively simple one, chances are that the structure is going to be symmetrically arranged with the "lone" (or minority) atom in the middle.

Hydrogen and elements in the halogen family cannot be in the middle of the molecule. They each need to share only one other electron in order

When charged particles in the sky collide, they create auroras. Such particles come from the Sun. Green auroras, such as this one, are from atomic oxygen.

to have a full valence level—if they can share with only one other atom at a time, then they cannot be in the middle of the molecule.

Once the element symbols are arranged, the valence electrons are drawn around each symbol. If an atom is going to have electrons that are "doubled up," do not put the double where the atom bonds to another atom. Rather, put the doubled pair on a side facing the outside of the molecule. An electron between two symbols is being shared by those two atoms, and both atoms may count it as part of their needed eight. Once all atoms have eight valence electrons (except hydrogen, which is full with two valence electrons), the molecule is correctly drawn.

Lone pairs

Sometimes atoms have electrons that are not being shared between two atoms—the pairs that were doubled up on an element and were not involved in bonding. These pairs of electrons not involved in bonding are called lone pairs.

Example 5.2D

Covalent Lewis Dot Structures

1. Draw the Lewis dot structure for methane, CH$_4$.

   • Carbon has four valence electrons, and each hydrogen atom has one valence electron. Hydrogen cannot be in the middle of the molecule, because hydrogen can bond to only one other atom.

   • When sharing electrons, each atom gets to count the ones that are shared. Therefore, the carbon now has eight electrons surrounding it, a full valence level for carbon, and each hydrogen has two, a full valence level for hydrogen.

$$\begin{array}{c} H \\ \vdots \\ H \cdot\cdot C \cdot\cdot H \\ \vdots \\ H \end{array}$$

2. Draw the Lewis dot structure for CBr$_4$.

   • Carbon has four valence electrons, and each bromine has seven. Bromine cannot be in the middle because bromine can bond to only one other atom.

   • When they share electrons, each has a total of eight-a full valence level. Each bromine has three lone pairs.

$$\begin{array}{c} \overset{..}{:}\overset{..}{Br}\overset{..}{:} \\ :\overset{..}{Br}\cdot\cdot\overset{..}{C}\cdot\cdot\overset{..}{Br}: \\ :\overset{..}{Br}: \end{array}$$

Double bonds   Double bonds are formed when two pairs of electrons are shared. Double bonds are shorter in length (the nuclei of the two elements are closer together) and stronger (they require more energy to break). A double bond needs to be formed when two atoms that are next to each other (they are already bonded together with a single bond) each has an unpaired electron (it is not already bonded to another atom or in a lone pair). The single electron from each atom involved is erased and redrawn between the two atoms. Now the two atoms are sharing four electrons—a double bond.

If two atoms have single, unpaired electrons but they are not located directly next to each other, other atoms need to be moved around so that the two atoms with unpaired electrons are next to each other and can form a double bond. This situation happens often in chains of carbon atoms.

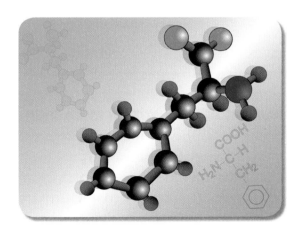

Phenylalanine is an amino acid. It is produced by plants, and it is also produced in the breast milk of mammals. Some people cannot metabolize phenylalanine. They must make sure they don't eat it—and it's in lots of food sweetened with aspartame (such as Equal or NutraSweet).

Example 5.2E

Double Bonds in Covalent Structures

Draw the Lewis dot structure for C_2H_4.

- Each carbon has four valence electrons, and each hydrogen atom has one valence electron. The hydrogen atoms cannot go in the middle of the molecule, so the two carbons are bonding together.

$$H \cdot \cdot \dot{C} \cdot \cdot \dot{C} \cdot \cdot H$$
$$H H$$

- The hydrogen atoms each have two electrons around them, so they have full valence levels; however, the carbons each have only seven valence electrons—not full valence levels. If the carbon atoms form a double bond by moving their single electrons in between to bond, they each achieve a full valence level.

$$H \cdot \cdot C :: C \cdot \cdot H$$
$$H H$$

Triple bonds   **Triple bonds** form when two elements share three pairs of electrons. Triple bonds are even shorter and stronger than double bonds. The idea is similar to that of forming a double bond. If two atoms are next to each other and they each have an unpaired electron, the unpaired electrons move in to form a double bond. If after forming a double bond each atom still has an unpaired electron, those are also erased and redrawn between the two atoms-forming a triple bond. As in the double bond, sometimes atoms have to be moved around in the molecule in order for two elements that have unpaired electrons to be directly next to each other.

Example 5.2F

Triple Bonds in Covalent Structures

Draw the Lewis dot structure for C_2H_2.

- Each carbon has four valence electrons, and each hydrogen atom has one valence electron. The hydrogen atoms cannot go in the middle of the molecule, so the two carbons bond together.

$$H \cdot \cdot \dot{C} \cdot \cdot \dot{C} \cdot \cdot H$$

- The hydrogen atoms each have two electrons around them, so they have full valence levels; however, the carbons each have only six valence electrons—not full valence levels. If the carbon atoms form a triple bond by moving their single electrons in to bond, they each achieve a full valence level.

$$H \cdot \cdot C ::: C \cdot \cdot H$$

Lewis structures that can be written more than one way

Many covalent molecules can have Lewis dot structures drawn correctly in more than one way. Sometimes these ways are not really different under closer inspection, but often they are quite different. If two structures with the same chemical formula are drawn differently, they are called **isomers.** Unless the way the chemical formula is written (or the chemical's name) shows exactly how the elements should be joined, each of the different isomer drawings is correct. See Figures 5–2 and 5–3 for examples of when two drawings are (and are not) isomers.

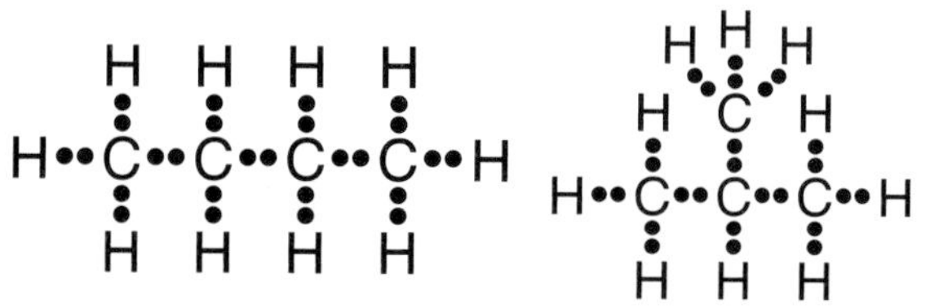

Figure 5–2. Examples of isomers. Butane (on the left) and 2-methylpropane (on the right) have the same chemical formula but different chemical structures.

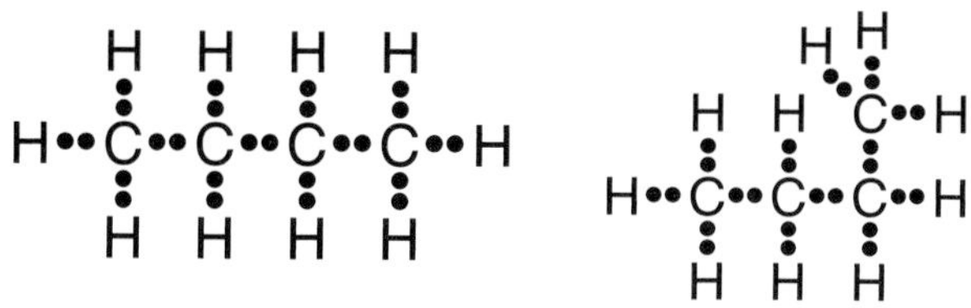

Figure 5–3. Example of drawings that are really the same. These pairs may look different, but they are not chemically different—the atoms are still bonded in the same order, so it does not matter which side they are bonded on.

Often the chemical formula does not differentiate between the isomers, but the chemical name does. For example, C_4H_{10} is the chemical formula for both butane and 2-methylpropane. (Chapter 11 will teach you how to understand these names.) Looking at the formula only, even experienced chemists would not be sure which isomer was being discussed. But by looking at the chemical name they would know for sure. For now, you will be given chemical formulas only from which to draw a structure. This means that, for now, you may draw different structures than your lab partner or neighbor when given a chemical formula, but you both could be correct!

The Atomium, which was built for the 1958 World's Fair in Brussels, Belgium.

Go Online
Animated examples
http://webcom4.grtxle.com/
khk12Chemistry

Lewis dot structures for polyatomic ions

Polyatomic ions were discussed in Chapter 2. They were "chunks" of more than one atom (polyatomic) that together had a charge (ion). Polyatomic ions combine the concepts of covalent bonding and ionic bonding.

The atoms *within* the polyatomic ion are covalently bonded to each other—the atoms share electrons rather than giving and taking them. However, in order to satisfy the octet rule for all the atoms in the polyatomic ion, one or more electrons must be removed (to form a polyatomic cation) or added (to form a polyatomic anion). The charge on the polyatomic ion indicates how many electrons were removed or added in order to satisfy the octets of all involved atoms.

The only polyatomic cations cited in this text are ammonium (NH_4^{+1}) and hydronium (H_3O^{+1}). Each had one electron removed (erased from the structure) in order to form full valence levels. Where did this electron go? It went to the associated anion, just as in the ionic compounds drawn earlier.

Many polyatomic anions are mentioned in this text. They had electrons added in order to form full valence levels. Where did those electrons come from? They came from the cation that lost electrons.

So the atoms are bonded covalently within the polyatomic ion, but the bond *between* the polyatomic ion and another ion is ionic.

Household ammonia is a solution of NH_3 in water.

Example 5.2G

Polyatomic Ion Structures

1. Draw the Lewis dot structure for CO_3^{-2}.

   • Carbon has four valence electrons, and each oxygen has six valence electrons.

   $$:\overset{..}{O}\!\cdot\!\cdot\!\overset{..}{C}\!\cdot\!\cdot\!\overset{..}{O}:$$
   $$:\overset{..}{O}:$$

   • This structure shows that none of the elements has full valence levels. The carbon can double bond with one of the oxygen atoms to satisfy the valence levels for the carbon and one of the oxygens.

   $$:\overset{..}{O}\!\cdot\!\cdot\!\overset{..}{C}\!::\!\overset{..}{O}:$$
   $$:\overset{..}{O}:$$

   • But the other two oxygen atoms still do not have full valence levels. Two electrons can be added, one to each oxygen atom. This situation causes an overall charge of –2 on the structure.

   $$\left(:\overset{..}{\overset{.}{O}}\!\cdot\!\cdot\!\overset{..}{C}\!::\!\overset{..}{O}:\ \ :\overset{..}{O}:\right)^{-2}$$

2. Draw the Lewis dot structure for SO_4^{-2}.

   • Sulfur has six electrons, and each oxygen has six electrons.

   • If an oxygen is placed on each side of the sulfur, two of the oxygens will be placed on sides where sulfur has a pair of electrons already. In these cases, the bond consists of the two atoms sharing the pair of electrons that came from sulfur-those two oxygen atoms will keep all of their six electrons to themselves as three lone pairs.

   $$:\overset{..}{O}:$$
   $$:\overset{..}{O}\!\cdot\!\cdot\!S\!\cdot\!\cdot\!\overset{..}{O}:$$
   $$:\overset{..}{O}:$$

   • Two of the oxygen atoms have only seven electrons each. The –2 charge on the ion means that you can add two electrons-one to each oxygen.

   $$\left(:\overset{..}{\overset{.}{O}}:\ :\overset{..}{O}\!\cdot\!\cdot\!S\!\cdot\!\cdot\!\overset{..}{O}:\ :\overset{..}{O}:\right)^{-2}$$

Exceptions to the octet rule

Some elements can bond and are stable with more or fewer than eight valence electrons (other than hydrogen, which needs only two). Boron and beryllium are often stable with only six valence electrons. Any element in the third period and below on the periodic table can bond to have more than eight valence electrons. For example, the elements in the 3p section of the periodic table have full 3s subshells and unfilled 3p subshells. They bond with other elements in order to fill their 3p subshell and have eight valence electrons. However, they also have a 3d subshell that is completely empty and could hold extra electrons. Therefore, they can bond with other elements and hold more than eight valence electrons.

PRACTICE 5.2

Lewis Dot Structures

One class of oil is paraffin. As a solid, paraffin is a wax and is used in making candles.

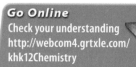

Go Online
Check your understanding
http://webcom4.grtxle.com/
khk12Chemistry

Draw the Lewis dot structures for each of the following molecules:

1. CCl_4
2. CH_3Cl
3. H_2O
4. NH_3
5. H_2Te
6. TeI_2
7. C_2H_6

8. C_2H_5Cl
9. C_3H_6
10. HCN
11. CS_2
12. C_2H_5OH
13. N_2
14. H_2NCH_2Br

15. CO_2
16. $HSCH_2OH$
17. Cl_2
18. NH_4^{+1}
19. CO_3^{-2}
20. NO_2^{-1}
21. PO_4^{-3}

22. Oils consist of mixtures of many hydrocarbon (hydrogen- and carbon-containing) compounds. Oils usually contain five or more carbons. There are four classifications of compounds that make up these mixtures. Two of the classes are paraffins and olefins. Paraffins contain single bonds only, whereas olefins contain at least one multiple bond. Draw the structure for the simplest five-carbon paraffin and olefin: C_5H_{12} and C_5H_{10}.

23. Draw the following ionic compounds' Lewis dot structures: LiCl, $CaCl_2$, SrO, Na_2O.

24. Draw the following ionic compounds' Lewis dot structures that contain polyatomic ions (that are covalently bonded within themselves): $(NH_4)_2S$, $NaNO_2$

Save this paper for assignments 5.3-5.5!

Molecules in 3D

Covalent Molecules in 3D

Purpose To build molecules in 3D space in order to determine their shapes

Materials Marshmallows, gumdrops, or Styrofoam balls of two different sizes (5 large and 20 small), and 20 toothpicks

Background information Covalent bonds are made of electrons, and electrons are all negative. Negative things repel other negative things. Therefore, negative electrons want to be as far apart as possible from each other. In this activity, the atoms will be the marshmallows/gumdrops/Styrofoam balls, and the bonds (electrons) will be the toothpicks. The toothpicks will connect the "atoms," which want to be as far away from each other as possible. Use a large "atom" as the central atom and the smaller "atoms" as the outside atoms bonded to the central atom. For this exercise, the central atom (the large one) will be called *A* and the out-

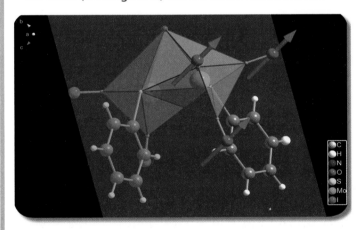

Computers help us to visualize the inside workings of molecules, such as in this graphicrepresentation of a molecule.

side atoms (the smaller ones) will be called *X*.

Part 1 Molecules with no lone pairs

Build the following molecules, getting the bonds as far away as possible. Stop after building each molecule

and compare with other groups and with the class. Have your teacher approve the model before you move on to the next one in order to make sure you built it correctly. Once each model has been discussed with the teacher and approved, write a description of how the atoms are arranged in 3D (do not look at the toothpicks now, just the "atoms"). Make a drawing of the model, representing or noting the 3D aspect of it as best as you can. Do not tear apart your model, because you will need it for Part 2, which follows; instead, use new materials for each molecule.

Construct: AX_2, AX_3, AX_4, AX_5, AX_6

Part 2 Molecules with lone pairs

A lone pair is a pair of electrons that is not being shared by two atoms. This case would be represented in the models by a toothpick sticking out of the central atom without an outside atom bonded to it. These molecules are based on the molecules you already built. (There are slight differences that will be discussed in the text after the lab.) Count the toothpicks that this new molecule will need, and choose the model you built in Part 1 that has the same number of toothpicks. The model of the molecule with the lone pair will be based on the one from Part 1 with the same number of electron pairs around the central atom. Once you have chosen the model from Part 1, remove the necessary outer atoms so that the central atom has the specified number of lone pairs. Stop and compare this new model with other groups and have it approved by your teacher. Once the model is discussed and approved by the teacher, write a description of what the atoms look like in 3D space (not the toothpicks, just the "atoms"). Make a drawing of the model, representing or noting the 3D aspect of it as best you can.

Construct: AX_2 with one lone pair, AX_2 with two lone pairs, AX_3 with one lone pair, AX_3 with two lone pairs

Geometry of covalent bonding

Covalent bonds are pairs of electrons, and those electrons are negatively charged. Those negative charges repel each other and want to be as far apart as possible. Many times this situation means that a molecule must take advantage of 3D space rather than remaining "flat." This tendency is called the **valence shell electron pair repulsion theory** (VSEPR theory, pronounced "vesper"), and it is the basis for how molecules arrange themselves in space. A VSEPR chart, Table 5–1, is found on the last page of this chapter.

That is, molecular bonds arrange themselves around a central atom so that the electron pairs are at the greatest angle from each other. The table at the end of this chapter shows the number of atoms that are bonded to the central atom, number of lone pairs, the 3D drawing of how the molecule exists, and the name for that 3D shape. Note that it is of little importance whether a bond is a single or a multiple bond; the fact that electrons are between those two atoms is what is important—so do not count individual bonds when analyzing a molecule. Instead, count the number of atoms and the number of lone pairs around the central atom. Lone pairs around the outside atoms are not considered—only those on the central atom.

Distortion of angles with lone pairs

When lone pairs are around a central atom, they take up a bit more space than a bond with an atom. In a bond with another atom, the electrons are shared between two atomic nuclei—the positive protons of the two nuclei are "controlling" the electrons forming the bond. When the electrons are lone pairs, they are controlled by a nucleus on only one side-from the central atom. This situation means that they expand and take up slightly more room than if they were controlled by two nuclei. There are greater repulsions between this lone pair and the surrounding bonded pairs. Therefore, the angles in molecules containing lone pairs are slightly distorted, compared with the no-lone-pair version that they are based on. The lone pairs take up more room and "push" the bonded pairs closer together, distorting the structure.

For example, a tetrahedral molecule has bond angles of 109.5° between each of the four bonds. However, water, a "bent" molecule with two bonds and two lone pairs (based on the tetrahedron shape) will have a higher angle between the lone pair and the bonds and slightly lower angles between the bonds themselves. The bond angle (H-O-H) in water is 105°. (See Figure 5–4.)

Ionic compound structures

Ionic compounds are formed by the attraction between the positively and negatively charged ions. These ions arrange themselves in a pattern in such a way that each negatively charged anion is surrounded by positively charged cations, and vice versa. This arrangement allows for opposite charges

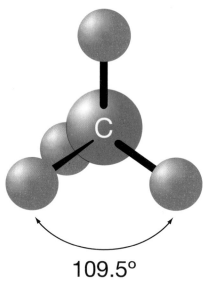

109.5°

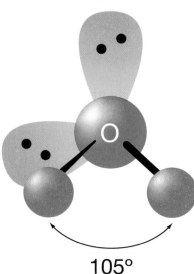

105°

Figure 5–4. Bond distortion with lone pairs. The methane molecule on top is a tetra-hedron with H-C-H angles of 109.5°, whereas the water molecule underneath has two lone pairs distorting the bond angles by taking up more space themselves. Water has bond angles of 105° between the hydrogen atoms.

to be closest to each other (opposites attract) and like charges to be as far from each other as possible (like charges repel). (See Figure 5–5.)

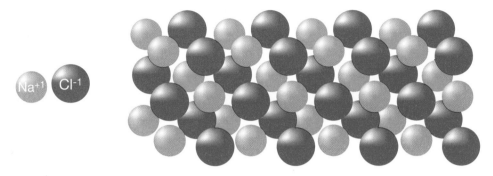

Figure 5–5. Ionic bonding. Sodium chloride is an ionic compound.

PRACTICE 5.3

VSEPR Theory

Give the molecular shapes for the structures you drew for the following questions in Practice 5.2: 1-6, 10, 11, 15, 18-21. (Hint-make sure the structure is drawn correctly first!)

SECTION 5.4

Polarity of Molecules

Electronegativity and the periodic table

Atoms have a property called electronegativity, which is the pull an atom exerts on an electron it is sharing in a bond with another element. If two elements have the same electronegativity, they pull evenly on the electron and it is shared perfectly evenly between those two atoms. However, if one atom has a higher electronegativity than the other, the electrons are shared unevenly-they are closer to the atom with the higher electronegativity.

Electronegativity is a trend that can be found in the periodic table, just as atomic radius and ionization energy (as discussed in Chapter 4). As the atomic radius of an atom decreases from left to right on the periodic table, the valence electrons (those involved in bonding) are closer to the nucleus, and they feel the pull of the nucleus charge more. Therefore, as atomic radius decreases, electronegativity increases from left to right across a period (see Figure 5–6). Likewise, as atomic radius increases down a group, the electrons are farther from the nucleus and more shielded from its pull by the core electrons. Therefore, as atomic radius increases down a group, electronegativity decreases.

H 2.1																	
Li 1.0	Be 1.5											B 2.0	C 2.5	N 3.0	O 3.5	F 4.0
Na 0.9	Mg 1.2											Al 1.5	Si 1.8	P 2.1	S 2.5	Cl 3.0
K 0.8	Ca 1.0	Sc 1.3	Ti 1.5	V 1.6	Cr 1.6	Mn 1.5	Fe 1.8	Co 1.9	Ni 1.9	Cu 1.9	Zn 1.6	Ga 1.6	Ge 1.8	As 2.0	Se 2.4	Br 2.8
Rb 0.8	Sr 1.0	Y 1.2	Zr 1.4	Nb 1.6	Mo 1.8	Tc 1.9	Ru 2.2	Rh 2.2	Pd 2.2	Ag 1.9	Cd 1.7	In 1.7	Sn 1.8	Sb 1.9	Te 2.1	I 2.5
Cs 0.7	Ba 0.9	Lu 1.0	Hf 1.3	Ta 1.5	W 1.7	Re 1.9	Os 2.2	Ir 2.2	Pt 2.2	Au 2.4	Hg 1.9	Tl 1.8	Pb 1.9	Bi 1.9	Po 2.0	At 2.2

Figure 5–6. Periodic table and electro-negativities.

Electronegativity and polarity of bonds

If the difference in electronegativities of two atoms involved in a bond is less than or equal to 0.4, then they are considered to be pulling on the electrons in similar enough amounts that the bond is nonpolar covalent. If the electronegativity difference is greater than 0.4 and less than 2.0, then the bond is polar covalent—they are not sharing the bonding pair evenly. If the difference is above 2.0, then the bond is an ionic bond (as occurs when a metal and a nonmetal bond). The difference is so great that they don't share at all—one atom takes the electrons from the other atom.

When a bond is polar and the electrons are shared unevenly, the negative electrons are closer to one atom than to the other. This situation means that the more electronegative element is taking on more than its share of the negative charge of the electrons, and that element has a slightly negative charge. It is not a full negative charge, as an anion would have when it completely takes electrons from a cation; instead, it is a partial negative charge. The less electronegative element has less than its share of the negative electron charge, and therefore it carries a partial positive charge. (See Figure 5–7.)

The polarity of a bond is shown by a symbol that looks like an arrow with a cross in the tail to look like a plus sign (+→). The arrow points toward the more electronegative element, and the plus in the tail points toward the less electronegative element. This direction means that the plus in the tail is pointing toward the partially positive atom.

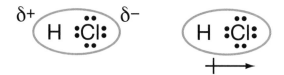

Figure 5–7. Polar bond. The two atoms share the electrons, but the atom on the right has a higher electronegativity and pulls the electrons closer to itself. There are two ways to show the polarity: (1) with the "δ" symbols, which mean "partial," shown on the left or (2) with the arrow with the plus-sign tail, shown on the right.

Example 5.4

Polar Bonds

1. Draw a polarity arrow for the bond C—S.

   • Carbon and sulfur both have an electronegativity of 2.5. Therefore, the difference between the two is zero. This is a nonpolar bond.

   C—S

2. Draw the polarity arrow for the bond between C and F.

   • Carbon has an electronegativity of 2.5, and fluorine has an electronegativity of 4.0. The difference between the two is 1.5—this is a polar bond. The arrow points toward the more electronegative element, with the plus sign pointing toward the element that has a partial positive charge (the less electronegative element).

   C—F
   ⊢→

Polarity of bonds and polarity of molecules

A molecule could have polar bonds and create an overall nonpolar molecule. If the polarities point in such a way that they cancel each other out, then the overall molecule will not show a polar split in the charges. However, if the polar bonds do not cancel each other out, then the entire molecule will be polar-one side will have a partial positive charge and the other will have a partial negative charge. In order to determine whether the polar bonds cancel out, the 3D shape of the molecule must be taken into consideration, not the way we draw it on flat paper. (See Figure 5–8.)

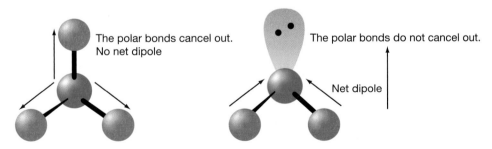

The polar bonds cancel out. No net dipole

The polar bonds do not cancel out.

Net dipole

Figure 5–8. Polar bonds and polar molecules. The molecule on the left has polar bonds, but they cancel each other out. The molecule on the right has a polar bond that is not canceled out; therefore, it is a polar molecule.

PRACTICE 5.4

Polarity of Molecules

1. For bonds between the following pairs of elements, indicate the polarity of the bond by drawing the arrow symbol (↦). If the bond has no polarity, say so: C-O, H-C, C-N, H-N, S-O, N-O, Cl-C.

2. For the following questions in Practice 5.2, draw the polarity arrow symbols for all the polar bonds: 1-6, 10, 11, 15, 18-21.

3. For the questions in Practice 5.2 listed previously, say whether the molecule has an overall polarity or if it is nonpolar.

4. Are paraffin and olefin molecules polar or nonpolar molecules? (Refer to question 22 in Practice 5.2 for explanations of these two classifications of compounds.)

SECTION 5.5

Intermolecular Forces

Intramolecular versus intermolecular forces

Forces inside a molecule (the forces that bond atoms together in a compound) are called **intramolecular forces.** The forces that cause two separate molecules to be attracted to each other are called **intermolecular forces.** Intermolecular forces (or **Van der Waals forces**) are not chemical bonds, but rather attractions between separate molecules.

Intramolecular forces are broken during a chemical change. Atoms are chemically bonded in one way, and then those bonds are broken and atoms are rearranged to form new compounds with new intramolecular forces. Intermolecular forces are broken during some physical changes-melting, boiling, evaporating, and dissolving. A sample may have more than one type of intermolecular force at the same time.

London dispersion forces

In atoms, electrons move around the nucleus. In a molecule, those electrons continue to move around the nucleus-only there are several nuclei in the molecule and many more electrons. Sometimes those electrons all end up on the same side of the molecule for a brief period of time. As they "gang up" on one side, that side becomes partially negative, leaving the other side partially positive. This produces a polar situation (as was discussed previously with polar bonds and molecules). The difference here is that it is a temporary dipole situation—when the electrons continue to move around the nuclei, they will spread out again (see Figure 5–9).

Figure 5–9. Temporary dipole. As the electrons "gang up" on the right side of the molecule on the left, it creates a slightly negative and a slightly positive area in the molecule. The molecule on the right has the same thing happen. The slightly negative area on the left molecule attracts the slightly positive area on the right molecule.

The polarity in the molecule is brief. But in that brief time, it could induce the molecule next to it to form a dipole-the positive area of the first molecule could attract the electrons from a neighboring molecule and cause them to "gang up" on one side of that molecule as well. Now there are two molecules next to each other that are attracted through their positive and negative areas. This situation can allow nonpolar gases, such as nitrogen or propane, to become liquids under certain conditions.

Such attractions between the temporarily polar molecules are called **London dispersion forces.** Because the force is an attraction between molecules, it is an intermolecular force-but a very weak one, because it is a temporary situation. All molecules have these forces, because they all have electrons that have the possibility of "ganging up" on one side. The strength of the London dispersion force is greater as the number of electrons in a molecule increases (when the molecule gets larger). If there is a greater number of electrons to "gang up," then there is a more dramatic polarity between the positive portion and the negative portion of the molecule.

Dipole–dipole interactions

When a molecule has a permanent polarity, it has a portion of the molecule with a partial positive charge and a portion with a partial negative charge. The partial positive portion of one molecule is attracted to the partial negative portion of another molecule. This case is similar to the London dispersion forces discussed previously, except that these dipoles are permanently in the molecule, so they always have the capacity to form these attractions. The attractions between polar molecules are called **dipole–dipole interactions.** They are also intermolecular forces, and all polar molecules have them. Dipole–dipole interactions are stronger than London dispersion forces because the molecules always have the capability of forming them with other polar molecules.

Hydrogen bonding

When a hydrogen atom bonds to a highly electronegative element (fluorine, oxygen, or nitrogen), the hydrogen is left with almost no share of the electrons—the electrons in the bond (which includes the only electron the hydrogen atom had) are held much more tightly by the other, more electronegative atom than by the hydrogen atom. The hydrogen atom has a partial positive charge, and the other atom has a partial negative charge

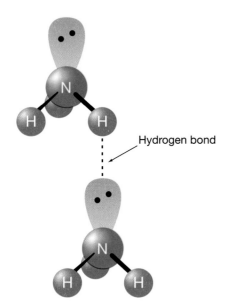

Figure 5–10. Hydrogen bonding. The hydrogen bonded to the nitrogen on the top molecule hydrogen bonds with the nitrogen on the bottom molecule (shown by the dotted line).

Hydrogen bond

Go Online
Check your understanding
http://webcom4.grtxle.com/
khk12Chemistry

(as with all polar molecules, but more strongly in this case). If that partial positive-charged hydrogen is near a highly electronegative element in a neighboring molecule, it is strongly attracted to the partial negative charge of the other molecule. This bond is not a full covalent bond—it is not an intramolecular force, but it is a strong attraction between a hydrogen atom on one molecule and an electronegative element on another molecule, called **hydrogen bonding** (Figure 5–10). Hydrogen bonding is the strongest of the types of intermolecular forces.

Hydrogen bonding is a specific, strong case of a dipole–dipole interaction. The reason that the bond is so strong is that when another electronegative element shares unevenly with hydrogen (when it pulls hydrogen's electron closer to itself in a bond), hydrogen has no other electrons around its nucleus to counteract the positive charge of the nucleus. There are no inner electrons neutralizing the positive charge of the proton in the nucleus. This lack of electrons makes an especially polar bond that leaves hydrogen vulnerable to attraction to negative atoms—such as a highly electronegative element on another molecule.

PRACTICE 5.5

Intermolecular Forces

1. For questions 1-6, 10, 11, and 15 in Practice 5.2 (you've already drawn the molecules), list the intermolecular forces that apply to that molecule.

2. Explain in your own words why hydrogen bonding is the strongest of the intermolecular forces, followed by dipole–dipole interactions and then London dispersion forces.

3. What type of intermolecular forces does water show? What type of intermolecular forces would paraffins and olefins (compounds found in oils) show? How might this force explain why oil and water do not mix?

SECTION 5.6

Intermolecular Forces and Properties

The number and strength of the intermolecular forces in a substance have effects on the properties that the substance displays. They are all based on the same principle: the more intermolecular forces a substance has with the molecules around it, the harder it is to separate those molecules.

Breaking bonds or intermolecular forces requires adding energy. When bonds or forces are reformed, energy is released. Think about magnets when trying to understand this concept. To pull apart two magnets that are stuck together, you have to use energy to break their attraction. However, when you bring two magnets close together, their attraction will join them together without your help.

Melting, evaporating, and boiling

In order to melt a solid or to evaporate or boil a liquid, the intermolecular attractions between molecules must be broken. In a solid, there are many points of intermolecular attraction between molecules. This situation is because those molecules are packed closely together and there is more opportunity to form attractions. To turn the solid into a liquid, some of those points of attraction must be broken to allow the molecules to move freely in the liquid. The rest of the intermolecular points of attraction are broken when the liquid is boiled or evaporated and turned into a gas.

You must add energy to break all intermolecular forces. Therefore, it takes more energy to melt or boil a sample that has stronger intermolecular forces than it does for one that has weaker intermolecular forces. As intermolecular forces increase, the melting and boiling points increase.

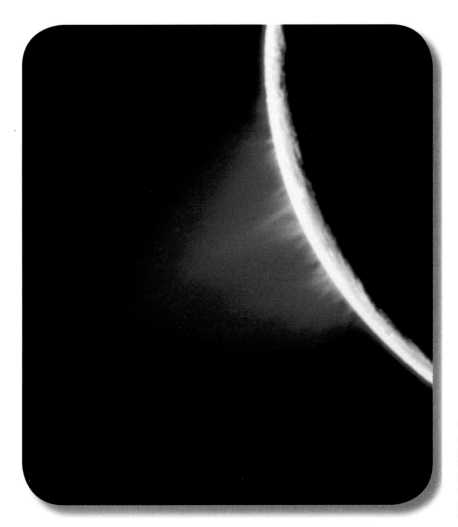

Water is essential to life on Earth, so scientists are eager to find other places in the solar system where water exists. Where there is water, there may be life. Geysers throwing ice and water vapor are shown here, coming from a moon of Saturn called Enceladus.

Importance of water's intermolecular forces to life

In general, smaller molecules have smaller intermolecular forces and lower melting and boiling points. Therefore, small molecules are usually found as gases at normal Earth temperatures and pressures. Water is a special molecule. It has such strong intermolecular forces—it has all three discussed already—that even though it is very small, it is still found as a liquid on Earth. Based only on its size (molecular mass), it should be a gas, but the intermolecular forces cause it to be a liquid. If water were not a polar molecule with hydrogen—bonding capability, life could not exist—water on Earth would be a gas!

Viscosity

Viscosity is the resistance of a liquid to flow. Molasses is a much more viscous substance than water. The greater the intermolecular forces in a sample, the more those molecules want to stick and clump together, and the less they want to slide past each other to flow or pour. Very large molecules are also more viscous because the molecules can intertwine with each other and not pour or flow easily (think of trying to pour a bowl of spaghetti—it all tangles together and does not flow very well).

Solubility

When making a solution, the solute is the substance being dissolved, and the solvent is the substance doing the dissolving. In order for a solute to be dissolved, the intermolecular forces that link the solvent molecules together must be broken, as well as the intermolecular forces between the solute particles. Once those forces are broken, there is room for the solute particles to fit in between the solvent molecules. The solute particles and the solvent molecules form new intermolecular forces with each other. (See Figure 5–11.) The new interactions need to be as strong, or stronger, than the old ones in order for the process to happen. Otherwise, the solute and solvent are more stable separately and will not form a solution. In general, if the energy required to break the bonds or forces is much greater than the energy released when new ones form, then it is an unfavorable situation. However, if the energy released is greater than the energy that had to be put in (or even if it is not a great deal less), the situation is favorable and therefore dissolution will occur.

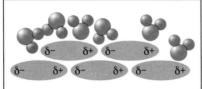
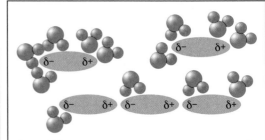

Figure 5–11. Molecules dissolving. The solvent and solute molecules must break their own intermolecular forces and form new intermolecular forces with each other.

Go Online
Molecular animations
http://webcom4.grtxle.com/
khk12Chemistry

Oil and water

Intermolecular forces explain why oil and water do not mix. Water uses all three types of intermolecular forces to link to other water molecules—London dispersion, dipole–dipole, and hydrogen bonding. Oil molecules are large, nonpolar molecules. They therefore can use only London dispersion forces to connect with other molecules. In order for the water molecules to separate and make room for the oil molecules to fit in, all three types of intermolecular forces must be broken between water molecules. Once the water intermolecular forces are broken, the water molecules can only connect with the oil molecules by London dispersion forces. Water molecules would be breaking all three types of intermolecular forces, and they can only reform the weakest type of forces with the oil molecules. Therefore, it is more favorable for the water molecules to connect with each other, and the oil molecules to separate out and float to the top (because they are less dense).

How soap affects solubility

Oil and water do not mix. So how can water be used to wash away oil, dirt, and grime? Soap forms a "bridge" between the two molecules. Soap molecules have one portion of the molecule that is nonpolar and forms London dispersion forces with the large, nonpolar oil and dirt molecules. The other end of the soap molecule contains a polar region or even regions with positive or negative charges. These polar or charged regions are strongly attracted to the water molecules. Several soap molecules surround the oil molecules with the nonpolar "tail" pointing toward the oil molecule and the polar "head" pointing toward water. This action forms what is called a **micelle**. The water molecules can now allow these micelles to fit in between because they are able to re-form strong interactions with the polar soap "heads" (unlike with the oil alone). (See Figure 5–12.)

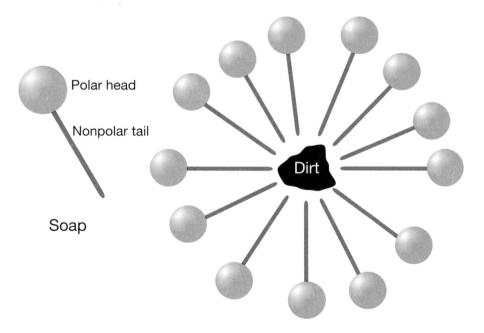

Figure 5–12. Surfactant molecules attract to both nonpolar dirt and polar water, forming a micelle. The "dirt" is in the middle. The nonpolar "tails" on the soap molecules are attracted to the nonpolar dirt. The polar "heads" on the soap molecules are attracted to the water molecules.

Soaps are alkali salts of fatty acids. By allowing oil and water to mix, soap removes oil, dirt, and grime.

Surface tension

Surface tension is the resistance of molecules to spreading out (increasing their surface area) or being penetrated, and such tension is caused by the attraction molecules have to the other molecules around them. It is the reason that water beads up on a waxed surface. The water molecules have strong attractions to other water molecules, as previously discussed. The attraction to other water molecules is stronger than the attraction to the waxed surface. The water molecules will pull together and form a bead rather than spreading out on the waxed surface. Surface tension makes drops spherical, whereas gravity makes drops flatten. The more spherical

Water droplets exhibit surface tension.

a drop is, the higher the surface tension. The stronger the intermolecular forces are in a substance, the greater the surface tension that substance will display, because the molecules are held tightly together.

Effect of soap on surface tension

Soap acts in a similar way with surface tension as with solubility. The soap molecules provide enough attraction with the water molecules to be let into the network and dissolve. However, the new attractions that are formed are not quite as strong as the ones with water alone, and therefore

A good soap can be judged by its ingredients and their proportions. In the early 1890s, one of the earliest product-research laboratories in the United States was at Procter and Gamble, set up to analyze and improve the soap-making process.

the new soap–water solution does not have as strong surface tension as the water alone. Surface tension must be broken in the water in order for the water to spread on the surface and clean it. (Think of water on a plate vs. soapy water on a plate: which covers the plate better?)

LAB 5.6

Intermolecular Forces and Evaporation

Purpose To sort volatile liquids based on strength of intermolecular forces

Background information A volatile liquid is one that evaporates easily. When a liquid evaporates, it requires energy to be put in to break the intermolecular forces connecting the liquid molecules. The energy necessary for these forces to be broken comes from the things surrounding the liquids—from the air and the surface that the liquid touches. (Energy and energy changes will be discussed in more detail in Chapter 7.)

Materials Thermometer (or temperature probes and data collection system), filter paper, small rubber band, tape, various volatile liquids in test tubes

! **Safety** The liquids used in this lab are flammable (no open flames in the lab!) and poisonous. Avoid inhaling the fumes. Notify your teacher if any sample comes in contact with your skin or clothes.

Procedure

1. If you are using temperature probes and a data collection system, set up the system.

2. Tear a piece of filter paper in half.

3. Wrap the filter paper around the end of the temperature probe or the thermometer so that the area that measures temperature is totally surrounded by the filter paper.

4. Secure the filter paper with a small rubber band.

5. Place the filter paper-covered thermometer in a test tube with the first volatile liquid. Allow the filter paper to soak up the volatile liquid for a minute.

6. Record the temperature reading.

7. Remove the thermometer from the test tube and lay it on the table so that the end with the filter paper is hanging off the edge of the table. Tape the thermometer in place.

8. Watch the temperature reading as the liquid evaporates. The liquid is removing energy from the filter paper and the air around it to gain energy to break the intermolecular forces in the liquid, so that the molecules can evaporate. The temperature reading will drop as the energy is removed from the air and filter paper and used to evaporate the liquid.

9. Record the lowest temperature reading you see.

10. Remove the filter paper from the thermometer and repeat with each of the volatile liquid samples you have.

LAB 5.6

Data Make a chart with the names of each of the volatile liquids down the side, and the beginning temperature and the lowest temperature across the top.

Procedure

1. Draw the Lewis dot structures for each of the volatile liquids.

2. For each of the drawings from question 1, indicate which intermolecular forces you think would be involved with the liquids.

3. Make a list of the liquids based on the information from question 2-order them from the liquid with the least intermolecular forces to the greatest intermolecular forces.

4. For each volatile liquid, find the temperature change that occurred during the evaporation of the liquid.

5. The more intermolecular forces between molecules, the more energy that will have to be absorbed into the liquid in order to break those forces and evaporate the liquid. That energy is being removed from the air and the filter paper. The more energy that is removed from the air and the filter paper, the greater the change in temperature of those objects will be. List the volatile liquids in order from the least intermolecular forces to the greatest intermolecular forces based on the temperature change you observed in the lab.

6. How does your list of volatile liquids in question 3 (based upon their Lewis dot structures) compare with the list in question 5 (from your lab data)? If there were some differences, why do you think that happened? Which do you think is more reliable—the lab data or your decisions based on the drawings?

7. Share your lists as a class. Use whiteboards if your teacher provides them. Are there any discrepancies? If so, discuss the evidence and come to a consensus.

(This lab is adapted with permission from "Experiment 9: Evaporation and Intermolecular Attractions" in Vernier Software and Technology's *Chemistry with Computers* Lab Book.)

PRACTICE 5.6

Intermolecular Forces and Properties

1. Describe how intermolecular forces affect melting and boiling points.

2. Explain how water's intermolecular forces are important to life.

3. Explain the three steps needed for something to dissolve.

4. Use the three steps of the dissolving process and the idea of intermolecular forces to explain why water alone will not wash away dirt and grime.

5. Explain why adding soap allows dirt and grime to be washed away. How does adding soap change the situation?

6. Explain why water beads up on waxed surfaces.

7. Explain why oil does not bead up on waxed surfaces.

Go Online
Check your understanding
http://webcom4.grtxle.com/
khk12Chemistry

Here is your chance to use the chemistry you know to create and evaluate the effectiveness of a soap.

Making and evaluating soap

Problem To make a soap and test its properties with a commercial soap.

Materials Vegetable oil, 10% solution of potassium hydroxide in ethanol, saturated sodium chloride solution, large test tube, 250 mL or 400 mL beaker for hot water bath, hot plate, test tube tongs, 3 100 mL beakers, 1 beaker to catch a filtrate, funnel/funnel rack/ring stand/filter paper, stir rod, 3 watch glasses or small pieces of glass.

> ⚠ **Safety** Wear goggles. Potassium hydroxide is caustic, so be cautious. Do not use open flames with ethanol in the room. Use caution with all glassware, especially hot glassware. Report any spills, breaks, or contact with skin or clothing to the teacher.

Procedure

Part 1 Making potassium soap

1. Add one plastic pipette full of vegetable oil to a large test tube. This is the "fat" needed for the soap.

2. Add 10 mL of 10% solution of potassium hydroxide in ethanol. This will add the charged region to the fat molecules. The non-polar oil and the polar ethanol solution will not be miscible at first.

3. Heat the test tube in a hot water bath for 3–5 minutes. (**Caution:** Do not use a Bunsen burner around ethanol—ethanol is highly flammable!) As the reaction proceeds, the insoluble ingredients will react to form the soluble soap. The solution will change colors to a dark yellow or orange as the reaction continues.

4. After the color has started to develop, periodically test to see if all the oil has reacted. Do this by dipping your stir rod into the test tube and then dipping the stir rod into a small beaker of fresh water (use any beaker you have—you'll

dump it out after the "test" anyway). If you see oil droplets on the top of the water, the reaction is not complete. If there are no oil droplets, then the reaction is complete (all of the oil has been reacted to form the soap) and you may move on.

5. When the reaction is complete, pour the mixture into a 100-mL beaker and put it in the boiling water bath. Make sure the level of the water bath is not so high as to overflow into the beaker; pour some out if it is too high. Watch until all the ethanol has evaporated. It will be thick and gooey, and boiling will cause thick foam. This is the potassium soap.

> **Safety** Do not touch it with your hands!
> ⚠

6. Remove the beaker from the hot water bath and allow it to solidify (this won't take long).

7. Add 40 mL of de-ionized water and stir to dissolve it. Label this beaker as "potassium soap." Write observations about how easily the soap dissolved in the water.

Part 2 Making sodium soap

1. Pour half of your potassium soap solution into another 100-mL beaker. To this second beaker, add 15 mL of saturated sodium chloride solution. Stir vigorously for 10 minutes. This makes sodium soap (the small curds that you see in the beaker).

2. Set up a filtration system and wet down the filter paper in the funnel.

3. Filter the solution away from the sodium soap (and into an empty beaker below the funnel). Once the solution has filtered through, remove the filter paper from the funnel and unfold it on a piece of paper towel.

4. Clean out the 100-mL beaker that the sodium soap came out of. Use a rubber policeman, spoon, spatula, or stir rod to scrape the soap off the filter paper (be careful not to tear the filter

paper apart) and place it in the now-clean 100-mL beaker. Label this beaker "sodium soap."

5. Dissolve the sodium soap in 20 mL of deionized water and write observation on the solubility of the soap in water.

Part 3 **Using commercial soap**

1. Add approximately 1 g of commercial soap to a 100-mL beaker. Label this beaker "commercial soap."

2. Dissolve the soap in 40 mL of deionized water. Write observations on the solubility of this soap in water.

Part 4 **Testing solubility of fat in each soap**

1. Spread a thin coating of the original vegetable oil on a watch glass. Test the ability of the potassium soap to wash the soap off the glass by dipping a paper towel in the soap solution and washing the greasy watch glass. Record observations.

2. Repeat the test with each of the other two soaps—preferably each on a different watch glass so you can compare them all in the end.

Observations Record your observations.

	Solubility in water	Ability to wash away fats
Potassium soap		
Sodium soap		
Commercial soap		

Conclusion Restate the purpose of the lab. Use your observations to make general judgments about the effectiveness of each type of soap. Which property do you think is most important in soap (solubility in water or ability to wash away fats)? Or are the properties equally important? Why? Use your understanding of solubility, bonding, and intermolecular forces to explain why the soaps you made needed a "fatty" component as well as a "charged" component. How might this type of experimentation or information be used in real life? What other type of experiment could you do?

Lab with permissions from *http://chem.csustan.edu*

Metals and nonmetals bond when a metal gives up electrons and a nonmetal takes the electrons. The giving and taking of electrons results in ions that are attracted to each other in an ionic bond. Ionic solids form networks of ions in such a way that an anion is surrounded by cations and vice versa. Ionic solids have high melting and boiling points, often dissolve in water, and conduct electricity when dissolved.

Metal atoms bond together in metallic bonding by sharing a large pool of electrons. This sharing of electrons with the entire network results in atoms being bonded to the network, not to specific other metal atoms. This situation allows metals to have properties such as malleability and ductility, and it allows them to conduct electricity as a solid.

Nonmetals bond with each other by sharing electrons in a covalent bond. If the electrons are shared evenly, when the electronegativities of both elements are similar, the bond is nonpolar. If the electronegativities of the elements are greatly different, one atom will pull on the electrons more than the other, and they will be shared unevenly—thus, it will be a polar bond. A molecule in which the polar bonds cancel each other out is still a nonpolar molecule. However, if they do not cancel out, the molecule will be polar. Polar molecules often dissolve in water, whereas nonpolar molecules do not. Neither is an electrolyte.

Molecules can be drawn on paper using Lewis dot structures. The element's symbol represents the nucleus and core electrons, and the valence electrons are drawn around the symbol. The elements give and take (ionic bonding) or share (covalent bonding) until all elements have full valence levels. Atoms can bond with single, double, or triple bonds. Multiple bonds are shorter and stronger than single bonds. Atoms can also have lone pairs, which are valence electrons not involved in bonding.

Lewis dot structures can be used to determine a molecule's structure in 3D using the valence shell electron pair repulsion theory. Once the 3D structure is known, the polarity of the overall molecule can be determined.

Intermolecular forces are the attractions between separate molecules. London dispersion forces are a result of the "ganging up" of electrons on one side of the molecule, resulting in a temporarily polar molecule that can then be attracted to other temporarily or permanently polar molecules. All molecules have London dispersion forces. Dipole–dipole interactions are the attractions between permanently polar molecules. Hydrogen bonding occurs when a hydrogen atom is bonded to a highly electronegative element and it comes close to a highly electronegative element in another molecule.

The stronger the intermolecular forces, the harder it is to separate the molecules. This difficulty means that higher intermolecular forces result in higher melting and boiling points, as well as higher surface tension and viscosity. Intermolecular forces also play a role in determining whether something is soluble or not. The intermolecular forces must be broken in the solute and solvent (requiring energy), and then new intermolecular forces are formed between the solute and solvent (releasing energy). If the amount of energy required is much more than the energy released, the two will not form a solution.

1. Compare and contrast covalent, polar covalent, ionic and metallic bonding.

2. Why are only the valance electrons drawn when drawing Lewis structures?

3. What things must be true to call two molecules isomers?

4. What is the octet rule and what are common exceptions to it?

5. Explain how both covalent and ionic bonding are involved with polyatomic ions.

6. What role does electronegativity play in determining if a bond is polar or non-polar?

7. What theory is used to determine the 3-D geometry of molecules?

8. Compare single, double, and triple bonds in the amount of electrons involved, the length of the bond, and the strength of the bond.

9. An unknown compound dissolves in water but does not conduct electricity. What type of bond is it most likely to be?

10. An unknown compound does not dissolve in water. What type of bond is it most likely to be?

11. An unknown compound dissolves in water and conducts electricity when dissolved. What type of bond is it most likely to be?

12. For each of the following, say whether it would be ionic or covalent (use your periodic table to figure out the answers).

    a. NaBr   **e.** MgO

    b. CH_4 **f.** CuCl

    c. SO_2 **g.** HCOOH

    d. NH_3 **h.** SF_6

13. For each of the following, draw the Lewis Dot Structure.

    a. CH_3Br **h.** NH_4^{+1}

    b. C_2H_6 **i.** H_3CSCH_2F

    c. CO_2 **j.** O_2

    d. PH_3 **k.** NCl_3

    e. H_2NCH_3 **l.** H_2NCOOH

    f. C_3H_6 **m.** C_3H_7OH

    g. NO_2^{-1} **n.** SO_4^{-2}

14. For the following from question 13, tell the shape of the molecule, draw the polarity arrows for any polar bonds, and tell if the overall molecule is polar: a, c, d, g, h, k, n.

15. Draw the following ionic compounds' Lewis dot structures:

    a. NaCl   **c.** $MgBr_2$

    b. CaO   **d.** Mg_3P_2

    e. Na_2SO_4 (which contains a polyatomic ion)

16. What's the difference between intermolecular and intramolecular forces?

17. Explain the differences between London dispersion forces, dipole–dipole interactions, and hydrogen bonding.

18. List the intermolecular forces that apply for molecules a, c, d, g, h, k, and n in question 13.

19. How do intermolecular forces affect what will dissolve in a substance?

20. How do intermolecular forces affect melting and boiling points?

21. What are viscosity and surface tension, and how does the strength of the intermolecular forces affect these two properties?

Table 5-1 Valence Shell Electron Pair Repulsion Theory			
Number of Atoms Bonded to the Central Atom	Number of Lone Pairs on the Central Atom	Picture	Molecular Shape Name
2	0		Linear
3	0		Trigonal planar
2	1		Bent
4	0		Tetrahedron
3	1		Trigonal Pyramidal
2	2		Bent
5	0		Trigonal bipyramidal
6	0		Octahedron

Soap bubbles reflecting and floating on the surface of the water.

CHAPTER 6

Sports Drinks

Fighting Dehydration with Chemistry

IN THIS CHAPTER

- Solutions and electrolytes
- Concentrations of solutions
- Acidity and pH
- Solubility and precipitation
- Stoichiometry
- Limiting reactants
- Properties of solutions

INTRODUCTORY ACTIVITY

What do you think are the benefits of drinking a sports drink while exercising, rather than plain water?

How are your ideas influenced by the marketing strategies of the companies that sell these drinks?

Share your ideas with a partner and then as a class.

to create a good-tasting carbonated beverage.

Introduction

Gatorade originated on the football fields of the University of Florida—well, actually it was in the laboratories at the University. But in 1965, the football players used it to prevent dehydration in the hot, humid Florida weather. In 1967, it came on the market, named after the Florida Gators football team.

When we exercise, we burn carbohydrates. When these carbohydrates are gone, the body begins finding energy in other ways, which produces lactic acid in the muscles. Lactic acid lowers the pH of the muscles and causes muscle fatigue and cramping. It is better to have enough carbohydrates to burn than to build up lactic acid.

When carbohydrates are used in the body, the body produces heat, which can raise the core temperature of the body. Sweat cools the body by absorbing the excess heat in order to evaporate. Therefore, sweat is a necessary body function to control overheating. However, if a person were to sweat so much that he or she lost 2% of body weight, it would put stress on the heart, raise body temperature, and lower performance.

Water is just as good for you as a sports drink.

Excessive sweating also results in loss of electrolytes. Two important electrolytes in the body are the sodium cation (Na^+) and the potassium cation (K^+). These electrolytes are necessary for storing and processing carbohydrates, transmitting nerve impulses to the brain, bringing nutrients into cells, and removing waste from cells. When one or both of these electrolyte levels begin to drop due to excessive sweating, negative consequences could include muscle fatigue, weakness, heat exhaustion, and heat stroke.

It's important to replace carbohydrates and lost water and electrolytes when exercising. But are sports drinks really better than plain water? Studies have shown that, in their ability to reduce core body temperature, heart rate, and rate of sweating, sports drinks are no better than plain water. Experts agree that it is most important to stay hydrated (and don't wait until you're thirsty to drink; you're already becoming dehydrated by that point). They also say that water rehydrates you as well as, if not better than, sports drinks. But water doesn't replace carbohydrates or electrolytes lost in sweating, you say? Those can be replaced more than adequately with a good diet before and after exercising.

So why is the sport drink industry a 700 million dollar gold mine? Because the drinks taste better! The better a drink tastes, the more likely people are to drink enough of it to stay properly hydrated. And although the sports drinks themselves don't actually improve performance, the fact that people drink more of them than they would plain water, and are therefore more hydrated, increases performance. So the sports drinks won't really increase your performance any more than maintaining a good diet and staying hydrated with water during exercise.

Electrolytes are the key to sports drinks and dehydration. But what are electrolytes, and how do they get into the drink? How do we measure how much of them are in the drink? What other reactions do they produce? And how do the properties of water change when electrolytes are added?

(Information from "Sports Drinks: Don't Sweat the Small Stuff" by Tim Graham, from the February 1999 issue of *ChemMatters*, a publication of the American Chemical Society.)

Sports Drinks

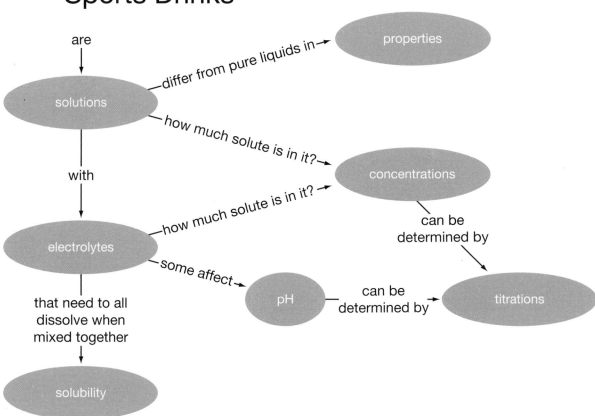

Solutions and Electrolytes

How ionic compounds dissolve in water

In the last chapter, you learned that water is a polar molecule. Many ionic compounds dissolve in water. The polar regions of the water are attracted to the charges of the ionic compound. The positive area of a water molecule is attracted to the negative anion in the ionic compound, and the negative portion of water is attracted to the positive cation. Water molecules surround the ions on the outer layers of the solid ionic compound. Once a cation is surrounded by enough water molecules that it has a greater attraction for the water molecules than for the anions in the ionic compound, it moves off, surrounded by those water molecules. The same process happens with the anions. As these ions move off with water molecules, a new layer of ions is exposed in the solid ionic compound and the process can continue. The process of water molecules pulling away the

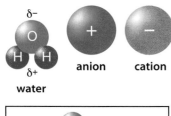

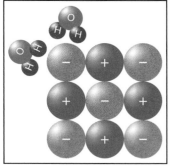

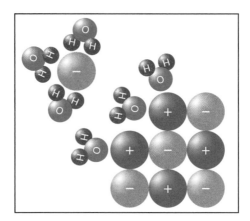

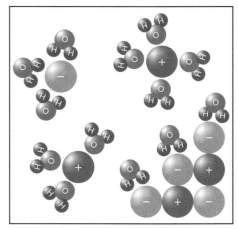

Figure 6–1. Hydration of an electrolyte. The water molecules' partially positive regions attach to anions and carry them away, while the water's partially negative regions attach to cations and carry them away. The positive and negative ions floating in water can now conduct electricity—they are **electrolytes.**

ions from an ionic compound is called **hydration,** and it is what occurs when an ionic compound dissolves in water (Figure 6–1).

A misconception about dissolving

Many people think that when a substance dissolves in water that it disappears somehow. This isn't true, of course—all the atoms are still there. However, before the substance dissolves, it is in one large mass; there are enough particles packed together that we can easily see them. As the water moves particles away from the mass one by one as described above, the particles become separate and we cannot see the individual particles anymore—they are much too tiny individually. So the substance has just been pulled into pieces that are too tiny for us to see anymore, rather than being in one large group—but they are all still there.

Forming electrolytes in water

Once the ions are hydrated, they are free-floating and move around independently of the other ions. The process of breaking up an ionic compound into the separate ions is called **ionization** or **dissociation.** Free-floating ions in water conduct electricity. When an ionic compound ionizes completely (all the ions separate), it is called a strong electrolyte, because the many free ions conduct electricity easily. An example of a strong electrolyte is table salt (NaCl). For a weak electrolyte, only a relatively few molecules ionize; most stay together. Therefore, only a few ions are available to conduct electricity, and they do so weakly. Vinegar (HCH_3COO) is a weak electrolyte.

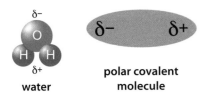

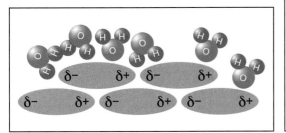

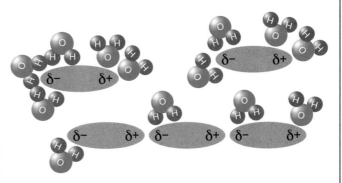

Figure 6-2. Hydration of a non-electrolyte. The water molecules' partially positive and negative regions are attracted to the regions of the opposite charge on the polar solute. Because there are no free-floating ions to conduct electricity, it is a non-electrolyte.

Non-electrolytes are substances that do not conduct electricity when dissolved in water. They do not ionize when they dissolve. Many polar covalent molecules dissolve in water, as you saw in the last chapter, but they do not conduct electricity. The hydration process occurs with these polar molecules as well—the positive portion of the water molecule is attracted to the negative portion of the polar solute molecule, and vice versa. These polar covalent molecules are separated from each other and carried away, surrounded by the water molecules. However, the polar covalent molecules are not made of ions; they share electrons with each other and therefore are not made up of cations and anions like ionic compounds. Because the polar covalent molecules do not separate into ions, dissolving them in water does not create free-floating charges that can conduct electricity. Therefore, polar covalent molecules can dissolve in water, but they do not conduct electricity (Figure 6–2). An example of a non-electrolyte is sugar ($C_6H_{12}O_6$).

Pure water also does not conduct electricity, because it is polar covalent. Tap water, however, may conduct electricity, if it has many electrolytes dissolved in it (tap water is a mixture, whereas pure water is a compound).

Clarification of terms

The terms can become confusing—"strong electrolyte," "weak electrolyte," or "non-electrolyte" refers to the entire compound, and describes whether it breaks up into ions when dissolved in water. However, the term *electrolyte* (as used when talking about the electrolytes in our body or sports drinks) refers to the free-floating ions, not to the whole compound from which it came.

Solution Saturation and Temperature

Purpose To observe the solubility of KBr as temperature changes

Instructions Design a lab to determine the mass of KBr that will dissolve in at least five different temperatures of water. Use no more than 10 mL of water for each trial in order to keep your usage of KBr reasonable. Your write-up must include:

- **Title**

- **Purpose**

- **Background information** (what you know about how molecules move at different temperatures, etc.)

- **Hypothesis** (make sure to include the "why")

- **Variables and constants**

- **Materials**

   ! **Safety** Use caution with any hot glassware or hot plate/Bunsen burner. Wear goggles when working with chemicals and hot water.

- **Procedure**

- **Observations**

- **Data table**

- **Results/Calculations** Make a solubility curve (a graph of amount of KBr dissolved versus temperature).

- **Conclusion** Restate the purpose. Give your results. Was your hypothesis supported? If not, what new explanations can you give for your results? Explain how you think the temperature, motion of the molecules, and ability to dissolve are related, and why. What are at least two possible sources of error in this lab? How could this type of information or investigation be used in the real world?

Making a solution

Solutions are made from a solvent and a solute. The solvent does the dissolving, whereas the solute is dissolved. This section has used water as the solvent. Water is often called the "universal solvent" because it is used to dissolve so many things.

When a solution has dissolved all the solute that it can hold, it is called a **saturated** solution. The solvent cannot hold even one more molecule of solute—if any more were added, it would remain a solid. If it is holding less than the maximum that can dissolve, the solution is called an **unsaturated** solution. In an unsaturated solution, if more molecules of the solute are added, they will dissolve into the solution until the maximum of solute particles is reached and the solution is saturated.

It is possible to get a solution to hold more than the maximum amount of solute at a certain temperature. For most substances, increasing the temperature will increase the amount of solute that dissolves. (There are a few substances that dissolve more in cooler temperatures, but those are far less common.) If the saturated solution is warmed, it no longer contains the maximum amount of solute—the maximum has been raised as the temperature has been raised, and it is now an unsaturated solution. More solute can be added to the solution at the higher temperature. When the solution is cooled back down again, it now has more solute particles dissolved than it ordinarily would have been able to hold at the lower temperature. This is called a **supersaturated** solution.

Example 6.1

Electrolytes

Break the following strong electrolytes into ions.

1. $NaNO_3$

$NaNO_3 \rightarrow Na^+ + NO_3^-$

2. $CaCl_2$

$CaCl_2 \rightarrow Ca^{+2} + 2\,Cl^-$

PRACTICE 6.1

Solutions and Electrolytes

1. Sodium is added to sports drinks in the form of sodium chloride (table salt). The salt is added to provide the sodium electrolyte that is lost through sweating. However, a major reason that it is added is to get someone to drink even more—salty foods make people thirsty! Break down NaCl into electrolytes.

2. Break down the following strong electrolytes: KNO_3, Na_2SO_4, $Ca(CH_3COO)_2$, LiBr.

3. Use particle visualizations to show how the electrolytes in question 2 break down.

4. In Section 2.8, kinetics and collision theory were discussed. Increasing surface area was said to increase the rate of reaction. Explain why, at the molecular level, increasing the surface area of the solid will increase the rate of dissolving.

5. Sun tea is made from placing a see-through container of water with tea bags in a sunny window or on a porch. The sun heats the water, and the tea brews. The tea is then refrigerated and served as iced tea. Explain why adding sugar to the sun tea during or immediately after removing it from the sunny place would result in a different-tasting drink than adding sugar right before you drink it.

Go Online
Check your understanding
http://webcom4.grtxle.com/khk12Chemistry

Salt crystals under a microscope.

Concentrations of Solutions

There are several ways to measure the concentration of a solution. **Concentration** describes how much solute is in how much solvent—the ratio of solute to solvent (Figure 6–3).

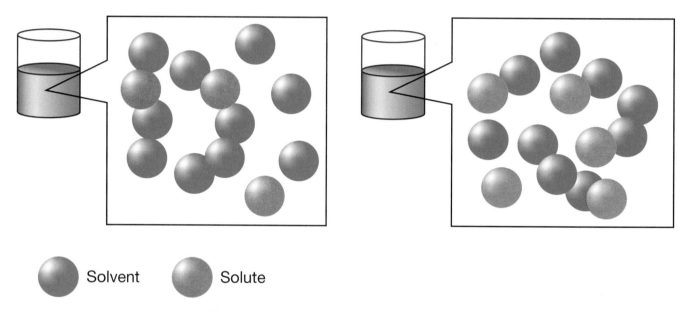

Solvent   Solute

Figure 6–3. Concentration. The solution on the left has less solute in the same volume of solution. The solution on the right has more solute. The solution on the right has a higher concentration.

Percent concentration

Go Online
Animated examples
http://webcom4.grtxle.com/
khk12Chemistry

Concentrations of solutions are often reported in percent weight per volume, %(W/V). Percent weight/volume is the percentage of the weight (more correctly, mass; although they are not scientifically the same thing, our language often interchanges the two) of the solute to the volume of the solution. The mass is in grams, and the volume in milliliters.

$$\%(W/V) = \frac{\text{mass solute}}{\text{volume solution}} \times 100$$

Example 6.2A

Concentration in %(W/V)

Find the %(W/V) of a sample that has 14.5 g solute in 150 mL of solution.

$$\%(W/V) = \frac{\text{mass solute}}{\text{volume solution}} \times 100 \qquad \%(W/V) = \frac{14.5\ g}{150\ mL} \times 100 = 9.67\%(W/V)$$

Molarity concentration

The %(W/V) unit is useful for making solutions because mass and volume are both easily measured in the lab. However, chemical equations don't use masses to balance, they use molecules or moles. Another unit for showing concentration that uses moles is molarity (M) (remember in these calculations that 0.001 L = 1 mL).

$$\text{Molarity} = \frac{\text{mole solute}}{\text{L solution}}$$

Example 6.2B

Concentration in Molarity

Find the molarity of a solution that has 26.5 g NaCl dissolved in 500 mL of solution.

- Change grams to moles for NaCl:

$$26.5\ g\ NaCl \times \frac{1\ mole\ NaCl}{58.44\ g\ NaCl} = 0.453\ mole\ NaCl$$

- Change mL to L:

$$500\ mL \times \frac{0.001\ L}{1\ mL} = 0.500\ L$$

- Find molarity:

$$\text{Molarity} = \frac{\text{mole solute}}{\text{L solution}}$$

$$\frac{0.453\ mole\ NaCl}{0.500\ L} = 0.906\ M\ NaCl$$

Converting between %(W/V) and molarity

%(W/V) uses mass in grams of the solute and volume in mL of the solution. Molarity uses moles of solute and liters of solution. We can convert back and forth between them because we can convert between grams and moles of solute, and we can also convert between milliliters and liters of solution.

Example 6.2C

Converting Between % and Molarity

A 750 mL sample is 0.55 M $CaCl_2$. Find the %(W/V).

- For %(W/V) we will need the grams solute and the mL solution.

- We already have the mL solution, so we'll need to use the molarity to find the grams solute.

- Use molarity and volume to find moles.

- First the volume needs to be in liters to be used with molarity: 750 mL = 0.750 L

$$Molarity = \frac{mole\ solute}{L\ solution}$$

$$0.55\ M\ CaCl_2 = \frac{x\ mole\ CaCl_2}{0.750\ L}$$

- Solve for moles:

$$(0.750\ L) \times (0.55\ M\ CaCl_2) = 0.41\ mole\ CaCl_2$$

- Change grams to moles:

$$0.41\ mole\ CaCl_2 \times \frac{110.98\ g\ CaCl_2}{1\ mole\ CaCl_2} = 46\ g\ CaCl_2$$

- Find %(W/V)—remember to use mL solution!

$$\%(W/V) = \frac{mass\ solute}{mL\ solution} \times 100 =$$

$$\frac{46\ g\ CaCl_2}{750.\ mL} \times 100 = 6.1\%\ (W/V)$$

Concentration of electrolytes

When ionic compounds dissolve and form electrolytes, the concentration for the individual electrolytes can be different from the concentration of the overall compound. You must take into consideration how the compound breaks up into electrolytes.

Example 6.2D

Concentration of Electrolytes

A solution is 0.55 M $CaCl_2$ (a strong electrolyte). Find the concentration of the ions.

$$CaCl_2 \rightarrow Ca^{+2} + 2\ Cl^-$$

- For every one $CaCl_2$, there will be 1 Ca^{+2} ion. You will get 1 Ca^{+2} mole for every 1 $CaCl_2$ mole. *The concentration of Ca^{+2} is 0.55 M.*

- For every one $CaCl_2$, there will be 2 Cl^- ions. You will get 2 Cl^- moles for every 1 $CaCl_2$ mole. *The concentration of Cl^- is 1.10 M.*

Concentrations of Solutions

Go Online
Check your understanding
http://webcom4.grtxle.com/
khk12Chemistry

1. The minimum recommendation for carbohydrates in a sports drink is 14 grams in a 240 mL serving. What is the concentration of carbohydrates in the drink in %(W/V)? The maximum recommendation is 20 grams in a 240 mL serving. What is this %(W/V)?

2. Use particle visualizations to show a solution before and after more solute has been added to the container.

3. The minimum recommendation for sodium in a sports drink is 50 mg in a 240 mL serving. What is the concentration of sodium in the drink in %(W/V)? (Hint: Change milligrams to grams first.) The maximum recommendation is 100 mg in a 240 mL serving. What is this concentration in %(W/V)?

4. A drink that is more than 3% salt will actually dehydrate you instead of rehydrating you. The excess electrolytes are eliminated from the body by the kidneys, through producing urine. Excess urination will dehydrate the body. What is the molarity of 240 mL of a 3%(W/V) NaCl solution?

5. What is the molarity of the solution produced when 145 g of sodium chloride is dissolved in enough water to make 2.75 L of solution?

6. How many grams of potassium chloride are needed to prepare 0.750 L of a 1.50 M solution?

7. What is the molarity of the solution produced when 85.6 g of HCl is dissolved in sufficient water to prepare 0.385 L of solution?

8. To produce 3.00 L of a 1.90 M solution of sodium hydroxide, how many grams of sodium hydroxide must be dissolved?

9. If 8.77 g of potassium iodide are dissolved in sufficient water to make 4.75 L of solution,

    a. what is the molarity of the solution,?

    b. what is the molarity of K^+ and I^- in the solution?

    c. what is the total ion molarity?

10. In order to prepare 2.00 L of a 3.00 M solution of iron(III) chloride, how many grams of iron(III) chloride must be used?

11. If 35.0 g $CaCl_2$ is added to 250.0 mL of water, what is the concentration in

    a. %(W/V)?

    b. Molarity?

    c. What are the molarities of Ca^{+2} and Cl^- in the solution?

    d. What is the total ion molarity?

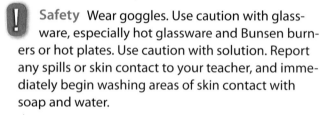
LAB 6.2

Concentration of Solutions

Problem To find the concentration of a $CuCl_2$ solution; the concentration is to be found in molarity and in %(W/V)

Instructions You will be given 50 mL of a $CuCl_2$ solution with unknown concentration. Design a lab to find the concentration of the solution that includes the following elements. (Remember that it sometimes helps to think about these problems backward—what quantities are needed to solve for the two concentration units? How can you design a procedure and data table to measure those needed quantities?)

- **Title**

- **Problem**

- **Background information** (about concentrations and the two units of concentration you'll use)

- **Materials**

> [!] **Safety** Wear goggles. Use caution with glassware, especially hot glassware and Bunsen burners or hot plates. Use caution with solution. Report any spills or skin contact to your teacher, and immediately begin washing areas of skin contact with soap and water.

- **Procedure**

- **Data table**

- **Results/Calculations**

- **Conclusion** Restate your problem, give your results, give two possible sources of error (be specific) and one way that this type of technique could be used in real life.

- **Create a class histogram of results.** (See Lab 2.7, Discussion question 5 for instructions.) Describe the class results. Is there a clear mode? If not, give possible reasons.

SECTION 6.3

Acidity and pH

In Chapter 2, pH was measured for various household substances. pH was also used in the final lab project to judge the effectiveness of antacids. But what does pH really measure?

Calculating pH from concentration of hydronium

You learned in Chapter 2 that acids donate an H^+ ion in water to form H_3O^+ (the hydronium ion); see Figure 6–4. A strong acid is one in which

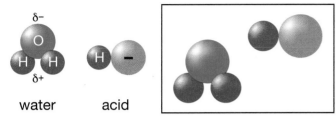

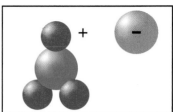

water   acid

Figure 6–4. Acid dissociating in water. From left to right, the water and acid approach each other; the partially negative portion of the water molecule is attracted to the partially positive portion of the acid (the hydrogen atom). The acid dissociates, leaving an H_3O^+ hydronium ion and the anion from the acid.

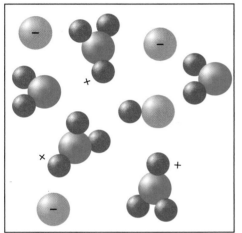
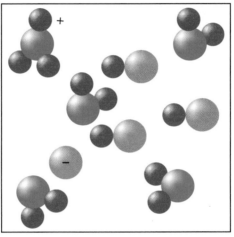

strong acid   weak acid

Figure 6–5. Strong versus weak acid. On the left is a strong acid; most of the acid molecules have dissociated. On the right is a weak acid; only a small portion of the acid molecules have dissociated in the water.

every molecule of the acid donates its hydrogen cation. A weak acid has only a few acid molecules that donate the hydrogen cation; the rest do not dissociate (Figure 6–5).

The "p" is a mathematical symbol that stands for "–log." A **logarithm (log)** is an exponent that helps us to compute. For example, a log helps you to measure the pH or acidity of a chemical solution. The pH is the negative logarithm of the concentration of free hydrogen ions, so the pH is the "–log H."

The pH is the –log of the concentration of the hydronium ion in water. The concentration is in molarity, and is symbolized by $[H_3O^+]$ in the pH equation. As $[H_3O^+]$ increases, the pH decreases (Figure 6–6).

$$pH = -\log[H_3O^+]$$

The log scale is based on 10's; $\log_{10}(x) = y$, where y is the power to which 10 is raised to obtain x. In other words, $10^y = x$. For example, $\log_{10}(100) = 2$ because $10^2 = 100$.

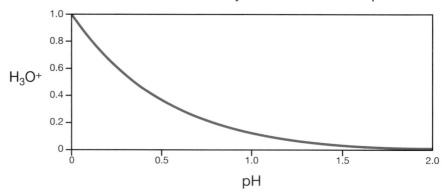

Concentration of hydronium ion versus pH

H_3O^+

Figure 6–6. When the concentration of hydronium ion is high, the pH is low, and vice versa.

The difference between each pH value means there is a difference in the concentration of the hydronium ion of 10 times (10×). For example, there are 10× as many hydronium ions in a solution that has a pH of 3 as in a solution with a pH of 4. Figure 6–7 shows the relationship between acidity and pH.

Log scales have no units—pH has no units.

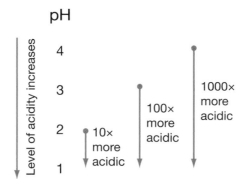

pH

Level of acidity increases

10× more acidic

100× more acidic

1000× more acidic

Figure 6–7. This chart shows how the level of acidity increases with each decrease in pH.

Solving for concentration of hydronium

Often the pH of a sample is known, but the concentration of the hydronium ion is what is needed. The pH equation can be rearranged algebraically to solve for the concentration of the hydronium ion.

$$[H_3O^+] = 10^{-pH}$$

Strength of acids and pH

Because most of the molecules of a strong acid produce hydronium ions in water, you don't need as many of the strong acid molecules to begin with before the concentration of hydronium starts to climb and the pH goes down. However, in a weak acid, relatively few molecules dissociate and produce hydronium ions—a lot of weak acid molecules must be added to the solution before very many of them produce hydronium. It takes a high concentration of a weak acid to lower the pH by the same amount as a small amount of strong acid.

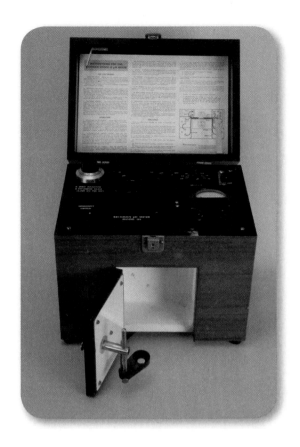

The Beckman pH-meter, Model G, was truly a revolution in pH measurement. Originally introduced as a way to measure the acidity of lemons, chemists soon realized its potential and began using it around the country. What made the Beckman G so revolutionary in the 1930s was its compact, self-contained system of electronics and electrodes that allowed chemists to easily and quickly determine the pH of almost any solution.

Bases

As you learned in Chapter 2, bases produce the hydroxide ion (OH^-) in water. As for the acids, a strong base is one in which all the molecules of the base produce hydroxide ions. A weak base has only a few of the base molecules producing hydroxide ions in water (Figure 6–8).

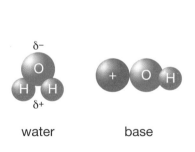

water   base

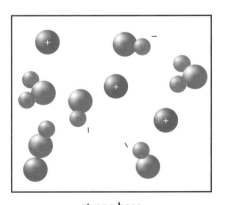

strong base

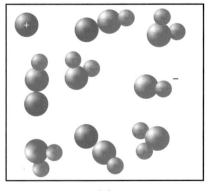

weak base

Figure 6–8. Strong versus weak base. The left shows a strong base; almost all the base molecules have dissociated in water. The right shows a weak base; a very small portion of the base molecules have dissociated.

Acids and bases are electrolytes

A strong acid is one that donates its hydronium ion to water; this means that it is dissociating the hydrogen cation from the anion. This forms electrolytes, as discussed in section 6.1. A strong acid is one that dissociates all its molecules. Therefore, a strong acid is a strong electrolyte, whereas a weak acid is a weak electrolyte.

Bases form the hydroxide ion in water; this means that bases are also electrolytes. Just as with acids, strong bases are strong electrolytes and weak bases are weak electrolytes.

Autoionization of water

Water will autoionize—it will split into ions on its own (2 $H_2O \rightarrow$ $H_3O^+ + OH^-$). Water will do this until the product of the hydronium ion concentration and the hydroxide ion concentration in a solution is equal to 1.0×10^{-14} at 25°C.

$$[H_3O^+] \times [OH^-] = 1.0 \times 10^{-14}$$

If the concentration of hydronium is greater than the concentration of hydroxide, the sample will be acidic. Likewise, if the concentration of hydroxide is greater than that of hydronium, the sample is basic. Both will be present because of the autoionization of water, but one may be in a higher concentration than the other. If the concentration of the two ions is equal, the solution is neutral, and the pH is 7.

Example 6.3

pH Calculations

1. Find the pH of a solution with a hydronium concentration of 1.5×10^{-4}.

$$pH = -\log[H_3O^+] = -\log(1.5 \times 10^{-4}) = 3.82$$

2. Find the hydronium concentration of a solution with a pH of 10.7.

$$[H_3O^+] = 10^{-pH} = 10^{-10.7} = 1.99 \times 10^{-11} \text{ M}$$

3. Find the hydroxide concentration of a solution with a pH of 12.5.

- First find the hydronium concentration:

$$[H_3O^+] = 10^{-pH} = 10^{-12.5} = 3.16 \times 10^{-13} \text{ M}$$

- Then use the hydronium concentration to find the hydroxide concentration:

$$1 \times 10^{-14} = [H_3O^+][OH^-],$$

$$1 \times 10^{-14} = [3.16 \times 10^{-13} \text{ M}][OH^-],$$

$$\frac{1 \times 10^{-14}}{3.16 \times 10^{-13}} = [OH^-] = 0.0316 \text{ M}$$

pH

1. What would you expect the pH of a lemon-lime flavored drink to be—above or below 7? Why?

2. The pH of a sports drink can be as low as 2.38. (Such an acidic drink can be harmful to your teeth!) What is the hydronium concentration in such a sample?

3. How many times more acidic is a solution with a pH of 2 compared to one with a pH of 6?

4. Use particle visualizations to draw a solution with a pH of 2 versus a solution with a pH of 3.

5. Use particle visualizations to draw a solution with a pH of 8 versus a solution with a pH of 7.

6. If pH of the body drops below 6.8 or rises above 7.8, death can occur. What are the hydronium ion concentrations for these pH's?

7. What are the corresponding hydroxide concentrations for question 6?

8. Find the pH if the $[H_3O^+]$ is:
   (a) 1.5×10^{-2} M; (b) 0.15 M; (c) 0.000045 M; (d) 2.9×10^{-4} M.

9. Find the $[H_3O^+]$ if the pH is:
   (a) 11.5; (b) 1.5; (c) 7.0; (d) 8.2.

10. Find the $[OH^{-1}]$ of the following:
    (a) pH = 8.9; (b) $[H_3O^+]$ = 0.000035 M; (c) pH = 2.6; (d) $[H_3O^+]$ = 2.65 M.

Go Online
Check your understanding
http://webcom4.grtxle.com/
khk12Chemistry

SECTION 6.4

Solubility and Precipitation

LAB 6.4

Solubility and Precipitation

Purpose To observe precipitation reactions and determine solubility rules

Materials Solutions of electrolytes, well-plate

Safety You will be using very small amounts in this lab, but you still need to use caution with the solutions. Silver nitrate (the Ag^+ solution, and the product in several of the other reactions) will stain your clothing and skin a black/brown color. Chromates (in the CrO_4^{-2} solution) are known carcinogens. Wear goggles at all times. Report spills or skin contact to your teacher, and immediately begin to wash areas of skin contact with soap and water.

(continues)

Solubility and Precipitation (*cont'd.*)

Procedure

1. It may help to place the well-plate on top of a white piece of paper so that you can see the colors of solutions and precipitates better.

2. Place 4–5 drops of each solution in the wells on the well-plate to match the data table below. The same anion is added in every well in a column, and the same cation is added in every well in a row.

3. Record observations about whether a precipitate forms, and, if so, what color it is.

Data table

	Cl^-	CrO_4^{-2}	SO_4^{-2}	NO_3^-
Na^+				
Ag^+				
Ba^{+2}				
Ca^{+2}				

Discussion

1. For each precipitation reaction that occurred, write the balanced equation. Use the cation and the anion as the reactants, and the precipitate as the product. Be sure to include the charges when writing cations and anions that are not in a compound.

2. For each of the anions used in the lab, make a list of cations that it is not soluble with—the cations with which it formed a precipitate. You've created a set of solubility rules.

3. Which anion(s) were the least likely to form a precipitate? Which were the likeliest? What about the cations?

4. AgCl is used in black-and-white photography; it is the chemical that coats the photographic paper. Use your observations in this lab to explain why you must use photographic paper in a darkroom.

5. Share your solubility rules with the class. Use a whiteboard if your teacher provides one. After sharing, do you want to make any changes to your set of rules? Were there any discrepancies? How did you use evidence to resolve them?

You can't go to a shelf in the chemical storeroom and find a bottle of solid ions—the solids in those bottles are in the form of neutral compounds, not charged ions. When they are not dissolved in water, electrolytes are in the form of solid ionic compounds. The ionic compound must be neutral; therefore, if the desired electrolyte is an anion, it bonds with a cation to form a neutral compound. When the desired electrolyte is a cation, it is bonded to an anion to form a neutral compound. A desired cation electrolyte and a desired anion electrolyte could bond together to form a neutral compound, as well. These compounds must be soluble in water in order to produce electrolytes.

Precipitation reactions

When you add these soluble ionic compounds to the water, they dissolve and produce electrolytes. However, the ions could bond with other ions in the solution and form an insoluble compound. The insoluble compound is called a **precipitate**. A precipitate is the insoluble compound that forms from the chemical reaction between two soluble salts. This reaction is then called a **precipitation reaction**. A precipitation reaction is another example of a double replacement reaction. (Acid–base neutralization was an example of a double replacement reaction discussed in Chapter 2.)

Go Online
Animated examples
http://webcom4.grtxle.com/
khk12Chemistry

When writing precipitation reactions, it helps to include the state of matter after each chemical. This lets the reader know which compounds are dissolved in water and which compounds are precipitates. Compounds that dissolve in water are labeled "aq" for "aqueous." The precipitates are labeled with an "s" to show that they are a solid, and are not dissolved in the water.

General form of double replacement reaction:

$$AX + BY \rightarrow AY + BX$$

Example of precipitation reaction:

$$AgNO_3 \text{ (aq)} + NaCl \text{ (aq)} \rightarrow AgCl \text{ (s)} + NaNO_3 \text{ (aq)}$$

Solubility of ionic compounds

Why are some ionic compounds soluble in water, whereas others are not? If the attraction between the ions in the ionic compound is greater than the attraction between the water and the ions, the water cannot "pull" hard enough on the ions to cause them to separate from the other ions. In other words, the ions of the ionic compound are more stable with each other than they are when hydrated by water molecules, and therefore they don't separate into electrolytes and dissolve.

Go Online
Molecular animations
http://webcom4.grtxle.com/
khk12Chemistry

Solubility rules

There are charts and tables that you can look at to determine whether a combination of a cation and an anion will dissolve or not. A table of solubility rules can be used when writing chemical reactions to determine whether a product will be insoluble and will form a precipitate. One such table is at the end of this chapter on page 249.

Example 6.4

Precipitation Reactions

Finish the following equation: $CaCl_2 + AgNO_3 \rightarrow$

- Indicate which products are aq (they dissolve in water) and which are precipitates (label as *s)*. If nothing precipitates, write "no ppt."

- First, finish the reaction by writing the products (it will be a double replacement reaction).

- Write the formulas of the products correctly by balancing charges:

$$CaCl_2 + AgNO_3 \rightarrow AgCl + Ca(NO_3)_2$$

- Then balance the chemical equation:

$$1\ CaCl_2 + 2\ AgNO_3 \rightarrow 2\ AgCl + 1\ Ca(NO_3)_2$$

- Then use the solubility rules to determine which compounds dissolve in water and which don't:

$$1\ CaCl_2\ (aq) + 2\ AgNO_3\ (aq) \rightarrow 2\ AgCl\ (s) + 1\ Ca(NO_3)_2\ (aq)$$

Go Online
Check your understanding
http://webcom4.grtxle.com/
khk12Chemistry

PRACTICE 6.4

Precipitation Reactions

Finish the following reactions and balance the equations. Remember that you must write chemical formulas correctly (by balancing their charges) before you balance the equation. Indicate which products are aq (they dissolve in water) and which are precipitates (s). If nothing precipitates, write "no ppt."

1. $NaNO_3 + K_2CO_3 \rightarrow$

2. $AgNO_3 + KBr \rightarrow$

3. $Cu(NO_3)_2 + NaOH \rightarrow$

4. $NaCH_3COO + NH_4NO_3 \rightarrow$

5. $K_2SO_4 + NaNO_3 \rightarrow$

6. $KI + Pb(NO_3)_2 \rightarrow$

7. $Pb(NO_3)_2 + CuCl_2 \rightarrow$

8. $K_2CO_3 + LiNO_3 \rightarrow$

9. $Ca(CH_3COO)_2 + Na_3PO_4 \rightarrow$

10. $Ba(OH)_2 + Na_2SO_4 \rightarrow$

Stoichiometry

LAB 6.5A

Introduction to Stoichiometry

Purpose To use acid/base neutralization reactions to introduce the idea of stoichiometry

Background information Acids react with bases. Phenolphthalein is used as an indicator—it's colorless in acids, and pink in bases. You will put the indicator in the NaOH (base), and add acid until all of the base has reacted and the solution is neutral (colorless).

Materials 0.1 M solutions of NaOH, HNO_3, HCl, H_2SO_4, test tube, test tube rack, 3 plastic pipettes, phenolphthalein indicator

> ⚠ **Safety** Use caution with glassware. These chemicals will cause harm. Report any spills or contact with skin to your teacher, and immediately begin washing any affected skin with soap and water.

Procedure

1. Be careful not to mix up the pipettes throughout the lab—keep them for use in only one chemical each. When adding drops, be sure that they go down to the bottom of the test tube and don't get stuck on the side.

2. Add 20 drops of NaOH solution to your test tube.

3. Add 1–2 drops of indicator to turn the basic solution pink.

4. Add HCl one drop at a time, shaking after each drop to mix the solution. Continue adding HCl slowly until the solution turns colorless. Try not to add extra acid—just enough to turn the solution colorless. Record the number of drops required.

(continues)

Introduction to Stoichiometry (*cont'd.*)

5. Wash out the test tube and repeat steps 2–4 with NaOH and HNO_3.

6. Wash out the test tube and repeat steps 2–4 with NaOH and H_2SO_4.

Data table

	HCl	HNO$_3$	H$_2$SO$_4$
Drops added			

Discussion

1. Write the balanced equation for the neutralization (double replacement reaction) between NaOH and HCl.

2. Write the balanced equation for the neutralization (double replacement reaction) between NaOH and HNO_3.

3. Write the balanced equation for the neutralization (double replacement reaction) between NaOH and H_2SO_4.

4. Determine the class average for drops of HCl, HNO_3, and H_2SO_4 that were required to neutralize the 20 drops of NaOH.

5. Because each solution had the same concentration (0.1 M), they each have the same number of molecules per drop. So we can think of the number of drops as counting the number of molecules. Use the class averages to find the ratio of HCl drops/NaOH drops. Repeat to determine the average HNO_3 drops/NaOH drops, and the average H_2SO_4 drops/NaOH drops.

6. What do you notice about these ratios and the balanced chemical equation?

7. If you had put in 30 drops of NaOH, how many drops of HCl, HNO_3, or H_2SO_4 would have been required to turn the solution neutral?

8. If the coefficients of a balanced equation tell us how many molecules of each reactant are needed to complete one and only one reaction, then we can also use them to tell moles of each chemical needed (remember, moles are a way of counting molecules in large groups). If you have 0.15 mole NaOH, how many moles HCl, HNO_3, and H_2SO_4 are needed to neutralize the reaction?

Go Online
Animated examples
http://webcom4.grtxle.com/
khk12Chemistry

Mole ratio in a balanced chemical equation

When compounds react, the balanced equation gives the ratio of the compounds that are reacted and the ratio of the compounds that are produced.

For example, in the equation $2 \ AgNO_3 + 1 \ BaCl_2 \rightarrow 2 \ AgCl + 1 \ Ba(NO_3)_2$, for every two molecules of silver nitrate that react, one molecule of barium chloride is reacted. And for every set of two silver nitrates and one barium chloride that react, two silver chlorides and one barium nitrate molecule will be produced. However, molecules are too tiny to count them one by one, so we use the counting unit of moles (as discussed in Chapter 3) to count molecules in larger groups. For example, for every two moles of silver nitrate molecules and one mole of barium chloride molecules that react, two moles of silver chloride molecules and one mole of barium nitrate molecules are produced. See the table below for how these proportions might play out in different situations.

	What's being reacted		What will be produced	
	2 AgNO$_3$ +	1 BaCl$_2$ $\rightarrow$	2 AgCl +	1 Ba(NO$_3$)$_2$
Situation 1	2 moles reacted	1 mole reacted	2 moles produced	1 mole produced
Situation 2	4 moles reacted	2 moles reacted	4 moles produced	2 moles produced
Situation 3	1 mole reacted	0.5 mole reacted	1 mole produced	0.5 mole produced

The mole ratio from a balanced equation can be used to determine information about one of the chemical compounds from information about a different compound in the same reaction. This is called **stoichiometry**. The key ingredient for success in stoichiometry is having a correctly written and balanced chemical equation to begin with.

Example 6.5A

Stoichiometry with Moles

- Based on the balanced equation 2 AgNO$_3$ + 1 BaCl$_2$ $\rightarrow$ 2 AgCl + 1 Ba(NO$_3$)$_2$, if you react 3.5 moles of AgNO$_3$, how many moles of barium nitrate will be produced?

- You must be in the units of mole to switch from one chemical to another. In this problem, you are in the units of mole, so you may immediately switch from AgNO$_3$ to Ba(NO$_3$)$_2$ using the ratio found in the balanced equation.

$$3.5 \text{ mole AgNO}_3 \times \frac{1 \text{ mole Ba(NO}_3)_2}{2 \text{ mole AgNO}_3} = 1.75 \text{ mole Ba(NO}_3)_2$$

Molecular mass and finding moles for stoichiometry

In Chapter 3, you learned how to convert between moles and mass using the molecular mass. Often the mass of a substance can be determined in the lab, but the moles are needed for stoichiometry. Therefore, the molecular mass is needed to convert back and forth. Remember that when you are converting between grams and moles, the molecular mass is always the number of grams equal to one mole—do not look at the balanced chemical equation when converting between grams and moles. The coefficient in the balanced equation is only used for switching between chemicals (in the unit of moles).

Example 6.5B

Stoichiometry with Masses

Based on the balanced equation 2 AgNO₃ + 1 BaCl₂ → 2 AgCl + 1 Ba(NO₃)₂, if you react 15.5 g of $AgNO_3$, how many grams of barium nitrate will be produced?

- You will need to compare one chemical to another in order to complete this problem.

- You may only compare chemicals in the unit of moles. This problem has the given information in grams. Therefore, you must convert grams to moles using the molecular mass—then you can compare chemicals and complete the problem.

$$15.5 \text{ g AgNO}_3 \times \frac{1 \text{ mole AgNO}_3}{169.91 \text{ g AgNO}_3} \times \frac{1 \text{ mole Ba(NO}_3)_2}{2 \text{ mole AgNO}_3} \times \frac{261.32 \text{ g Ba(NO}_3)_2}{1 \text{ mole Ba(NO}_3)_2} = 11.9 \text{ g Ba(NO}_3)_2$$

Molarity and finding moles for stoichiometry

Go Online
Animated examples
http://webcom4.grtxle.com/
khk12Chemistry

Earlier in this chapter, the unit of molarity was discussed. Molarity is the ratio of moles of solute to liters of solution. Therefore, molarity can be used to convert between volume and moles. Once we know how many moles are in the solution, we can use this information for stoichiometry.

Example 6.5C

Stoichiometry with Solutions

What volume of a 0.10 M solution of NaOH is needed to completely react with 250 mL of a 0.10 M solution of H_2CO_3? The chemical reaction is 1 H₂CO₃ + 2 NaOH → 1 Na₂CO₃ + 2 H₂O.

- Because the question is asking for information about the NaOH, you should begin the problem with the other chemical (H₂CO₃), which we know more about. You can use the molarity to convert

between the L and moles, but you need the volume to be in L in order to do that (so 250 mL = 0.250 L).

- Once you have converted between L and moles, you can use the balanced equation to compare chemicals. Once you are at the correct chemical, you can use the molarity of NaOH to convert back to volume.

$$0.250 \text{ L H}_2\text{CO}_3 \times \frac{0.10 \text{ mole H}_2\text{CO}_3}{1 \text{ L H}_2\text{CO}_3} \times \frac{2 \text{ mole NaOH}}{1 \text{ mole H}_2\text{CO}_3} \times \frac{1 \text{ L NaOH}}{0.10 \text{ mole NaOH}} = 0.500 \text{ L NaOH}$$

Combining molecular mass and molarity in stoichiometry problems

A problem doesn't have to begin and end with the same unit. A stoichiometry problem could begin with the mass of one compound and end with the concentration of another, or vice versa.

Example 6.5D

Combination Stoichiometry

How many grams of NaOH are needed to neutralize 250 mL of a 0.10 M H_2CO_3 solution? The balanced equation is $1\ H_2CO_3 + 2\ NaOH \rightarrow 1\ Na_2CO_3 + 2\ H_2O$.

- Again, the question is asking about NaOH, so begin with the information you know about the H_2CO_3. Use the molarity to convert between the volume (changed to liters) and moles.

- Then use the balanced equation to compare chemicals once you're in moles.

- Finally, convert moles NaOH back to grams using the molecular mass of NaOH.

$$0.250\ L\ H_2CO_3 \times \frac{0.10\ \text{mole}\ H_2CO_3}{1\ L\ H_2CO_3} \times \frac{2\ \text{mole}\ NaOH}{1\ \text{mole}\ H_2CO_3} \times \frac{40.00\ g\ NaOH}{1\ \text{mole}\ NaOH} = 2.00\ g\ NaOH$$

Stoichiometry with gases

In Chapter 3, you learned about gas behavior and gas laws. Using the ideal gas law, you can calculate that any gas will be 22.4 L if there is one mole of particles and they are at standard temperature (0°C and 1 atm). Therefore, at STP, 1 mole = 22.4 L of a gas. This equality can also be used in stoichiometry to convert between grams and liters of gases.

Go Online
Animated examples
http://webcom4.grtxle.com/
khk12Chemistry

If a problem asks for a volume of a gas at non-STP conditions, go ahead and use stoichiometry to find the volume at STP, and then use the combined gas law to convert the volume to the desired nonstandard conditions.

Example 6.5E

Stoichiometry with Gases

1. How many liters of oxygen are needed to completely combust 1.5 L of methane (CH_4) at STP? The balanced equation is CH_4 (g) + 2 O_2 (g) → CO_2 (g) + 2 H_2O (g).

   - Use the fact that 1 mole of gas at STP = 22.4 L to convert between L and moles.

   $$1.5\text{ L }CH_4 \times \frac{1\text{ mole }CH_4}{22.4\text{ L }CH_4} \times \frac{2\text{ mole }O_2}{1\text{ mole }CH_4} \times$$

   $$\frac{22.4\text{ L }O_2}{1\text{ mole }O_2} = 3.0\text{ L }O_2$$

2. How many liters of oxygen would be needed at 25°C and 1.2 atm? (See Section 3.7 for explanation of the gas laws.) Use the combined gas law.

   $$\frac{P_1 V_1}{T_1} = \frac{P_2 V_2}{T_2}$$

   $$\frac{(1.0\text{ atm} \times 3.0\text{ L})}{273\text{ K}} = \frac{(1.2\text{ atm} \times V_2)}{298\text{ K}}$$

   - The temperature must be in Kelvin to use the gas laws:

     $$(25°C + 273 = 298\text{ K})$$

   - Solve for V_2:

     $$\frac{(1.0\text{ atm} \times 3.0\text{ L} \times 298\text{K})}{(273\text{ K} \times 1.2\text{ atm})} = V_2 = 2.73\text{ L}$$

Keeping equalities straight

Use the table below to help you remember how to convert between different quantities.

To go between	Use the equality
Grams and moles	Molecular mass in grams = 1 mole
Moles and liters of a solution	Molarity in moles = 1 L
Moles and liters of a gas at STP	1 mole = 22.4 L at STP
Two different chemicals in a reaction	Coefficient ratio from balanced equation

Titration

Titration is a lab technique in which a solution of known concentration reacts with a solution of unknown concentration. The two solutions are reacted until every single molecule in the unknown solution has been exactly reacted with the known solution. There are no extra molecules of either reactant in the flask—they all have been matched up in the exact mole ratio from the balanced equation. This point is called the **stoichiometric point** or the **end point.**

An indicator is used to show when this point has been reached. If the stoichiometric point happens at a specific pH, then the indicator is a pH indicator, as was used in Chapter 2. There are other ways of determining when a titration is over if pH isn't a factor. Sometimes the color of one of the reacting solutions itself will change once all the molecules have been reacted. Other types of indicators can tell the presence of a certain molecule. For example, iodide indicates the presence of starch by turning blue-black. Once all the iodide is reacted, a starch solution would no longer be black.

Percent yield

Because of errors in lab technique and measurements, and reactions that don't go to completion (which will be discussed in Chapter 8), reactions don't always produce 100% of what they are supposed to based on the stoichiometry. **Percent yield** = amount actually produced/amount predicted through stoichiometry if all the reactants react × 100.

PRACTICE 6.5

Stoichiometry

Use the following equation for problems 1–6:

_____ N_2O_5 + _____ H_2O → _____ HNO_3

1. How many moles of nitric acid will be produced when 0.51 mole of dinitrogen pentoxide reacts?

2. How many moles of water are needed to produce 1.25 mole of nitric acid?

3. How many moles of water are needed to react completely with 0.78 mole of dinitrogen pentoxide?

4. How many grams of nitric acid will be produced when 0.25 mole of water reacts?

5. What is the percent yield of the last reaction if 24.25 g nitric acid are actually produced?

6. How many moles of dinitrogen pentoxide are needed to produce 5.25 g of nitric acid?

7. _____ C_6H_{14} + _____ O_2 → _____ CO_2 + _____ H_2O.
   How many grams of hexane (C_6H_{14}) would be needed to make 860.0 g of carbon dioxide?

8. What is percent yield of the last reaction if only 800 g of CO_2 reacted in the lab?

Go Online
Check your understanding
http://webcom4.grtxle.com/
khk12Chemistry

(continues)

Stoichiometry (cont'd.)

9. _____ $Al(OH)_3$ + _____ $CaCO_3 \rightarrow$ _____ $Al_2(CO_3)_3$ + _____ $Ca(OH)_2$.
How many grams of calcium hydroxide would result from 250 grams of calcium carbonate?

10. _____ $(NH_4)_2Cr_2O_7$ + _____ $Pb(NO_3)_4 \rightarrow$ _____ NH_4NO_3 + _____ $Pb(Cr_2O_7)_2$.
How many grams of lead(IV) dichromate will be produced from 45.50 g of lead(IV) nitrate?

11. _____ Li_3N + _____ $H_2O \rightarrow$ _____ NH_3 + _____ $LiOH$.
What mass of lithium hydroxide will be produced with 0.38 g of lithium nitride reacting?

12. _____ NaI + _____ $Cl_2 \rightarrow$ _____ $NaCl$ + _____ I_2.
What mass of sodium chloride is produced when 0.29 g of sodium iodide is reacted with chlorine?

13. _____ HCl + _____ $NaOH \rightarrow$ _____ $NaCl$ + _____ HOH.
How many mL of 0.100 M HCl are needed to react completely with 50.00 mL of 0.200 M NaOH?

14. _____ HNO_3 + _____ $NaOH \rightarrow$ _____ $NaNO_3$ + _____ HOH.
How many mL of 0.150 M HNO_3 are needed to react completely with 150.00 mL of 0.250 M NaOH?

15. _____ CH_3COOH + _____ $NaOH \rightarrow$ _____ $NaCH_3COO$ + _____ HOH.
How many mL of 0.200 M CH_3COOH are needed to react completely with 70.00 mL of 0.155 M NaOH?

16. _____ HCl + _____ $Ba(OH)_2 \rightarrow$ _____ $BaCl_2$ + _____ HOH.
How many mL of 0.0500 M $Ba(OH)_2$ are needed to react completely with 55.00 mL of 0.450 M HCl?

17. _____ H_2SO_4 + _____ $NaOH \rightarrow$ _____ Na_2SO_4 + _____ HOH.
If 10.2 mL of H_2SO_4 are needed to react completely with 75.00 mL of 0.340 M NaOH, what is the concentration of the acid?

18. _____ H_3PO_4 + _____ $NaOH \rightarrow$ _____ Na_3PO_4 + _____ HOH.
If 37.8 mL of H_3PO_4 are needed to react completely with 115.00 mL of 0.250 M NaOH, what is the concentration of the acid?

19. _____ $C_6H_{12}O_6 \rightarrow$ _____ C_2H_6O + _____ CO_2.
What mass of sugar ($C_6H_{12}O_6$) is required to produce 1.82 L of carbon dioxide gas at STP?

20. _____ S_8 + _____ $O_2 \rightarrow$ _____ SO_2.
How many liters of oxygen are necessary to combust 425 g of sulfur at STP? How many liters of oxygen would be needed if you were reacting at 25°C and 0.95 atm?

21. _____ C_6H_6 + _____ $O_2 \rightarrow$ _____ H_2O + _____ CO_2.
Find the mass of benzene (C_6H_6) needed to produce 2.66 L of carbon dioxide gas at STP.

Stoichiometry: Titration

Purpose To use solution stoichiometry to find the concentration of citric acid in a drink sample

Background information Citric acid is a triprotic acid, meaning it has three hydrogens that are "acidic"—they react with bases. Phenolphthalein is used as an indicator—it's colorless in acids and pink in bases. When the reaction reaches the stoichiometric point, all of the acidic hydrogens will have reacted with NaOH. The next drop of NaOH will cause the solution to be basic, and the phenolphthalein will turn pink.

Materials Drink sample, standardized NaOH, burette, flask, phenolphthalein indicator, graduated cylinder, beaker, funnel

> **!** **Safety** Use caution with glassware. NaOH is caustic—wear goggles at all times. Report any spills or contact with skin to your teacher, and immediately begin washing any contacted skin with soap and water.

Procedure

1. Obtain about 50 mL of the NaOH solution in a beaker.

2. Close the stopcock on the burette. With a small amount of NaOH, rinse the burette, swirling it around while tilting it to rinse the entire length of the burette. Drain the NaOH out of the stopcock to rinse it out as well.

3. Fill the burette with NaOH. Drain some out until the level of the NaOH is below the top mark on the burette. Record the exact volume of the NaOH.

4. Add approximately 30 mL of the drink solution to your flask. Before you add it to the flask, record the exact amount that is added, using the graduated cylinder.

5. Add 1–2 drops of phenolphthalein indicator—remember, it is colorless in acids and pink in bases. Swirl the flask to distribute the indicator.

6. Begin adding NaOH from the burette very slowly, swirling the flask the entire time. Continue adding the base slowly until one drop makes the solution in the flask turn pink. This indicates that you have

added enough of the base to reach the stoichiometric point and then go slightly over into the basic side.

7. Continue swirling the flask for 30 seconds. If after 30 seconds of swirling, the light pink color remains, you're done; record the volume of NaOH in the burette. (NOTE—In colorless solutions, the indicator will turn pale pink when the sample is basic; what color will it be if the pale pink was added to the original color of your drink sample? Look at the example your teacher shows, if any, to be sure that the color has changed.) If the color fades and disappears, continue adding base as in step 6 until the color remains for 30 seconds of swirling.

8. Empty and rinse the flask. If you have used only about 1/3 of the burette for the first trial, it is probably not necessary to refill it for the next

(continues)

Stoichiometry: Titration (cont'd.)

trial. However, if the burette is less than about 2/3 full, refill it with NaOH until it is near the top line of the burette (you do not need to empty and rinse it, just refill). Record the exact volume of the burette.

9. Repeat steps 4–7 for a total of three trials.

10. Empty and rinse all glassware, and leave them as you found them.

Data table

	Trial 1	Trial 2	Trial 3
Volume of drink (mL)			
Molarity of standardized NaOH			
Initial volume of burette (mL)			
Final volume of burette (mL)			

Calculations

1. The reaction between citric acid ($H_3C_6H_5O_7$) and sodium hydroxide produces sodium citrate ($Na_3C_6H_5O_7$) and water. Write the formula equation and balance it.

2. For each of the three trials, find the volume of NaOH used in the titration. Convert these volumes to liters.

3. Convert the volumes of drink sample in each trial into liters.

4. Use the concentration and the volume of NaOH used in the titration to find the molarity of the citric acid in each trial.

5. Find the average molarity of the citric acid in the drink sample.

Conclusion In complete sentences, restate the purpose of the lab, give your results, give two possible sources of error. Give one way in which this type of technique could be used in real life. Share your results as a class by creating a histogram (see Lab 2.7, Discussion question 5). Describe the class results. Is there a clear statistical mode? If not, give possible reasons.

Stoichiometry: Gravimetric

Purpose To determine the concentration of sodium ions in a drink sample and compare it to the concentration advertised on the drink label

Background information Sodium ions are a desired electrolyte in sports drinks. In order to get the sodium ion into the drink, table salt (NaCl) is added. The chloride ion in table salt will precipitate with silver ions. If the amount of chloride ions that precipitates can be determined, then the amount of sodium ions can also be known.

Materials Drink sample, silver nitrate solution, graduated cylinder, 2 beakers, funnel, funnel rack (or ceramic triangle and ring), ring stand, filter paper, balance

Safety Use caution with all glassware. Wear goggles at all times. Silver nitrate causes brown spots on skin that will remain until the layers of skin are shed—avoid contact with silver nitrate.

Procedure

1. Measure out approximately 100 mL of a drink sample in a graduated cylinder. Record the exact amount.

2. Pour the drink sample into a beaker.

3. Measure out approximately 25 mL of the 0.10 M silver nitrate solution. Add to the drink solution. The silver chloride will precipitate and form a white, cloudy-looking solid.

Stoichiometry: Gravimetric (*cont'd.*)

4. Warm the solution for about 30 minutes—DO NOT BOIL! (You can complete steps 5–9 while waiting.)

5. Set up a funnel in a funnel rack (or in a ceramic triangle on a ring) and connect to ring stand.

6. Fold a piece of filter paper into quarters. Write your name on the filter paper <u>in pencil</u>.

7. Find the mass of the dry filter paper.

8. Open one side of the folded filter paper, place it in funnel, and wet it down with water.

9. Place an empty beaker under the funnel so that the tip of the funnel is inside the beaker and touching the side of the glass.

10. Decant the *cooled* solution into the funnel and allow the filtrate to drain through into the bottom beaker. Try to keep the solid precipitate in the beaker as much as you can, because it will clog the filter paper and take longer to drain.

11. When the beaker is close to empty, pour all the contents (including the precipitate) into the filter paper. Rinse the beaker out with a small amount of water, and pour the rinse water into the filter paper. Repeat the rinse a few times until all the precipitate is in the filter paper.

12. Allow the filter paper to drain.

13. Remove the filter paper, and lay on a piece of paper towel in the area designated by your teacher.

14. Clean all glassware, and leave it as you found it.

Day 2

1. Find the mass of the filter paper with the silver chloride.

2. Throw the filter paper and silver chloride in the designated trash container.

Data

Volume of drink sample _____

Concentration of silver nitrate solution _____

Mass of dry filter paper _____

Mass of filter paper and dried silver chloride _____

From the drink label, mg of sodium in one serving _____

From the drink label, mL of drink in one serving _____

Calculations

1. Write and balance the formula equation for this reaction.

2. From your data table, find the mass of silver chloride produced.

3. Use the mass of silver chloride produced to find the concentration (in molarity) of sodium chloride reacted in the drink sample using stoichiometry.

4. Write the balanced equation for the dissociation of NaCl in water.

5. When dissolved in water, sodium chloride breaks up into electrolytes (it's a strong electrolyte). Use the molarity of sodium chloride to find the molarity of sodium ions.

6. Change the molarity of sodium chloride into the %(W/V) concentration of sodium ions in the drink sample using the equation in the last question.

7. Make a list on the classroom board of the %(W/V) found for chloride ions for each type of drink sample used (if all the class used the same drink, just one list). Find the average of all the results for the type of drink that you used.

8. Figure the %(W/V) of sodium in the drink according to the information on the label.

9. Find the percent error between the average %(W/V) concentration of sodium ions and the value you figured from the bottle label.

10. Look at the ingredients on the bottle label. Is there any other possible source of Na^+ other than NaCl? How could you account for that concentration of Na^+?

Conclusion In complete sentences: restate purpose, give results, give two possible sources of error, and give one application of this type of technique in the real world. Share your results as a class by creating a histogram (see Lab 2.7, Discussion question 5). Describe the class results. Is there a clear mode? If not, give possible reasons.

Limiting Reactants

LAB 6.6

Limiting Reactants

Purpose To determine which reactant is limiting

Materials Solutions of hydrochloric acid and sodium hydroxide, graduated cylinder, beaker, materials to find the pH of a solution

Safety Use caution with glassware. Wear goggles at all times. Hydrochloric acid causes burns, and sodium hydroxide is caustic. Report all spills or exposure to skin to your teacher, and immediately begin washing exposed area with soap and water.

Procedure

1. Measure out approximately 20 mL of HCl in a graduated cylinder. Record the exact amount in the data table. Pour into clean beaker.

2. Measure out approximately 20 mL of NaOH in a graduated cylinder. Record the exact amount in the data table. Pour into beaker to react with HCl.

3. Find the pH of the solution using materials available.

4. Dispose of solution as indicated by your teacher, clean glassware, and leave it as you found it.

Data

Volume of acid reacted: _____

Concentration of acid: _____

Volume of base reacted: _____

Concentration of base: _____

pH of products: _____

Discussion

1. Write the balanced equation for the chemical reaction you performed.

2. If the two reactants in this reaction were present in exactly the amounts called for by the balanced equation (called **stoichiometric proportions**), meaning that when the reaction was complete there would be none of either reactant left over, what compounds would be in the beaker at the end of the reaction? How do you know? What would be the pH of the final solution if the reactants were present in stoichiometric proportions?

3. Using your measured pH, what compounds were present in your beaker? Explain how you know.

4. Use the answer to question 3 to determine which reactant was left over in the reaction. This reactant is said to be "in excess."

5. Use the answer to question 3 to determine which reactant ran out in the reaction and limited how far the reaction could go. This reactant is called the "limiting reactant."

6. Draw a particle visualization showing what is in the container after the reaction is complete.

7. Using the volume and concentration of each of the reactants, use stoichiometry to determine the mass of salt that would have been produced if each of the reactants reacted completely (you will do two stoichiometry calculations).

8. Question 7 gave you two possibilities for how much salt would be produced. Which of those answers do you think will prove true? Explain why you chose your answer.

9. Was the limiting reactant from your calculations the same as the limiting reactant from your pH readings? Should they be the same? Why or why not?

10. Use your volume and concentration of the excess reactant and your concentration of the limiting reactant to determine what volume of the limiting reactant would have been needed for the reactants to be present in stoichiometric proportions.

Limiting and excess reactants

In titrations, the reactants are added so as to have exactly enough, and all molecules are reacted. However, not all reactions are done in this manner. Sometimes there are too few molecules of one of the reactants, and it runs out. This is called a **limiting reactant**: a reactant that runs out during a chemical reaction and limits how much product is made. The other reactant is said to be "in excess"—after the limiting reactant has run out and the reaction has stopped, there is excess of the other reactant.

This idea can be shown easily in the grocery store. When you buy a package of bratwurst, you get five in a package. When you shop for the buns, they come eight to a package. You can only make five sets of bratwurst and buns, regardless of the extra three buns. Therefore, the brats are the limiting reactant and the buns are the reactant in excess—there are some left over.

Limiting and excess reactants are concepts illustrated by grocery items. The brats (sold as five to a package) are the limiting reactant. The buns (sold as eight to a package) are the reactant in excess.

Chemistry students working on labs in 1929.

Example 6.6

Limiting Reactants

1. If 14.5 g $AgNO_3$ and 14.5 g $BaCl_2$ react, how many grams of $AgCl$ will be produced?

$$2 \, AgNO_3 + 1 \, BaCl_2 \rightarrow 2 \, AgCl + 1 \, Ba(NO_3)_2$$

- Both reactants in the products have given information. Use both of these pieces of information for stoichiometry to find the mass of $AgCl$ if each of the reactants was totally reacted.

$$14.5 \text{ g } AgNO_3 \times \frac{1 \text{ mole } AgNO_3}{169.91 \text{ g } AgNO_3} \times$$

$$\frac{2 \text{ mole } AgCl}{2 \text{ mole } AgNO_3} \times \frac{143.35 \text{ g } AgCl}{1 \text{ mole } AgCl} = 12.2 \text{ g } AgCl$$

- If all the silver nitrate reacted, 12.2 g of silver chloride would be produced.

$$14.5 \text{ g } BaCl_2 \times \frac{1 \text{ mole } BaCl_2}{208.23 \text{ g } BaCl_2} \times$$

$$\frac{2 \text{ mole } AgCl}{1 \text{ mole } BaCl_2} \times \frac{143.35 \text{ g } AgCl}{1 \text{ mole } AgCl} = 20.0 \text{ g } AgCl$$

- If all the barium chloride reacted, 20.0 g of silver chloride would be produced. As the silver chloride begins to be produced in the reaction, the silver nitrate and barium chloride begin to be used up. When 12.2 g of silver chloride is produced, all of the silver nitrate is gone. Once one of the reactants has run out, the reaction stops—it can't keep going without one of the reactants. Therefore, *12.2 g of silver chloride* will be produced.

2. What was the limiting reactant in question 1?

- The silver nitrate is the reactant that will be totally gone once 12.2 g of silver chloride is produced—therefore, *silver nitrate is the limiting reactant*. Barium chloride will be left over once the reaction has stopped.

PRACTICE 6.6

Limiting Reactants

1. _____ Ba + _____ $N_2 \rightarrow$ _____ Ba_3N_2.
   What mass of barium nitride is produced with 22.6 g of barium and 4.2 g of nitrogen reacted?

2. _____ $Pb(NO_3)_2$ + _____ KI $\rightarrow$ _____ PbI_2 + _____ KNO_3.
   What mass of lead(II) iodide will be produced when 16.4 g of lead(II) nitrate and 28.5 g of potassium iodide are reacted?

3. What is the limiting reactant in the previous problem?

4. _____ H_2O + _____ Na $\rightarrow$ _____ NaOH + _____ H_2.
   What is the limiting reactant when 10.0 g of water is reacted with 4.5 g of Na? (Show your work—don't just write the limiting reactant!)

5. Explain why there is no limiting reactant in a titration that is correctly done.

Properties of Solutions

Properties of Solutions

Purpose To determine how dissolved substances affect properties such as freezing and boiling point

Materials 2 beakers, test tube, 2 thermometers or temperature probes, rock salt, ice, Bunsen burner, drink sample and pure water sample, graduated cylinder

⚠ **Safety** Use caution with glassware, especially hot glassware. Wear goggles at all times. Always point test tube away from people when heating.

Procedure

1. Thoroughly clean and rinse with distilled water two test tubes, two thermometers, and a graduated cylinder.

2. Determine the freezing point:

   a. Label one test tube *water*. Add 10 mL of distilled water to the test tube. Place a thermometer into the test tube.

   b. Label the other test tube *sports drink*. Add 10 mL of the drink sample to the test tube. Place a thermometer into the test tube.

   c. Make an ice bath by adding ice, enough water to cover the ice, and rock salt to a beaker. Stir the mixture.

   d. Place both test tubes in the ice bath—be careful not to get any of the salty ice water in them. Stir the sample tube (gently!) with the thermometer occasionally, until it freezes.

   e. Remove the test tubes from the ice bath, and record the temperatures when reading is stable.

   f. Do not empty the test tubes—use them for part 3.

3. Determine the boiling point:

   a. Place the test tubes in warm water until the frozen drink sample melts. (Be careful not to get any water inside the test tubes.) Continue warming the test tubes until they no longer feel cold—do not put cold glass in hot water or a flame, or on a hot plate.

   b. Add one or two clean boiling stones or glass beads to each test tube to promote smooth boiling.

   c. Gently heat one of the test tubes over a Bunsen burner flame. Always point the opening in the test tube away from all people (preferably toward a wall or window). Hold the test tube with test tube tongs and move it in and out of the flame to prevent it from heating too quickly.

   d. After the sample begins to boil, record the temperature when the reading is stable. Do not let the thermometer sit on or touch the side of the glass—take the temperature of the boiling liquid inside.

   e. Repeat steps c and d for the other test tube.

   f. Clean the test tubes after allowing them to cool. Be careful not to place a hot test tube into cold water.

Data

Freezing point of drink sample: _____

Boiling point of drink sample: _____

Freezing point of distilled water: _____

Boiling point of distilled water: _____

(continues)

Properties of Solutions (*cont'd.*)

Discussion

1. Classify the two samples you used as pure element, pure compound, homogeneous mixture, or heterogeneous mixture. (See Section 2.1 if you don't remember.)

2. What trend did you notice in the freezing point of a substance as solutes are added to it?

3. What trend did you notice in the boiling point of a substance as solutes are added to it?

4. Share your results from questions 2 and 3 with the class. Use whiteboards, if provided. Are there any discrepancies? If so, discuss them. How can evidence be used to resolve discrepancies?

5. When you make homemade ice cream, you put rock salt in the water surrounding the ingredients container. Use the findings from the lab to explain why you added rock salt to the ice water bath.

Go Online
Molecular animations
http://webcom4.grtxle.com/
khk12Chemistry

Vapor pressure

The kinetic energy of molecules is related to the temperature of those molecules—the higher the temperature, the more kinetic energy they have, and the faster they move. However, temperature is related to the *average* kinetic energy of the molecules. Therefore, there are some molecules that are moving around faster and have more energy than the average, and some that are below the average.

In a liquid, there may be some molecules that are so much above the average that they have enough energy to become gas molecules. (See Figure 6–9.) If those molecules are on the top layer of the liquid—on the surface—they can "escape" the liquid, becoming a gas. That is, some of

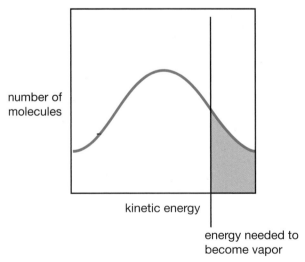

Figure 6–9. Graph showing the number of molecules that have each amount of energy. The average energy is shown, and the energy necessary to become vapor is also shown. Note that although the majority of molecules do not have the energy needed to become vapor, some do.

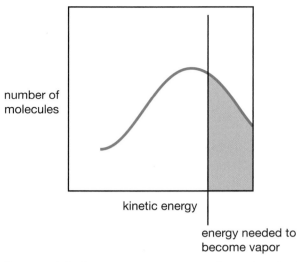

Figure 6–10. As the average energy increases, the number of molecules that have the minimum energy needed to become vapor also increases.

the molecules on the surface of a liquid have enough energy to break the intermolecular forces that hold the liquid together and pop off to become a gas. This process is **evaporation.** The gas molecules above the liquid exert pressure (you learned in Chapter 3 that all gas molecules do). The pressure of those molecules is called **vapor pressure.**

When temperature increases, the average kinetic energy increases. As the average increases, the number of molecules that have the minimum energy needed to break the forces of the liquid and become vapor also increases (Figure 6–10). Therefore, as temperature increases, vapor pressure also increases.

Vapor pressure of a solution

In an ionic solution, many of the water molecules are "tied up" with the solute particles. They are connected to the solute particles with intermolecular forces (see Section 5.5 for information on intermolecular forces). The water molecules evaporate less easily when they are interacting with the solute particles in this way. *The vapor pressure of a solution (with a nonvolatile solute) is always lower than the vapor pressure of the pure solvent.*

The more solute particles there are, the more water molecules are "tied up," and therefore the lower the number of water molecules that are available to evaporate. So the more solute that is added, the lower the vapor pressure will become.

Effects of electrolyte versus non-electrolyte solutes

If the solute is a strong electrolyte, adding one molecule of the strong electrolyte compound would produce more than one solute particle. For example, adding one NaCl unit produces two particles in the water:

When hot lava from a volcano meets the cool ocean, you can see evaporation of the water as steam.

1 NaCl → 1 Na$^+$ + 1 Cl$^-$. For every unit of salt that's added, you get twice the effect because you'll get two particles in the water.

Since non-electrolytes do not dissociate in solution, the effect is one to one—for every one molecule of non-electrolyte that's added, you only get one particle in the water.

Boiling point of a solution

When a liquid boils, it bubbles. Those bubbles are little pockets of molecules that have gone from the liquid phase to the gas phase. The bubbles rise because the gas is less dense than the liquid. They rise to the top until they "pop" and join with the rest of the gas above the liquid. The gas molecules in the bubbles exert the same pressure as the vapor pressure of the liquid.

If the atmospheric pressure pushing down on a sample of liquid is greater than the pressure that the bubbles would have, the bubbles cannot form. However, if the vapor pressure of the liquid increases so that the pressure of the bubbles would be at least equal to the atmospheric pressure, then the bubbles can form and the sample will boil. The way to increase the vapor pressure of the liquid is to increase the temperature. So, when the temperature increases, so that the vapor pressure increases enough that the bubbles can push against the atmospheric pressure enough to form, the solution will boil.

The vapor pressure of a solution is lower than that of the pure solvent (as discussed above). Therefore, there is a greater difference to be made up between the vapor pressure of the solution and the atmospheric pressure in order to boil the solution. This means that we have to raise the temperature even higher in order to get the vapor pressure of the solution equal to the atmospheric pressure. *Solutions always boil at higher temperatures than does a pure solvent.*

Calculating boiling point of an aqueous solution

$$\Delta T = K_B M$$

For every mole of particles that is added to a pure solvent, the boiling point increases by the **boiling point elevation constant**. For water, at sea level, the boiling point elevation constant is 0.52°C/mole. There are different constants for each solvent. This means that for every mole of particles that is added to water, the boiling point increases by 0.52° from its 100.00°C boiling point (at sea level). For 1.0 M sugar in water, the boiling point would be 100.52°C, because sugar is a non-electrolyte. For 1.0 M NaCl, which is an electrolyte producing two ions, the boiling point would be 101.04°C.

Go Online
Molecular animations
http://webcom4.grtxle.com/
khk12Chemistry

When water boils, bubbles rise to the surface.

Freezing point of a solution

A substance is at its freezing point when the solid phase and liquid phase are in equilibrium. That means that every time a molecule breaks free of the solid phase and becomes a liquid phase molecule, a different liquid phase molecule joins the solid and becomes a solid phase molecule.

The overall number of solid and liquid phase molecules doesn't change. If the sample is at the freezing point, the two states of matter are in equilibrium—ice water at 0°C is in equilibrium; the amount of solid ice will stay the same. If the sample drops below the freezing point, molecules will leave the solid more slowly than they are joining the solid; eventually they will all be solid molecules—the sample completely freezes. If the sample rises above the freezing point, then molecules will leave the solid faster than the liquid molecules can join the solid; eventually they will all be liquid molecules, and the sample completely melts.

In order to understand freezing points of solution, think of an ice cube in a glass of sugar water. The solid phase ice molecules on the surface of the ice cube can break free and join the liquid phase molecules. However, the sugar molecules that are floating around in the solution get in the way of liquid phase molecules' joining the solid ice cube and becoming solid

Why does freezing preserve food and keep it from decaying? The freezing stops bacteria from growing because chemical reactions are slowed down.

phase molecules. Therefore, the molecules are leaving the solid to become liquid faster than the liquid is joining the solid—eventually all the solid molecules will leave and there will be no solid left, only liquid.

If you lower the temperature even further, the solid molecules leave the solid phase at a lower rate—a rate that can be matched by the liquid molecules joining the solid. Therefore, the rates will be at an even lower temperature for a solution than it was for a pure liquid. *The freezing point of a solution will always be lower than for the pure liquid.*

Calculating freezing point of an aqueous solution

For every mole of particles that is added to a pure solvent, the freezing point decreases by the **freezing point depression constant**. For water, at sea level, every 1 mole of particles decreases the freezing point by 1.85°C. A 1.0 M solution of sugar water (a non-electrolyte) would lower the freezing point from 0°C to –1.85°C. A 1.0 M solution of NaCl (which produces twice as many particles because it is an electrolyte) would lower the freezing point to –3.70°C.

$$\Delta T = K_f m$$

**Go Online**
Check your understanding
http://webcom4.grtxle.com/
khk12Chemistry

PRACTICE 6.7

Properties of Solutions

1. Explain why vapor pressure increases as the temperature of a solution increases.

2. Explain why the vapor pressure is always lower for a solution than the pure liquid.

3. Explain why road crews put salt on the roads in winter.

4. Why would $CaCl_2$ have more of an effect on the roads than NaCl?

5. Explain why it is possible to get a sports drink below the freezing point of water, and still be able to drink it.

6. Why do people put salt in their water when cooking spaghetti? (Hint: It's not for taste alone! It shortens either the time to boil the water or the time to cook the pasta once the water is boiling. Which is it? Explain how you know.)

7. What concentration of particles is present in a 1.0 M solution of $AlCl_3$? What would be the boiling point and freezing point (at sea level) of a 1.0 M $AlCl_3$ aqueous solution?

8. What concentration of particles is present in a 2.0 M solution of $CaCl_2$? What would be the boiling point and freezing point (at sea level) of a 2.0 M solution of $CaCl_2$ in water?

Here is your chance to use the chemistry you know to create a good-tasting carbonated drink.

Carbonated beverage

Purpose To use stoichiometry to make a carbonated beverage

Background information When citric acid and sodium bicarbonate (baking soda) react, they produce carbon dioxide gas, which is what "carbonates" a carbonated drink.

Materials Small paper cups for weighing ingredients, one medium paper cup for making beverage, baking soda, citric acid, powdered drink mix, measuring cup (with metric units), plastic spoon

! **Safety** *Do not* do this lab in the regular laboratory, because you will be tasting the sample produced! *Do not* use regular lab equipment (except the balance which none of your ingredients or equipment other than the outside of a cup should touch at any time). Ingestion of excessive amounts of baking soda may be harmful.

Pre-lab calculations Using the information on the powdered drink mix package, find the following for one serving:

1. Mass of powdered drink mix, in grams

2. Mass of sugar, in grams (1 cup of sugar = 200 grams)

3. Volume of water, in mL

4. Write the balanced formula equation for the reaction. Citric acid ($H_3C_6H_5O_7$) and sodium bicarbonate react to produce carbon dioxide gas, water, and sodium citrate ($Na_3C_6H_5O_7$).

5. Use the balanced equation and stoichiometry to determine the mass of citric acid needed to react with 1.0 g of sodium bicarbonate.

Procedure

Part 1

1. Use the small paper cups and the balance to measure out the four solid ingredients needed (based on pre-lab calculations). Record observations of each of the ingredients. Add each ingredient to the large paper cup after measuring.

2. Use the measuring cup to measure the needed water.

3. Add water to the solid ingredients in the larger paper cup. Stir until all solid ingredients dissolve. Record observations during and after the reaction.

4. Taste test the drink—pour into separate cups for each lab partner. You and your partners may finish off the drink sample if you wish. Record observations about the taste.

Part 2

1. Repeat Part 1, but this time use half as much citric acid as in Part 1.

2. This time, taste test only a **small** amount of the drink.

Part 3

1. Repeat Part 1, but this time use half as much sodium bicarbonate as in Part 1.

Now that you know about stoichiometry, what do you think ecological stoichiometry is about? There is chemistry in all of life. Ecological stoichiometry studies how elements in the environment balance. The correct balance of available resources is necessary for each being's survival. The Earth's living creatures and the Earth's elemental cycles are connected. For example, how might global warming affect sea temperature, which would affect coral reefs, on which fish species depend?

2. This time, taste test only a **small** amount of the drink

Observations Record observations of ingredients before, during, and after reaction (including taste afterward).

Discussion

1. Explain why the reaction did not occur until the water was added—why didn't they react as solids? Use your knowledge of kinetics and collision theory (from Chapter 2) and of how solutions are made (from this chapter) to answer thoroughly.

2. In Part 2, what was the limiting reactant? What was the excess reactant? How did that affect the taste?

3. In Part 3, what was the limiting reactant? What was the excess reactant? How did that affect the taste?

4. Why were you allowed to drink as much of the sample as you wanted in Part 1, but in Part 2 and Part 3 you were cautioned to taste only a small amount? (Hint: Look at the safety information.)

5. Where else would stoichiometry apply to everyday life?

(This activity adapted with permission from "Fizzy Drinks: Stoichiometry You Can Taste" by Brian Rohrig, published in *The Journal of Chemical Education*, December 2000, page 1608A.)

Strong electrolytes are ionic compounds that almost completely dissociate into ions when dissolved in water. Weak electrolytes are ionic compounds that only partially dissociate into ions when dissolved in water. When ions (which are charged) are free-floating in water, they can conduct electricity. Strong electrolytes conduct electricity well when dissolved in water, and weak electrolytes conduct electricity weakly. Non-electrolytes are covalently bonded compounds that dissolve in water but do not form free-floating charges, and therefore cannot conduct electricity.

A solution is composed of the substance that is dissolved, the solute, and the substance doing the dissolving, the solvent. A solution that still has room to hold more solute particles is called unsaturated, and a solution that is holding all the solute particles possible to hold at that temperature is saturated. A supersaturated solution is one that has been heated to a higher temperature (which generally allows a solvent to hold more solute particles) to increase the amount of solute in the solution, and then cooled down to a temperature that ordinarily would not allow the solution to hold that much solute.

The concentration of a solution describes how much solute is in how much solvent. Concentration can be given in percentage of weight/volume or molarity. The concentration of electrolytes is determined from the number of ion particles that are formed from the original ionic compound and the concentration of the original ionic compound.

pH is a measure of the acidity of a solution. $pH = -\log[H_3O^+]$. As the concentration of the hydronium ion increases, the pH decreases. Acids and bases are also electrolytes. Strong acids and strong bases dissociate almost completely in water—therefore, they are strong electrolytes. Weak acids and weak bases dissociate only slightly, and are therefore weak electrolytes.

Not all ionic compounds are soluble in water. If two soluble compounds are mixed, it is possible that a new combination of ions that is not soluble in water will form; this is a precipitate. A series of reactions between different ions produces solubility rules that describe which ionic compounds are soluble.

Stoichiometry uses a balanced equation, with a ratio of moles of the compounds involved, to determine information about one compound involved in the reaction from information about another compound involved in the reaction. If one reactant runs out before the other reactants, it is called a limiting reactant, because the reaction stops. Stoichiometry can be used to determine the limiting reactant.

Liquids have a vapor pressure—the pressure created by those liquid molecules with enough energy to break free from the surface of the sample and become gas molecules. As temperature increases, the vapor pressure of a liquid increases. A solution always has a vapor pressure that is less than that of the original solvent, because there are fewer solvent molecules on the surface available for evaporation. A liquid boils at the temperature at which the vapor pressure of the liquid and the atmospheric pressure of the surroundings are equal. Solutions will have higher boiling points and lower freezing points than the pure solvent due to the presence of the solute particles.

1. Explain the difference between a strong electrolyte, a weak electrolyte, and a non-electrolyte.

2. Define solute and solvent.

3. Explain the difference between saturated, unsaturated, and supersaturated solutions.

4. What is pH? How is it found?

5. What is the difference between a strong acid and a weak acid? Between a strong base and a weak base?

6. What is the difference between an acid and a base?

7. What is a precipitate, and when does it form?

8. What is a limiting reactant? How does it affect how much product is made?

9. What is the vapor pressure of a liquid? Explain how temperature affects this property.

10. Break up the following strong electrolytes.
    a. $CaCl_2$
    b. $Sr(NO_3)_2$
    c. Na_2SO_4
    d. K_3PO_4

11. If you needed to make a 0.250 M solution of NaOH that was 500 mL, how many grams of NaOH would you need?

12. If 62.0 g of $ZnCl_2$ is added to 0.100 L water, what is the molarity of the solution? What is the %(W/V)?

13. If you had 0.025 L of a 0.125 M solution of K_2CrO_4 and heated it until all the water was gone, how many grams of K_2CrO_4 would you have? What was the %(W/V) of the original solution?

14. You have 500 mL of a 12.5%(W/V) solution of NaOH. What is the molarity of the solution?

15. If you need 25 mL of a 1.5 M solution of NaCl, what is the %(W/V)?

16. Find the pH for the following if the concentration of H_3O^+ is equal to:
    a. 1.75×10^{-3} M
    b. 4.67×10^{-4} M

c. 8.92×10^{-5} M

d. 0.00175 M

e. 0.0000475 M

f. 1.5×10^{-12} M

17. Find the $[H_3O^+]$ for the following.
    a. pH = 1.65
    b. pH = 7.95
    c. pH = 5.67
    d. pH = 12.75
    e. pH = 3.25

18. Finish each equation and indicate which are insoluble (a precipitate) with an (s) and which are soluble with an (aq). If there is not an insoluble product, write "no reaction" next to the equation. (Remember to reference the solubility table at the end of the chapter.)
    a. $NH_4Cl + KBr \rightarrow$
    b. $Pb(NO_3)_2 + NaCl \rightarrow$
    c. $KCl + Na_2SO_4 \rightarrow$
    d. $CuCl_2 + Na_2CO_3 \rightarrow$
    e. $Pb(NO_3)_2 + Na_2CrO_4 \rightarrow$
    f. $Ba(NO_3)_2 + Na_2SO_4 \rightarrow$

Use the following equation for problems 19–26.

_____ Li + _____ $H_3PO_4 \rightarrow$ _____ H_2 + _____ Li_3PO_4

19. How many moles of lithium would react with 4 moles of phosphoric acid?

20. How many moles of phosphoric acid would react to produce 0.4 moles of lithium phosphate?

21. If 2.5 moles of phosphoric acid react, how many grams of lithium are needed?

22. If 17.95 g of lithium react, how many grams of lithium phosphate will form?

23. If you want to make 22.2 g of lithium phosphate, how many grams of phosphoric acid would you need to react?

24. If you react 12.5 g of lithium, how many liters of hydrogen will you make at STP? How many liters would you make if it were at 30°C and 1.9 atm?

25. If you react 15.75 g of phosphoric acid and 22.2 g of lithium, how many grams of lithium phosphate will you make?

26. What is the limiting reactant in the last problem?

27. _____ NaOH + _____ HCl → _____ NaCl + _____ H_2O. How many mL of 0.25 M HCl will be needed to neutralize 8.97 mL of 0.15 M NaOH?

28. _____ $Sr(OH)_2$ + _____HCl → _____$SrCl_2$ + _____ H_2O. What is the concentration of HCl if it takes 32.6 mL to neutralize 25.0 mL of 0.115 M $Sr(OH)_2$?

29. _____ NaOH + _____ H_2CO_3 → _____ Na_2CO_3 + _____ H_2O. What is the concentration of H_2CO_3 if it takes 14.5 mL to neutralize 57.0 mL of 0.548 M NaOH?

30. _____ NaOH + _____ H_3PO_4 → _____ Na_3PO_4 + _____ H_2O. What is the volume of NaOH needed to neutralize 12.5 mL of 0.275 M H_3PO_4? The NaOH is 0.97 M.

31. Solutions always have a _____ vapor pressure than the pure liquid.

32. Solutions always have a _____ freezing point than the pure liquid.

33. Solutions always have a _____ boiling point than the pure liquid.

34. How would $NaNO_3$ affect the freezing point of water as compared to Na_2CO_3 if both chemicals are added in equal concentrations? Explain.

35. If the boiling point elevation constant for water at sea level is 0.52°C/mole particles, how many moles of particles are needed to raise the boiling point to 101.6°C? What concentration of $CaCl_2$ would be needed to raise the boiling point this much?

36. If the freezing point depression constant for water at sea level is 1.85°C/mole particles, what is the freezing point of a 2.0 M solution of NaCl in water?

Solubility Rules

These anions	Form soluble compounds with these cations	Form insoluble compounds with these cations
NO_3^- (nitrate)	Most cations	No common cations
CH_3COO^- (acetate)	Most cations	Ag^+
Cl^- (chloride)	Most cations	Ag^+, Pb^{2+}, Hg_2^{2+}, Tl^+
Br^- (bromide)	Most cations	Ag^+, Pb^{2+}, Hg_2^{2+}, Tl^+
I^- (iodide)	Most cations	Ag^+, Pb^{2+}, Hg_2^{2+}, Tl^+
SO_4^{2-} (sulfate)	Most cations	Ba^{2+}, Sr^{2+}, Pb^{2+}, Ag^+, Ca^{2+}
CrO_4^{2-} (chromate)	Most cations	Ba^{2+}, Sr^{2+}, Pb^{2+}, Ag^+
S^{2-} (sulfide)	NH_4^+, cations of column 1, cations of column 2	Most other cations
OH^- (hydroxide)	NH_4^+, cations of column 1, and Ba^{2+} and Sr^{2+}	Most other cations
CO_3^{2-} (carbonate)	NH_4^+, cations of column 1 except Li^+	Most other cations
PO_4^{3-} (phosphate)	NH_4^+, cations of column 1 except Li^+	Most other cations

Hot and Cold Packs

Chemistry Aids Injury and Maintains Food Temperature

IN THIS CHAPTER

- Endothermic and exothermic
- Calorimetry and heat capacity
- Changes in state
- Enthalpy of a chemical reaction
- Hess's law

CHAPTER 7

INTRODUCTORY ACTIVITY

How many objects or products can you think of in everyday life that either give off heat or absorb heat?

Which of these items involve physical processes?

Which of them are chemical processes?

Share with your partner and then with the class.

to determine, from the standpoint of a product developer, which reaction would produce the best hot or cold pack for the cost.

Introduction

You are high in the mountains on a camping trip, and it begins to snow. Your hands are cold, and you reach for a hand warmer package. You shake the contents as instructed, and place the hot pack inside your gloves. How does it work?

You're running in a track meet and injure your ankle. The athletic trainer snaps a cold pack and places it on your ankle. How does it work?

Why do some packs produce heat, and others produce cold? What is inside the hot and cold packs? How do the properties of hot and cold packs depend on the identity and amount of the chemicals inside? Are they all chemical processes, or are some of them physical processes?

Physical and chemical processes both can either produce heat (which will make it feel hot, as in a "hot pack") or absorb heat (which will make it feel cold, as in a "cold pack"). A cold pack doesn't really produce cold—it absorbs the heat from your body (or whatever object it touches), and as the heat leaves your body, you feel cold.

Some hot and cold packs involve a physical process of a change in state—such as the cold pack that is filled with gel and placed in the freezer. When you need one, you simply remove it from the freezer; as the frozen gel melts, it absorbs energy from your body (or your food) and therefore makes your body (or food) feel cold. Likewise, a hot pack can be placed in the microwave or in boiling water to heat the gel. The pack then gives off that heat to your body (or food) as it cools, and you (or your meal) feel hot.

Some hot and cold packs use a different physical process—that of dissolving. When some substances dissolve in water, they give off or absorb heat. For example, heat packs that have a little metal disk in them that you "snap" back and forth to activate the hot pack use the dissolving process. The snapping of the disk creates a disturbance that causes a supersaturated solution to crystallize—producing heat.

Hot/Cold Packs

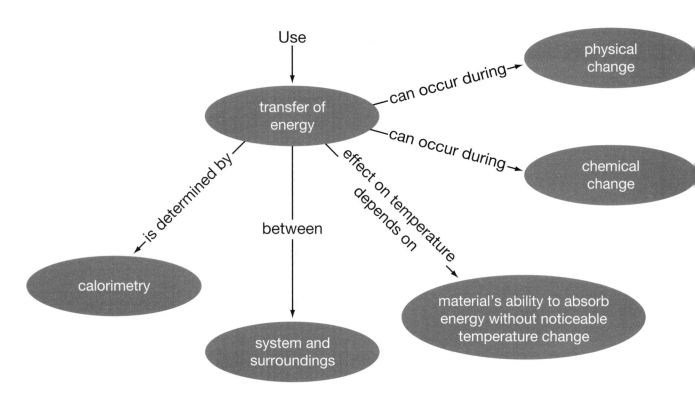

Other products use chemical processes. The packaging of the hot or cold pack keeps the reactants of the chemical process separated, and by snapping or shaking the package, you mix the reactants together, allowing the reaction to occur.

This chapter will explain both the physical and chemical processes and the energies associated with them.

SECTION 7.1

Endothermic and Exothermic

Go Online
Animated information
http://webcom4.grtxle.com/
khk12Chemistry

Changes, both physical and chemical, can be classified as being endothermic or exothermic. **Endothermic** means energy is taken in, or absorbed, into the system, whereas **exothermic** means energy is released from the system. Where does the energy come from or go? The energy goes from, or into, the surrounding matter.

System versus surroundings

Students often have too broad a view of a system. For example, a student might be shown a beaker with a reaction occurring inside it, and he or she might label the beaker as the system and the air as the surroundings. However, it's actually much narrower than that. Say, for example, you are watching a chemical reaction between silver nitrate and copper to produce copper(II) nitrate and silver. The specific molecules involved are the system. Everything else, including the water molecules in which they are dissolved, the glass of the beaker, any thermometer or stirring rod that is placed in the beaker, and the air surrounding the beaker are all the surroundings.

Endothermic processes

An endothermic process is one that takes in energy during the change. This means that energy leaves the surroundings and enters the system. When sweat is on your skin, the droplets of water (sweat) take in energy to evaporate. Where does that energy come from? The energy comes mainly from your skin, with some also coming from the air surrounding the droplet. Your skin (the surrounding) loses energy, while the sweat droplets (the system) gain the energy. This is an endothermic physical process explaining how sweat cools the body.

Sweating during physical exertion is an endothermic process to keep you cool.

When an endothermic process occurs in a beaker, the energy goes into the system—the specific molecules reacting. Where does that energy come from? The surrounding molecules in the beaker; for example, water molecules, if the solvent is water. If energy is lost from the overall solution (the surroundings) to go into the system (the specific molecules reacting), then the solution will cool down. A thermometer placed in a beaker during an endothermic reaction will show a drop in temperature.

For some endothermic reactions, taking energy from the surrounding water isn't enough—you have to provide heat to some reactions to get them going.

Exothermic processes

An exothermic process is one that gives off energy during the change. When you put a hot piece of metal into a cool container of water, the metal (the system) cools off, while the water (the surroundings) warms up. The metal loses energy as the surroundings gain energy. This is an exothermic physical process.

When hydrochloric acid reacts chemically with a metal, the solution warms up. The chemicals reacting (the acid molecules and the metal atoms) lose energy as the water molecules (the surroundings) gain energy. The thermometer will show the solution (the surroundings) gaining the energy. Exothermic processes show a rise in the temperature of their surroundings.

PRACTICE 7.1

Endothermic and Exothermic

1. What is the difference between exothermic and endothermic?

2. You hold a beaker in your hand as a reaction proceeds inside the beaker. The beaker begins to feel cool in your hand. (a) Is the reaction endothermic or exothermic? (b) Where is heat coming from? (c) Where is the heat going?

3. You put a thermometer into a solution where a reaction is occurring. The thermometer shows that the temperature is rising. (a) Is the reaction endothermic or exothermic? (b) Where is the heat coming from? (c) Where is the heat going?

4. Is a hot pack the result of an exothermic or endothermic process? Explain how you know.

5. Say whether each of the following is endo- or exothermic: (a) melting ice; (b) boiling water; (c) freezing water; (d) dry ice turning into a gas.

SECTION 7.2

Calorimetry and Heat Capacity

Energy changes can occur during physical changes. These energy changes result in the change of temperature of a substance, or the change of state of a substance—melting, boiling, freezing, or condensing.

The temperature of a substance is directly proportional to the average kinetic energy of the particles. That means that the higher the temperature of a substance, the faster its molecules are moving. When we observe the temperature change of a substance, we know that the molecules are changing their speeds—speeding up when temperature rises, and slowing down when temperature drops.

Heat, energy, and enthalpy

Heat is the flow of energy from an object with higher temperature to one with a lower temperature. **Enthalpy** is a quantity that takes into account the internal energy of a system, as well as the pressure and volume of the system. As long as the system pressure does not change, the enthalpy is equal to the energy flow (or heat) of the system. All the work in this chapter, both in problems and labs, will take place in an "open system"—meaning that it's open to the room and atmosphere around us. Because the problems will be occurring in the open air, the pressure changes will be very, very small. **Therefore, for everything done in the open air, enthalpy and heat are essentially the same thing.** This chapter will use the term *enthalpy* as scientists commonly use it, but you can always think of enthalpy as "heat" or as the flow of energy from the hotter object to the colder object, if it occurs in the open.

Go Online
Calorimetry
Go to: www.scilinks.org
Code: Chem1e257

SCiINKS
NSTA

Units for measuring energy

Energy is measured in several quantities. The SI unit for energy is **joules** (J). It is often used with the metric prefix "kilo" (kilojoule or kJ) to talk about large quantities of energy.

Another common unit for energy is **calorie** (cal). The calorie is defined as the amount of energy needed to heat 1 gram of water by 1°C. It can also be used with the "kilo" prefix—kilocalorie (kcal). One kilocalorie is equal to one "**food calorie**" (Cal, with the uppercase C), which is what's on the back of your food package.

Heat capacity

Why does it take some pans a long time to heat on the stove, when others get hot very quickly? Some molecules or atoms can absorb a lot of energy

Go Online
Animated examples
http://webcom4.grtxle.com/
khk12Chemistry

within their own structures before extra added energy causes them to move faster. When they do reach the point where they begin to move enough faster for the thermometer to detect a change, their temperature will rise to reflect this faster motion. (Think of how some people can "absorb" larger amounts of caffeine before it affects them and they begin to "move faster.")

$$4.18 \text{ J} = 1.00 \text{ cal}$$

$$1000 \text{ cal} = 1 \text{ Cal}$$

A substance's ability to absorb energy before it changes temperature observably is called its heat capacity. **Heat capacity** is the amount of energy a substance can absorb before a noticeable increase in temperature. Scientists have defined **specific heat capacity** (symbolized C_p) as the amount of energy 1 gram needs to absorb in order to raise the temperature by 1°C. (Note that the unit of "calorie" was defined by the amount of energy to raise 1 gram of water by 1°C—one calorie was defined by the specific heat capacity of water.)

A substance with a very high heat capacity can absorb a lot of energy before the temperature rises. The air in springtime becomes warm much earlier than the water in swimming pools. The air has a much lower heat capacity; the energy of the sun is enough to warm the air. The water in the pool has a much higher heat capacity—much more energy is needed to raise the temperature of the pool (as will happen when longer, hotter days string together with warmer, shorter nights).

Also, the greater the mass of a substance is, the greater the energy that is needed to raise the temperature of the entire substance. For example, it takes much longer to raise the temperature of a large pot of water to the boiling point than it does for a small cup of water.

Using heat capacity in calculations

If the specific heat capacity is the amount of energy needed to raise 1 gram by 1°C, then the equation that relates heat capacity and energy absorbed is $\Delta H = m \times C_p \times \Delta T$. The change in enthalpy is ΔH, and it uses energy units. The mass of the substance is m, and it is measured in grams (g). The specific heat capacity is C_p, and its units are J/g°C or cal/g°C. The change in temperature is ΔT, measured in °Celsius (°C).

Whenever "change in" is used in math and science (symbolized by Δ), it always indicates that you use "final condition minus initial condition" ($T_2 - T_1$ for ΔT). This will result in a positive sign for change in enthalpy when the temperature increases (energy is absorbed), and a negative sign for change in enthalpy when the temperature decreases (energy is lost).

Lavoisier designed this calorimeter in 1782 to measure the total amount of heat or "caloric" releases during a given operation. With a calorimeter, still used today in a modern version, the amount of heat given out by a heated object as it cools can be measured.

Example 7.2A

Heat Capacity Calculations

1. How many joules are needed to warm 45.0 g of water from 15°C to 57°C?

   $\Delta H = m \times C_p \times \Delta T$ mass = 45.0 g

   $T_1 = 15°C$ $T_2 = 57°C$

   - The specific heat capacity of water is 1.00 cal/g°C or 4.18 J/g°C. Choose the one with the unit containing joules, because the problem asked for the energy in joules.

   $\Delta H = (45.0 \text{ g}) \times \dfrac{4.18 \text{ J}}{\text{g°C}} \times (57°C - 15°C)$

   $\Delta H = 7900 \text{ J}$

2. If 458 calories of energy are added to 120.0 g of water at 25°C, what will the final temperature be?

   $\Delta H = 458$ calories   mass = 120.0 g $T_1 = 25°C$

   - Use the 1.00 cal/g°C for the specific heat of water, because the energy is given in calories for this problem.

   $\Delta H = m \times C_p \times \Delta T$

   $458 \text{ cal} = 120.0 \text{ g} \times \dfrac{1.00 \text{ cal}}{\text{g°C}} \times (T_2 - 25°C)$

   - Solve for T_2:

   $\dfrac{458 \text{ cal}}{120.0 \text{ g} \times 1.00 \text{ }^{cal}/_{g°C}} = T_2 - 25°C$

   $\dfrac{458 \text{ cal}}{120.0 \text{ g} \times 1.00 \text{ }^{cal}/_{g°C}} + 25°C = T_2$

   $T_2 = 28°C$

Go Online
Check your understanding
http://webcom4.grtxle.com/
khk12Chemistry

PRACTICE 7.2A

Heat Capacity Calculations

Note that the specific heat capacity for water is 1.00 cal/g°C (which is equal to 4.18 J/g°C).

1. How many calories are in 5.79 J?

2. How many calories are in 3.97 kJ?

3. How many food calories are in 6.87 kJ?

4. How many joules are in 12.7 cal?

5. How many joules are in 14.5 Cal?

6. Define specific heat capacity in your own words.

7. Explain why, when you take clothes that are still damp out of a clothes dryer, they don't feel hot, but if you wait until they're dry to take them out, they feel quite hot. (Hint—Where is the energy from the dryer going with the damp clothes? Where is it going with the dry clothes? Use the idea of specific heat capacity in your explanation.)

8. A diaper company has recently come out with training pants that let toddlers know they're wet by making them feel cold. Explain what happens when the pants get wet that causes them to make the child feel cold.

9. How many calories would be required to change the temperature of 750.0 g of water from 15°C to 90°C?

10. How many calories would be required to change the temperature of 250.0 g of aluminum from 15°C to 75°C? The specific heat of aluminum is 0.214 cal/g°C.

11. Given 800.0 g of water at 22°C, calculate the final temperature of the water after it absorbs 3600 calories.

12. How many joules are taken in if 854 g of water went from 23.5°C to 85.0°C?

13. How much heat is required to raise the temperature of 96.7 g of phosphorus trichloride from 31.7°C to 69.2°C? The specific heat of phosphorus trichloride is 0.874 J/g°C.

14. Two objects placed together at different temperatures will come to thermal equilibrium—heat will flow until they are the same temperature. Would an object with a high specific heat capacity or one with a low specific heat capacity come to thermal equilibrium faster? Explain how you know.

15. Some hot packs feel similar to beanie bags. They are filled with wheat. The water inside the wheat absorbs energy when the hot pack is heated, such as in a microwave. When the warmed hot pack is placed on your skin, explain where the heat is coming from and where it goes.

Heat Capacity Calculations (*cont'd.*)

16. Why does the hot pack in question 15 eventually stop feeling hot to your skin?

17. If you want a hot pack to last for a very long time after it's been heated, would you want it to have a small specific heat capacity or a large specific heat capacity? Explain your choice.

Calorimetry

Calorimetry is the laboratory technique of observing energy changes when two substances are combined. For example, when a piece of hot metal is placed into a cup of cool water, the hot metal will lose energy, while the cool water gains energy. This energy exchange will occur until thermal equilibrium is reached. Thermal equilibrium is when both substances are the same temperature. The energy that is lost by the hot metal as it cools is transferred directly into the cool water, which causes its temperature to rise. The energy lost by the metal is equal to the energy gained by the water: $\Delta H_{metal} = -\Delta H_{water}$. Therefore, $m_{metal} \times C_{p\ metal} \times \Delta T_{metal} = -m_{water} \times C_{p\ water} \times \Delta T_{water}$. If the two objects are allowed to come to thermal equilibrium (if you wait long enough, they will), then their T_2 values will be the same. So for the above equation, the final temperature of the metal and the water will be the same.

Example 7.2B

Calorimetry Calculations

A hot pack with a mass of 25.0 g and a temperature of 95°C is added to a 150.0 g sample of water at 25°C. The final temperature of the system is 75°C. What is the specific heat capacity of the hot pack? (Find it with the units of cal/g°C.)

$$m_{hot\ pack} \times C_{p\ hot\ pack} \times \Delta T_{hot\ pack} = -m_{water} \times C_{p\ water} \times \Delta T_{water}$$

- The T_2 for both substances is the same.

- Use 1.00 cal/g°C for the specific heat of water because the units match the ones that the problem specifies.

$m_{hot\ pack} = 25.0\ g$ $T_{1\ hot\ pack} = 95°C$ $T_{2\ hot\ pack} = 75°C$

$m_{water} = 150.0\ g$ $T_{1\ water} = 25°C$ $T_{2\ water} = 75°C$

$$C_{p\ water} = 1.00\ cal/g°C$$

$$25.0\ g \times C_{p\ hot\ pack} \times (75°C - 95°C) = -150.0\ g \times 1.00\ ^{cal}/_{g°C} \times (75°C - 25°C)$$

- Solve for $C_{p\ hot\ pack}$:

$$C_{p\ hot\ pack} = \frac{-150.0\ g \times 1.00\ ^{cal}/_{g°C} \times (75°C - 25°C)}{25.0\ g \times (75°C - 95°C)}$$

$$C_{p\ hot\ pack} = 15\ cal/g°C$$

Calorimetry Calculations

1. Some food containers include a hot pack that can be placed in the microwave and heated up. The hot pack can then be placed in an insulated pouch next to the food. If the hot pack has a mass of 30.0 g and it is heated to a temperature of 85°C, what is the heat capacity (in cal/g°C) of the pack if it can warm 500.0 g of water from 25°C to 40°C?

2. If a piece of aluminum that is 3.90 g and at 99.3°C is dropped into 10.0 g of water at 22.6°C, what will be the final temperature? The specific heat of aluminum is 0.902 J/g°C.

3. If a piece of cadmium with mass 65.6 g at a temperature of 100.0°C is dropped into 25.0 g of water at 23.0°C, what is the final temperature? The specific heat of cadmium is 0.2311 J/g°C.

4. A piece of unknown metal with a mass of 23.8 g is heated to 100.0°C and is dropped into 50.0 g of water at 24.0°C. The final temperature is 32.5°C. What is the specific heat of the metal?

LAB 7.2

Calorimetry

Purpose To find the specific heat capacity of an unknown piece of metal and use it to identify the metal

Materials Hot plate/Bunsen burner setup, two beakers 400 mL or larger, one piece of unknown metal, two Styrofoam cups, thermometer or temperature sensors with data collection method (computer or calculator)

Safety Wear goggles. Use caution with Bunsen burner (open flame) or hot plate. Use caution with boiling water, hot glassware, and hot metal.

Procedure

1. Record the mass of the piece of metal.

2. Place a beaker ¾ full of water on the hot plate or Bunsen burner to boil. While you're waiting for it to boil, you can go on to the next step, but once the water begins to boil, slowly lower the piece of metal into the boiling water. (If there's a string tied to the metal, use the string to lower it in and then lay the string over the edge of the beaker so that you can use it to pull the metal out; be careful the string doesn't come in contact with the hot plate or a flame from the Bunsen burner. If there is no string, use tongs to lower and remove the metal.)

3. Record the mass of a pair of Styrofoam cups (stack one inside the other).

4. Add approximately 100 mL of water to the cups. Record the mass of the cups and the water.

5. Place the stacked cups inside a larger beaker for stability during the experiment.

6. Record the temperature of the boiling water—this is the same as the temperature of the metal. Check with your teacher to see how long the metal you're working with should stay in the water.

7. Place the hot metal into the water in the cups and allow the energy to transfer from the metal to the water. To measure the energy change:

   a. **If you're using thermometers:** Record the temperature of the water in the cups just before you put the metal into the cup, and continue to watch the thermometer while you stir the water. Once the temperature stops increasing, or begins to decline, record the highest temperature you saw.

Calorimetry (*cont'd.*)

b. If you're using temperature probes with a data collection method (calculator or computer): Begin the data collection just before you place the metal in the water in the cups. Stir the water and watch as the temperature climbs. When the temperature has leveled off, or begins to decrease, stop the data collection. Record the lowest and the highest temperatures on the graph (usually you can do this by pressing a "statistics" button and reading the maximum and minimum) as the initial and final temperatures.

8. Repeat the process for a second trial (and a third if there's time). (Hint—The mass of the metal and the Styrofoam cups should be the same for all three trials.)

Data table

	Trial 1	Trial 2	Trial 3
Mass of metal (g)			
Mass of Styrofoam cups (g)			
Mass of cups and water (g)			
Initial temperature of metal (°C)			
Initial temperature of water (°C)			
Final temperature of water and metal (°C)			

Results Use the data table to find the specific heat capacity of the metal for each trial (find the specific heat capacity of the metal in the units of J/g°C). Find the average value for specific heat capacity.

Conclusion Restate the purpose. Use the known specific heat capacities of different metals to identify the metal. Identify at least two possible sources of error in this experiment. How can this type of experiment or information be used in real life? Create a class histogram of results (see Lab 2.7, Discussion question 5). Describe the class results. Is there a clear mode? If not, suggest possible reasons.

SECTION 7.3

Changes in State

Temperature does not change during change in state

When an ice cube melts, it is absorbing energy. We know this is true because liquid molecules have more energy (move more and exist at higher temperatures) than solid molecules. Therefore, the molecules must absorb energy to transition from a solid to a liquid.

When the temperature of a substance changes (as with the equations used in the previous section), the energy that is absorbed is used to make the molecules move faster. However, when energy is added to a substance that is changing state, the temperature does not change. For example, while ice is melting—while it's transitioning from solid to liquid—the temperature will not change. So if the energy being added to the system is not being used to move the molecules faster, what is it doing? It's being used to overcome intermolecular forces (Chapter 5 discussed intermolecular forces). Many intermolecular forces are broken when a substance melts, and all the intermolecular connections are broken when a substance is boiled.

Enthalpy changes during change in state

Melting and freezing   When a sample is being melted or frozen, the energy change is described by the enthalpy of fusion equation $\Delta H = m \times H_{fus}$. The change in enthalpy is ΔH, m is mass, and H_{fus} is the enthalpy of fusion of the substance. The enthalpy of fusion is the amount of energy needed to overcome the intermolecular forces per gram of substance, in units of cal/g or J/g.

If the sample is being melted, it is absorbing energy to overcome the intermolecular forces, and the change in enthalpy will therefore be positive. If the sample is being frozen, it is releasing energy in order to form new intermolecular forces. The release of energy is shown by a negative change in enthalpy.

Boiling and condensation   When a sample is being condensed or boiled, the energy change is described by the enthalpy of vaporization equation $\Delta H = m \times H_{vap}$. The change in enthalpy is ΔH, m is the mass, and H_{vap} is

Go Online
Animated examples
http://webcom4.grtxle.com/
khk12Chemistry

Strong geothermal activity creates boiling lakes and springs.

the enthalpy of vaporization of the substance. The enthalpy of vaporization is given in cal/g or J/g and is the amount of energy per gram of substance needed to overcome intermolecular forces.

As with the enthalpy of fusion equation, if a substance is being boiled it is absorbing energy to overcome the rest of intermolecular forces, and it will have a positive change in enthalpy. If the substance is being condensed, it is becoming a liquid and forming new intermolecular forces, which releases energy; therefore, the change in enthalpy is negative.

Example 7.3A

Changes in State Enthalpy Calculations

1. How many calories are needed to melt 28.0 g of ice? The enthalpy of fusion of ice is 80.87 cal/g.

    $\Delta H = m \times H_{fus}$ $m = 28.0$ g $H_{fus} = 80.87$ cal/g

    $\Delta H = 28.0$ g $\times 80.87 \,^{cal}/_g$

    $\Delta H = 2260$ cal

2. What is the enthalpy of vaporization of a substance if it takes 28,215 joules to boil away 15.0 g of the substance?

$\Delta H = m \times H_{vap}$ $m = 15.0$ g $\Delta H = 28,215$ J

$28,215 \text{ J} = 15.0 \text{ g} \times H_{vap}$

$\dfrac{28,215 \text{ J}}{15.0 \text{ g}} = H_{vap}$

Solve for H_{vap}:

$H_{vap} = 1880$ J/g

Heating curves—adding energy to a substance

As energy is added to a solid below the freezing point, the energy is being used to increase the speed of the molecules, which increases the temperature. The temperature increases until the melting point of the solid is reached. At the melting point, the intermolecular forces are broken with the energy being added (the temperature is no longer changing), and the solid begins to melt and become liquid. As long as both solid and liquid are in the sample, the temperature will not change—it will not go above the melting point because all energy being added is used to overcome intermolecular forces. Figure 7–1 shows how energy input affects water.

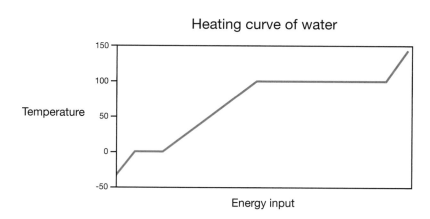

Heating curve of water

Temperature

Energy input

Figure 7–1. Heating curve of water. As energy is added to the sample of ice, the temperature increases until it reaches the melting point. While the ice melts, the temperature remains constant. Once all of the sample is liquid, the temperature begins to increase again until it reaches the boiling point. While the liquid boils, the temperature does not change. Once all the sample is a gas, the temperature can then increase again.

Once enough intermolecular forces are broken that the entire solid has melted and become a liquid, the energy being added once again causes the molecules to move faster, increasing the temperature. Once the liquid reaches the boiling point, the energy added is used to overcome the remaining intermolecular forces so that the liquid can boil and become a gas. As long as there are both liquid and gas, the temperature will not go above the boiling point, because all the energy being added is being used to overcome intermolecular forces.

Once all the intermolecular forces are broken and the liquid has completely become a gas, the temperature of the gas can continue to increase as more energy is added, and that energy causes the molecules to move faster.

The specific heat capacities of a substance in the solid, liquid, and gas states are different. This can be seen by the different slopes in the heating curve above. Make sure, when working these types of problems, that you use the correct specific heat capacity for the state of matter that you're dealing with at that time.

Also note that the heating curve shows that much more energy is needed to boil the water than to melt it. This is because the enthalpy of vaporization is much greater than the enthalpy of fusion. In order to vaporize water, *all* of the intermolecular forces must be broken. This requires much more energy than overcoming just some of the forces to melt the ice.

Cooling curves—removing energy from a substance

The opposite processes can happen as well. As energy is removed from a gas, it begins to cool down (molecules move more slowly as the sample releases energy) until it reaches the boiling point. Intermolecular forces re-form (releasing even more energy), and the gas condenses into a liquid. The liquid can then cool until it reaches the freezing point, at which time it re-forms the remaining intermolecular forces, freezing into a solid. The solid can then continue to cool to an even lower temperature. All of these

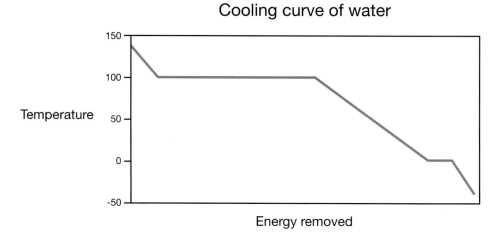

Figure 7–2. Cooling curve of water. The temperature changes are the opposite of those shown in Figure 7–1.

processes are exothermic; energy is released, and they will therefore give a negative value for ΔH.

This explains why steam burns are worse than water burns. The steam has an enormous amount of energy compared to water at 100°C (because of the high heat of vaporization of water), and when it condenses back to liquid as it touches your skin, that enormous amount of heat is transferred to you.

Example 7.3B

Heating Curve Calculations

How many calories are needed to warm 15.0 g of water from –20°C to steam at 135°C? The specific heat of ice is 0.51 cal/g°C. The specific heat of steam is 0.48 cal/g°C. The heat of vaporization of water is 547.2 cal/g, and the heat of fusion of ice is 80.87 cal/g.

- To warm the ice: $\Delta H = m \cdot C_p \cdot \Delta T$

- Use the specific heat capacity of solid water, $m = 15.0$ g, $T_1 = -20°C$, and $T_2 = 0°C$ (because that's the melting point of ice—the highest temperature it can go as "ice").

  $\Delta H = 15.0 \text{ g} \times 0.51 \,^{cal}/_{g°C} \times (0°C - (-20°C)) = 153$ cal

- To melt the ice,

  $\Delta H = m \cdot H_{fus}$

  $\Delta H = 15.0 \text{ g} \times 80.87 \,^{cal}/_{g°C} = 1213$ cal

- To warm the water from its current temperature (0°C) to the highest temperature at which it can be liquid

- (100°C), using the specific heat capacity of liquid water (1.00 cal/g°C), $\Delta H = m \cdot C_p \cdot \Delta T$

  $\Delta H = 15.0 \text{ g} \times 1.00 \,^{cal}/_{g°C} \times (100°C - 0°C) = 1500$ cal

- To boil the water,

  $\Delta H = m \times H_{vap}$

  $\Delta H = 15.0 \text{ g} \times 547.2 \,^{cal}/_{g°C} = 8208$ cal

- To warm the steam from its current temperature (100°C) to its final temperature (135°C), using the specific heat capacity of gaseous water,

  $\Delta H = m \times C_p \times \Delta T$

  $\Delta H = 15.0 \text{ g} \times 0.48 \,^{cal}/_{g°C} \times (135°C - 100°C) = 252$ cal

- Add up the total energy change for the entire process: 153 cal + 1213 cal + 1500 cal + 8208 cal + 252 cal = 11,326 cal, which is *11,000 cal* with 2 significant figures.

PRACTICE 7.3

Changes in State

1. Explain the difference between heat capacity, heat of fusion, and heat of vaporization.

2. How many calories would be required to vaporize 100.0 g of Freon if the enthalpy of vaporization is 35.0 cal/g?

3. How many calories does it take to melt 2.78 g of sodium chloride if the heat of fusion is 397.32 kcal/g?

Go Online
Check your understanding
http://webcom4.grtxle.com/
khk12Chemistry

(continues)

Changes in State (*cont'd.*)

4. How much energy is needed to melt 25.4 g of iodine if the enthalpy of fusion is 61.7 J/g?

5. How much energy is needed to melt 4.24 g of lead if the enthalpy of fusion is 162 J/g?

6. It takes 79.91 cal to melt 1.0 gram of an unknown substance. What is the enthalpy of fusion of the substance?

7. A cold pack filled with gel, with a mass of 15 g, is frozen. It's placed in 1000.0 g of water at 50°C. When the ice pack is completely thawed, the water is at 22°C. What is the enthalpy of fusion of the ice pack? (Hint— This problem combines the ideas of calorimetry from Practice 7.2B with the ideas of enthalpy of fusion from this section.)

8. Use your answer from the last question to explain why the cold packs are made with this type of gel rather than with ice.

9. Draw a heating curve for water from –15°C to 125°C. Label each section of the graph with the phases of water that are present and which equation you would use to find the enthalpy for that section.

10. Use this information for the three questions below. The specific heat of ice is 0.51 cal/g°C. The specific heat of steam is 0.48 cal/g°C. The enthalpy of vaporization of water is 547.2 cal/g, and the enthalpy of fusion of ice is 80.87 cal/g.

    a. Calculate the total heat absorbed in the graph from question 9 for 25.0 g of water.

    b. Calculate the energy needed to change 70.0 g of ice at –64°C to steam at 522°C.

    c. How many calories will be released when the temperature of 1000.0 g of steam at 180°C is changed to water at 35.0°C?

LAB 7.3

Enthalpy of Fusion of Ice

Purpose To find the enthalpy of fusion of ice and compare it to the theoretical value

Hints Remember that sometimes, before writing up your procedure, it helps to write the mathematical equations you will need in order to solve for the heat of fusion of ice. Then, from the equations, you can make a data table, and from that you can write a procedure.

It's difficult to measure the mass of ice because its mass is constantly changing as it melts. It's easier to use ice in the experiment and then find its mass after it has melted and served its purpose in the experiment.

Enthalpy of Fusion of Ice (*cont'd.*)

The mass of the ice before the experiment will be the same as the mass of the melted ice (water) after the experiment because of the law of conservation of mass (mass does not change during chemical and physical changes).

Procedure Design a lab using calorimetry to find the heat of fusion of ice. The write-up should include:

- **Title**

- **Purpose**

- **Background information** (Include information about how calorimetry works, defining the enthalpy of fusion, and giving the theoretical value for the enthalpy of fusion of ice.)

- **Materials**

- **Procedure** (Perform more than one trial.)

- **Data table** and **observations** (Remember—no calculations here, just raw data)

- **Results/calculations** (Show all equations used, show work, average your final results for enthalpy of fusion of ice, calculate the percent error with the theoretical value.)

- **Conclusion** Restate the purpose and answer it completely. Give at least two possible sources of error. How can this type of experiment or this type of information be used in real life? What other type of experiment could you do?

Create a class histogram (see Lab 2.7, Discussion question 5). Describe the class results. Is there a clear mode? If not, suggest possible reasons.

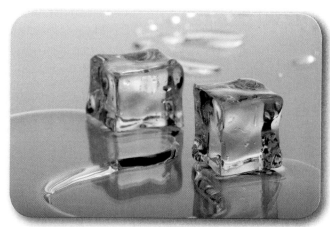

When ice is transitioning from solid to liquid (melting), the temperature will remain stable.

SECTION 7.4

Enthalpy of a Chemical Reaction

Enthalpy changes also occur during chemical reactions. The bonds in the reactants need to be broken (which takes energy), and the bonds in the products need to be formed (which releases energy). If more energy is put in to break bonds than is released when bonds form, the reaction is endothermic. If more energy is released when new bonds form than is put in to break the old bonds, the reaction is exothermic.

Enthalpy of formation

The **enthalpy of formation (H_f)** is the enthalpy change when a compound is formed from the elemental state. For example, the following reaction forms CaC_2 (s) from the elemental states of calcium and carbon (graphite):

$$Ca\ (s) + 2\ C\ (graphite) \rightarrow CaC_2\ (s).$$

This value can be found by looking up CaC_2 (s) in an enthalpy of formation table (in the Appendix pp. 438). For the reaction given above, the value is –59.8 kJ/mole.

If you were interested in the reverse reaction—breaking a compound down into its elemental forms—it would be the opposite of the value found on enthalpy of formation table (the opposite process has the opposite result in enthalpy change). Therefore, for breaking CaC_2 (s) down into its elemental states, the reaction would be CaC_2 (s) $\rightarrow$ Ca (s) + 2 C (graphite), and the enthalpy change would be +59.8 kJ/mole.

When using the enthalpy of formation table, it's very important to be sure to match up the correct states of matter. For example, the formation of *liquid* water has an enthalpy change of –285.8 kJ/mole, whereas the formation of *gaseous* water has an enthalpy change of –241.8 kJ/mole.

Enthalpy of reaction

The **enthalpy change during a chemical reaction** is symbolized with ΔH_{rxn}. The enthalpy change during any chemical reaction can be found in two ways: (1) the reaction can be done and the enthalpy change measured as in the calorimetry experiments earlier in the chapter, or (2) enthalpies of formation can be used to calculate the theoretical enthalpy change for the reaction. The first method is fine, except that you'd have to experimentally measure the heat of reaction for every possible reaction one at a time. The second method allows you to use one set of data (the enthalpy of formation table) to calculate the enthalpy change of any reaction possible—you don't have to actually do each reaction in the lab.

For the purposes of using enthalpies of formation, a chemical reaction can be thought of as a two-step process: (1) the reactants are broken down into their elemental states and then (2) those elemental states are formed into the products. (This is not the way chemical reactions actually occur—they do not break down into single elements and then reform all at once—rather, whole molecules collide and transition into new molecules, as discussed in Chapter 2. But for the purposes of talking about energy changes, this is an acceptable way of representing the energy changes that do take place.)

If we add up all the enthalpy changes that occur during these two steps, we'll get the total enthalpy change for the chemical reaction. When the elements are formed into the products, the values that appear on the enthalpy of formation table correctly describe the process. However, when the reactants are broken down into the elements, the values we need are the opposite of what appears on the enthalpy of formation table.

Go Online
Topic: energy of chemical reactions
SC INKS
NSTA
Go to: www.scilinks.org
Code: Chem1e270

Go Online
Animated examples
http://webcom4.grtxle.com/khk12Chemistry

Therefore, we need to "add the opposite" of the heat of formation table value when talking about the reactants. The equation becomes **Enthalpy change for the reaction = Total enthalpy of formation of the products plus the opposite of the total enthalpy for formation of the reactants**, or

$$\Delta H_{rxn} = \Sigma H_{f\ products} - \Sigma H_{f\ reactants}$$

(The Σ symbol means "sum of all the" or "total.")

Taking into account the number of moles of the compound in the reaction

The table of enthalpy of formations gives the enthalpy change for the chemical reaction just as it is written. The units are kJ/mole. It gives the enthalpy change (in kJ) for 1 mole of the reactant being produced. What if your chemical reaction uses two moles of the compound? Then you need to multiply the enthalpy of formation by two, because when you produce twice the amount of compound, you'll get twice the amount of energy.

Example 7.4A

Enthalpy of Reaction

Find the enthalpy of reaction for the following reaction: $2\ CH_3OH\ (l) + 3\ O_2\ (g) \rightarrow 2\ CO_2\ (g) + 4\ H_2O\ (l)$

- Look up the enthalpy of formation for each of the reactants and products:

  $CH_3OH\ (l) = -239$ kJ/mole; $O_2\ (g) = 0$ kJ/mole; $CO_2\ (g) = -394$ kJ/mole; $H_2O\ (l) = -286$ kJ/mole

- Use the following equation to find enthalpy of reaction: $\Delta H_{rxn} = \Sigma H_{f\ products} - \Sigma H_{f\ reactants}$

- Remember to multiply each enthalpy of formation by the numbers of moles found in the balanced equation:

  $\Delta H_{rxn} = [2$ moles $\times (H_f\ CO_2) + 4$ moles $\times (H_f\ H_2O)] - [2$ moles $\times (H_f\ CH_3OH) + 3$ moles $\times (H_f\ O_2)]$

  $\Delta H_{rxn} = [2$ moles $\times -394$ kJ/mole $+ 4$ moles $\times -286$ kJ/mole)] $- [2$ moles $\times -239$ kJ/mole $+ 3$ moles $\times 0$ kJ/mole)]

  $\Delta H_{rxn} = [-1932$ kJ] $- [-478$ kJ] $= -1450$ *kJ* (an exothermic reaction)

PRACTICE 7.4A

Enthalpy of a Reaction

Use enthalpy of formation table to find the enthalpy of reaction for each of the following.

1. $2\ CaC_2\ (s) + 5\ O_2\ (g) \rightarrow 2\ CaO\ (s) + 4\ CO_2\ (g)$

2. $CaCO_3\ (s) \rightarrow CaO\ (s) + CO_2\ (g)$

Go Online
Check your understanding
http://webcom4.grtxle.com/khk12Chemistry

(continues)

Enthalpy of a Reaction (*cont'd.*)

3. $4 C_2H_5OH (l) + 13 O_2 (g) \rightarrow 8 CO_2 (g) + 10 H_2O (l)$

4. $4 NH_3 (g) + 5 O_2 (g) \rightarrow 4 NO (g) + 6 H_2O (g)$

5. $6 FeCl_2 (s) + 2 Al_2O_3 (s) + O_2 (g) \rightarrow 2 Fe_3O_4 (s) + 4 AlCl_3 (s)$

6. $2 HNO_3 (aq) + Ag (s) \rightarrow AgNO_3 (s) + NO_2 (g) + H_2O (l)$

Remember for the next four problems that you must first write the chemical formulas correctly, and then balance the equation before determining the enthalpy of reaction.

7. Solid sodium metal reacts with liquid water to form an aqueous sodium hydroxide and hydrogen gas.

8. Aqueous sodium hydroxide reacts with aqueous hydrochloric acid to form solid sodium chloride and water.

9. Aqueous potassium hydroxide reacts with aqueous hydrochloric acid to produce solid potassium chloride and water.

10. Solid sodium carbonate reacts with aqueous hydrochloric acid to form aqueous sodium chloride, liquid water, and gaseous carbon dioxide.

11. Which of the above processes in questions 1–10 could possibly be used to make a cold pack? Explain why you chose the ones that you did.

12. Of the reactions from questions 1–10 that you said could be used in a cold pack, which would have the most practical reactants and products? Explain your choice.

Enthalpy and stoichiometry

Go Online
Animated examples
http://webcom4.grtxle.com/
khk12Chemistry

Energy can be used in a balanced equation along with the mole ratio of the compounds for use in stoichiometry. You can use the enthalpy of formation information to calculate the enthalpy of reaction for a given reaction. But what actual energy change will occur if you react a specific mass of the reactant?

Example 7.4B

Enthalpy and Stoichiometry

For the following reaction, how much energy is released if 11.5 g of CH_3OH reacts:

$$2 CH_3OH (l) + 3 O_2 (g) \rightarrow 2 CO_2 (g) + 4 H_2O (l)$$

$$\Delta H = -1454 \text{ kJ}$$

- Use stoichiometry beginning with the mass of the methanol reacted. Change grams to moles

using the molecular mass; once you have moles, you can use the balanced equation to convert between moles and energy.

$$11.5 \text{ g } CH_3OH \times \frac{1 \text{ mole } CH_3OH}{32.05 \text{ g } CH_3OH} \times \frac{-1454 \text{ kJ}}{2 \text{ mole } CH_3OH}$$

$$= 261 \text{ kJ}$$

Enthalpy and Stoichiometry

Go Online
Check your understanding
http://webcom4.grtxle.com/
khk12Chemistry

1. Using the following equation,

   $4 NH_3 + 5 O_2 \rightarrow 4 NO + 6 H_2O$, $\Delta H_{rxn} = -904.4$ kJ

   a. How many moles of NH_3 will be needed to release 452.2 kJ?

   b. How many moles of oxygen will be needed to release 1808.8 kJ?

   c. How many moles of water will be produced when 678.3 kJ is released?

2. How much heat will be released if 6.0 g of carbon reacts with oxygen in the following equation? $C + O_2 \rightarrow CO_2$, $\Delta H_{rxn} = -394$ kJ

3. How much heat will be released if 9.75 g of aluminum reacts with ammonium nitrate in the following equation?
   $2 Al + 3 NH_4NO_3 \rightarrow 3 N_2 + 6 H_2O + Al_2O_3$, $\Delta H_{rxn} = -2030$ kJ

4. How much heat will be absorbed if 27.1 g of iodine reacts with hydrogen according to the following? $H_2 + I_2 \rightarrow 2 HI$, $\Delta H_{rxn} = +26.5$ kJ

5. Explain how stoichiometry can be used to determine the mass of the reactants a manufacturer would put in a hot pack if they wanted it to produce a certain amount of energy.

LAB 7.4

Enthalpy of a Reaction

Purpose To find the heat of reaction between aqueous hydrochloric acid and solid sodium hydroxide, and compare it to the theoretical value found from the enthalpy of formation table

Materials Two Styrofoam cups, 400 mL beaker, thermometer or temperature sensors with data collection method (calculator or computer), 1.0 M HCl, solid NaOH, balance, and weighing dishes

! Safety Wear goggles. Hydrochloric acid causes burns. Sodium hydroxide is caustic. Report any spills or contact with skin or clothing to your teacher immediately. Use caution with glassware.

Procedure

1. Find the mass of two Styrofoam cups (one inside the other).

2. Add approximately 100 mL of 1.0 M HCl to the Styrofoam cups. Find the mass of the cups and the HCl.

3. Place the Styrofoam cups with the acid inside a beaker for stability throughout the experiment.

4. In a weighing dish, find the mass of about 2 grams of solid sodium hydroxide. (Note—Sodium hydroxide is hygroscopic, which means that it absorbs moisture from the air. Never leave a bottle of solid NaOH without a lid on it. Work quickly to find the mass of the pellets.)

5. Find the initial temperature of the hydrochloric acid and the final temperature after the reaction:

   a. If you're using thermometers: Record the temperature of the acid just before you put the sodium hydroxide into the cup, and continue to watch the thermometer while you stir the reaction. Once the temperature stops increasing, or

(continues)

begins to decline, record the highest temperature you saw.

b. **If you're using temperature probes with a data collection method (calculator or computer):** Begin the data collection just before you place the sodium hydroxide in the acid in the cups. Stir the reaction and watch as the temperature climbs. When the temperature has leveled off, or begins to decrease, stop the data collection. Record the lowest and the highest temperatures on the graph (usually you can do this by pressing a "statistics" button and reading the maximum and minimum) as the initial and final temperatures.

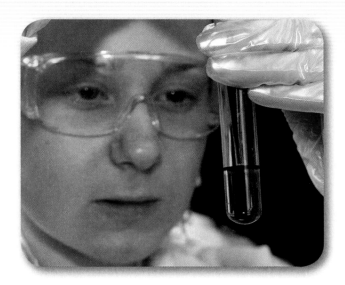

6. Empty the cup down the drain with the water running (the acid and base have now neutralized each other). Repeat for a second trial (and a third if there's time).

Data table

	Trial 1	Trial 2	Trial 3
Mass of Styrofoam cups (g)			
Mass of cups and HCl (g)			
Mass of solid NaOH (g)			
Initial temperature of reaction (°C)			
Final temperature of reaction (°C)			

Results/Calculations

1. Write the complete, balanced chemical equation (including states of matter) for the reaction.

2. Find the mass of the hydrochloric acid solution used in each trial.

3. The hydrochloric acid is almost all water, and therefore it will have a specific heat capacity very close to water's specific heat capacity. Use the mass of the acid (water), the specific heat capacity of water (in J/g°C) and the temperature change of the reaction (the water) to find the energy gained by the acid solution for each trial.

4. Change the energy gained by the water to kJ for each trial.

5. The energy gained by the water is the opposite of that lost by the reaction. Write the energy change for the reaction for each trial.

6. Before we can compare our experimental value for energy change during the reaction with the theoretical value, we must get them into the same units. The theoretical value is in kJ/mole reactants. NaOH is the limiting reactant in this experiment (there was extra acid in the cup). Use the mass of NaOH in each trial to find the moles of NaOH.

7. Find the kJ/mole NaOH for each trial.

8. Find the average kJ/mole NaOH for the experiment. This is your actual enthalpy of reaction for your experiment.

9. Find the theoretical enthalpy of reaction for the reaction (using the balanced equation in question 1) by using the enthalpy of formation table.

10. Find your percent error between your actual value and the theoretical value.

Conclusion Restate the purpose and answer it completely. Give at least two possible sources of error for this experiment. Tell how these types of experiments led to the development of the enthalpy of formation table. Create a class histogram (see Lab 2.7, Discussion question 5). Describe the class results. Is there a clear mode? If not, suggest possible reasons.

Hess's Law

Hess's law says that if you add up the enthalpy changes for each of a series of chemical reactions, the overall change in enthalpy is the same as if you went straight from the starting point to the finishing point. You just need to manipulate the stepwise chemical reactions so that when you add them all up, you get exactly the same thing as the overall one-step reaction. Whatever manipulation you do to the chemical reactions, you must also do to the enthalpy change for that chemical reaction. Then you add up all the enthalpy changes, and you'll get the enthalpy change for the overall one-step reaction.

Manipulating the equations so that they add up to the overall one-step equation is sometimes not as easy as it sounds. Follow these steps to make the manipulations easier.

Steps for completing a Hess's law problem

Go Online
Animated examples
http://webcom4.grtxle.com/
khk12Chemistry

1. Label each of the stepwise equations with letters (A, B, etc.) if it hasn't been done already.

2. Look at your overall equation.

   a. Look at the first reactant in the overall equation.

   b. Find the stepwise equation that has the same reactant in it (same chemical *and* same state of matter). It doesn't need to have the same number of moles of that compound, just the same chemical. It doesn't even need to be on the reactant side of the equation in the stepwise equation; just find where the same chemical and the same state of matter are.

   c. Determine whether the chemical in the stepwise equation is on the correct side of the stepwise equation; is it on the reactant side?

   d. If it is, write down this stepwise equation and its label (A, B, etc.) off to the side.

   e. If it isn't, write down the opposite of the stepwise equation (flip the reactants and the products) and write the –label (–A, –B, etc.) off to the side.

3. Repeat step 2 for each of the *reactants* in the overall equation. If a reactant appears identically in more than one stepwise equation, skip it for now; the problem will most likely get worked out on its own later. If the reactant appears in a stepwise equation that you've already written down, don't write it down again.

4. Repeat step 2 for each of the *products* in the overall equation. Check to make sure that the product is on the product side of the stepwise

equation. If it's not, flip the equation when you write it down and also write the –label beside the stepwise equation.

5. Once all the stepwise equations have been written down, you must begin to cancel out things that do not appear in the overall equation. Something will cancel out if the chemical formula and state of matter are identical and it appears on the reactant side of one stepwise equation and the product side of another. If a chemical appears identically on opposite sides, but the number of the compound doesn't match up (for example, you have two of them on the reactants side but only one on the product side), then you must multiply one of the stepwise equations by a coefficient in order to get the chemical to cancel out. You must multiply everything in the stepwise equation by that coefficient and also write that coefficient in front of the label off to the side of the stepwise equation.

6. Once all the chemicals are cancelled out that do not appear in the overall equation, add up the remaining chemicals—you should get an identical copy of the overall equation. If you did, add up all the "labels" and it will give you the formula that you need to plug the stepwise equations' enthalpy of reactions into in order to get the enthalpy of reaction for the overall equation.

Chemistry students around 1900, performing a lab about ceramics.

Example 7.5

Hess's Law

Use Hess's law to find the heat of reaction for the following overall reaction given the step reactions:.
Overall reaction: N2 (g) + 2 O$_2$ (g) → 2 NO$_2$ (g)

(A) N$_2$ (g) + O$_2$ (g) → 2 NO (g) ΔH = 180 kJ

(B) 2 NO$_2$ (g) → 2 NO (g) + O$_2$ (g) ΔH = 112 kJ

Follow the numbered steps in the preceding text.

1. Already done for us above.

2. The first reactant in the overall equation is N$_2$ (g). It appears in stepwise reaction A. It is on the reactant side of the overall equation and also on the reactant side of the stepwise reaction, so we write it just as it appears: (A) N$_2$ (g) + O$_2$ (g) → 2 NO (g)

3. The next reactant is O$_2$ (g)—it already has been written down in stepwise equation A, so we'll skip it and move on to the next reactant or product. We're done with the reactants now.

4. The only product is NO$_2$ (g). It appears in the stepwise reaction B. However, it is on the product side of the overall reaction and the reactant side of the stepwise reaction. Therefore, we need to flip the stepwise reaction when we write it down: (−B) 2 NO (g) + O$_2$ (g) → 2 NO$_2$ (g)

5. Add up the two equations.

    (A) N$_2$ (g) + O$_2$ (g) → 2 NO (g)

    + (−B) 2 NO (g) + O$_2$ (g) → 2 NO$_2$ (g)

    _____

    N$_2$ (g) + 2 NO (g) + O$_2$ (g) + O$_2$ (g) →
    2 NO (g) + 2 NO$_2$ (g)

6. Combine like chemicals and cancel out anything that appears on both sides exactly the same.

    N$_2$ (g) + 2 O$_2$ (g) → 2 NO$_2$ (g)

This now matches the overall equation given in the problem. In order to correctly add the stepwise equations to equal the overall equation, we added equations A and −B. Do the same thing with the enthalpies of reaction for these two stepwise reactions:

    A + (−B) = (180 kJ) + (−112 kJ) = 68 kJ

The enthalpy of reaction for the overall reaction is *68 kJ*.

PRACTICE 7.5

Hess's Law

Use Hess's law to find the heat of reaction for the overall reaction, given the step reactions.

1. Overall reaction: S (s) + O$_2$ (g) → SO$_2$ (g)

    (A) 2 S (s) + 3 O$_2$ (g) → 2 SO$_3$ (g) ΔH = −790.4 kJ

    (B) 2 SO$_2$ (g) + O$_2$ (g) → 2 SO$_3$ (g) ΔH = −198.2 kJ

2. Overall reaction: 2 C (s) + H$_2$ (g) → C$_2$H$_2$ (g)

    (A) 2 C$_2$H$_2$ (g) + 5 O$_2$ (g) → 4 CO$_2$ (g) + 2 H$_2$O (l) ΔH = 2600 kJ

    (B) C (s) + O$_2$ (g) → CO$_2$ (g) ΔH = −394 kJ

    (C) 2 H$_2$ (g) + O$_2$ (g) → 2 H$_2$O (l) ΔH = −572 kJ

3. Overall reaction: NO (g) + O (g) → NO$_2$ (g)

    (A) 2 O$_3$ (g) → 3 O$_2$ (g) ΔH = −427 kJ

    (B) O$_2$ (g) → 2 O (g) ΔH = 495 kJ

    (C) NO (g) + O$_3$ (g) → NO$_2$ (g) + O$_2$ (g) ΔH = −286 kJ

Go Online
Check your understanding
http://webcom4.grtxle.com/
khk12Chemistry

FINAL CHAPTER PROJECT

7

Here is your chance to use the chemistry you know to determine, from the standpoint of a product developer, the most cost-effective materials for a hot or cold pack.

Making a hot or cold pack

Purpose To determine which chemical produces the most efficient hot or cold pack for the cost of reactants

Materials 2 Styrofoam cups, 1 large beaker, thermometer or temperature probe and data collection device, balance

You will be assigned either a list of chemicals (calcium chloride, lithium bromide, and lithium chloride) or three of the following four chemicals: potassium nitrate, ammonium nitrate, sodium acetate, and potassium chloride. You will use about 2 grams of each chemical for each trial (about 4 grams of each chemical total).

! **Safety** Wear goggles while in lab. Avoid contact with or inhalation of chemicals. Wash hands after lab and report any incidents to your teacher.

Procedure

1. Find the mass of 2 Styrofoam cups stacked together (your calorimeter).

2. Add between 2 and 3 grams of your assigned chemical to the cup. Record the exact mass of the cup with the chemical.

3. Place the cups in a larger beaker for stability.

4. Add about 50 mL of water to a graduated cylinder. You don't need to record the volume; you'll find the mass in a later step. Leave the water in the graduated cylinder for now.

5. If using thermometers:

   a. Record the initial temperature of the water in the graduated cylinder.

   b. Add the water to the Styrofoam cup and stir with the thermometer.

   c. Observe the temperature as it begins to change while stirring the water in the calorimeter. If it is increasing, record the highest temperature it reaches. If the temperature is decreasing, record the lowest temperature it reaches.

6. If using temperature probes with a data collection device:

   a. Place the probe into the graduated cylinder. Start the data collection.

   b. Add the water to the Styrofoam cup and stir with the temperature probe.

   c. Observe the temperature readout until it levels off. Stop the data collection.

7. Use the "statistics" function of your data collection device to find the minimum and maximum temperatures during collection. You will need to decide, based on your graph/data, which is the initial temperature (the min or max) and which is the final temperature (the min or the max). Record the two temperatures appropriately.

8. Find and record the mass of the two cups with the chemical and the water.

9. Repeat the process so that you have completed two trials for each of the three chemicals you were assigned. Make sure you thoroughly dry the cup between each trial (or use a new cup).

Data table

	Chemical 1: ____		Chemical 2: ____		Chemical 3: ____	
Price of chemical ($)						
How many grams for that price?						
	Trial 1	Trial 2	Trial 1	Trial 2	Trial 1	Trial 2
Mass of calorimeter (g)						
Mass of calorimeter and chemical (g)						
Initial temp of water (°C)						
Final temperature of water (°C)						
Mass of calorimeter, chemical, and water (g)						

Results/Calculations

1. Find the mass of water that changed temperature in the calorimeter for each trial.

2. Find the enthalpy change of the water in the calorimeter for each trial.

3. Find the mass of chemical used for each trial.

4. Find the cost of the chemicals used for each trial.

5. Find the enthalpy change per cost of chemicals used for each trial.

6. Find the average enthalpy change per cost of chemicals for each chemical.

Discussion

1. Did you produce a hot pack in your experiment or a cold pack? Give evidence to support your answer.

2. Was the process endothermic or exothermic?

3. Did the hot or cold pack use a chemical process or a physical process? Explain what occurred during the process to produce or remove energy from the calorimeter.

4. Which of the chemicals makes the best hot/cold pack for the price—which chemical would you choose to make a hot or cold pack?

5. Look at the information in the following table. Would you still choose the same chemical as your top choice? Why or why not?

Chemical	Hazardous if Ingested? (yes/no)	Listed symptoms
$CaCl_2$	Yes	Nausea and vomiting
LiBr	Yes	Nausea, vomiting, rash, ringing in ears, diarrhea, drowsiness, coma
LiCl	Yes	Gastrointestinal irritation
KNO_3	Yes	Violent gastroenteritis
NH_4NO_3	Yes	Gastrointestinal discomfort
$NaC_2H_3O_2$	No	Some irritation
KCl	Yes	Gastrointestinal irritation, vomiting, circulatory problems, heart problems; may be fatal

6. Explain how you would change the setup of the process to make a real hot pack or cold pack; instead of using cups and pouring the water in, how could you use the chemical and the water to make a realistic hot/cold pack? Describe how it would work.

7. Create two class histograms (one for "cold" and one for "hot") to see if the class is in agreement about the most efficient chemical (see Lab 2.7, Discussion question 5). Describe the class results. Is there a clear mode? If not, suggest possible reasons.

Endothermic processes absorb energy, whereas exothermic processes release energy. The system and surroundings must be carefully defined when discussing whether a process is endothermic or exothermic.

Energy is measured in joules, calories, or food calories.

Heat is the flow of energy from an object with a higher temperature to one with a lower temperature. If the process occurs in open air and there are no pressure changes, then enthalpy is the same thing as heat. The amount of energy that 1 gram of a substance can absorb before its molecules begin to move faster and the temperature of the substance is raised by 1°C is known as the specific heat capacity. Specific heat capacity, mass, and temperature change of the substance and the energy absorbed or released are related to each other in the equation $\Delta H = m \times C_p \times \Delta T$. The specific heat capacity is different for each state of matter of a substance; therefore, it is necessary to make sure that the correct specific heat capacity is used for the state of matter in the problem.

Calorimetry is a laboratory technique that uses the energy change of one substance to compare with the energy change of another substance. Calorimetry uses the idea that if two objects at different temperatures are put together, they will come to thermal equilibrium—they'll lose or gain energy until they have the same temperature. The amount of energy that one object gains is equal to the amount of energy the other object loses.

While a substance is going through a change in state, the energy being added or released does not affect the temperature of the substance—the molecules are not changing the average speed at which they move. Rather, the energy absorbed or released relates to the breaking or forming of intermolecular forces that occurs during a change in state. A heating curve can show how the energy absorbed or released affects the temperature of a substance over time.

The energy change during melting or freezing is related to the mass of the substance and the enthalpy of fusion (the amount of energy needed to break enough intermolecular forces in 1 gram of the substance in order to melt it) with the equation $\Delta H = m \times H_{fus}$. The energy change during boiling or condensing is related to the mass of the substance and the enthalpy of vaporization (the amount of energy needed to break enough intermolecular forces in 1 gram of the substance to boil it) with the equation $\Delta H = m \times H_{vap}$.

The energy change during a chemical reaction can be found through experiment (with calorimetry) or by using the enthalpy of formation (the energy change involved in forming a chemical compound from its elemental components): $\Delta H_{rxn} = \Delta H_{f\ products} - \Delta H_{f\ reactants}$.

The energy change of a reaction can be used along with the balanced equation for the reaction in stoichiometry to determine the energy change for a specific mass of reactant used or product produced.

Hess's law shows that the overall energy change in a chemical reaction is equal to the sum of all the stepwise reactions that add up to the overall chemical reaction.

Use the following information for the review questions.

Enthalpy of fusion of water:	80.87 cal/g
Enthalpy of vaporization of water:	547.2 cal/g
Specific heat capacity of liquid water:	1.00 cal/g°C
	or 4.18 J/g°C
Specific heat capacity of ice:	0.51 cal/g°C
Specific heat capacity of steam:	0.48 cal/g°C

1 cal = 4.18 J   1000 cal = 1 Cal   1000 J = 1 kJ

1. Explain the differences between systems and surroundings. Give an example from your life.
2. Explain exothermic and endothermic. Give an example of each type of process in your life.
3. Explain the differences between specific heat capacity, heat of fusion, and heat of vaporization.
4. How does specific heat capacity relate to the amount of time needed to heat up a substance?
5. Define calorimetry and explain how it is used to determine information about a substance's properties or a chemical reaction's enthalpy of reaction.
6. How many joules are in 2.34 cal?
7. How many calories are in 12.5 joules?
8. How many calories are in 1.45 kJ?
9. How many joules are in 15.4 Cal?
10. Explain heat capacity in your own words.
11. Two objects with the same mass are sitting in a warm, sunny window. Which would be cooler to the touch after a very short time (not long enough to reach thermal equilibrium): the object with the higher heat capacity or the object with the lower heat capacity? Explain how you know.
12. How many calories are needed to heat 45.4 g of water from 15.0°C to 45.0°C?
13. How many joules are needed to heat 53.5 g of aluminum from 37.2°C to 64.5°C? The specific heat capacity of aluminum is 0.902 J/g°C.
14. What is the specific heat capacity of a metal if it takes 842 J to heat 15.4 g from 22.3°C to 34.5°C?
15. How many grams of water are there if it takes 24.5 cal to heat the water from 13.7°C to 87.6°C?
16. What is the final temperature of water if 845.2 joules are added to 45.3 g of water at 10.0°C?
17. In calorimetry, explain why we can use the energy changes in one material to determine information about the energy changes of another material.
18. A metal block of aluminum with a mass of 45.5 g is at 97.2°C. It is added to 75.5 g of water at 22.0°C. What is the final temperature of the block and the water? The specific heat of aluminum is 0.902 J/g°C.
19. A 4.55 g block of iron is at 62.2°C and is added to 12.2 g of water at 25.0°C. What is the final temperature of the iron and the water? The specific heat of iron is 0.107 cal/g°C.

20. A piece of aluminum is 34.5 g and is at 65.4°C. It is added to an unknown amount of water at 23.4°C. The final temperature of the aluminum and the water is 37.5°C. What is the mass of the water? The specific heat of aluminum is 0.902 J/g°C.
21. An unknown metal is 24.5 g and is at 75.4°C. It is added to 45.2 g of water at 24.5°C. The final temperature of the metal and the water is 55.8°C. What is the specific heat of the metal in cal/g°C?
22. Explain why the temperature does not change in a substance when it is going through a change in state—if the energy added isn't changing the temperature, then where is it going?
23. How many kcal are needed to melt 34.5 g of sodium chloride if the heat of fusion is 397.32 kcal/g?
24. How many joules are needed to melt 14.2 g of iodine if the heat of fusion is 162 J/g?
25. How many calories are needed to boil 14.3 g of H_2O?
26. How many calories are needed to change 12.5 g of ice at −10°C to steam at 145°C?
27. How many calories are released when 17.8 g of 155°C steam is changed to ice at −23°C?
28. How many calories are needed to change 78.2 g of water at 55°C to steam at 134°C?
29. You can tell an equation is exothermic by
    a. is the ΔH positive or negative?
    b. is energy a product or reactant?
30. Use heat of formation tables to find the heat of reaction for the following equations.
    a. C_2H_4 (g) → 2 C (s) + 2 H_2 (g)
    b. 2 Fe (s) + 3 CO_2 (g) → Fe_2O_3 (s) + 3 CO (g)
    c. Br_2 (g) + 3 F_2 (g) → 2 BrF_3 (g)
31. BCl_3 + 3 H_2O → H_3BO_3 + 3 HCl $\Delta H = -112$ kJ
    How much energy is released if
    a. four moles of water react?
    b. 14.5 g of HCl is produced?
32. 2 HgO → 2 Hg + O_2 $\Delta H = +181$ kJ
    a. How many grams of HgO are used when 475 kJ is reacted?
    b. How many grams of O_2 are absorbed when 179 kJ is produced?
33. S_2Cl_2 + CCl_4 → CS_2 + 3 Cl_2 $\Delta H = +112$ kJ
    a. How many grams of chlorine are absorbed when 145 kJ is produced?
    b. If 14.5 g of S_2Cl_2 is used, how much energy is produced?
34. $CaCO_3$ + 2 NH_3 → $Ca(CN)_2$ + 3 H_2O $\Delta H = -90.0$ kJ
    a. How many grams of NH_3 are used when 798 kJ is released?
    b. How much energy is released if 19.7 g of water is produced?

CHAPTER 8

Chemistry in Industry
Chemistry Making Money

IN THIS CHAPTER

- Equilibrium
- Equilibrium constants
- Reaction quotients
- Le Chatelier's principle
- Environmental concerns

INTRODUCTORY ACTIVITY

What do you think a chemical engineer does—for example, in a manufacturing plant?

What do you think are a chemical manufacturer's main concerns?

What do you think environmental chemistry is all about?

Think about these questions, share ideas with a partner, and then with the class.

**to use equilibrium to determine the energy flow
in a reaction as a research scientist.**

Introduction

Chemical manufacturers are in business to make money. Making money involves having efficient processes, with little waste and as much product produced as possible. This goal is one of the problems chemical engineers work on: creating or improving the processes through which a product is made. They can also use chemistry and problem solving to develop new or better products, select or improve the materials used, and engineer drugs.

Environmental chemistry is concerned with how things affect our environment at a chemical level. Often, chemical engineers work on problems of protecting the environment and regulating industries that may affect the environment.

The worlds of the manufacturing chemical engineer and the environmental scientist overlap—in fact, they often must work together to accomplish a goal. The manufacturer wants to minimize waste production for economic reasons, whereas the environmental chemist wants to minimize waste production to protect the environment—both work toward the same goal. However, they may believe that different paths are best to get there, and compromises must be made in order to come to an agreement.

This chapter will discuss some of the ideas that a chemical engineer must take into account when trying to make the most product with the least waste possible—ideas about equilibrium and Le Chatelier's principle. The chapter will also discuss some important issues concerning environmental chemistry in our world.

Chemistry in Industry

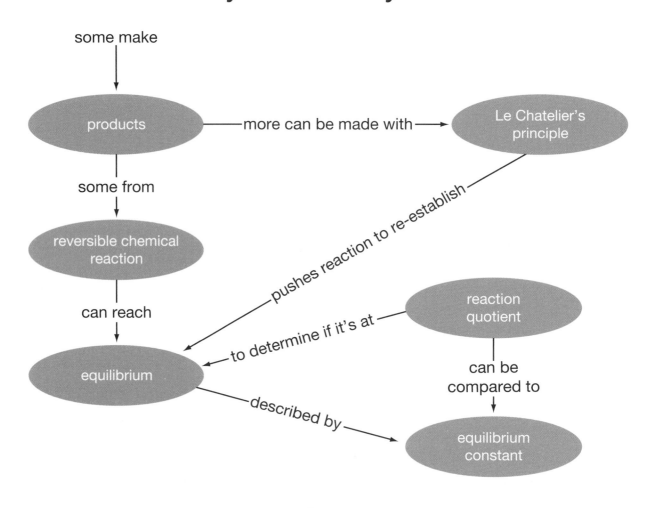

Equilibrium

Reversible reactions

Some reactions are reversible. In a chemical reaction, reactants collide and react to form the products. In a **reversible reaction**, after some products have been formed they can collide again and re-form the reactants.

For example, for the forward reaction A + B → C + D, the reactants (A and B) collide and react to form the products (C and D). However, once a supply of products has been made, they can collide and react to re-form the reactants: C + D → A + B. When a chemical reaction is reversible, it is written with a double-sided arrow: A + B ↔ C + D, which shows that it can proceed in both directions.

Establishing equilibrium

Chemical equilibrium occurs when the rate of the forward reaction equals the rate of the reverse reaction. This means that every time a set of reactants reacts to form a set of products, a set of products also reacts to form a set of reactants.

If the forward reaction rate is the same as the reverse reaction rate, chemical equilibrium has been reached. **The reaction then occurs at the same rate.**

In order for a reaction to happen, the molecules reacting must collide with the minimum energy and the correct orientation to each other (this is known as **collision theory,** which you learned about in Chapter 2). The more molecules there are, the more often they will collide. The more often they collide, the more often a collision will have the needed energy and orientation to produce a reaction. Therefore, the more molecules there are to react, the faster they will do so—the rate of reaction will be higher. (Section 2.8 discussed rate of reaction.)

As reactants form products, fewer reactant particles are available to collide with each other. Therefore, as the reactants are used up, and their concentration decreases, the rate of the forward reaction slows down.

When reactants are first mixed together, only the forward reaction is possible—there are no products present to collide and form reactants. Therefore, at first only the forward reaction takes place. The rate of the reverse reaction is zero, because it is not taking place. As more and more products are made, however, more collisions can occur to re-form the original reactants. Therefore, as more products are made, the rate of the reverse reaction increases.

Go Online
Molecular animation
http://webcom4.grtxle.com/khk12Chemistry

After a period of time, the number of reactant molecules has lowered enough (lowering the rate of the forward reaction) and the number of product molecules has increased enough (raising the rate of the reverse reaction), that the forward and reverse reaction rates are equal. Every time a set of reactants forms a set of products, a set of products also re-forms a set of reactants. Figure 8–1 shows these two processes reaching equilibrium.

Go Online
Topic: equilibrium
Go to: www.scilinks.org
Code: Chem1e287

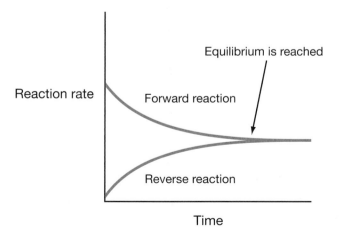

Figure 8–1. Diagram showing the reverse reaction rate increasing, and the forward reaction rate decreasing. In this way equilibrium is reached.

Some reactions come to equilibrium very quickly, while others can take quite awhile to establish equilibrium. The speed at which equilibrium is established depends on how easily each side reacts to form the other.

Dynamic equilibrium

When the forward reaction rate equals the reverse reaction rate, the reaction is at equilibrium. However, this does not mean that reactions have stopped. The forward and reverse reactions are still occurring—they are just occurring at the same rate. This means that the number of reactant molecules and the number of product molecules do not change, but the reaction does continue.

Think about two toddlers playing with a basket of toys. One toddler likes to take toys out of the basket, and the second toddler likes to put toys back in the basket. (This is a realistic scenario with small children!) The basket initially contains 25 toys. The first toddler (the "forward reaction") gets to the basket first and takes out 9 toys, leaving 16 toys in the basket. Then the second toddler (the "reverse reaction") begins to put toys back into the basket. They work at the same speed—every time the first toddler takes a toy out, the second toddler puts another toy back in. As long as they work at the same speed, the number of toys inside and outside the basket will remain the same—9 outside and 16 inside—and neither side will gain any ground. But even though the *number* of toys in the basket will remain the same, *which* specific toys are in the basket will change. For example, the first toddler removes a ball and the second one puts in a car, then the first one takes out a block and the second one puts in a stuffed

A research substrate, such as the one shown here, is the base on which an experimental material can be grown and cultured. Actelion is a pharmaceutical company that uses such substrates to conduct research into drug treatments. For example, they make drugs to help people with lung and heart hypertension. How do you think that for-profit companies should decide what their chemists should research? Actelion's aim is to see which health problems have scientific merit, unmet medical need, and commercial potential.

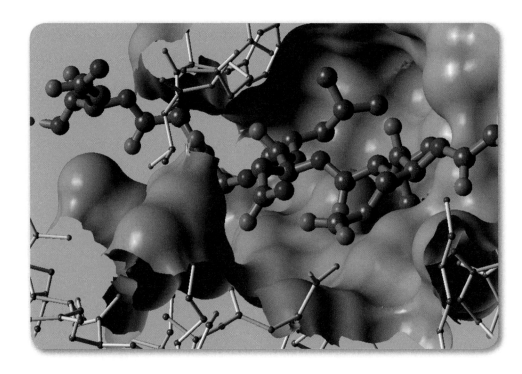

animal. The ratio of toys on the outside and toys on the inside does not change, but the "reactions" continue.

The same thing happens with a chemical reaction at equilibrium—the ratio of the number of products to reactants doesn't change, because every time it removes reactants to form products it also removes products to form reactants. The specific molecules do react and change, but the overall ratio doesn't. This idea is known as **dynamic equilibrium**. "Dynamic" indicates that it is constantly changing (the reactions are constantly going on), yet "equilibrium" means that it stays the same (the ratio of products to reactants stays the same).

Determining whether a system is at equilibrium

The number, or concentration, of the reactants and products can be measured over a period of time. At first, the reactants will decrease and the products will increase. However, as the products begin to react, the numbers of both will level off and remain constant. If the concentrations of the reactants and products are measured over a period of time and they remain constant, then the system is at equilibrium.

PRACTICE 8.1

Equilibrium

1. Explain what *dynamic equilibrium* means in your own words.

2. Describe how *forward reaction rate* and *reverse reaction rate* are similar and different.

3. During equilibrium, how do the forward and reverse reaction rates compare?

4. Why does it take time for a reaction to reach equilibrium? (Some do this faster than others, but none is instantaneous.)

Go Online
Check your understanding
http://webcom4.grtxle.com/khk12Chemistry

SECTION 8.2

Equilibrium Constants

At equilibrium, the number of product molecules and the number of reactant molecules have stabilized—they stay constant. In the toddler example above, even as both continued to play ("react"), the ratio of toys inside the basket to toys outside the basket remained 16:9. It's the same with all equilibrium systems—the ratio of the products to the reactants will always be the same. The ratio is dependent on the balanced equation of the reaction, known as the **equilibrium constant,** with the symbol K_{eq}.

Writing equilibrium constant expressions

The **equilibrium constant expression** is the mathematical formula that shows the ratio of products to reactants at equilibrium. If the numbers of the product and reactant molecules remain constant and the volume of the reaction is constant, then the concentrations (the molarities) also remain constant. The molarity is often used in equilibrium constant expressions because it is easier to work with in a lab setting than "number of molecules" (or even "moles"). Concentration is symbolized with brackets—[A] symbolizes "concentration of A." The ratio depends on the coefficients of the balanced equation.

For the reaction a A + b B $\leftrightarrow$ c C + d D, the lowercase letters are the coefficients of the balanced equation and the uppercase letters are the chemical formulas of the reactants and products. For this reaction, the equilibrium constant expression would be

$$K_{eq} = \frac{[C]^c[D]^d}{[A]^a[B]^b}$$

Equilibrium constants use powers and multiplication (rather than addition) because the equilibrium concentrations relate to reaction rates (a system is at equilibrium when the forward and reverse reaction rates are the same), and reaction rates follow collision theory. The math of collision theory (the frequency with which collisions are successful in producing a reaction) uses powers and multiplication.

Go Online
Animated examples
http://webcom4.grtxle.com/
khk12Chemistry

Example 8.2A

Writing Equilibrium Constant Expressions

Write the equilibrium expression for the following reaction:

$$2 \text{ NOCl (g)} \leftrightarrow 2 \text{ NO (g)} + \text{Cl}_2 \text{ (g)} \qquad K_{eq} = \frac{[NO]^2[Cl_2]^1}{[NOCl]^2}$$

Not all reactants and products are included in the equilibrium constant expression

Aqueous solutions and gases   Concentration is used in K_{eq} expressions. Aqueous solutions have concentrations—how many moles of the solute are in what volume of solvent? Gases also have concentrations—how many moles of gas are in what volume container? Both gases and aqueous solutions have concentrations that can change as a reaction proceeds. Therefore, they both affect the ratio of concentrations of products to reactants at equilibrium—they are both involved in the equilibrium constant expression.

Pure solids However, concentration (moles/L) equals density (g/L) divided by molecular mass (g/moles) for pure solids. Density and molecular mass are both intensive properties—they do not change no matter what size sample you have.

This means that, for a pure solid, because the density and molecular mass never change, the concentration will also never change. If the concentration never changes, then it is constant and does not affect the ratio of the concentration of the products to the concentrations of the reactants. Therefore, pure solids do not affect the equilibrium expression.

Pure liquids Pure liquids follow the same rules as for pure solids. The density and molecular mass also do not change as the reaction proceeds; therefore, the concentration is constant and does not affect the equilibrium constant expression.

Example 8.2B

Heterogeneous Equilibrium Calculations

Write the equilibrium expression for the following reaction:

$$Fe_2O_3 \text{ (s)} + 3\,H_2 \text{ (g)} \leftrightarrow 2\,Fe \text{ (s)} + 3\,H_2O \text{ (g)}$$

$$K_{eq} = \frac{[H_2O]^3}{[H_2]^3}$$

Fe_2O_3 and Fe are not included because they are pure solids.

Using equilibrium constant expressions in calculations

The **equilibrium constant expression** is the mathematical formula that shows the ratio of products to reactants. The **equilibrium constant** itself is the number that is found when equilibrium concentrations are plugged into the equilibrium constant expression. You can use the equilibrium constant expression to solve for the equilibrium constant if you know the concentrations at equilibrium, or you can use it to solve for equilibrium concentrations if you know the equilibrium constant.

Example 8.2C

Equilibrium Constant Calculations

1. For the reaction below, at equilibrium, the concentrations present are as follows: N_2 is 0.48 M, O_2 is 0.75 M, and NO is 0.030 M. Find K_{eq}.

   • First, write the K_{eq} expression:

   $$N_2 \text{ (g)} + O_2 \text{ (g)} \leftrightarrow 2\,NO \text{ (g)}$$

   $$K_{eq} = \frac{[NO]^2}{[N_2]^1[O_2]^1}$$

   • Then, plug in values of the equilibrium concentrations:

   $$K_{eq} = \frac{[0.030\text{ M}]^2}{[0.48\text{ M}]^1[0.75\text{ M}]^1} = 0.0025$$

(continues)

Example 8.2C

Equilibrium Constant Calculations (*cont'd.*)

2. For the reaction below, find the concentration of NO if the K_{eq} is 0.0025 and the concentrations of N_2 and O_2 at equilibrium are respectively 0.55 M and 0.92 M.

$$N_2\text{ (g)} + O_2\text{ (g)} \leftrightarrow 2\text{ NO (g)}$$

- First, write the K_{eq} expression:

$$K_{eq} = \frac{[NO]^2}{[N_2]^1[O_2]^1}$$

- Plug in values of the equilibrium concentrations and K_{eq}:

$$0.0025 = \frac{[NO]^2}{(0.55\text{ M})^1(0.92\text{ M})^1}$$

- Solve for [NO]:

$$0.0025 \times (0.55\text{ M})(0.92\text{ M}) = [NO]^2$$

$$0.00127 = [NO]^2$$

$$0.036\text{ M} = [NO]$$

Units of equilibrium constants

Because every K_{eq} has a different expression, every K_{eq} would have different units. For example, the K_{eq} in the example problem above,

$$K_{eq} = \frac{[NO]^2}{[N_2]^1[O_2]^1}$$

would have no units (M^2/M^1M^1 = no units). The units all cancel out. However, another K_{eq} expression might be different. For example, if

$$K_{eq} = \frac{[CO_2]^2}{[CO]^2[O_2]^1}$$

then the units would be $M^2/M^1M^1 = 1/M$. Because each K_{eq} would have a different unit, the chemistry community has decided not to use units with equilibrium constants.

Meaning of an equilibrium constant

This section gives general statements about the size of K_{eq}. Because K_{eq} uses exponents, there are some exceptions to these general statements, but they are valid for most situations.

When thinking about K_{eq} and whether it's large or small, remember that it is the ratio of products/reactants. If the concentration of the products is higher than that of reactants, the top of the fraction is larger, and the K_{eq} will be larger. If the concentration of the reactants is larger than that of the products, the bottom of the fraction is larger, and the K_{eq} will be smaller.

If K_{eq} is very large, then the ratio of products to reactants at equilibrium is large. This means that when the reaction reaches equilibrium, there are more products than there are reactants. The reaction is said to "lie to the right," meaning that when it's at equilibrium, the products (on the right side of the reaction) are in greater concentration than the reactants.

Cold facilitates some reactions. This product experiment is in a cold nitrogen container.

If K_{eq} is very small, then the ratio of products to reactants at equilibrium is small. This means that when the reaction reaches equilibrium, there are fewer products than reactants. The reaction is said to "lie to the left," meaning that when it's at equilibrium, the reactants (on the left side of the reaction) are in greater concentration than the products.

Note that $K_{eq} = 1$ does *not* necessarily mean that reactant concentration = product concentration. Because the equilibrium constant expression contains powers, you might get an equilibrium constant of 1 even when the concentrations are not equal. Take, for example, the reaction 2 A $\leftrightarrow$ B with equilibrium concentrations of [A] = 2 M and [B] = 4 M. The equilibrium constant would be $(4)/(2)^2 = 1$, even though there is a higher concentration of products than reactants.

Equilibrium constants and temperature

Temperature affects the ratio of products to reactants at equilibrium. Some reactions happen more easily in higher temperatures, and some reactions happen more easily in lower temperatures. (This idea will be discussed more in Section 8.4.) If a forward reaction happens more easily in higher temperatures, then the reverse reaction will happen less easily in those higher temperatures. Therefore, raising the temperature will make the forward reaction happen more than the reverse reaction—there will be a higher ratio of products to reactants. This change in temperature changes the ratio of products to reactants, and therefore changes the K_{eq}. (It does not change the equilibrium expression; the equation is the same, but it does change the number that is the equilibrium constant.)

The opposite is also true. If a forward reaction happens less easily in higher temperatures, then the reverse reaction will happen more easily in those higher temperatures. Therefore, the reverse reaction will happen more often and there will be a lower ratio of products to reactants. This temperature change will again change the K_{eq} value.

Every reaction has a different equilibrium constant value at each different temperature—however, the equilibrium expression (the mathematical formula) doesn't change; it's based only on the balanced equation.

PRACTICE 8.2

Equilibrium Constants

1. What can you tell about a reaction from a large equilibrium constant?

2. What can you tell about a reaction from a small equilibrium constant (a decimal)?

3. From an economic standpoint, why would a chemical manufacturer want to find a way to produce the company's products with reactions that have large K_{eq}?

4. Write equilibrium constant expressions for the following.

   a. $2 CO (g) + O_2 (g) \leftrightarrow 2 CO_2 (g)$

   b. $2 SO_2 (g) + O_2 (g) \leftrightarrow 2 SO_3 (g)$

   c. $CO (g) + 3 H_2 (g) \leftrightarrow CH_4 (g) + H_2O (g)$

   d. $C (s) + H_2O (g) \leftrightarrow CO (g) + H_2 (g)$

   e. $NH_4NO_3 (s) \leftrightarrow N_2O (g) + 2 H_2O (g)$

   f. $ZnCO_3 (s) \leftrightarrow ZnO (s) + CO_2 (g)$

5. Use the following lab data about the reaction $2 NO_2 (g) \leftrightarrow N_2O_4 (g)$.

Trial	Equilibrium [NO$_2$]	Equilibrium [N$_2$O$_4$]
1	0.0172 M	0.00140 M
2	0.0243 M	0.00280 M
3	0.0310 M	0.00452 M

   a. Write the equilibrium expression for the reaction.

   b. Find the value of K_{eq} for each trial.

   c. Find the average value of K_{eq}.

6. For the reaction $N_2O_4 (g) \leftrightarrow 2 NO_2 (g)$, $K_{eq} = 8.75 \times 10^{-2}$. If the concentration of N_2O_4 is 1.72×10^{-2} M, what is the concentration of NO_2?

7. For the reaction $2 SO_2 (g) + O_2 (g) \leftrightarrow 2 SO_3 (g)$, the $K_{eq} = 85.0$. If at equilibrium the concentrations of both SO_2 and O_2 are 0.050 M, what is the concentration of SO_3?

LAB 8.2

Equilibrium Constants

Purpose To determine the equilibrium constant for the reaction $Fe^{+3} (aq) + SCN^- (aq) \leftrightarrow FeSCN^{+2} (aq)$

Background information The product of the reaction ($FeSCN^{+2}$) is colored (reddish-orange). The more product you have, the darker the solution. This means that the amount of light the solution absorbs (as shown by a darker color) and the concentration of the product are directly related. (This direct relationship between the concentration of a colored compound

LAB 8.2

Equilibrium Constants (*cont'd.*)

in a solution and amount of light it absorbs is known as **Beer's law.**)

A set of samples of known concentration of $FeSCN^{+2}$ will be tested to see how much light they absorb. A calibration curve will be made by graphing the known concentration of the sample against the amount of light absorbed. We can then test an unknown sample of $FeSCN^{+2}$ to see how much light it absorbs. We then use the calibration curve and the amount of light absorbed by the unknown sample to determine the concentration of $FeSCN^{+2}$ in that sample.

Materials Spectrophotometer or colorimeter with data collection device, test tubes or cuvettes to use with the spectrophotometer or colorimeter, standard solutions provided by the teacher with known concentrations of $FeSCN^{+2}$, solutions of 2×10^{-3} M Fe^{+3} and 2×10^{-3} M SCN^{-1} in small beakers, two very small graduated cylinders or graduated pipettes, 3 test tubes for mixing the test solutions, test tube rack

! **Safety** Use caution with all chemicals, especially those whose properties are unknown, and with glass. Report spills or contact with skin or clothing to your teacher.

Procedure for using a spectrophotometer

Part 1

Find the absorption of each of the known solutions

1. Allow the spectrophotometer to warm up.

2. Set the spectrophotometer to read absorption and set the wavelength dial to 445 nm.

3. Fill the test tube or cuvette with distilled water. Carefully wipe off any fingerprints, insert it into the spectrophotometer, and close the lid. "Zero" the spectrophotometer with the zero dial.

4. Empty the test tube or cuvette and shake it dry. (Careful not to break it!) Fill it with the first known $FeSCN^{+2}$ solution. Wipe any fingerprints off the glass, insert it into the spectrophotometer, and close the lid. Record the concentration of the known solution and the absorption in the data table for Part 1.

5. Rinse the test tube or cuvette and repeat step 4 for each of the known solutions.

Part 2

Find the absorption of the unknown solutions

6. In a test tube rack, add 5 mL of the 2.0×10^{-3} M Fe^{+3} solution to each of the three test tubes.

7. Add the 2.0×10^{-3} M SCN^{-1} solution to each of the test tubes: 3 mL in the first, 4 mL in the second, and 5 mL in the third.

8. Stir the solution in each test tube (rinse the stir-rod in between uses).

9. Pour a sample from the first test tube into the test tube or cuvette for the spectrophotometer. Wipe fingerprints off, insert into the spectrophotometer, and close the lid. Record the absorption in the data table for Part 2.

10. Rinse the test tube or cuvette (and shake dry) and repeat step 4 for the other two test solutions.

Procedure For using a colorimeter and data collection device (calculator or computer)

Part 1

Find the absorption of each of the known solutions

1. Set up the colorimeter with the data collection device. Use the colorimeter on the blue LED position (470 nm).

2. Fill the cuvette with distilled water, and wipe away any fingerprints. Place it inside the colorimeter. If your colorimeter has a CAL button, push it. If not, follow the steps given by your instructor to calibrate the colorimeter.

3. Set up the data collection device to record data with input ("Events with entry"). You will enter the concentrations, and it will record the absorption.

4. Start the data collection.

5. Empty the cuvette and shake it dry. (Be careful not to break it!) Add the first known solution to the cuvette, wipe away any fingerprints, and insert it into the colorimeter. Wait for the readout of the absorption to settle down, click "KEEP," and enter in the concentration of the known solution. You don't need to complete the data table for Part 1 because you're using the data collection device.

(continues)

Equilibrium Constants (*cont'd.*)

6. Rinse the cuvette and repeat step 5 for each of the known solutions.

7. When done with all of the samples, stop the data collection.

8. Use your data collection device to perform a linear fit on the graph of the data. Print this graph, or if you're unable to print the graph, record the linear equation ($y = mx + b$, with m being the slope) under question 1 in the Results/Calculations.

Part 2

Find the absorption of the unknown solutions

9. In a test tube rack, add 5 mL of the 2.0×10^{-3} M Fe^{+3} solution to each of the three test tubes.

10. Add the 2.0×10^{-3} M SCN^{-1} solution to each of the test tubes: 3 mL in the first, 4 mL in the second, and 5 mL in the third.

11. Stir the solution in each test tube (rinse the stir-rod between uses).

12. Pour a sample from the first test tube into the cuvette for the colorimeter. Wipe fingerprints off, and insert into the colorimeter. Watch the live readout of the absorption, and record the absorption in the data table for Part 2.

13. Rinse the test tube or cuvette, and repeat step 4 for the other two test solutions.

Data tables

Part 1

Concentration of $FeSCN^{+2}$ in known solution	Absorption

Part 2

Trial #	mL of 2.0×10^{-3} M Fe^{+3}	mL of 2.0×10^{-3} M SCN^{-1}	Total volume (mL)	Absorption
1	5	3	8	
2	5	4	9	
3	5	5	10	

Results/Calculations

1. Use these results tables to organize your results as you calculate them below. Work through the questions (showing your work as you go), and the questions will tell you how and when to fill in the results tables. (Make tables for Trials 2 and 3 as well.)

Trial 1

	Fe^{+3}	$SCN^{-1} \rightarrow$	$FeSCN^{+2}$
Initial			0 M
Change	−	−	+
Equilibrium			

2. Find the line equation.

   For spectrophotometer: Use graph paper or a computer program to make a graph with absorption on the y axis and concentration of the known solutions on the x axis. Use your information from the data table of Part 1 to plot the graph. Draw a best-fit line through your data points (it should go through (0,0) because with 0 concentration you'd have 0 absorption). Find the slope of the best-fit. Write the line equation here ($y = mx + b$), with m being the slope).

   For colorimeter with data collection device: If you used the colorimeter with the data collection device, you already made the calibration curve (the graph of absorption versus concentration). Record the line equation here.

3. Use the line equation from your calibration curve ($y = mx + b$) where y is the absorption, m is the slope, and x is the concentration of $FeSCN^{+2}$. Find the concentration of $FeSCN^{+2}$ for the three test trials. Record these values in the "**Equilibrium FeSCN^{+2}**" space in the results table for each trial.

4. Each of the trial samples used 0.005 L of 2.0×10^{-3} M e^{+3}. Use the dilution equation ($M_1V_1 = M_2V_2$) to find the M_2 for Fe^{+3} for each of the three trials if the V_2 values are 0.008, 0.009, and 0.010 mL for the three trials. Record these values as the "**Initial Fe^{+3}**" concentration in the results table for each trial.

Equilibrium Constants (*cont'd.*)

5. The SCN^{-1} was originally 2.0×10^{-3} M. If the first trial used 0.003 mL, the second trial used 0.004 mL, and the third trial used 0.005 mL, use the dilution equation ($M_1V_1 = M_2V_2$) to find M_2 for each of the three trials if the final volumes were 0.008, 0.009, and 0.010 mL for the three trials. Record these values in the results table for each trial as the **Initial SCN^{-1}** concentrations.

6. Determine the **Change $FeSCN^{+2}$** for each of the three trials by remembering that the reaction began with 0 M of the products. Fill in this value in your results table.

7. The balanced equation shows that the ratio is 1:1:1. This means that the concentration of $FeSCN^{+2}$ that was gained in each trial (which you determined in question 6) is the same as the concentration of both Fe^{+3} and SCN^{-1} that was lost in each trial. Fill in the **Change** spaces for Fe^{+3} and SCN^{-1} for each trial in the results table.

8. Use the **Initial** and **Change** values in your results table to determine the equilibrium concentrations for Fe^{+3} and SCN^{-1} in each of the three trials. Record these values in your results table.

9. Write the K_{eq} expression for the reaction (the balanced equation is given in the Purpose).

10. Use the equilibrium values in your results tables to determine the value of K_{eq} for each of the three trials.

11. Solve for average K_{eq} at this temperature.

Conclusion Restate the purpose and give your results that answer the purpose. What are two or three possible sources of error that could happen in this lab? Create a class histogram (see Lab 2.7, Discussion question 5). Describe the class results. Is there a clear mode? If not, suggest possible reasons.

SECTION 8.3

Reaction Quotients

Equilibrium constants use the concentrations of products and reactants at equilibrium. How do we know if our reaction is at equilibrium yet? One way was discussed in Section 8.1: measure the concentrations of the reactants and products over time, and when they remain constant, the reaction is at equilibrium. Measuring the concentrations several times can be very time consuming, though. There's another way that usually requires fewer measurements.

If you already know the equilibrium constant for that temperature, and you know the current concentrations in the system, you can compare them. If you use the current concentrations in the equilibrium constant expression and the ratio ends up equaling the equilibrium constant, then the system is at equilibrium. If the current ratio does not equal the equilibrium ratio, then equilibrium has not been established yet, and you need to keep waiting. This can reduce the number of measurements needed because you don't have to wait until two measurements taken at different times are equal. As long as you get one that equals the equilibrium constant, you're done. You don't have to wait for a second one to confirm the fact.

Reaction quotient

The **reaction quotient (Q)** is found when you use the equilibrium constant expression with current concentrations. If equilibrium concentrations are plugged into the expression, then you're solving for K_{eq} (the equilibrium constant). However, if you are unsure whether you're at equilibrium, and you plug in current concentrations that may or may not be at equilibrium, then you're solving for Q (the reaction quotient).

Think of Q in the same way as K_{eq}—if the concentration of the products is larger, the top of the fraction is larger and Q is larger; if the concentration of the reactants is larger, the bottom of the fraction is larger and Q is smaller.

Which way to go to get to equilibrium

If Q is larger than K_{eq}, then the current ratio of products to reactants is too high. In order to come to equilibrium, there need to be fewer products and more reactants. The reaction needs to proceed toward the reactants (products need to react to re-form reactants). It needs to "proceed to the left" to come to equilibrium.

If Q is smaller than K_{eq}, then the current ratio of products to reactants is too low. In order to come to equilibrium, there need to be more products and fewer reactants. The reaction needs to proceed toward the products (reactants need to react to form products). The reaction needs to "proceed to the right" to come to equilibrium.

If Q is equal to K_{eq}, then the current ratio of products to reactants is equal to the ratio at equilibrium. Therefore, the reaction is currently at equilibrium.

Example 8.3

Reaction Quotient

For the reaction below, $K_{eq} = 0.0025$. If the following concentrations are present, is the reaction at equilibrium?

N_2 is 0.55 M, O_2 is 0.35 M, and NO is 0.04 M

If not, which way will it proceed to reach equilibrium? $N_2 \, (g) + O_2 \, (g) \leftrightarrow 2 \, NO \, (g)$

- First, write the K_{eq} expression:

$$K_{eq} = \frac{[NO]^2}{[N_2]^1 [O_2]^1},$$

which is the same as the Q expression.

- Then, plug in values of the current concentrations to solve for Q:

$$Q = \frac{[0.04 \text{ M}]^2}{[0.55 \text{ M}]^1 [0.35 \text{ M}]^1} = 0.0083$$

The $Q > K_{eq}$. Therefore, the reaction is *not* at equilibrium. It will need to increase the bottom of the fraction (and at the same time decrease the top) in order to become equal to K_{eq}. Therefore, the reaction needs to produce more reactants (and remove some products), so the reaction will *proceed to the left*.

Reaction Quotient

1. What is the difference between the reaction quotient (Q) and the equilibrium constant (K_{eq})?

2. What will happen in a reaction if Q is larger than K_{eq}?

3. What will happen in a reaction if K_{eq} is larger than Q?

4. Why might a chemical manufacturer solve for Q and compare it to K_{eq} when making a chemical in the factory?

5. For the following reaction, $COCl_2$ (g) $\leftrightarrow$ CO (g) + Cl_2 (g), $K_{eq} = 170$. If the concentrations of CO and Cl_2 are each 0.15 M and the concentration of $COCl_2$ is 0.0011 M, is the reaction at equilibrium? If not, which way will it proceed to reach equilibrium?

6. For the following reaction, H_2 (g) + I_2 (g) $\leftrightarrow$ 2 HI (g), $K_{eq} = 50.5$. Find Q and predict which way the reaction will proceed if $[H_2] = 0.150$ M, $[I_2] = 0.175$ M, and $[HI] = 0.950$ M.

Go Online
Check your understanding
http://webcom4.grtxle.com/
khk12Chemistry

SECTION 8.4

Le Chatelier's Principle

LAB 8.4

Changes to Equilibrium

Purpose To study how a reaction at equilibrium will change if reactants are added or removed, using the reaction Fe^{+3} (aq) + SCN^- (aq) $\leftrightarrow$ $FeSCN^{+2}$ (aq)

Materials 4 test tubes, test tube rack, 150 mL beaker, 25 mL graduated cylinder, 0.20 M $Fe(NO_3)_3$ solution, 0.002 M KSCN solution (or 0.02 M solution), small samples of solid $Fe(NO_3)_3$, KSCN, and Na_2HPO

Safety Wear goggles. Use caution with glassware, and report any spills or incidents to your teacher.

Background information The reaction that you will use is Fe^{+3} (aq) + SCN^- (aq) $\leftrightarrow$ $FeSCN^{+2}$ (aq).

The product ($FeSCN^{+2}$) is a red-brown color.

Procedure

1. Pour 25 mL of distilled water into the beaker. Add 5 drops of 0.20 M $Fe(NO_3)_3$ solution. Record observations.

2. Measure out 25 mL of 0.002 M KSCN solution. Record observations before adding it to the beaker (OR measure out 2.5 mL of 0.02 M KSCN solution in the graduated cylinder and dilute with distilled water to a total volume of 25 mL).

3. Add the KSCN solution to the beaker and stir. The system is now at equilibrium. Record observations.

4. Pour about an inch of solution into each of the four test tubes.

(continues)

Changes to Equilibrium (*cont'd.*)

5. The first test tube will be the control to compare with changes in the other three.

6. To the second test tube, add a few crystals of $Fe(NO_3)_3$. This is adding a reactant—adding Fe^{+3}. Compare it to the first test tube and record observations.

7. To the third test tube, add a few crystals of KSCN. This is adding a reactant—adding SCN^{-1}. Compare it to the first test tube and record observations.

8. To the fourth test tube, add a few crystals of Na_2HPO_4. Adding the PO_4^{-3} ion will cause a precipitate with the Fe^{+3} ion. This is the same as removing the Fe^{+3} from the solution (removing a reactant). Record observations by comparing it to the first test tube.

Observations Record all observations about the reactants before mixing, the solution at equilibrium after mixing, and the effect of adding each reactant or removing a reactant.

Discussion

1. Write the K_{eq} expression for the reaction.

2. What color change would lead you to believe that a change caused more products to form (resulting in less reactant)? What color change would lead you to believe that more reactants formed (resulting in less product)?

3. If more products are formed, the reaction is said to have "shifted to the right." If more reactants are formed, the reaction is said to have "shifted to the left." For each of the Procedure steps 6–8, write whether the reaction shifted toward the right or toward the left.

4. Write a general statement about how a reaction at equilibrium behaves if reactants are added to the system and if reactants are removed from the system.

5. Solids are not supposed to affect equilibrium, yet in steps 6–8 you added solids to the test tubes that *did* affect the equilibrium position (as evidenced by color change). Why did those solids affect the equilibrium position?

Why is equilibrium important to industry? If the K_{eq} of a reaction is very small, then the ratio of products to reactants is small—there are few products and many reactants. The reaction does not go to completion, meaning that not all of the reactants are used up to produce as many products as possible. If a company is trying to produce a chemical with a reaction that has a small K_{eq}, it will have many reactants left over with few products being produced. Chemical engineers try to find the most efficient way to produce a chemical, but sometimes the best way possible is through a reaction with a small K_{eq}. Companies need to make money, and if they have a lot of reactants left over and not much of the product they are trying to produce, then they aren't making the most money possible.

Le Chatelier's principle

Le Chatelier's principle says that if a system at equilibrium is disturbed, the reaction will proceed in one direction or another in order to re-establish equilibrium. This rule means that if the current ratio of products to reactants is equal to the equilibrium constant and that ratio is somehow disturbed or changed, the reaction will either produce more products or more reactants in order to re-establish the equilibrium ratio. At first, the Q is equal to the K_{eq}; then when we disturb the system, the Q is changed so that it is no longer equal to K_{eq}. The reaction continues until the Q equals K_{eq} again.

Another way to think about Le Chatelier's principle is that the equilibrium system will attempt to undo whatever change has occurred to get to equilibrium again.

Effect of changing concentrations

If the concentration of one of the reactants or products changes, either by adding or removing some molecules, the Q will no longer equal K_{eq}, and the reaction will shift one way or another in order to re-establish equilibrium.

Adding reactants/products (increasing concentration) If a system is at equilibrium and more reactants are poured into the system, there are now too many reactants. The ratio of products to reactants will be too small. The value of Q will now be lower than K_{eq}. In order for the Q to become equal to K_{eq} again, the reaction will reduce the number of reactants and increase the number of products. The reaction will shift toward the right (to produce more products) in order to reach equilibrium.

Likewise, if a system is at equilibrium and more products are poured into the system, there are now too many products. The ratio of products to reactants will be too large. The value of Q will now be higher than K_{eq}. In order for Q to become equal to K_{eq} again, the reaction will reduce the number or products and increase the number of reactants. The reaction will shift to the left (to produce more reactants) in order to reach equilibrium.

A manometer measures gas pipe-line pressures in inches of water, abbreviated WC for water column.

You can also think of it in terms of "undoing." When you increase the concentration of reactants, the system undoes that change by decreasing the reactants and producing more products. When you increase the number of products, the system undoes that by removing products (which makes more reactants).

Removing reactants/products (decreasing concentration)   If a system is at equilibrium and reactants are removed from the system, there are now too few reactants. The ratio of products to reactants will be too large. The value of Q will now be higher than K_{eq}. In order for Q to become equal to K_{eq} again, the reaction will reduce the number of products and increase the number of reactants. The reaction will shift to the left (to produce more reactants) in order to reach equilibrium.

If products are removed from a system at equilibrium, there are now too few products. The ratio of products to reactants will be too small. The value of Q will now be lower than K_{eq}. In order for Q to become equal to K_{eq} again, the reaction will reduce the number of reactants and increase the number of products. The reaction will shift to the right (to produce more products) in order to reach equilibrium.

The undoing principle can be applied here as well. If you remove reactants, the system undoes that change by making more reactants (a shift to the left); and if you remove products, the system undoes that by making more products (a shift to the right).

Effect of changes in volume (changes in pressure)

When the volume of a gas is changed, the pressure is also changed in an indirect relationship (see Section 3.5 for an explanation of gas behavior). If the pressure of the reactants or products is changed, the system will shift one way or another to reduce the impact of the pressure change.

Increasing the volume   If the volume of the system is increased, the pressure is decreased. In order for the system to undo the change, it will shift to increase the pressure again by shifting to the side with more moles of gas molecules (the higher number of molecules results in higher pressure). For example, for the equilibrium $2\,CO\,(g) + O_2\,(g) \leftrightarrow 2\,CO_2\,(g)$, an increase in volume (reducing pressure) would push the reaction to the left, where there are three moles of gases as opposed to the two moles of gases on the right, to create more pressure.

Decreasing the volume   If the volume of the system is decreased, the pressure is increased. In order for the system to bring the pressure of the system back down again, it will shift toward the side of the equation with the smaller number of gas molecules (lower number of molecules results in lower pressure). If you decrease the volume in the equilibrium

2 CO (g) + O$_2$ (g) $\leftrightarrow$ 2 CO$_2$ (g), the pressure will increase and the reaction will shift to the right to decrease the new pressure.

When changes in volume have no effect   What if both sides of the chemical reaction have the same number of moles of gas molecules? Then the change in volume (the change in pressure) will have no effect. A shift to either side of the reaction will not re-adjust the pressure in the system, so there is no gain to be had by shifting. The amount of products and reactants will stay the same.

Effect of changing temperature

In an endothermic reaction   An endothermic process is one in which energy is absorbed. The overall energy change of the process is positive. You can also think of these types of processes as having energy as a reactant. If energy is a reactant and you increase the energy in the system by raising the temperature, it's just like increasing the concentration of a reactant. The reaction will shift to the products side. Likewise, removing energy from the system (by dropping the temperature) is the same as removing a reactant—the reaction will shift to the left.

In an exothermic reaction   An exothermic process is one in which energy is released. The overall energy change of the process is negative. These processes can be thought of as having energy as a product. If you

This chemical sensor, using laser beams, locates and identifies chemical spills (and ground contamination) from a safe distance. The laser beams identify substances by their distinct chemical "fingerprints."

increase the energy by raising the temperature, it's the same as increasing a product—the reaction will shift to the left. Likewise, if you remove energy (by dropping the temperature), it's like removing a product—the reaction will shift to the right.

When changes do not disturb the equilibrium

Any change that does not disturb the equilibrium constant does not cause the reaction to shift in any way. Only reactants and products in an equilibrium constant expression can affect the equilibrium position of the reaction. Adding, removing, or otherwise changing substances that are not included in the equilibrium constant expression does not disturb the system at equilibrium. Therefore, changes in pure solids or liquids do not disturb the equilibrium that has been established. An exception to this rule is when you add a solid into an aqueous system and that solid dissolves and becomes a part of the aqueous system—now the aqueous compound *can* affect the equilibrium position. You observed this exception in Lab 8.4.

Also, adding a gas that is not involved in the reaction (such as a noble gas) does not change the pressure of the gases involved in the equilibrium itself, and therefore does not disturb the equilibrium.

Speeding up the time it takes to reach equilibrium

Adding a catalyst (see Section 2.8 for a discussion on catalysts) speeds up the rate of reaction. Therefore, products begin to accumulate faster because the forward reaction is happening at a higher rate. The sooner the products show up, the sooner they can begin reacting back to re-form reactants. This means that the system can come to equilibrium faster than without the catalyst. Catalysts are not included in the equilibrium constant expression, and therefore they do not affect the ratio of products to reactants at equilibrium at all—only how fast the system reaches equilibrium.

Go Online
Check your understanding
http://webcom4.grtxle.com/
khk12Chemistry

PRACTICE 8.4

Le Chatelier's Principle

For questions 1–15, say whether the reaction will shift **to the reactants** or **to the products** to re-establish equilibrium.

1. Increase concentration of a reactant (not pure liquid or solid)

2. Increase concentration of a product (not pure liquid or solid)

3. Decrease concentration of a gaseous product

4. Decrease concentration of an aqueous reactant

5. Increase concentration of a pure solid product

Le Chatelier's Principle (*cont'd.*)

6. Increase concentration of a pure solid reactant

7. Decrease the volume of the following reaction: $2\,NO_2\,(g) \leftrightarrow N_2O_4\,(g)$

8. Increase the volume of the following reaction: $H_2\,(g) + I_2\,(g) \leftrightarrow 2\,HI\,(g)$

9. Increase the volume of the following reaction:
   $NH_4Cl\,(s) \leftrightarrow NH_3\,(g) + HCl\,(g)$

10. Add a noble gas to a reaction to increase the overall pressure

11. Increase the temperature of an endothermic reaction

12. Decrease the temperature of an endothermic reaction

13. Increase the temperature of an exothermic reaction

14. Decrease the temperature of an exothermic reaction

15. Add a catalyst

16. How is Le Chatelier's principle important in industry from an economic standpoint?

17. List three ways to increase the production of products for the following equation: $2\,SO_2\,(g) + O_2\,(g) \leftrightarrow 2\,SO_3\,(g)$ (an exothermic reaction).

SECTION 8.5

Environmental Concerns

We all live on planet Earth together. However, we also all produce a large amount of waste and remove a large amount of resources.

Earth

Waste   Waste production is a major concern—landfills are filling up quickly with material that won't degrade for many lifetimes. In 2003, United States residences, businesses, and institutions created more than 236 million tons of municipal solid waste (trash), which is about 4.5 pounds of trash per person per day (an increase from 4.4 pounds per person in 2001; www.epa.gov). This growing trash problem is being addressed in two ways: (1) stopping trash from getting into the system and (2) taking care of it better once it's there.

Source reduction is stopping the trash before it's even made—reducing packaging and changing product design and manufacturing processes to create less trash in the first place. Recycling can reduce the amount of paper, glass, plastic, and metal that make it into the trash flow. Composting

How can you keep trash from ending up in a landfill?

can take care of organic (carbon-based) trash, such as food waste or lawn clippings, and further reduce the amount of trash each day.

Once the trash is in the system, more is being done to store it efficiently. Landfills have safeguards and liners in place to prevent contamination of the ground and water surrounding them. They are also being engineered in ways to maximize the capacity of the land. Combustion of trash, burning it at high temperatures, can reduce the load that landfills must support, as well as provide electricity.

Currently in the United States, 30% of waste is recovered (and recycled or composted), 15% is burned in combustion facilities, and 55% ends up in landfills (www.epa.gov).

The problem becomes even more complicated when the waste is toxic—from manufacturing or nuclear power sources. Where do you put it then? Who's willing to live near toxic dumps? How do we know that it will remain contained and not contaminate the water, ground, and air surrounding it?

Renewable and nonrenewable resources Many of our past and current energy resources are nonrenewable. Ninety percent of the energy the

United States uses is from nonrenewable sources. We may be using these energy sources much more quickly than they can be replaced; hence, they are considered nonrenewable. Estimates indicate that petroleum resources will be gone in 70–100 years, and natural gas within the next two centuries, at best. The coal supplies of the world may last another three centuries. Throughout the world, almost all of our energy is from one of these three resources. As supplies diminish and their availability runs out, they will become more and more costly to consumers. Rising costs and diminishing supplies lead people to investigate other renewable resources, such as water, solar power, nuclear power (which would alleviate production of CO_2 but then contribute to the waste problem discussed above), hybrid- and fuel-cell–powered cars, and wind.

Go Online
SC LINKS
NSTA
Topic: environmental chemistry
Go to: www.scilinks.org
Code: Chem1e307

Water The hydrologic cycle includes water evaporating into the atmosphere and falling back to the ground as precipitation (rain, sleet, snow). Once it falls back to the ground, it can fall directly into water sources such as oceans, rivers, or streams, or it can fall on solid ground. If it falls on solid ground, it can either run off the surface into water sources or soak into the ground (becoming groundwater) and work its way through underground water sources (aquifers).

Although water is a renewable resource in the sense that it cycles through the hydrologic cycle, it still must be used carefully. It may seem as if there is an abundance of water on the planet. However, consider that 97.2% of that water is salt water. Although salt water can be desalinated (the salt removed), this is an expensive process. Despite the cost, the popularity of desalination of water is increasing across the globe as people

Chemical spills require residents to evacuate, while specialists trained in various types of chemicals can clean up the accident.

Environmental chemistry seeks to protect our planet.

look for new sources of water. The other 2.8% of water on the planet is fresh water. However, 2.14% of that fraction is in the polar ice caps and glaciers. This leaves us with less than 1% of the world's water supply that is in the atmosphere as water vapor, in the ground, and in fresh-water lakes, rivers, and streams. The entire population of the world depends on this tiny fraction of the world's water supply.

Not only do people use water in obvious ways (drinking, cooking, bathing, etc.), but water is also used in household appliances, in toilet flushing, and in ways that we don't even see. Every product that you use throughout the day required water at some point in order for it to be made. This includes water used in electrical plants, water that goes into manufacturing processes and products, water used to clean vats at food production plants, water used to irrigate grasses to feed the livestock that supply our milk and meat.

Water resources are being polluted in any number of ways—from waste being poured directly into water sources, to the oil dripped on roads from our cars and washed away with the rain. Contaminants that are buried can work their way into the groundwater and pollute our resources as well. Other sources of contamination include agricultural runoff and household chemical use (such as lawn care products and detergents).

Water sources that can be reached, such as rivers and lakes, can be cleaned if they are contaminated. This is a very costly and time-consuming process, but it can be done if necessary. General Electric's Hudson River plants contaminated the Hudson River from 1947 to 1977 with PCBs (polychlorinated biphenyls, an industrial chemical mixture once used as lubricants or coolants, no longer in use in the United States). The Environmental Protection Agency (EPA) held the company responsible in 2002, rather than using taxpayer money to clean up the river. Plans were made to begin dredging the river in two phases, beginning in 2008— a very expensive proposition for the electric company. More information can be found about this process at http://www.epa.gov/hudson.

If groundwater gets contaminated (from buried waste or leaching through the ground), it's much more complicated. Even if the source of the contamination is removed, it can take a very long time for all the contamination to work its way out of the ground and into water sources, where it can be cleaned.

Air

Air moves around the entire planet. Therefore, air pollution is never only a local problem, but a global one. Pollution produced on another continent can be measured in the air in North America. This means that everyone must work together to minimize air pollution. To help with the problem, the United States government passed the Clean Air Act in 1970, and has amended it several times since then to keep up with current demands and technologies.

A smoggy day in Los Angeles, California.

Air pollutants that are too small for us to see can attract water droplets and form **aerosols** that can be seen as fog or smoke. These aerosols can remain in the air for quite awhile, participating in chemical reactions. **Particulates** are larger pollutant particles, and they will settle out to the ground. They aren't involved in chemical reactions in the air as much as aerosols, because they do settle out, but they can reduce visibility while they are in the air (the particles are large enough for us to see). Particulates can be prevented from reaching the atmosphere with techniques such as smokestack filtering or scrubbing.

Industrial smog comes from the burning of coal and oil, and produces a high number of particulates. It often contains sulfur dioxide, which accumulates in water droplets in the air and produces sulfuric acid. This contributes to acid rain problems, and breathing even small amounts of sulfuric acid can be dangerous. **Photochemical smog** is made up of compounds that need exposure to sunlight to start a chemical reaction. These pollutants primarily come from internal-combustion engines (car and diesel engines) and leaking tank farms (places where oil or fuel are stored), and include nitrogen oxides and hydrocarbons. Over the years, cars have become more efficient, and state and national governments have pressured car manufacturers to drastically lower emissions from internal-combustion engines.

Ozone

Many people have heard of the ozone layer, the ozone hole, and the threat of global warming. Ozone (O_3) is found in our atmosphere, and it absorbs ultraviolet light from the sun—protecting us from the damage that UV light would cause. The process is cyclical—ozone is broken down by UV light into molecular oxygen (O_2) and an oxygen atom (O), and then those products eventually collide and re-form the ozone (releasing heat). In other words, ozone recycles itself, as shown in Figure 8–2. The concentration of ozone in the stratosphere is quite small, yet it can absorb 95% of the UV radiation from the sun.

The problem arises when chlorofluorocarbons (CFCs) decompose the ozone in the atmosphere. Although they have been prohibited for

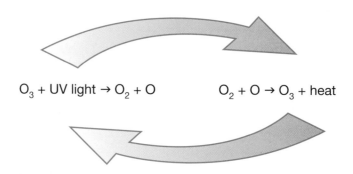

$O_3 + UV\ light \rightarrow O_2 + O$ $O_2 + O \rightarrow O_3 + heat$

Figure 8–2. The ozone reaction cycle.

The forests of South America help remove the planet's carbon dioxide. But roads continue to be built through the jungle, and deforestation follows the roads.

about 30 years, CFCs can remain in the atmosphere for a very long time and can destroy many ozone molecules each, making even a small amount of CFCs very dangerous. This has produced the ozone hole in the atmosphere, which reduces protection from the sun's dangerous UV light. The increased intensity of UV radiation reaching Earth's surface is believed to have caused the mutations in frogs and toads observed in rivers in the Northern Hemisphere.

Greenhouse gases and global warming

Greenhouse gases produce the "greenhouse effect." The ground absorbs energy from the sun during the day and is warmed. The warm ground radiates infrared waves (heat). Those waves are absorbed and emitted again by carbon dioxide, water, and other gases in the atmosphere, known as **greenhouse gases.** The greenhouse gases emit the heat back down toward the Earth, which can then reabsorb it and be warmed again. This process traps heat in the atmosphere, much as a greenhouse would with its glass walls and roof.

Carbon dioxide is the number-one concern among the gases emitted by human activity (especially the burning of fossil fuels). As more carbon dioxide accumulates in the atmosphere, more energy can be absorbed and released back toward Earth. Therefore, more and more heat will be re-emitted toward Earth as more and more carbon dioxide is produced, which leads to the global warming effect. Carbon dioxide is removed from the atmosphere by plant respiration. However, as the planet becomes more and more deforested, the number of plants available to remove carbon dioxide from the atmosphere diminishes. So at the same time that humans are expelling more carbon dioxide to the atmosphere, we are also taking away some of the planet's ability to reduce it by cutting down trees.

That global warming *could* occur is widely debated. Many variables could affect any overall temperature change—the sun's intensity, the ocean's ability to absorb greenhouse gases and heat, cloud cover, atmospheric particles, and other factors. Possible effects of global warming have already been seen in shrinking polar icecaps and loss of glacier mass, and release of this fresh water into the oceans has been predicted to cause the ocean level to rise as much as 10 feet in the course of the next century. This could not only cause flooding of lands below sea level, but also disrupt ocean currents that depend on temperature and salinity—which in turn help regulate our weather patterns.

Your job

What can you, as an ordinary citizen, do to help with these problems?

Reduce—reduce the amount of trash you produce and the amount of resources you consume.

Reuse—reuse working items, repair broken items, donate unwanted items.

Recycle—recycle glass, plastics, paper, and metal.

Become involved in public policy issues, and exercise your privilege to vote.

Go Online
Check your understanding
http://webcom4.grtxle.com/
khk12Chemistry

PRACTICE 8.5

Environmental Concerns

1. Explain how chemical manufacturers might use Le Chatelier's principle to address waste problems.

2. Explain why manufacturers might not always be able to do everything that environmental scientists suggest they do. How can a balance be struck to meet the needs of manufacturers and environmentalists? Should there be a balance, or do the needs of one group outweigh the other's?

3. Describe how the information you learned in this section compares to the knowledge you had previously, any differing opinions you hold, or concerns of which you were completely unaware. Consider each of these—Earth, water, and air.

4. List ways that you could reduce, reuse, or recycle in your life today. Make a list with at least five different ways. Share with your lab partners and discuss your ideas.

FINAL CHAPTER PROJECT

Here is your chance to use the chemistry you know to work as a research scientist to determine whether a reaction is endo- or exothermic.

An endo- or exothermic reaction?

Purpose To determine whether a chemical reaction is endothermic or exothermic based on Le Chatelier's principle. The reaction is $CoCl_4^{-2}$ (aq) $\leftrightarrow$ $[Co\cdot(H_2O)_6]^{+2}$ (aq) + 4 Cl^{-1} (aq); reactants are blue, and products are pink.

Materials Your instructor will give you a test tube with the reaction at equilibrium at room temperature. Determine the rest of the materials on your own.

⚠ **Safety** The solution is made with ethanol, which is highly flammable. Therefore, there are to be NO OPEN FLAMES during this lab! Wear goggles when working with chemicals. Use caution with glassware. Add any other safety information you think is necessary based on your procedure.

Instructions Design a lab to determine whether the reaction is endothermic or exothermic. Your write-up should include:

- **Purpose**

- **Background information** about endothermic and exothermic reactions and how Le Chatelier's principle applies to them

- **Materials**

⚠ **Safety** Remember—no open flames in the room!

- **Procedure**

- **Observations**

- **Results** Summary of findings in complete sentences; no conclusions, just summary

- **Conclusion** Restate the purpose, and answer the purpose using your results and Le Chatelier's principle as evidence. How can Le Chatelier's principle be used in other ways? How could it be used in a chemical manufacturing setting?

Some chemical reactions are reversible. At first, the forward reaction happens as the reactants collide to form products. However, after some products are made they can collide to re-form reactants. When the rate of the forward reaction equals the rate of the reverse reaction, the ratio of the concentration of products to reactants will not change. The system is then at equilibrium. It is a dynamic equilibrium, however, as the reactions continue—they just do so at the same rate, so they appear to have stopped as the ratio of concentrations remains constant.

The equilibrium constant expression (K_{eq}) can be written from the balanced equation as the ratio of the concentrations of products to reactants, with the coefficients of the balanced equation as the powers of the concentrations. Pure solids and pure liquids are not included in the K_{eq} expression, because their concentrations do not change and therefore do not affect the ratio.

The equilibrium constant is the numerical value found when concentrations of reactants and products at equilibrium are plugged into the K_{eq} expression. K_{eq} values have no units. Equilibrium constants are temperature dependent.

A very large K_{eq} indicates a larger ratio of products to reactants at equilibrium, and the reaction is said to lie to the right. A very small K_{eq} shows a smaller ratio of products to reactants at equilibrium, and the reaction is said to lie to the left.

The reaction quotient (Q) is found using the K_{eq} expression, but plugging in current concentrations. If $Q = K_{eq}$, then the system is at equilibrium. If $Q < K_{eq}$, then more products need to be made (and reactants removed) to reach equilibrium, so the reaction will shift to the right. If $Q > K_{eq}$, then more reactants need to be made (and products removed) to reach equilibrium, so the reaction will shift to the left.

Le Chatelier's principle states that if a system is at equilibrium and something is done to disturb the equilibrium, the system will re-adjust itself to reach equilibrium. This means that if you change something in a system at equilibrium, the system will attempt to undo it. Changes that affect equilibrium include adding or removing reactants or products (not a pure solid or liquid), changes in pressure of a gas reactant or product (as a result of a volume change), or changes in temperature. Changes that do *not* affect the equilibrium include adding a pure solid or liquid (even if it is a reactant or product), adding a compound that is not involved in the reaction, or adding a catalyst.

Our environment consists of the earth, water, and air. Environmental concerns include rising waste production and safe disposal, wise use of water and protection against contamination of water, choosing energy sources wisely, and how the compounds released in the air affect our protection from the sun's rays and global conditions. The concept map at the beginning of the chapter can help you review the chemistry of reactions and the factors that lead to equilibrium, and the constants, principles, and reaction quotient formulas that humans use to manipulate chemistry.

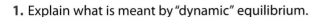
1. Explain what is meant by "dynamic" equilibrium.

2. Compare and contrast the equilibrium constant expression and the equilibrium constant.

3. Compare and contrast the equilibrium constant and the reaction quotient.

4. What does it mean to say that an equilibrium "lies to the left"? What does it mean when an equilibrium "lies to the right"?

5. What does each of the following tell you?

   a. A large K_{eq}

   b. A small K_{eq}

6. Write equilibrium constant expressions for the following.

   a. $2 H_2 (g) + O_2 (g) \leftrightarrow 2 H_2O (g)$

   b. $2 NO (g) + Br_2 (g) \leftrightarrow 2 NOBr (g)$

   c. $NaCl (s) + H_2SO_4 (l) \leftrightarrow HCl (g) + NaHSO_4 (s)$

   d. $P_4 (s) + 6 NO (g) \leftrightarrow P_4O_6 (s) + 3 N_2 (g)$

7. For the following reaction, $2 SO_2 (g) + O_2 (g) \leftrightarrow 2 SO_3 (g)$, the equilibrium concentrations are $[SO_2] = 0.175$ M, $[O_2] = 0.35$ M, and $[SO_3] = 0.70$ M. Find K_{eq}.

8. For the following reaction, $N_2 (g) + O_2 (g) \leftrightarrow 2 NO (g)$, $K_{eq} = 1.2 \times 10^{-4}$. If the concentration of N_2 is 0.166 M and the concentration of O_2 is 0.145 M, what is the concentration of NO?

9. Solve for Q and determine which way the reaction will proceed for each of the following.

   a. $CaCO_3 (s) \leftrightarrow CaO (s) + CO_2 (g)$
      $[CO_2] = 0.0004$ M, $K_{eq} = 5.10$

   b. $Fe_2O_3 (s) + 3 H_2 (g) \leftrightarrow 2 Fe (s) + 3 H_2O (g)$
      $[H_2] = 0.45$ M, $[H_2O] = 0.37$ M, $K_{eq} = 0.064$

   c. $N_2 (g) + O_2 (g) \leftrightarrow 2 NO (g)$
      $[N_2] = 0.81$ M, $[O_2] = 0.75$ M,
      $[NO] = 0.030$ M, $K_{eq} = 0.0025$

10. For each of the following changes in the reaction $2 SO_2 (g) + O_2 (g) \leftrightarrow 2 SO_3 (g)$, will they make the reaction shift toward the reactants, the products, or no change?

    a. O_2 is added

    b. SO_3 is removed

    c. SO_3 is added

    d. Volume is decreased

11. Will adding heat to an endothermic reaction make a reaction at equilibrium proceed toward the products or reactants?

12. For each of the concerns below, summarize the problem, what's causing the problem, and what can be done to alleviate the problem.

    a. Landfills becoming full

    b. Rising costs of fuel sources

    c. Groundwater contamination

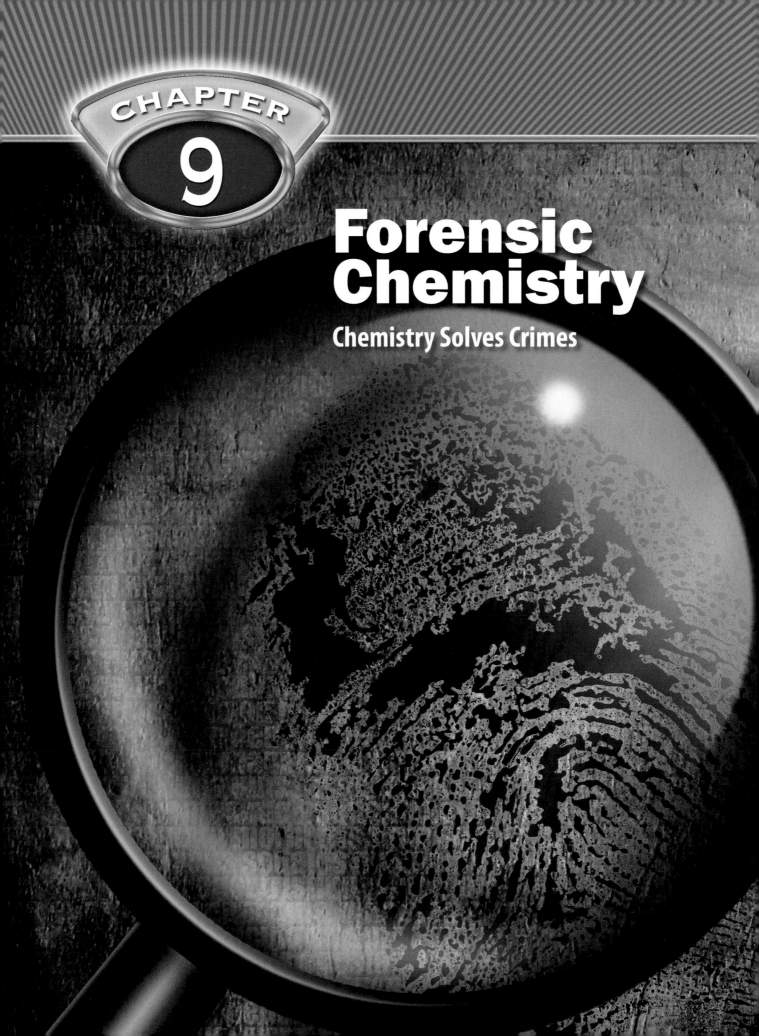

CHAPTER 9

Forensic Chemistry

Chemistry Solves Crimes

IN THIS CHAPTER

- Analysis using solubility
- Analysis using chromatography
- Analysis of a chemical formula

INTRODUCTORY
ACTIVITY

What is forensic science?

Where have you been exposed to forensic science?

What do you think those scientists do?

What types of science are involved in forensic work?

What other types of scientists might also do similar work?

Think about these ideas, share them with a partner, and then with the class.

to write a short story describing a crime scene and the chemistry used to solve the crime.

Introduction

Scientists of all types are often interested in the composition of a substance. Geologists can use the composition of a rock to identify its origin; chemists analyze substances to determine exactly how a chemical reaction proceeds; pharmaceutical scientists identify the substances in a drug sample over a period of time to set expiration dates; and forensic scientists identify substances to connect suspects to crimes or to determine how a crime happened.

Crime investigation TV shows and movies have brought forensic science into the spotlight. Many of the tests they show technicians performing involve chemistry. For example, they use a substance called Luminol to test for the presence of blood: Luminol and blood react to form a compound that glows when excited by UV radiation. Often, the stories show crime scene specialists bringing samples back to the lab for analysis in any one of several large machines that seem to print out a report in a matter of seconds. It's actually a little more complicated than that. But there are many ways in which chemists can analyze a substance to determine its composition. Often, once they determine its composition, they can compare it to samples that they have already analyzed. Then, if they find a match between their sample analysis from the crime scene and an analysis of a "known" sample, they can identify the origin of the test sample collected at the crime scene.

This chapter discusses several ways in which a chemist can identify what is in a sample.

Forensic Chemistry

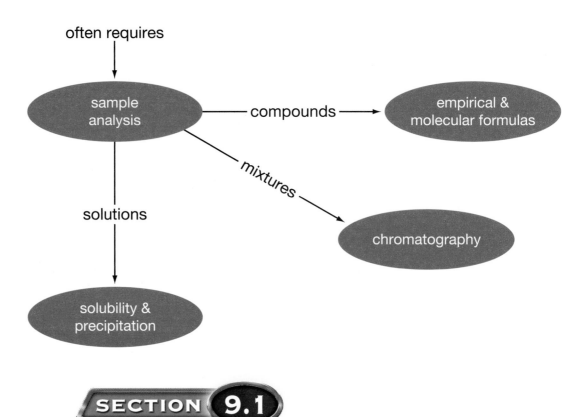

often requires

sample analysis

compounds

empirical & molecular formulas

mixtures

chromatography

solutions

solubility & precipitation

SECTION 9.1

Analysis Using Solubility

Remember that this section assumes that you have completed Chapter 8 or have an understanding of equilibrium, equilibrium constants, and reaction quotients.

What substances will dissolve in water?

Go Online
Topic: forensic chemistry
Go to: www.scilinks.org
Code: Chem1e320

*SC*INKS
NSTA

Go Online
Molecular animations
http://webcom4.grtxle.com/
khk12Chemistry

Section 6.1 describes how many ionic substances and polar substances dissolve in water, whereas most nonpolar substances do not dissolve in water. Why don't *all* ionic and polar substances dissolve in water? In order for a substance to dissolve, the intermolecular forces between the water molecules (which are very strong) must be broken, the intermolecular forces between the solute particles must be broken, and the solute and solvent must form new intermolecular forces together. Breaking attractions requires energy to be put into the system, and forming new attractions releases energy. If much more energy is needed to break the old attractions than is gained when new ones are formed, then the solute and solvent are more stable separately than they are together. Therefore, a solution will not form.

Why do copper II nitrate (on the right in the left photo) and sodium hydroxide (on the left in the left photo) dissolve in water, but when mixed, they form a precipitate (a solid that doesn't dissolve, as shown in the right photo)?

Many ionic substances will dissolve slightly in water; if only a few of the solute–solute interactions and only a few of the water–water interactions are broken, the solution will tolerate dissolving a few solute particles. The greater the difference between solute–solute/water–water interaction and solute–water interaction stability is, the less solute that will dissolve in the water.

Dissolving a substance and equilibrium

When a solid dissolves in water, the solid particles are surrounded by water molecules, and then the particles move off and are evenly dispersed through the water (see Section 6.1 for a more thorough explanation). Every once in a while, the solid molecules that are hydrated by water molecules and moving through the solution come in contact with each other and re-form their intermolecular forces, making them solid again. The more solute particles that are dissolved in the solution, the more often they will come in contact with each other and re-form into solid solute again.

If the rate at which solid particles dissolve into the solution is greater than the rate at which they re-form, the solid will continue to dissolve. This is the case in an unsaturated solution—you could still add more solute, and it would continue to dissolve faster than it would re-form into a solid.

If the rate at which solid solute dissolves into the solution is lower than the rate at which the solute re-forms, there will be a net gain in "solid." This would result in a solution that has too much solute to dissolve. (Think

Forensic technicians use chemistry to identify crime clues. They may use Luminol on evidence (which glows if blood is present). Blood can then be analyzed for its DNA.

about adding sugar to iced tea. If you add more than will dissolve, you will end up with some solid sugar that sits at the bottom of your glass.)

When the rate at which water molecules carry the solid particles away equals the rate at which the solid molecules re-form, the process of dissolving is at equilibrium. This is the case in a saturated solution; the solution is holding all that it will hold, without any excess that remains solid at the bottom of the container. *A saturated solution is at equilibrium.*

Writing equations and equilibrium constant expressions for dissolving a substance

Go Online
Animated examples
http://webcom4.grtxle.com/
khk12Chemistry

An equation can be written showing the process of a solid dissolving in water. For solid NaCl, the equation would be NaCl (s) $\rightarrow$ Na$^+$ (aq) + Cl$^-$ (aq). If a saturated solution of NaCl is at equilibrium, then the equation for the process can be written with a double arrow (to indicate equilibrium): NaCl (s) $\leftrightarrow$ Na$^+$ (aq) + Cl$^-$ (aq). If the process is at equilibrium, then an equilibrium constant expression can be written for the process. The equilibrium constant expression is the ratio of concentration of products to reactants with the balanced equation coefficients as the "powers" of each concentration (see Section 8.2). The equilibrium constant is symbolized by K. Because this is the equilibrium of solubility, it is symbolized as K_{sp} (the "sp" is for "solubility product"). The equilibrium constant expression for the solubility of NaCl would be

$$K_{sp} = \frac{[\text{Na}^+][\text{Cl}^-]}{1}$$

(Remember that pure solids and liquids are not included in equilibrium constant expressions, so the solid reactant, NaCl, is not included.)

Example 9.1A

Writing K_{sp} Expressions

1. Write the equation for the process of dissolving $Ca(NO_3)_2$.

   $Ca(NO_3)_2 \ (s) \leftrightarrow Ca^{+2} \ (aq) + 2 \ NO_3^- \ (aq)$

2. Write the solubility equilibrium constant expression for the above process.

   $K_{sp} = [Ca^{+2}][NO_3^{-1}]^2$

LAB 9.1A

Finding a Solubility Product

Purpose To find the solubility product of $Ca(OH)_2$

Materials 2 plastic pipettes, 3 test tubes, test tube rack, saturated $Ca(OH)_2$ solution, 0.10 M HCl solution, phenolphthalein

! Safety Use caution with all chemicals and with glassware. Report spills or chemical contact with skin or clothing to your teacher.

Background information A saturated solution has exactly the maximum number of ions that will dissolve in that amount of water—one more ion would cause precipitation. The K_{sp} is the equilibrium constant using the values of a saturated solution. Therefore, if you have a saturated solution and you can figure out how many ions are in it, you can solve for the solubility product. This lab will find the K_{sp} for $Ca(OH)_2$.

The reaction you will be performing is $Ca(OH)_2 + 2 \ HCl \rightarrow CaCl_2 + 2 \ H_2O$.

$Ca(OH)_2$ is a base, so it will be pink with phenolphthalein. When every molecule of $Ca(OH)_2$ has been reacted away (and therefore "counted"), the solution will no longer be pink. We can "count" the molecules by knowing how much HCl we added to take away the pink color and by using stoichiometry.

Procedure

1. Obtain a small amount of saturated $Ca(OH)_2$ solution in a beaker.

2. Use a pipette to add 50 drops of $Ca(OH)_2$ to each of the three test tubes.

3. Add one drop of phenolphthalein to each test tube. Swirl the test tube to mix. The solution will now be pink, because $Ca(OH)_2$ is basic.

4. Obtain a small amount of 0.10 M HCl in a beaker.

5. Using the other pipette, add HCl to a test tube, drop by drop, swirling after each drop. Try to drop the solution directly into the liquid below—don't let the drops slide down the side of the test tube. Stop adding when the solution turns colorless. Record the number of HCl drops needed to remove the pink color. Repeat with the other two test tubes.

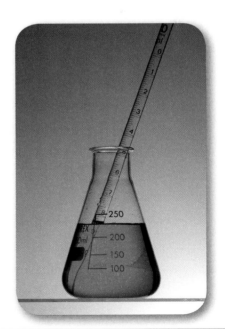

(continues)

Finding a Solubility Product (*cont'd.*)

of HCl for each of the three trials. There are about 15,000 drops in 1 liter.

2. Use the liters of 0.10 M HCl used in a trial (from result 1), the balanced equation in the background information, and the liters of $Ca(OH)_2$ used (from result 1) to find the concentration of $Ca(OH)_2$ in each trial through stoichiometry.

3. Average the concentrations of $Ca(OH)_2$ from the three trials.

4. Write the balanced equation for the dissolving process (**dissolution**) of $Ca(OH)_2$ (s).

5. Use the average concentration of $Ca(OH)_2$ to find the average concentrations of Ca^{+2} and OH^- in the saturated solution.

6. Write the K_{sp} expression for the dissolution of $Ca(OH)_2$.

7. Use the average concentrations of Ca^{+2} and OH^- to solve for K_{sp}.

Conclusion Restate purpose and answer the purpose with your results. What are three possible sources of error? Create a class histogram (see Lab 2.7, Discussion question 5). Describe the class results. Is there a clear mode? If not, suggest possible reasons.

Data table

Trial	Drops of HCl added
1	
2	
3	

Results/Calculations

1. Convert "drops of solutions" to "liters of solutions" for the original 50 drops of $Ca(OH)_2$ and the drops

Determining whether a substance will precipitate out

How can you tell if you've added too much solute to a solution so it will have excess solute at the bottom of the beaker? How can you tell if you've added enough that it will be a saturated solution?

Just as in other examples of equilibrium in Chapter 8, you can calculate the reaction quotient (Q) with concentrations at any given time (see Section 8.3). If the reaction quotient is equal to the equilibrium constant, then the process is at equilibrium. If you're working with dissolving a substance and the $Q = K_{sp}$, then the solution is saturated.

If $Q < K_{sp}$, then there are too few products (the top of the ratio is too small) in the current solution to be at equilibrium. For dissolving substances, the "products" are the ions that are dissolved. Therefore, if $Q < K_{sp}$, there are too few particles dissolved to be at equilibrium, and the solution is unsaturated.

If $Q > K_{sp}$, then there are too many products (the top of the ratio is too large), meaning there are too many particles dissolving and the solution can't hold them all. Therefore, the extra particles will re-form into "solid" and either make the solution cloudy (the result of solid particles' being mixed throughout the sample) or sink to the bottom (if the density and particle size are large enough and if you wait long enough). This is called forming a **precipitate**. The particles that do dissolve form a saturated solution—the solution itself is holding all the solute particles it can, making it saturated, and the extra particles that the solution cannot hold form a solid, the precipitate.

A geothermal lake in New Zealand has formed a sinter precipitate of silica.

Example 9.1B

Using Q with K_{sp}

1. A solution of $Mg(OH)_2$ at equilibrium contains the following concentrations: $[Mg^{+2}] = 4 \times 10^{-5}$ M and $[OH^-] = 8 \times 10^{-5}$ M. Find the K_{sp} for $Mg(OH)_2$.

   - First write the equation for the dissolving process:

     $$Mg(OH)_2 \text{ (s)} \leftrightarrow Mg^{+2} \text{ (aq)} + 2\,OH^- \text{ (aq)}$$

   - Then write the K_{sp} expression:

     $$K_{sp} = [Mg^{+2}][OH^-]^2$$

   - Then plug in the concentrations to solve for K_{sp}:

     $$K_{sp} = (4 \times 10^{-5} \text{ M})(8 \times 10^{-5} \text{ M})^2 = 2.6 \times 10^{-13}$$

2. If you try to form a solution of $Mg(OH)_2$ with the following concentrations, will it be unsaturated, saturated, or contain a precipitate if $K_{sp} = 2.6 \times 10^{-13}$?

   $$[Mg^{+2}] = 2 \times 10^{-5} \text{ M and } [OH^-] = 2 \times 10^{-4} \text{ M}$$

   The equation and the K_{sp} expression are the same as in the previous question.

   Use the current concentrations to solve for Q:

   $$Q = [Mg^{+2}][OH^-]^2 =$$
   $$(2 \times 10^{-5} \text{ M})(2 \times 10^{-4} \text{ M})^2 = 8 \times 10^{-13}$$

   Because $Q > K_{sp}$, the solution is *saturated, with a precipitate.*

Precipitation reactions

A precipitate can also form when two soluble compounds are dissolved in water separately and then the two solutions are combined. The cation of one soluble compound, when combined with the anion of the other soluble compound, can form a new compound that is less soluble in water than the original two compounds. Therefore, the new, less-soluble compound will form a precipitate. Precipitation reactions are double replacement reactions.

A chart with solubility rules (a list of rules to determine whether a double replacement reaction will form a precipitate or not) can be found at the end of Chapter 6. But even with these solubility rules, the compounds that form precipitates in large concentrations may not form a precipitate if the concentrations are low enough. If the Q is lower than or equal to the K_{sp} for that compound, then the newly formed solute will dissolve.

The insoluble compound formed when sodium hydroxide and copper(II) nitrate are mixed is a precipitate.

Example 9.1C

Precipitation Reactions

Write the double replacement reaction for the combination of the following two soluble compounds: $AgNO_3$ and $BaCl_2$

- First, write the double replacement reaction, balancing ion charges to write correct chemical formulas:

$$AgNO_3 + BaCl_2 \rightarrow AgCl + Ba(NO_3)_2$$

- Next, balance the equation:
$$2\,AgNO_3 + BaCl_2 \rightarrow 2\,AgCl + Ba(NO_3)_2$$

- Finally, use solubility rules to determine which products are soluble and which are not.

- $AgCl$ is insoluble, and $Ba(NO_3)_2$ is soluble:
$$2\,AgNO_3\ (aq) + BaCl_2\ (aq) \rightarrow 2\,AgCl\ (s) + Ba(NO_3)_2\ (aq)$$

Using solubility information for analysis of a sample

Solubility rules and solubility equilibrium can be used to determine what's in a solution of unknown composition. For example, if you think there might be chloride ions (Cl^-) in the solution, you could add silver ions (Ag^+) to the sample. If chloride ions were indeed present, the AgCl would form an insoluble compound (a precipitate). The precipitate would be a positive test for Cl^- ions.

However, it's not always that easy. What if the solution was thought to contain both chloride ions and sulfate ions (SO_4^{-2})? Silver ions precipitate with both of those anions, forming AgCl or Ag_2SO_4. How would you know which one caused the precipitate, chloride or sulfate? You could use two tests, in the correct order. First, add calcium ions, which precipitate with the sulfate ion (forming $CaSO_4$) but not with chloride ($CaCl_2$ is soluble). If the addition of the calcium ions results in a precipitate, you have a positive test for sulfate ion. You can filter out any precipitate that did form in the sample (which would contain the sulfate ions if there were any) and then add the silver ions, which would precipitate with any chloride ions that are in the solution. With the sulfate ions removed from the solution, you would know that the silver ions were indeed precipitating with chloride and not the sulfate.

There is another way in which you could test for different ions. If you were testing for more than one ion and they do not precipitate out with the same chemicals, then you could test for one ion in one test tube and then test for the other ion in a fresh test tube. For example, if you were testing for Cl^- and SO_4^{-2}, you could have two test tubes, each with a sample of the test solution. To the first test tube add Ba^{+2}, which will precipitate with SO_4^{-2} but not with Cl^-. A precipitate would be a positive indicator for the presence of SO_4^{-2}. To the second test tube you could add Tl^+, which precipitates with Cl^- but not with SO_4^{-2}. A precipitate in the second test tube would be a positive indicator for the presence of Cl^-.

Qualitative and quantitative analysis

When a mixture contains many possible ions, the process begins to get much more complicated, and requires many steps to systematically remove one ion at a time. This process can be done qualitatively or quantitatively. If someone is testing just to see if chloride ion is there or not, he or she is doing **qualitative analysis**—testing for what is and isn't there. However, a person could add enough cation to be sure that all the chloride ions in the sample have precipitated out, then filter, dry, and find the mass of the precipitate and use the results to calculate how much chloride ion was in the sample. When measuring exactly how much of something is in a sample, it is called **quantitative analysis**.

In the 1970s, forensic light sources were big and costly. They used argon-ion lasers cooled by water. Today's more compact version weighs in at 18 pounds and uses strong incandescent bulbs with filters. Evidence such as fingerprints show up because organic materials absorb and fluoresce at different wavelengths.

Analysis with Solubility

Problem To identify which ions are in a water sample; possibilities include Ca^{+2}, Mg^{+2}, and Ag^+. Determine which, if any, of these cations are in your sample.

Instructions Design a lab to qualitatively identify the ions in the water sample. Your write-up must include:

- **Title**

- **Problem**

- **Background information** (about how solubility can be used to determine what ions are in a sample; include the reasoning for why you test for them in the order in which you decide to do it.)

- **Materials** (You will have access to solutions of the following anions, but you may or may not need to use them all: Cl^-, CH_3COO^-, NO_3^-, SO_4^{-2}, CrO_4^{-2}, OH^-. You will also have access to the usual lab equipment, so make a complete list of what you will need.)

 Safety

- **Procedure**

- **Data table/Observations**

- **Results** (A sentence summary of what happened; no conclusions yet!)

- **Conclusion** (Restate the purpose, give your findings with evidence from your results, include two possible sources of error, and describe a situation in which this could be used in a crime scene investigation.)

PRACTICE 9.1

Analysis with Solubility

1. Compare and contrast the equilibrium constant and equilibrium constant expression you learned about in chapter 8 with solubility product expression and solubility product.

2. Write the balanced equation and the K_{sp} expression for each of the following compounds' dissolution.

   a. $AgCl$ (s)

   b. $CaCl_2$ (s)

   c. Ag_2CrO_4 (s)

3. True or False: Solubility product remains the same no matter what temperature you're working at.

Go Online
Check your understanding
http://webcom4.grtxle.com/
khk12Chemistry

Analysis with Solubility (*cont'd.*)

4. True or False: The higher the value of the solubility product, the more soluble the solid is in water.

5. Find the value of K_{sp} for the following (you'll need to write the balanced equation and K_{sp} expression for each solid first).

   a. $Cd(OH)_2$ (s): at equilibrium, $[Cd^{+2}] = 1.7 \times 10^{-5}$ M and $[OH^-] = 3.4 \times 10^{-5}$ M.

   b. $Ce(OH)_3$ (s): at equilibrium, $[Ce^{+3}] = 5.2 \times 10^{-6}$ M and $[OH^-] = 1.6 \times 10^{-5}$ M.

6. What is a saturated solution?

7. True or False: Solubility equilibrium does not use the idea of "reactant quotient" as does reaction equilibrium.

8. Define *precipitation* in your own words. (Not dealing with weather!)

9. Why do some compounds dissolve while others are precipitates (don't dissolve)?

10. For the following, determine whether a precipitate will form or not (you'll need to write the balanced equation and K_{sp} expression for each solid first).

    a. $[Mg^{+2}] = 1.8 \times 10^{-4}$ M, $[OH^-] = 3.0 \times 10^{-4}$ M. For $Mg(OH)_2$, $K_{sp} = 8.9 \times 10^{-12}$.

    b. $[Ca^{+2}] = 1.5 \times 10^{-4}$ M, $[F^-] = 2.7 \times 10^{-4}$ M. For CaF_2, $K_{sp} = 3.9 \times 10^{-11}$.

    c. $[Ba^{-2}] = 4.0 \times 10^{-10}$ M, $[CrO_4^{-2}] = 1.0 \times 10^{-11}$ M. For $BaCrO_4$, $K_{sp} = 2.0 \times 10^{-10}$.

11. For each of the following, complete the double replacement reaction with a balanced equation that indicates which products form precipitates. If no precipitation occurs, write "no reaction."

    a. $KI + Pb(NO_3)_2$

    b. $Pb(NO_3)_2 + CuCl_2$

    c. $K_2CO_3 + LiNO_3$

    d. $Ca(CH_3COO)_2 + Na_3PO_4$

    e. $Ba(OH)_2 + Na_2SO_4$

12. For the following mixture, in what order would you introduce which anions to selectively precipitate out the cations one at a time: Ca^{+2}, Ag^+, Pb^{+2}, Cu^{+2}? For each anion you list, indicate which of the cations it would be precipitating out.

Go Online
Topic: chromatography
Go to: www.scilinks.org
Code: Chem1e330

SC*INKS*
NSTA

Investigator searching for fingerprints on wood by using an iodine fuming tube.

SECTION 9.2

Analysis Using Chromatography

Chromatography is a separation technique. Many different types of mixtures can be separated and analyzed by chromatography to determine what was in the mixture.

There are many types of chromatography, but they all work on the same principle. There are two phases in a chromatography system—a **stationary phase** and a **mobile phase**. What makes up these phases depends on the type of chromatography (which will be discussed below), but each type has both phases. The test sample is a mixture, which means it contains more than one compound or element physically mixed together (not bonded with chemical bonds, just physically mixed). The different components of the mixture are attracted to the stationary phase and the mobile phase differently.

These attractions depend on the size of the molecules in the mixture and the intermolecular forces that can be formed between the molecules in the test sample and the molecules that make up the stationary phase and the mobile phase (see Section 5.5 for information on intermolecular forces). If a molecule in the test sample is strongly attracted to the stationary phase, it will move very slowly—it will "stick" to the stationary phase and spend less time moving along with the mobile phase. If a molecule in the test sample is strongly attracted to the mobile phase, it will move very quickly—it will spend most of its time in the mobile phase and very little time "stuck" to the stationary phase.

The size of the components can also play a part in determining how fast they move. Small particles move much faster than larger particles.

These differences in attraction for the two phases (and differences in component molecule size) will separate the mixture—some things will move very quickly, some very slowly, and others somewhere in between. The type of chromatography selected to separate a mixture and what is used for the stationary phase and mobile phase must be chosen carefully. If all the components of the test sample are almost equally attracted to the mobile phase and not to the stationary phase, then they will all move through quickly, and very little separation between the components will occur. However, if components are too strongly attracted to the stationary phase, they will not move through fast enough, and each component will become spread out over the stationary phase.

Paper chromatography

Paper chromatography uses paper as the stationary phase. The paper can be special chromatography paper, or even a coffee filter. The test sample is dabbed on one end of the paper, and then the paper is dipped into a solution (the mobile phase). The solution then moves up the paper, carrying with it the test sample. The components in the test sample separate and form various spots on the paper (Figure 9–1). When the spots have all separated from each other, the paper is removed from the mobile phase and allowed to dry. It's very important to mark the spot where the test sample originally started, as well as where the mobile phase stopped moving forward (the **leading edge** of the mobile phase).

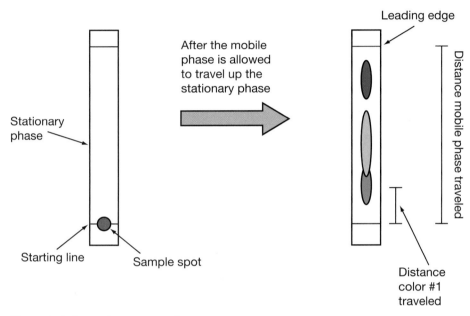

Go Online
Molecular animations
http://webcom4.grtxle.com/khk12Chemistry

Figure 9–1. Paper chromatography.

First, measure the distance that each component traveled from the original spot of the test sample. Also measure the distance the solvent traveled from the original spot of the test sample. Find the ratio, called the **retention factor (R_f)**:

$$R_f = \frac{\text{length traveled by component}}{\text{length traveled by mobile phase}}$$

The R_f depends on how attracted the component is to the mobile phase—the more attracted to the mobile phase, the more time it will spend in the mobile phase (as opposed to the stationary phase, the paper), and it will travel farther. The closer the R_f is to 1, the greater the attraction to the mobile phase.

The R_f of each component can then be compared to R_f values of known components to determine which components were in the original test sample. The R_f depends on the attraction between the component and the mobile phase versus the component and the stationary phase. Therefore, if you change the mobile phase or the stationary phase, then the R_f will

change. This means that the known R_f that you use to compare with your unknown components' R_f will need to be found using the same stationary phase and the same mobile phase as the test sample you investigated.

Paper chromatography is often used to separate colored dyes, such as inks or plant dyes, but it can also be used to separate amino acids and with RNA techniques.

Thin layer chromatography

Thin layer chromatography (TLC) is similar to paper chromatography. It uses a plastic or glass plate that contains an absorbent material (the stationary phase). The rest of the process is very much like that for paper chromatography. This technique can be used to check for the purity of an organic compound, for detecting pesticides or insecticides, or to determine the components in fiber samples.

Liquid chromatography

Liquid chromatography or **column chromatography** is a technique that uses a tube (column) packed with a material. The test sample is added to one end of the column. The mobile phase is then continuously added to the column. The test sample and the mobile phase travel through the column. The sample and mobile phase can travel down through a vertical column because of gravity (known as **column chromatography**), or the mobile phase can be pushed through a column with high pressure (known as **high-pressure liquid chromatography, HPLC**). The larger component molecules will get trapped in the packing material more often and take longer to travel down the column, whereas the smaller component molecules can move more quickly through the column. Also, there are interactions between the component molecules and the stationary phase (the packing material) and the mobile phase, just as there are in paper chromatography, which affect the rate at which a component travels through the column.

The time that a component of the sample comes off the column can be compared with the time that other known samples come off the same column (stationary phase) using the same mobile phase and, in the case of HPLC, the same pressure.

Sometimes, a sample container is placed at the end of the column to catch the mobile phase with the components that are washing through the column. The container is changed every so often to catch different components as they wash off the column at different times (depending on how fast or slow they moved through the column). The containers can then be analyzed using other lab techniques to determine exactly what is in each container. This technique can also be used to separate dyes, and each container would therefore hold a different dye (and be a different

Blood splatter tells a lot about how a fight took place.

color), to analyze water for contaminants, or to test a pharmaceutical drug for purity.

Gas chromatography

Gas chromatography is used to analyze volatile substances (those that easily turn into a vapor). It uses a column packed with an absorbent material (the stationary phase), and helium (or other gas)—the mobile phase—is flushed through the column. The test sample separates into its components based upon molecule size and attraction to the two phases. The various gases in the sample have different thermal conductivities or combustion enthalpies, and this is recorded electronically as the gases come off the column. This technique can be used to detect bomb materials and drugs and to compare fibers.

A *gas chromatograph* is an extremely hot oven that holds a hollow-coiled column. This historical picture of a chromatograph was made by Perkin-Elmer, a firm that began making chromatographs in the 1950s and still makes them today.

Column Chromatography

Purpose To analyze the food colors in a powdered drink by column chromatography

Materials Column (wide-stem plastic pipette, super jumbo plastic pipette, or short-stemmed Pasteur pipette), glass wool or cotton, sand, silica or alumina slurry, 5–10 small test tubes, small graduated cylinder, drink samples

 Safety Be careful with glassware. Do not drink the samples!

Procedure

1. Prepare the sample

   a. If using a powdered drink mix, add 1 gram of powdered drink mix to 10 g of water and stir—the color should be very intense.

   b. If using a soda, make sure that it is flat (no more bubbles) by letting it set out or by stirring it with a magnetic stirrer. Use it as is once it is flat.

   c. If using juice, it may be used "straight" (not diluted).

   d. Prepare your sample collection tubes.

   e. Fill each test tube with 5 mL of water and draw a line across the test tube at the water level. Empty all of the test tubes.

2. Either use a column that is already prepared or follow these steps to prepare a new column. The more level your layers, the better your separation will be.

   a. Cut the bulb off a wide-stem plastic pipette or the very top of the bulb off a super jumbo pipette so that you have access to the bulb from the top, or use a Pasteur pipette.

   b. Pack a small amount of glass wool or cotton in the bottom of the wide part of the column. It will filter out any solids as the sample flows through—you need just enough so that the sand and slurry you're about to add won't flow through.

   c. Add a small amount of sand to the column. It will provide a flat base for the stationary phase.

   d. Add silica slurry or alumina slurry to fill the column about ½ full. Stir the slurry right before you pour it into the column!

   e. Add a second layer of sand on top as a shock absorber to prevent disturbing the slurry.

   f. Add water to the top of the column, being careful not to disturb the layer of sand on top. You may want to use a pipette to add liquid to the top of the column. From this point on, do not let the column "dry out"—keep some water at the top at all times to prevent air bubbles from traveling down into the column. Have a beaker or test tube below the column to catch what flows through the column.

3. **Run the sample:** *Read the next two steps thoroughly before beginning* so that you understand all that you need to do.

   a. Wait until the water you've added is almost gone from the top of the column. Add the sample onto the column, being careful not to disturb the sand layer. Add as much as you can for your size of column. When the sample level is almost down to the sand layer, begin adding water to ensure that the column never runs dry (always being careful not to disturb the sand layer). It is important to have no air bubbles!

   b. Catch what begins to flow through in the first test tube. When the liquid level reaches the line on the test tube, put that test tube in the test tube rack and use the next one. Any test tubes from the beginning that are totally clear can be emptied and reused, because they were catching the water that was in the column before you added the drink mix.

   c. If there is time, let water flow through the column until all of the colors have come through, and then add another type of drink (colored pop that is flat—no bubbles—or another color of powdered drink mix prepared as above).

Data table

Make a list of what color fills each test tube. Be as descriptive as possible.

LAB 9.2A

Column Chromatography (*cont'd.*)

Discussion

1. What was the stationary phase in this experiment?

2. What was the mobile phase?

3. Which was more polar—the stationary phase or the mobile phase?

4. List the colors of the drink from most polar to least polar.

5. Explain why you made the color list the way you did. What science concepts did you use to determine the relative polarity of the colors?

LAB 9.2B

Analysis with Paper Chromatography

A crime scene has a note written in pen by the kidnappers. The investigators believe that if they can narrow down what kind of pen the writer used, they may be able to trace it to the suspects.

Purpose To identify the source of an unknown ink sample by comparing it to known ink samples using paper chromatography

Materials Four strips of chromatography paper about 15 cm long (one of which has the ink sample from the "crime scene" already on it), three known samples of ink to test, denatured alcohol, watch glass, 400 mL beaker, tape

 Safety Be careful with glassware.

Procedure

1. Lay the strips of paper down vertically. Make a horizontal *pencil* (not pen) line 2 cm from the bottom of the paper (this has already been done for you on the strip that has the unknown sample).

2. For each of the three test inks, label the top of each strip of paper (in pencil) with a name to identify which ink is being tested on which strip.

3. Make a *small* ink dot in the center of the pencil line for each of the three test inks. Let the dot air dry. Repeat in the same spot. Keep the ink spots as small as possible. Repeating several small dots in the same spot after drying the one before keeps the dot from spreading while still getting plenty of ink on the strip.

4. Fill your beaker about an inch high with denatured alcohol (or other solvent).

5. Place each of the four chromatography strips in the beaker so that the tip is in the water, but the water level does not touch the ink dots. Fold the top end over the beaker and tape it to the outside of the beaker to ensure that it doesn't slip in.

6. Place the watch glass on top of the beaker to keep the alcohol from evaporating from the test strip too soon.

(continues)

Analysis with Paper Chromatography (*cont'd.*)

7. Make observations as the solvent is absorbed up through the strips of paper.

8. When the solvent almost reaches the top of the paper, remove the paper from the beaker and lay it on a piece of paper towel. Draw a pencil line along the leading edge of the solvent (where the solvent stopped moving).

9. Measure and record the distance between the bottom line and the top line—this is the distance the solvent traveled.

10. Measure and record the distance between the bottom line and the center of the first color—this is the distance that color #1 traveled. Repeat for each color on the strip.

11. Repeat the measurements for each of the four strips.

Calculations

Calculate the R_f value for each color on each strip of paper.

Conclusion Restate the purpose. Use your data and observations to identify the unknown ink sample. Explain why the starting and finishing lines on the strips of paper are drawn in pencil. Explain why you don't have to make sure that the solvent travels the same distance on each strip of paper—each strip can have a different solvent distance, and you can still draw valid conclusions from the experiment. What other kinds of things could you test in this manner?

Data table

	Test strip #1	Test strip #2	Test strip #3	Unknown sample from crime scene
Type of ink				N/A
Distance solvent traveled (cm)				
Color #1				
Distance color #1 traveled (cm)				
Color #2				
Distance color #2 traveled (cm)				
Continue this table in the same manner (color #3 and so on) for each color that appears on the strips.				

Go Online
Check your understanding
http://webcom4.grtxle.com/
khk12Chemistry

PRACTICE 9.2

Analysis with Chromatography

1. A substance has an R_f value of 0.45 in water and an R_f value of 0.65 in propanol. Explain why the same substance would have a different R_f value in different solvents.

2. To which mobile phase in question 1 is the substance more attracted?

Analysis with Chromatography (*cont'd.*)

3. Explain the similarities and differences between at least three types of chromatography. Give an example of the type of sample each type of chromatography could be used for.

4. A crime scene investigator finds a stain that he believes is fruit juice at a crime scene. Describe how chromatography could be used to determine which juice it was that caused the stain. Is there more than one type of chromatography that could be used? Describe each type that could be used.

5. Determine the R_f value of the sample shown in Figure 9–2. You can measure it as if it were a real sample.

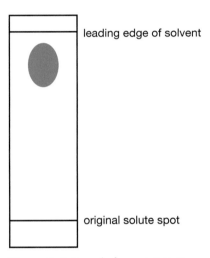

leading edge of solvent

original solute spot

Figure 9–2. Sample for question 5.

SECTION 9.3

Analysis of a Chemical Formula

There are several ways to express the composition of an unknown sample. The individual elements in a sample can be removed and analyzed. Once the masses of each individual element in the sample are found, the percent composition, empirical formula, or molecular formula can be determined.

Percent composition

Percent of anything is

$$\frac{\text{part}}{\text{whole}} \times 100$$

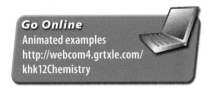

Go Online
Animated examples
http://webcom4.grtxle.com/
khk12Chemistry

For **percent composition**, the "part" is the mass of the individual element or substance, and the "whole" is the mass of the whole sample. Percent composition calculations can be performed on each individual element in a chemical compound or on each substance in a mixture.

Example 9.3A

Percent Composition

1. What is the percent composition of a 3.00 g sample that contains 1.45 g of carbon and 1.55 g of hydrogen?

$$\%C = \frac{1.45 \text{ g}}{3.00 \text{ g}} \times 100 = 48.3\%$$

$$\%H = \frac{1.55 \text{ g}}{3.00 \text{ g}} \times 100 = 51.7\%$$

2. What is the percent composition of $Ca(NO_3)_2$?

- Use the molecular mass for the "sample's" mass and the amounts that the individual elements contribute to the molecular mass for the "element's" mass.

Molecular mass:

$1 \times Ca = 1 \times 40.08 = \quad 40.08$

$2 \times N = \quad 2 \times 14.01 = \quad 28.02$

$6 \times O = \quad 6 \times 16.00 = \quad \underline{96.00}$

$\qquad\qquad\qquad\qquad 164.10 \text{ g/mole}$

$$\%Ca = \frac{40.08 \text{ g/mole}}{164.10 \text{ mole}} \times 100 = 24.4\%$$

$$\%N = \frac{28.02 \text{ g/mole}}{164.10 \text{ mole}} \times 100 = 17.1\%$$

$$\%O = \frac{96.00 \text{ g/mole}}{164.10 \text{ mole}} \times 100 = 58.5\%$$

PRACTICE 9.3A

Percent Composition

1. A gas container found at a crime scene is believed to be important to solving the crime. The lab reported that the gas contained 82.6% carbon and 17.4% hydrogen. Use percent composition to determine whether the sample was propane (C_3H_8) or butane (C_4H_{10}).

2. Find the percent composition of a compound that contains 1.94 g of carbon, 0.48 g of hydrogen, and 2.58 g of sulfur in a 5.00 g sample of the compound.

3. A sample of an unknown compound has a mass of 0.847 g with the following composition: 50.51% F and 49.49% Fe. What were the masses of F and Fe in the sample?

4. Find the percent composition of a compound that contains 2.63 g C, 0.370 g H, and 0.580 g O in a 3.58 g sample.

Go Online
Check your understanding
http://webcom4.grtxle.com/
khk12Chemistry

Percent Composition (*cont'd.*)

5. A sample of an unknown compound with a mass of 2.876 g has the following composition: 66.07% C, 6.71% H, 4.06% N, and 23.16% O. What is the mass of each element in the sample?

6. A sample of a compound that has a mass of 0.432 g is analyzed. The sample is found to be made up of oxygen and fluorine only. If the sample has 0.128 g of oxygen, find the percent composition.

7. Find the percent composition of the following.

   a. $Co(NH_2)_2$

   b. Al_2S_3

   c. $(NH_4)_2C_2O_4$

Empirical formulas

The word *empirical* means that the results came from data that were collected in the lab or in the field. The **empirical chemical formula** (or just **empirical formula**) is the ratio of the elements in a chemical formula. Specifically, it is the lowest possible whole-number ratio of the elements in a chemical formula. You can think of it as the ratio of atoms or the ratio of moles, since the unit of moles is just a way of counting a lot of atoms at once.

Masses of the elements can often be easily measured in a lab. The masses must be converted into the number of moles of each element. The number of moles of the elements can then be compared to the smallest number of moles in the sample—this will produce the lowest possible ratio. If the comparison results in ratios that are not whole numbers, the ratio is then multiplied by whatever factor is necessary to produce the lowest possible whole-number ratio.

Go Online
Animated examples
http://webcom4.grtxle.com/khk12Chemistry

Example 9.3B

Empirical Formulas

Find the empirical formula of a sample that has 40.92 g C, 4.58 g H, and 54.50 g O.

- Change grams to moles for all components.

$$40.92 \text{ g C} \times \frac{1 \text{ mole C}}{12.01 \text{ g C}} = 3.407 \text{ mole C}$$

$$4.58 \text{ g H} \times \frac{1 \text{ mole H}}{1.01 \text{ g H}} = 4.54 \text{ mole H}$$

$$54.50 \text{ g O} \times \frac{1 \text{ mole O}}{16.00 \text{ g O}} = 3.406 \text{ mole O}$$

(continues)

Example 9.3B

Empirical Formulas (*cont'd.*)

- Compare all the components' number of moles to the smallest number of moles (3.406 moles in this problem) to get the lowest possible ratio.

$$\frac{3.407 \text{ mole C}}{3.406 \text{ mole}} = 1.000 \text{ C}$$

$$\frac{4.54 \text{ mole H}}{3.406 \text{ mole}} = 1.33 \text{ H}$$

$$\frac{3.406 \text{ mole O}}{3.406 \text{ mole}} = 1.000 \text{ O}$$

- This ratio (1.00:1.33:1.00) is not a whole-number ratio. Therefore, we need to multiply each number by a factor that will make them all the smallest whole numbers possible. In this case, that factor is 3.

$$1.00 \text{ C} \times 3 = 3.00 \text{ C}$$

$$1.33 \text{ H} \times 3 = 4.00 \text{ H}$$

$$1.00 \text{ O} \times 3 = 3.00 \text{ O}$$

- Write the formula with the lowest possible whole-number ratio: $C_3H_4O_3$

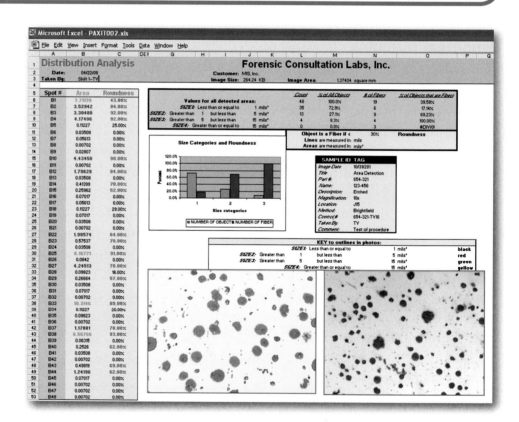

Computer software aids forensic chemists in analyzing evidence such as fibers and splatters.

Go Online
Animated example
http://webcom4.grtxle.com/
khk12Chemistry

Molecular formulas

The empirical formula is the lowest possible whole-number ratio of the atoms in a molecule. An example of an empirical formula is CH_3. But the actual molecule could be CH_3, C_2H_6, C_3H_9 or any other multiple. How do we know which chemical formula makes up the actual sample? What is the actual formula, the **molecular formula**?

The molecular mass of a substance can be determined by several laboratory methods—with sophisticated instruments, titrations, or precipitation reactions. Once the molecular mass has been determined, the empirical formula mass can be compared to it. How many times larger is the actual molecular mass than the empirical formula's mass? That's the same number of times larger the actual molecule is than the empirical formula.

Camel hair brushes have a gentle stroke that helps apply powder to look for fragile latent prints.

Example 9.3C

Molecular Formulas

The molecular mass of a compound is 176.14 g/mole. The empirical formula of the compound is $C_3H_4O_3$. Find the molecular formula.

- First, find the molecular mass of the empirical formula.

  $3 \times C = 3 \times 12.01 = 36.03$

  $4 \times H = 4 \times 1.01\ \ = 4.04$

  $3 \times O = 3 \times 16.00 = \underline{48.00}$

  88.07 g/mole

- Then, compare the empirical formula's mass to the molecular formula's mass.

  $$\frac{176.14 \text{ g/mole}}{88.07 \text{ g/mole}} = 2.00$$

- The molecular mass is twice as big, so the molecular formula must be twice as big as well.

  $C_6H_8O_6$

PRACTICE 9.3B

Empirical and Molecular Formulas

1. A gas container found at a crime scene is believed to be important to solving the crime. The lab reported that the gas contained 83.2% carbon and 16.8% hydrogen. Find the empirical formula of the sample.

2. Determine the empirical formula of a compound containing 0.928 g of gallium and 0.412 g of phosphorus.

3. Determine the empirical formula of a compound containing 1.723 g of carbon, 0.289 g of hydrogen, and 0.459 g of oxygen.

4. Find the empirical formula of a compound, given that a 48.5 g sample of the compound contains 1.75 g of carbon and 46.75 g of bromine.

Go Online
Check your understanding
http://webcom4.grtxle.com/khk12Chemistry

(continues)

Empirical and Molecular Formulas (*cont'd.*)

5. Determine the empirical formula of a compound containing 20.23% aluminum and 79.77% chlorine.

6. Determine the empirical formula of a compound containing 4.288 g of carbon and 5.712 g of oxygen.

7. Find the molecular formula of a compound that has 42.56 g of palladium and 0.80 g of hydrogen. The molecular mass of the compound is 216.8 g/mole.

8. Find the molecular formula of a compound that contains 30.45% N and 69.55% O. The molecular mass of the compound is 92.02 g/mole.

9. Find the molecular formula of a compound with a 212.1 g sample that has 42.4 g of hydrogen and 169.7 g of carbon, and the molecular mass is 30.0 g/mole.

10. A compound is known to have a molecular mass of 391.5 g/mole. Find the molecular formula of the compound, given that analysis of a 310.8 g sample revealed that the sample contains only boron and iodine. The mass of iodine in the sample is found to be 302.2 g.

11. Find the molecular formula of a compound that contains 56.36 g of oxygen and 43.64 g of phosphorus. The molar mass of the compound is 283.9 g/mole.

LAB 9.3A

Empirical Formulas

Purpose To determine the empirical formula of zinc chloride

Materials 150 mL beaker, mossy zinc, 3 M HCl, hot plate in a fume hood, balance, beaker tongs/hot pad/ "Hot Hands"

⚠ Safety Use caution with glassware, especially hot glassware. Be very careful with the HCl—it will burn. Do not heat the HCl solution in the open room—use a fume hood.

Procedure

1. Find the mass of a clean, dry 150 mL beaker. Write your name on it.

2. Measure a few pieces of zinc metal into the beaker. (Use a very small amount—the more you use, the longer you'll have to wait for it to react and then evaporate out the extra solution.) Record exact mass.

3. ⚠ Measure out about 25 mL of 3 M HCl. *Use caution with acid!*

4. Slowly pour the acid into the beaker.

5. Allow the reaction to proceed for 15 minutes or until all the zinc is gone.

6. ⚠ Place the beaker on a hot plate *in a fume hood* and begin to boil away the water and excess HCl.

Empirical Formulas (*cont'd.*)

7. A solid will form (crusty white/yellow). The reaction is complete when that solid melts again.

8. Remove the 150 mL beaker from the hot plate using beaker tongs.

   ⚠ CAUTION: very hot! Leave the beaker in the fume hood as it cools to ensure that you don't bring HCl fumes into the open classroom.

9. Allow the beaker to cool until it feels cool to your hand.

10. Find the mass of beaker and zinc chloride residue.

11. Zinc chloride is water soluble; you should be able to dissolve it down the drain and clean the beaker with soap and water.

Data table

Mass of beaker: _____

Mass of beaker and zinc: _____

Mass of beaker and zinc chloride: _____

Results/Calculations

1. Find the mass of the zinc and the chlorine reacted using your data table.

2. Use the mass of zinc and the mass of chlorine reacted to determine the empirical formula of zinc chloride.

3. Write the chemical formula for zinc chloride based on ionic charges—this is the correct formula for the compound.

Conclusion Restate the purpose and give your result. How close did you come to having whole-number values for the mole ratio in the empirical formula? What does this say about how accurate your lab technique was? Was your empirical formula the same as the one written based on ionic charges? Why or why not?

Alternative light sources are used to evaluate crime scene evidence.

Go Online

Animated examples
http://webcom4.grtxle.com/
khk12Chemistry

Hydrates

A **hydrate** is a molecule that has water molecules physically attached to it. Usually, when people are given this definition, they immediately assume the hydrate must be a liquid because it has water molecules attached to it. However, the substance is not dissolved in water—rather, it has a few water molecules attached to the "main" molecule by a physical attraction. Hydrates can be solids or even gases.

If the water molecules are removed, the leftover molecule (the "main" molecule) is called an **anhydride**. Because the water molecules are only physically attached in the hydrate, they can be removed to leave the anhydride in a physical change; simply heating the sample will drive off the water, leaving the anhydride behind.

Hydrate formulas

Hydrate formulas are written with this format: anhydride·nH$_2$O. The n is a coefficient that indicates how many water molecules are attached to each anhydride molecule. For example, Epsom salt (used for soaking swollen or sore parts of the body) is a hydrate of magnesium sulfate. The formula for Epsom salt is MgSO$_4$·7H$_2$O; there are seven water molecules attached to each magnesium sulfate molecule.

The coefficient can represent the number of molecules of water attached to one anhydride molecule or the number of moles of water attached to one mole of anhydride molecule (remember, using moles is a way of counting large numbers of molecules). The masses of the anhydride and the water are changed to moles, and the lowest whole-number ratio is found. This whole-number ratio is used to write the hydrate formula.

Example 9.3D

Hydrate Formulas

Find the formula of the barium iodide (BaI_2) hydrate. The hydrate sample had a mass of 10.407 g. After heating, the sample had a mass of 9.520 g.

- For hydrate problems, the mass of the anhydride (after heating, after the water is gone) and the mass of the water that left must be changed to moles.

- Mass of hydrate (anhydride + water) – Mass of anhydride = Mass of water lost

  10.407 g – 9.520 g = 0.887 g water lost

- Then, change the mass of anhydride and mass of water lost to moles.

$$9.520 \text{ g BaI}_2 \times \frac{1 \text{ mole BaI}_2}{391.13 \text{ g BaI}_2} = 0.0243 \text{ mole BaI}_2$$

$$0.887 \text{ g H}_2\text{O} \times \frac{1 \text{ mole H}_2\text{O}}{18.02 \text{ g H}_2\text{O}} = 0.0493 \text{ mole H}_2\text{O}$$

- Then compare the moles of anhydride and water lost to find the lowest possible whole-number ratio.

$$\frac{0.0493 \text{ mole H}_2\text{O}}{0.0243 \text{ mole BaI}_2} = 2.03$$

2.03 is very close to 2.00, so the hydrate formula is $BaI_2 \cdot 2H_2O$.

PRACTICE 9.3C

Hydrates

1. How can you turn a hydrate into an anhydride?

2. What is the hydrate formula if there are 0.391 g of Li_2SiF_6 and 0.0903 g of water?

3. What is the formula of the hydrate if there are 76.9 g of $CaSO_3$ and 23.1 g of water?

4. What is the formula of the hydrate if there are 0.737 g of $MgSO_3$ and 0.763 g of water?

5. What is the formula of the hydrate if there are 89.2 g $BaBr_2$ and 10.8 g of water?

Go Online
Check your understanding
http://webcom4.grtxle.com/khk12Chemistry

Hydrate Formulas

Purpose To determine the formula of a hydrate (Your teacher will tell you which hydrate you'll be working with.)

Instructions Design a lab to determine the formula of the hydrate. Your write-up must include:

- **Title**

- **Purpose**

- **Materials** Use an evaporating dish to hold the sample during the lab. Determine what other materials you will need.

> **!** **Safety** Your teacher will provide safety information specific to the hydrate you're working with. You should include any other important safety reminders, as well.

- **Procedure** Write a clear, concise procedure with numbered steps. Complete multiple trials if there will be time to do so (check with your teacher). One thing to keep in mind: how will you know when all of the water has been driven out of the hydrate and that the sample you have left is completely an anhydride? Make sure you write steps in your procedure to ensure this.

- **Data table**

- **Results/Calculations** Solve for the hydrate formula.

- **Conclusion** Restate the purpose and give your result for the hydrate formula. Give two or three possible sources of error that may have occurred in the lab. How can this type of experiment be used in a different situation?

Forensic police discover chemical fire-accelerants at this burned building, indicating that the fire was caused by an arsonist.

FINAL CHAPTER PROJECT

Here is your chance to use the chemistry you know to write a story using chemistry to solve a crime.

Forensics writing project

Write a short story about a crime scene investigation in which analysis of unknown samples is featured. Briefly describe the crime scene and the circumstances surrounding the crime. Include as many types of analysis learned in this chapter as you can. Mention each significant sample found at the crime scene, where or how the investigators found it, what kind of analysis you would perform on the sample, and how you might be able to use the results of that analysis to solve the crime. It can be a serious crime or even a humorous one—be creative!

Stories will be graded on number of different kinds of analysis used, accurate description of and use of analysis techniques, plausibility (could it really happen?), and creativity.

Many types of scientists need to determine what components are in a sample. There are several ways in which to do this.

A saturated solution is a solution at equilibrium. An equilibrium constant (K_{sp}) can therefore be written for the equation showing the dissolving process. A reaction quotient (Q) can be calculated from current concentrations of ions. If the $Q > K_{sp}$, there are too many ions for the solvent to hold, and some will precipitate out. If $Q < K_{sp}$, there is still room in the solution for more ions to dissolve, and the solution is unsaturated. If $Q = K_{sp}$, the solution is at equilibrium, meaning it is a saturated solution.

Precipitation reactions are double replacement reactions in which two soluble ionic compounds react to form at least one insoluble compound that precipitates in the solution. Precipitation reactions can be used to identify what ions are dissolved in a solution. The analysis can be qualitative or quantitative.

Chromatography is a separation technique using the attractions the components of the test sample have with a stationary phase and a mobile phase. There are several types of chromatography: paper, thin layer, column, high-pressure liquid, and gas. Once the components have been separated, they may be analyzed to determine what they are made of or be compared to known samples.

A chemical formula can be determined by analyzing how much of each individual element is present in the sample. The information can be used to calculate percent composition (the percent of the individual component compared with the overall sample) or empirical formula (the lowest possible whole-number ratio of atoms in a chemical

formula). If the empirical formula's molecular mass is compared with the actual molecular mass of the sample, the molecular formula (the actual ratio of atoms in the compound) can be determined.

A hydrate is a compound that has water molecules physically attached to it. After the water has been driven off by heating, the anhydride is left. By finding the whole-number ratio of the number of molecules of anhydride to the number of molecules of water, the hydrate formula can be determined.

1. Explain the difference between K_{sp} and Q. How is Q used to determine whether a solution is saturated?

2. What is the difference between the mobile phase and the stationary phase in chromatography?

3. Describe, in your own words, how chromatography works.

4. Explain the difference between empirical formula and molecular formula.

5. Write the solubility product expressions for each of the following.

   a. $SrSO_4$ (s)

   b. $MgCl_2$ (s)

   c. $Al_2(SO_4)_3$ (s)

6. Find the K_{sp} for the following.

   a. $AgBr$ (s) $\leftrightarrow Ag^+$ (aq) $+ Br^-$ (aq); at equilibrium, $[Ag^+] = 7.07 \times 10^{-7}$ M and $[Br^-] = 7.07 \times 10^{-7}$ M

   b. $MgCO_3$ (s) $\leftrightarrow Mg^{+2}$ (aq) $+ CO_3^{-2}$ (aq); at equilibrium, $[Mg^{+2}] = 4.9 \times 10^{-3}$ M and $[CO_3^{-2}] = 4.9 \times 10^{-3}$ M

7. Write whether each would be soluble in water.

   a. NH_4Br

   b. $PbCl_2$

   c. K_2SO_4

   d. $CuCO_3$

   e. $PbCrO_4$

   f. $BaSO_4$

8. Describe how you can use solubility rules to identify or separate a mixture of ions.

9. Find the percent composition of $Al(OH)_3$.

10. Find the percent composition of iron(III) carbonate.

11. Find the percent composition of a 6.00 g sample that contains 4.20 g C, 0.80 g O, and 1.00 g H.

12. The active ingredient in photographic fixer solution contains 0.979 g Na, 1.365 g S, and 1.021 g O. What is the empirical formula?

13. A compound that contains only nitrogen and oxygen is 30.4% N. The molecular mass is 92 g/mole. Find the empirical and molecular formula of the compound.

14. A sample of hydrated $CaSO_4$ has a mass of 26.50 g. After the solid is heated for a long time, the solid (now an anhydride) weighs 13.87 g. Find the formula for the hydrate.

CHAPTER 10

Batteries

Chemistry Provides Electricity

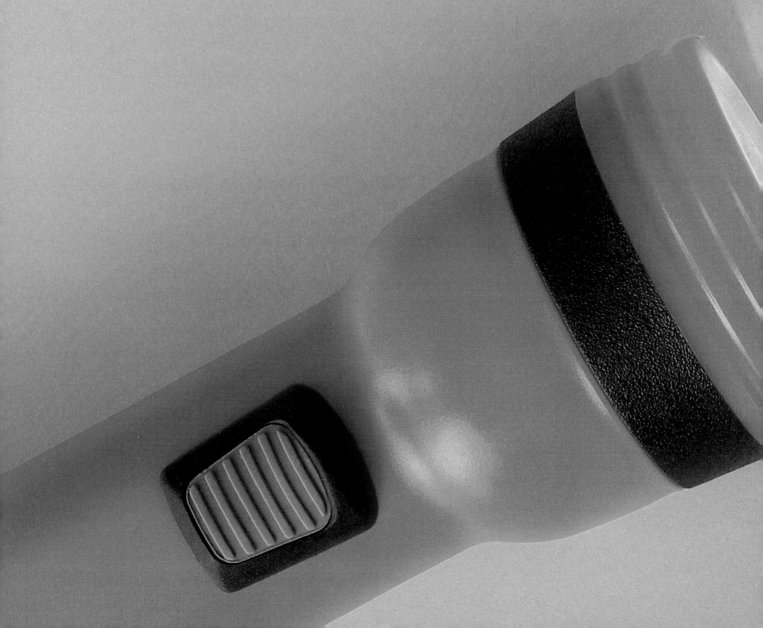

IN THIS CHAPTER

- Reduction and oxidation
- Redox reactions
- Batteries and redox reactions

INTRODUCTORY ACTIVITY

Can you think of a situation when a chemical reaction is used to produce electricity?

Can you think of a situation when electrical energy is used to produce a chemical reaction?

In those instances when electricity isn't being produced by a chemical reaction, how is it produced?

Think about these questions, share them with a partner, and then with the class.

to describe a type of battery to your classmates.

Introduction

Oxidation and reduction reactions (redox reactions) are ones in which electrons transfer from one atom or ion to another atom or ion. They occur everywhere around us, probably without your even knowing it. **Combustion reactions**—when something is added to oxygen and produces carbon dioxide and water (such as when something burns)—are redox reactions. When a metal rusts (oxidizes), a redox reaction has taken place. Some metals form undesirable rust when they oxidize (such as iron), whereas others (such as copper) form beautiful patinas during oxidation. Bleach removes stains (or sometimes simply makes them colorless so that we can't see them anymore), and that is also a redox reaction. Redox reactions are very common in living organisms—metabolism and respiration are both examples. Batteries are another common example of a redox reaction—one in which we harness the energy produced by moving electrons and use it in the form of electricity.

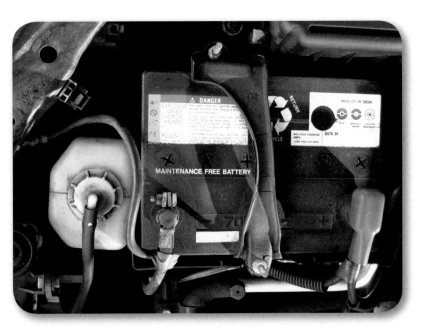

Car batteries are usually lead-acid batteries and can be recycled at auto repair centers. As you might know already, they're heavy, containing about 21 pounds of lead, about 3 pounds of plastic, and one gallon of sulfuric acid. Plastic can be recycled into other products. All of the lead can be reused for more batteries. Sodium sulfate is sometimes made from the sulfuric acid and is useful in fertilizers.

Batteries

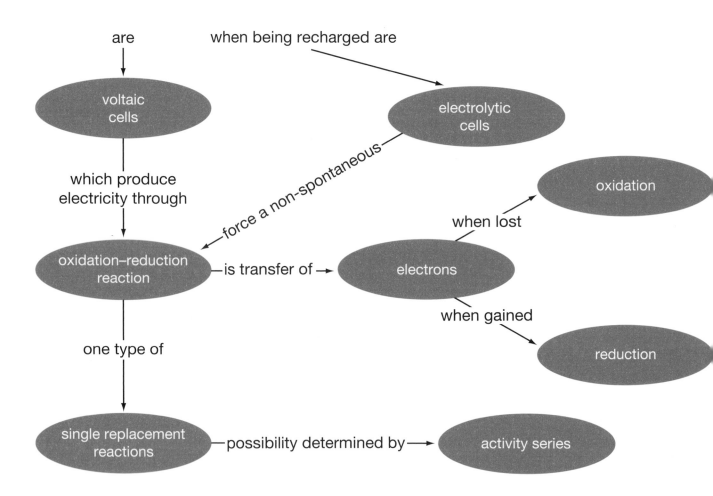

Reduction and Oxidation

A particular type of chemical reaction occurs when electrons move from one atom to another. A change in the number of electrons that an atom has means a change in the atom's charge. (Remember—the number of protons never changes in an atom, except in nuclear reactions.)

Defining reduction and oxidation

Reduction is the gaining of electrons. If an atom gains electrons, which are negatively charged, the charge will be reduced. For example, if the original reactant had a charge of +3 and it gained one electron in the reaction, the product would have a charge of +2, as in the equation $Fe^{+3} + e^- \rightarrow Fe^{+2}$. The charge on the iron ion has been reduced; therefore, this is a reduction equation. Another example of reduction occurs when a neutral atom becomes negative after the addition of electrons, as in $S + 2\,e^- \to S^{-2}$. Reduction, in other words, is the decrease of a positive charge.

Oxidation is the removal of electrons. If something loses electrons, it is being oxidized. Oxidation is the opposite of reduction. Examples of oxidation equations would be $Cu^+ \to Cu^{+2} + e^-$ and $2\,F^- \to F_2 + 2\,e^-$.

Reduction and oxidation happen simultaneously

You cannot have reduction without oxidation—you cannot add electrons to one thing without their coming from somewhere else. Anytime one atom or ion is reduced, you can find another one in the system that is oxidized. The complete process is known as a **reduction–oxidation reaction**, or a **redox reaction**. Chemical equations have to balance not only the number of atoms on each side but also the overall charge on each side.

Determining oxidation number

The **oxidation number** is the apparent charge on an atom when lone pairs or bonding electrons are assigned to it.

In an ionic compound, assigning the oxidation number is relatively easy—the metal atom has given away its valence electrons to the nonmetal atom (see Sections 5.1 and 5.2 for more information on ionic bonding). Therefore, the charge can be determined by the number of electrons given away or added to form a stable octet. For example, in the compound $CaCl_2$, the calcium atom had 2 valence electrons that it gave away. Each chlorine atom had 7 valence electrons, and each accepted one more from the calcium atom. This leaves the calcium ion with a charge of +2 and each chloride ion with a charge of –1. These are the same charges that you used to write ionic chemical formulas in Chapter 2.

However, in a covalent molecule, the atoms share the electrons. How can we determine the charge on an atom if it is sharing an electron with another atom? We have a set of rules to determine which atom is "assigned" shared electrons for the purpose of determining whether something gains or loses electrons in a chemical reaction. These rules are based on electronegativity: the atom with the higher electronegativity is assigned the electrons (see Section 5.4 for information on electronegativities).

Rule 1: *The oxidation number of any free element is zero.* This applies to any pure element, whether monoatomic (such as sulfur, which has the chemical symbol S) or diatomic (such as the HOFBrINCl elements, which when not bonded with another element come in 2s, such as Cl_2).

Rule 2: In an ionic compound, *the oxidation number of a monoatomic ion is the charge.* Thus, in $CaCl_2$, Ca would have an oxidation number of +2 and each Cl would have an oxidation number of –1.

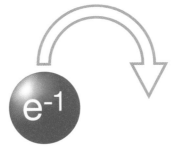

Electrons moving from one atom to another is reduction–oxidation, or "redox."

Go Online
Animated examples
http://webcom4.grtxle.com/
khk12Chemistry

Rule 3: *The oxidation number of hydrogen in most compounds is +1.* The exceptions are when hydrogen is with a less electronegative element (such as in LiH, where the charge on hydrogen is –1).

Rule 4: *Ions of elements in Group 1 (alkali metals) are +1.* Ions of elements in Group 2 (alkaline earth metals) are +2.

Rule 5: *The oxidation number of oxygen is –2.* The exception is when it's in a peroxide (such as hydrogen peroxide, H_2O_2, where the oxidation number of oxygen is –1).

Rule 6: *The sum of the oxidation numbers of all atoms in a compound must be zero.*

Rule 7: *The sum of the oxidation numbers of all atoms in a polyatomic ion must equal the charge on that polyatomic ion.*

Example 10.1A

Assigning Oxidation Numbers

Determine the oxidation number of each element in the following compounds.

1. Na_2SO_4

   - Na: Rule 4—It's in Group 1, so the oxidation number is +1. (Note that this could also be determined by Rule 2, because it's a monoatomic ion with a charge in an ionic compound, and the charge is +1.)

   - O: Rule 5—The oxidation number of oxygen is –2.

   - S: Rule 7—SO_4^{-2} is a polyatomic ion. Therefore, the oxidation numbers of the sulfur and the oxygen must add up to equal –2, so $1 \times (S) + 4 \times (O) = -2$. If each oxygen has an oxidation number of –2, then the problem becomes $1 \times (S) + 4 \times (-2) = -2$. This can be rearranged to become $S = (-2 + 8)/1 = +6$. (Note that this could also be figured out using Rule 6, where

   all atoms in the whole compound must add up to zero; then you'd include the 2 Na's with a charge of +1 in the equation as well.)

   - Na = +1   S = +6   O = –2

2. $CaCrO_4$

   - Ca: Rule 4—It's in Group 2, so the oxidation number is +2.

   - O: Rule 5—The oxidation number of oxygen is –2.

   - Cr: Rule 6—The compound must add up to zero, so $1 \times (Ca) + 1 \times (Cr) + 4 \times (O) = 0$. Therefore, $1 \times (+2) + 1 \times (Cr) + 4 \times (-2) = 0$, which can be rearranged to be: $Cr = (0 + 8 - 2)/1 = +6$. (Note that this could also be figured out using Rule 7 and adding up the polyatomic ion CrO_4 to equal –2.)

   - Ca: +2   Cr: +6   O: –2

Identifying what element is being reduced or oxidized in a reaction

Once the oxidation numbers have been assigned for each element on both sides of a chemical reaction, it can be determined which element is being reduced (the oxidation number is being lowered, or reduced, with the addition of electrons) and which element is being oxidized (the oxidation number is increasing with the removal of electrons).

If there are no elements changing oxidation numbers, then there are no elements gaining or losing electrons, and it is not a redox reaction.

Oxidizing agent and reducing agent

If an element is being reduced, the reduction is being caused by the other compound (the one that contains the element being oxidized). If an element is being oxidized, the oxidation is being caused by the other compound (the one that contains the element being reduced).

The **reducing agent** is the compound that is causing the reduction (it contains the element being oxidized). The **oxidizing agent** is the compound that is causing the oxidation. Note that the reducing and oxidizing agents are the entire compounds—not just the single element involved in the oxidation number change.

Example 10.1B

Identifying Species in a Redox Reaction

Which elements are being oxidized or reduced in the following: Fe_2O_3 (s) + 3 CO (g) → 2 Fe (l) + 3 CO_2 (g)? What are the oxidizing agent and the reducing agent in the reaction?

- First, assign the oxidation numbers to each element as in the previous example.

  For the reactants: Fe = +3; O in Fe_2O_3 = −2; C = +2; O in CO = −2

  For the products: Fe = 0; C = +4; O = −2

- The element that has a dropping oxidation number is being reduced. That is Fe, as it

drops from +3 → 0. Therefore, *iron is being reduced.*

- The element that has an increasing oxidation number is C, as it goes from +2 → +4. Therefore, *carbon is being oxidized.*

- Because the iron is being reduced, the carbon-containing compound is the reducing agent: *CO is the reducing agent.*

- Because the carbon is being oxidized, the iron-containing compound is the oxidizing agent: *Fe_2O_3 is the oxidizing agent.*

PRACTICE 10.1

Reduction and Oxidation

1. Determine the oxidation numbers for each element in the following.

   a. $Ni(OH)_2$ (which is used in NiCad batteries, such as in cell phones)

   b. $Cd(OH)_2$ (also used in NiCad batteries)

   c. $KMnO_4$

   d. Na_2CO_3

   e. HSO_4^-

Go Online
Check your understanding
http://webcom4.grtxle.com/
khk12Chemistry

(continues)

Reduction and Oxidation (*cont'd.*)

    f. $H_2S_2O_7$

    g. Al_2S_3

2. For each of the following, determine which element is being reduced and which is being oxidized, or state that it is not a redox reaction. Also state which compound is the reducing agent and which compound is the oxidizing agent for each redox reaction.

    a. H_2 (g) + N_2 (g) $\rightarrow$ NH_3

    b. $AgNO_3$ (aq) + $FeCl_3$ (aq) $\rightarrow$ AgCl (s) + $Fe(NO_3)_3$ (aq)

    c. H_2CO_3 (aq) $\rightarrow$ H_2O (l) + CO_2 (g)

    d. H_2O_2 (aq) + PbS (s) $\rightarrow$ $PbSO_4$ (s) + H_2O (l)

    e. HNO_3 (aq) + I_2 (s) $\rightarrow$ HIO_3 (aq) + NO_2 (g) + H_2O (l)

    f. $FeBr_2$ (aq) + Br_2 (l) $\rightarrow$ $FeBr_3$ (aq)

3. Explain why reduction and oxidation must always occur together.

4. Write a chemical reaction for the formation of rust from iron metal when it reacts with oxygen (O_2) to form iron(III) oxide (which is the "rust"). Which element is being oxidized? Which is being reduced?

5. Is it accurate to say that a metal has "oxidized" when it rusts? Explain.

SECTION 10.2

Redox Reactions

Single replacement reactions

Single replacement reactions are those in which one reactant is in its elemental form and the other reactant is a compound. The reactant in its elemental form (the "single" element) replaces one of the elements in the compound. The general form of a single replacement reaction is:

$$A + BX \rightarrow B + AX$$

An example of a single replacement reaction is:

$$Mg + CuSO_4 \rightarrow Cu + MgSO_4$$

A second example of single replacement is shown in Figure 10–1.

Go Online
Topic: redox reactions
Go to: www.scilinks.org
Code: Chem1e358

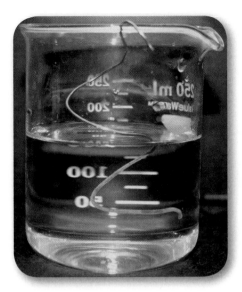

Figure 10–1. The copper wire reacts with silver nitrate solution (left, colorless) to form silver crystals and copper nitrate solution (right, blue): $Cu + 2\ AgNO_3 \rightarrow 2\ Ag + Cu(NO_3)_2$.

In single replacement reactions, the "single" element has an oxidation number of 0. After becoming part of the compound in the products, its oxidation number is no longer 0. The element that it "replaced" has gone from a nonzero oxidation number to a 0 as an element in the products. (In the example above with magnesium and copper sulfate, Mg goes from $0 \rightarrow +2$ and Cu goes from $+2 \rightarrow 0$). Therefore, all single replacement reactions are redox reactions. (There are redox reactions that are not single replacement reactions, but all single replacement reactions are redox reactions.)

LAB 10.2

Activity Series

Purpose To determine which elements are capable of reducing which elements in single replacement reactions

Materials Well-plate; four small samples each of copper, aluminum, zinc, and iron metals; 1 M solutions with droppers of $CuCl_2$, $Al(NO_3)_3$, $Zn(NO_3)_2$, and $Fe(NO_3)_3$

 Safety Wear goggles. Report any spills to your teacher. Avoid contact with the solutions.

Procedure

1. Use the data table as a guide to add solutions to the well-plate.

2. Use the data table as a guide to add metal pieces to the well-plate.

3. Wait a few minutes for the reactions to occur. Record any changes or signs of reaction in the data table.

(continues)

Activity Series (*cont'd.*)

Data table

	Cu	Al	Zn	Fe
CuCl$_2$				
Al(NO$_3$)$_3$				
Zn(NO$_3$)$_2$				
Fe(NO$_3$)$_3$				

Results

1. For each reaction that occurred, write the balanced single replacement reaction equation.

2. Rank the metals from most reactive to least reactive.

Discussion

1. For each reaction you wrote in Results question 1, identify which element is being reduced and which element is being oxidized.

2. For each reaction you wrote in Results question 1, identify the oxidizing agent and the reducing agent.

3. Share your answers (Results question 2) with the class. Use whiteboards if provided. Are there any discrepancies? If so, discuss them.

4. Why do you suppose the Statue of Liberty was built of copper rather than zinc?

Activity series

An activity series is a list of metals from the most likely to react in a chemical reaction to the least likely to react. The more likely a metal is to react, the more likely it is to be found in a compound rather than in its pure element form. You can find an activity series at the end of this chapter.

If one metal is more likely to react (and to be in a compound) than another metal that is currently in a compound, the first metal will replace the second one and a single replacement reaction will occur.

Chalcanthite, or "copper flower," is a mineral commonly found in the late-stage oxidation zones of copper deposits.

Example 10.2A

Using an Activity Series

Will the following single replacement reactions occur? If so, write the products.

1. $Mg + CuSO_4 \rightarrow$

   • Mg is higher on the activity series than Cu; therefore, it is more likely to be in a compound than Cu. Mg will replace Cu, and a single replacement reaction will occur.

   • $Mg + CuSO_4 \rightarrow Cu + MgSO_4$

2. $Cu + FeSO_4 \rightarrow$

   • Fe is higher on the activity series than Cu; therefore, it is more likely to be in a compound than Cu. Cu will not replace the Fe in the compound.

   • No reaction

Balancing redox reactions

Writing half-reactions   As mentioned in Section 10.1, not only does a redox reaction need to be balanced to make sure that the number of atoms of each element is the same on both sides, but the charges (and therefore the number of electrons transferred) need to be balanced as well. There are two sets of rules to accomplish this, depending on whether the reaction is occurring in an acidic solution or a basic solution. However, both sets of rules start out with the step of writing a half-reaction.

Half-reactions are the result of splitting the chemical reaction into two—one that shows the reduction process, and one that shows the oxidation process. To write a half-reaction, first determine which element is being reduced and which element is being oxidized, as in Section 10.1. Write the chemical compounds that include the element being reduced in a reduction half-reaction, and write the chemical compounds that contain the element that is being oxidized in an oxidation half-reaction.

Example 10.2B

Writing Half-Reactions

Write the half-reactions for the following reaction:
$I_2 + HClO \rightarrow HIO_3 + HCl$

- Determine the oxidation numbers of each element.

  For the reactants: $I = 0$; $H = +1$; $Cl = +1$; $O = -2$

  For the products: H in $HIO_3 = +1$; $I = +5$; $O = -2$; H in $HCl = +1$; $Cl = -1$

- The iodine is being oxidized (oxidation number changes from $0 \rightarrow +5$), and the chlorine is being reduced (oxidation number changes from $+1 \rightarrow -1$).

- The oxidation half-reaction would be:
  $I_2 \rightarrow HIO_3$

- The reduction half-reaction would be:
  $HClO \rightarrow HCl$

Balancing redox reactions in an acidic solution

The process for balancing a redox reaction in an acidic solution is as follows.

1. Write the half-reactions for the oxidation and reduction processes.

2. Balance the half-reactions with respect to the atoms involved (except for hydrogen and oxygen).

3. Balance the oxygen atoms by adding H_2O molecules to the side that needs more oxygen.

4. Balance the hydrogen atoms by adding H^+ to the side that needs more hydrogen atoms.

Go Online
Animated examples
http://webcom4.grtxle.com/
khk12Chemistry

5. Balance the charges by adding electrons to one side or the other.

6. Balance the electron change in the two half-reactions by multiplying the two half-reactions by the least common multiple.

7. Add the two half-reactions back together.

8. Cancel anything out that appears on both sides of the final equation (at the very least, the electrons should cancel out if you multiplied the half-reactions by the correct least common multiple).

Because the reaction is occurring in an acidic solution, we use the H^+ (which is what makes a solution "acidic"—see Section 6.3) to balance the hydrogen atoms.

Michael Faraday was an English chemist and physicist who during the mid 1800s contributed much to the fields of electrochemistry and electromagnetism. As a chemist, he was busy inventing the early bunsen burner and discovering benzene (now used as a solvent). From Faraday we get the terms *ion, electrode, cathode,* and *anode*.

Example 10.2C

Balancing a Redox Reaction in Acid

Balance the following redox reaction in an acidic solution:
$I_2 + HClO \rightarrow HIO_3 + HCl$. (The oxidation numbers and half-reactions were determined in Exercise 10.2B.)

Step 1: $I_2 \rightarrow HIO_3$

$HClO \rightarrow HCl$

Step 2: $I_2 \rightarrow 2 HIO_3$

$HClO \rightarrow HCl$

Step 3: $6 H_2O + I_2 \rightarrow 2 HIO_3$

$HClO \rightarrow HCl + H_2O$

Step 4: $6 H_2O + I_2 \rightarrow 2 HIO_3 + 10 H^+$

$2 H^+ + HClO \rightarrow HCl + H_2O$

Step 5: $6 H_2O + I_2 \rightarrow 2 HIO_3 + 10 H^+ + 10 e^-$

$2 e^- + 2 H^+ + HClO \rightarrow HCl + H_2O$

Step 6: $1 \times (6 H_2O + I_2 \rightarrow 2 HIO_3 + 10 H^+ + 10 e^-)$

$= 6 H_2O + I_2 \rightarrow 2 HIO_3 + 10 H^+ + 10 e^-$

$5 \times (2 e^- + 2 H^+ + HClO \rightarrow HCl + H_2O)$

$= 10 e^- + 10 H^+ + 5 HClO \rightarrow 5 HCl + 5 H_2O$

Step 7: $6 H_2O + I_2 + 10 e^- + 10 H^+ + 5 HClO \rightarrow 2 HIO_3 + 10 H^+ + 10 e^- +$

$5 HCl + 5 H_2O$

Step 8: $1 H_2O + 1 I_2 + 5 HClO \rightarrow 2 HIO_3 + 5 HCl$

Balancing redox reactions in a basic solution

The process for balancing a redox reaction in a basic solution is as follows.

1. Write the half-reactions for the oxidation and reduction processes.

2. Balance the half-reactions with respect to the atoms involved (except for hydrogen and oxygen).

3. Balance the oxygen atoms by adding *twice* as many OH^- as you need to the side that needs more oxygen.

4. Balance the hydrogen atoms by adding H_2O to the side that needs more hydrogen atoms.

5. Balance the charges by adding electrons to one side or the other.

6. Balance the electron change in the two half-reactions by multiplying the two half-reactions by the least common multiple.

7. Add the two half-reactions back together.

8. Cancel anything out that appears on both sides of the final equation (at the very least, the electrons should cancel out if you multiplied the half-reactions by the correct least common multiple).

Since the reaction is occurring in a basic solution, we use the OH^- (which is what makes a solution "basic"—see Section 6.3) to balance the oxygen atoms.

Go Online
Animated examples
http://webcom4.grtxle.com/
khk12Chemistry

Acid or gel batteries power these scooters. Safety is the advantage of the gel, but longevity of charge is the plus behind the acid type.

Example 10.2D

Balancing a Redox Reaction in Base

Balance the following reaction in basic solution:

$$C_2O_4^{-2} + MnO_4^- \rightarrow MnO_2 + CO_3^{-2}$$

Oxidation numbers:

- For the reactants, C = +3; O in $C_2O_4^{-2}$ = –2; Mn = +7; O in MnO_4^- = –2.

- For the products, Mn = +4; O in MnO_2 = –2; C = +4; O in CO_3^{-2} = –2.

- C is changing from +3 → +4; it is being oxidized.

- Mn is changing from +7 → +4; it is being reduced.

Step 1: $C_2O_4^{-2} \rightarrow CO_3^{-2}$

$MnO_4^- \rightarrow MnO_2$

Step 2: $C_2O_4^{-2} \rightarrow 2\,CO_3^{-2}$

$MnO_4^- \rightarrow MnO_2$

Step 3: $4\,OH^- + C_2O_4^{-2} \rightarrow 2\,CO_3^{-2}$

$MnO_4^- \rightarrow MnO_2 + 4\,OH^-$

Step 4: $4\,OH^- + C_2O_4^{-2} \rightarrow 2\,CO_3^{-2} + 2\,H_2O$

$2\,H_2O + MnO_4^- \rightarrow MnO_2 + 4\,OH^-$

Step 5: $4\,OH^- + C_2O_4^{-2} \rightarrow 2\,CO_3^{-2} + 2\,H_2O + 2\,e^-$

$3\,e^- + 2\,H_2O + MnO_4^- \rightarrow MnO_2 + 4\,OH^-$

Step 6: $3 \times (4\,OH^- + C_2O_4^{-2} \rightarrow 2\,CO_3^{-2} + 2\,H_2O + 2\,e^-)$

$= 12\,OH^- + 3\,C_2O_4^{-2} \rightarrow 6\,CO_3^{-2} + 6\,H_2O + 6\,e^-$

$2 \times (3\,e^- + 2\,H_2O + MnO_4^- \rightarrow MnO_2 + 4\,OH^-)$

$= 6\,e^- + 4\,H_2O + 2\,MnO_4^- \rightarrow 2\,MnO_2 + 8\,OH^-$

Step 7: $12\,OH^- + 3\,C_2O_4^{-2} + 6\,e^- + 4\,H_2O +$

$2\,MnO_4^- \rightarrow 6\,CO_3^{-2} + 6\,H_2O + 6\,e^- +$

$2\,MnO_2 + 8\,OH^-$

Step 8: $4\,OH^- + 3\,C_2O_4^{-2} + 2\,MnO_4^- \rightarrow 6\,CO_3^{-2} +$

$2\,H_2O + 2\,MnO_2$

PRACTICE 10.2

Redox Reactions

1. Which of the following reactions will occur in a NiCad battery? Ni + $Cd(OH)_2$ or Cd + $Ni(OH)_2$? Write the complete chemical reaction that occurs.

2. For each of the following, decide whether the reaction will happen. If so, write the products. If not, write "no reaction."

   a. $AlCl_3 + Ni \rightarrow$

   b. $AgNO_3 + Co \rightarrow$

   c. $SnCl_2 + Pb \rightarrow$

   d. $Au^{+3} + Fe \rightarrow$

   e. $Cu + Zn^{+2} \rightarrow$

3. Balance the following redox reactions in acidic solutions.

   a. $HMnO_4 + H_2SO_3 \rightarrow Mn^{+2} + HSO_4^-$

Go Online
Check your understanding
http://webcom4.grtxle.com/
khk12Chemistry

(continues)

PRACTICE 10.2

Redox Reactions (*cont'd.*)

    b. $Cr_2O_7^{-2} + I^- \rightarrow Cr^{+3} + I_2$

    c. $As_2O_3 + HNO_3 \rightarrow H_2AsO_4 + NO$

    d. $I_2 + H_2SO_3 \rightarrow HI + H_2SO_4$

    e. $H_3AsO_4 + Zn \rightarrow AsH_3 + Zn^{+2}$

4. Balance the following redox reactions in basic solution:

    a. $Al + MnO_4^- \rightarrow MnO_2 + Al(OH)_4^-$

    b. $NO_2 \rightarrow NO_2^- + NO_3^-$ (Hint—split the reaction as follows for the half-reactions: (1) $NO_2 \rightarrow NO_2^-$ and (2) $NO_2 \rightarrow NO_3^-$.)

    c. $CN^- + MnO_4^- \rightarrow CNO^- + MnO_2$

5. Balance the redox reaction you wrote in question 1 that occurs in NiCad batteries. This reaction occurs in a basic solution.

SECTION 10.3

Batteries and Redox Reactions

Electricity is the flow of electrons. Electrons are transferred in redox reactions. Therefore, if those electrons are transferred over a wire from the element being oxidized to the element being reduced, then electricity is flowing through the wire.

Voltaic cells

Go Online
Molecular animation
http://webcom4.grtxle.com/
khk12Chemistry

Go Online
Topic: batteries
Go to: www.scilinks.org
Code: Chem1e366
SC INKS
NSTA

Batteries are voltaic cells. **Voltaic cells** (also called **galvanic cells**) use the natural flow of electrons from an element that is more easily oxidized to an element that is more easily reduced. This flow of electrons produces electricity (when done over a wire), which can then be used to run your electronic devices. A voltaic cell consists of several parts: a solution with the substance being oxidized, a solution with the substance being reduced, metal electrodes in each solution connected by a wire, and a salt bridge. Figure 10–2 shows the setup of a voltaic cell.

    The first two components (the solutions) are there for obvious reasons: you need the elements or compounds being oxidized or reduced. If the two substances were in the same compartment (together in a beaker, for example), the reaction would still occur, but the energy would be released as heat to the surrounding molecules (warming the temperature of the solution). Electricity could not be harnessed from that process. By separating the two substances and forcing the electrons to transfer over a wire, usable electricity is produced.

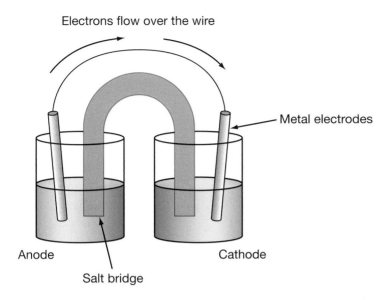

Electrons flow over the wire

Metal electrodes

Anode

Cathode

Salt bridge

Figure 10–2. Voltaic cell.

The metal electrodes and the wire are there to conduct the electrons from one side to the other (see Section 5.1 for information about why metals can conduct electricity). The electrode that is in the side being reduced is called the **cathode**; reduction occurs at the cathode. The electrode that is in the side being oxidized is called the **anode**; oxidation happens at the anode. The electrons flow from the substance being oxidized (losing electrons) through the anode (where the oxidation occurs), through the wire to the cathode (where the reduction occurs) and to the substance being reduced (gaining electrons). Chemical changes occur at the electrodes.

Over time, a charge builds up on one side; if electrons keep flowing to the side that is being reduced, eventually there will be a large negative charge built up on one side. Once the negative charges build up on one side, the electrons stop flowing; the negative charge is too large to continue adding more electrons to that side. Therefore, a **salt bridge** is added. The salt bridge consists of a salt, which is an ionically bonded compound that has cations (positively charged ions) and anions (negatively charged ions). The salt bridge does not allow the solutions being oxidized or reduced to flow back and forth, but it does allow the ions of the salt to go to the side where each (anion or cation) is needed (anode or cathode). As cations go to the side being reduced (and a negative charge begins to build up), the anions in the salt bridge go to the side being oxidized. This reduces the negative charge buildup on the side with the cathode by balancing it with the anions being added to the side with the anode. The salt bridge completes the circuit that allows the electrons to continue to flow across the wire.

Line notation

Chemists use a shorthand way of writing the components of a cell, called **line notation**. The oxidation reaction (that occurs at the anode) is always

Batteries of the mid 20th century.

written first, then the reduction reaction follows. The two sides are separated by a double vertical line (||).

Each side has the reactant written first, followed by the product. If the reactant and the product are the same state (solid, liquid, gas, or aqueous), they are separated by a comma. If they are different states, they are separated by a single vertical line (|).

Example 10.3A

Line Notation

1. Write the line notation for a voltaic cell that has the following overall reaction:

   $Zn \ (s) + Cu^{+2} \ (aq) \rightarrow Zn^{+2} \ (aq) + Cu \ (s)$.

   - The Zn is going from an oxidation number of 0 to +2; it's being oxidized. Therefore, it will be written first.

   - The reactant is the Zn, and the product is the Zn^{+2}; they are different states of matter, so they will be separated by a vertical line.

   $Zn \ | \ Zn^{+2}$

Example 10.3A

Line Notation (*cont'd.*)

- The Cu is going from an oxidation number of +2 to 0; it's being reduced. Therefore, it will be written second.

- The reactant is the Cu^{+2}, and the product is Cu; they are different states, so they will be separated by a vertical line.

  Cu^{+2} | Cu

  Zn | Zn^{+2} || Cu^{+2} | Cu

2. Write the complete equation for the cell with the following line notation: Fe | Fe^{+2} || Br_2 | Br^-.

   - The oxidation half-reaction is $Fe \rightarrow Fe^{+2} + 2\,e^-$.

   - The reduction half-reaction is $Br_2 + 2\,e^- \rightarrow 2\,Br^-$.

   - The overall reaction is *$Fe + Br_2 \rightarrow Fe^{+2} + 2Br^-$*.

LAB 10.3

Making a Battery

Purpose To determine the relationship between the number of cells in series and the potential difference

Background information A simple voltaic cell can be made by using pennies, nickels, and filter paper soaked in salt solution.

To create a one-cell battery, place a nickel on the table. Soak a coin-sized piece of filter paper in a saturated NaCl solution and place it on top of the nickel. Put a penny on top of that. Connect a voltmeter (set to measure low voltage, in the 1 V range) with one lead touching the nickel and the other lead touching the penny. Multicell batteries would have more than one of these "cells" stacked on top of each other (do not put filter paper between the "cells" when stacking them), with the voltage difference being read between the top coin and the bottom coin.

Instructions Design an experiment to answer the purpose based on the information above. Your write-up must include:

- Title

- Purpose

- **Background information** (Use the information above as a starting point; add information you know

about how a voltaic cell works and the purpose of each of the components in the simple battery setup.)

- **Materials**

 Safety

- **Procedure** (You should test a simple cell, as described above, and then several different setups that include multiple cells.)

(continues)

Making a Battery (*cont'd.*)

- **Data table**

- **Results** (Graph your data. Is it a direct or indirect relationship? Is it a linear relationship or exponential? Write a sentence summary of any trends in your data—no conclusions!)

- **Conclusions** (Restate the purpose. Answer the purpose using your data and results as evidence. How does this information add to what you understand about how batteries work? What might be the difference between various "voltage" batteries you can buy in stores? How do you think the voltage would be different if aluminum foil was used instead of the nickels? What if dimes were used? Share results as a class. Are there any discrepancies? If so, discuss them.)

If you have time, and if your teacher requests it, design and conduct an experiment to determine how the voltage changes if another metal is used.

Go Online
Animated examples
http://webcom4.grtxle.com/
khk12Chemistry

Calculating cell potential

Electrons have potential energy, or energy due to position, in addition to the energy created by their motion (kinetic energy). Electrons will flow until they are at the position with the lowest possible potential energy. There is a difference in the potential energy the electrons have on the cathode side of a cell and the anode side of the cell. This difference, known as the electrical **potential difference**, can be measured in **volts** by using a voltmeter attached to the two electrodes in the cell.

Standard reduction potentials

It is impossible to measure the potential difference of just one half of the cell; you need two sides to measure a difference. A table of the potential differences that shows each element in a cell with hydrogen is known as a **standard reduction potential table**. (See the Appendix pp. 437.) The hydrogen half-cell is used as a "reference" half-reaction, meaning it has been assigned a reduction potential energy of 0, and everything else is compared to it. The standard reduction potential table gives the **standard reduction potential** for a half-reaction, which is the potential difference measured between that element and hydrogen if the temperature is 25°C, the pressure is 101.3 kPa, and the concentration of the ions in the cell is 1 M.

The lower the standard reduction potential of an element, the less likely it is to be reduced (the less likely it is to accept electrons). It will more likely be oxidized and release electrons.

Cell potential

The **cell potential** is the potential difference between the two half-reactions in a cell. The overall potential of a cell is found by adding the potentials of the two half-reactions. Look up the reduction half-reaction of the cell on the standard reduction potential table to find the potential.

Also look up the oxidation half-reaction, except it will appear as the opposite (the reactants and products will be opposite on the table, because it is a *reduction* table, and we want our half-reaction to be oxidation). This means that when you look up the oxidation half-reaction as a reduction potential, you must use the *opposite* of the reduction potential to calculate the overall cell potential.

$$\text{Cell potential} = \left(\begin{array}{c}\text{reduction potential for}\\ \text{reduction half-reaction}\end{array}\right) + \left(\begin{array}{c}-\text{ reduction potential for}\\ \text{oxidation half-reaction}\end{array}\right)$$

Standard reduction potential is an intensive property

An intensive property (see Section 3.2) is one for which size doesn't matter, such as color, taste, or melting point. All these properties are the same for a small piece of a substance as they are for a large piece of the same substance. Standard reduction potential is also an intensive property.

In order to balance a redox reaction, the half-reactions may need to be multiplied by the lowest common multiple. However, this multiplication of the half-reaction does *not* affect the standard reduction potential. This is because it doesn't matter how many times a reaction occurs (how many times you have to add it in to balance the equation); all that matters is the difference in potential energy of an electron before the half-reaction is complete versus the potential energy of the electron after the half-reaction is complete. Therefore, when calculating the cell potential *you do not need to multiply it by the least common multiple that was used in the balanced equation.*

Example 10.3B

Calculating Cell Potential

Find the cell potential for the following cell:
$Fe \mid Fe^{+2} \parallel Br_2 \mid Br^-$.

- This line notation shows that Fe is being oxidized to Fe^{+2} and Br_2 is being reduced to Br^-.

- The standard reduction potential for Br_2 being reduced is $Br_2 + 2\,e^- \rightarrow 2\,Br^-$, 1.065 V.

- The standard reduction potential for Fe^{+2} being reduced is $Fe^{+2} + 2\,e^- \rightarrow Fe$, −0.44 V.

- The cell potential = (reduction potential for reduction half-reaction) + (− reduction potential for oxidation half-reaction).

- Cell potential = (1.065 V) + (−(−0.44 V)) = 1.065 V + 0.44 V = *1.51 V.*

Nonstandard cells

Everything up to this point has used the standard reduction potential, meaning that the potential was measured at 25°C with gases at a pressure of 1 atm and solutions having a concentration of 1 M. What if these conditions aren't true in a particular case?

Watch out for random blasts of nanowires! The tiny wires were created from a solution of cobalt, iron, and boron ions, which then overflowed their template array. CoFeB nanowires are often used on thin films, part of electronic devices such as computer memory. Much about nanoresearch is unpredictable, which makes it an exciting field.

The concepts of Le Chatelier's principle (see Section 8.4) can be used to determine what will happen to the cell potential in nonstandard situations. If a change is made that would push the reaction toward the products, then the cell potential would be *higher* than the standard cell potential. If a change is made that would push the reaction toward the reactants, then the cell potential would be *lower* than the standard cell potential.

Concentration cells

A **concentration cell** is when a cell contains the same reactants and products on each side of the cell. However, one side has a higher concentration of the ion than the other side. The cell will transfer ions until both sides have the same concentration of the ion. For example, a concentration cell containing silver electrodes and solutions of Ag^+ ions is shown in Figure 10–3.

The left side has a concentration of 0.1 M Ag^{+1}, whereas the right side has a concentration of 1.0 M Ag^{+1}. The cell will transfer ions until both sides have the same concentration. This means that the concentration of the silver ion needs to increase on the left and decrease on the right in order for them to become equal. The reaction that will occur on the left to increase the concentration of the ion will be $Ag \rightarrow Ag^+ + e^-$. This means that an oxidation reaction will occur on the left, so this side will be the anode. The reaction that will occur on the right to decrease the concentration of the ion will be $Ag^+ + e^- \rightarrow Ag$. This means that a reduction reaction will occur on the right, so this side will be the cathode. Ions will flow from the left to the right side. The ions will continue to flow until the two sides have equal concentrations of the ion; then the ions will stop transferring.

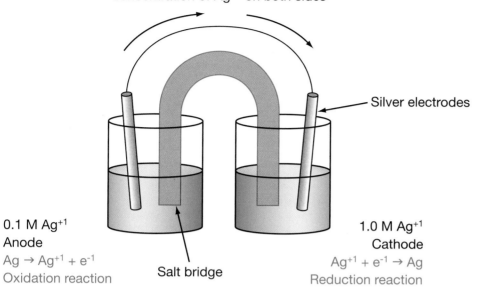

Electrons flow over the wire to equalize concentration of Ag^{+1} on both sides

Silver electrodes

0.1 M Ag^{+1}
Anode
$Ag \rightarrow Ag^{+1} + e^{-1}$
Oxidation reaction

Salt bridge

1.0 M Ag^{+1}
Cathode
$Ag^{+1} + e^{-1} \rightarrow Ag$
Reduction reaction

Figure 10–3. Concentration cell.

Electrolytic cells

An **electrolytic cell** is similar to a voltaic cell in its components. However, instead of the redox reaction occurring on its own and producing a flow of ions across a wire (producing electricity), electricity is put into the system to force the electrons to flow in the opposite way. This forces a redox reaction to occur that would not occur on its own; in fact, it goes in the opposite direction as would occur on its own. **Electrolysis** is when electricity causes a chemical reaction to occur.

Segways use lithium-ion batteries.

The potential that needs to be put into an electrolytic cell to push the electrons in the opposite direction is at least the opposite of the potential that would be gotten out of the cell if the electrons were allowed to flow on their own. You have to push with at least as much force on them as they would be pushing in the natural direction to get them to go against their usual direction.

Example 10.3C

Electrolytic cells

Find the potential that needs to be added to the following electrolytic cell: $Ag \mid Ag^+ \parallel Cu^{+2} \mid Cu$.

voltaic cell was found in Example 10.3B. It is 1.258 V.

- This is the opposite of the voltaic cell (which would have electrons flowing on their own) $Cu \mid Cu^{+2} \parallel Ag^+ \mid Ag$. The cell potential for this

- Therefore, *at least 1.258 V* would have to be put into the electrolytic cell.

PRACTICE 10.3

Go Online
Check your understanding
http://webcom4.grtxle.com/
khk12Chemistry

Batteries

1. Write the line notation for and find the standard cell voltage produced from a NiCad battery (see your answer to question 1 in Practice 10.2 for the chemical reaction).

2. Find the standard cell voltage produced from each of the following cells.

   a. $Zn \mid Zn^{+2} \parallel Fe^{+2} \mid Fe$

   b. $Mn \mid Mn^{+2} \parallel Br_2 \mid Br^-$

   c. $Ni \mid Ni^{+2} \parallel Hg_2^{+2} \mid Hg$

   d. $Pb \mid Pb^{+2} \parallel Cl_2 \mid Cl^-$

3. For each of the following standard electrolytic cells, indicate the minimum voltage that would need to be added.

   a. $Sn^{+2} \mid Sn^{+4} \parallel Pb^{+2} \mid Pb$

   b. $Cu \mid Cu^{+2} \parallel Ni^{+2} \mid Ni$

   c. $Ag^{+1} \mid Ag \parallel Fe \mid Fe^{+2}$

4. A battery is a voltaic cell. Explain how rechargeable batteries work, using the ideas of voltaic and electrolytic cells.

5. Why can a battery sit on a shelf without losing energy? Why does it need to be put into an electronic device and the power turned on before electricity flows?

FINAL CHAPTER PROJECT

Here is your chance to use the chemistry you know to describe a battery type to your classmates.

Battery research

Research one of the following types of batteries (or another topic that your teacher approves): fuel-cell batteries, nickel cadmium batteries (NiCd), nickel metal hydride batteries (NiMH), lithium ion batteries, lithium photo batteries, zinc carbon batteries, alkaline batteries, lead acid batteries, or metal chloride batteries.

Prepare a Microsoft PowerPoint® presentation or poster presentation (your teacher will let you know

which one) that gives the following information about your topic:

- Explains the components of the cells in this particular type of battery

- Gives chemical reactions that occur

- Lists applications for this battery type

- If the battery is rechargeable, how does it work? If not, why not?

- Lists the advantages and disadvantages of this type of battery as compared to other types

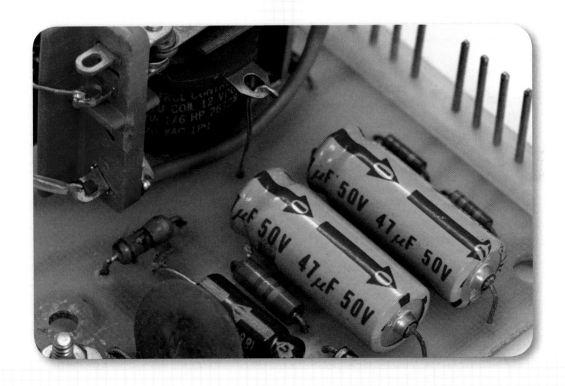

Oxidation is the loss of electrons, and reduction is the gaining of electrons. Oxidation and reduction must happen simultaneously in an oxidation–reduction reaction (redox reaction). The oxidation number of each element in a chemical reaction can be determined by following rules that assign electrons to atoms in a molecule. Once the oxidation numbers for each element before and after the reaction have been determined, the element that is being reduced is the one with the charge that was lowered (reduced), and the element being oxidized is the one with a charge that was raised. The oxidizing agent is the compound that caused the oxidation (it contains the element being reduced), and the reducing agent is the compound that caused the reduction (it contains the element being oxidized).

There are many types of redox reactions. Single replacement reactions are one type of redox reaction. A single replacement reaction involves an element in its elemental form replacing an element in a compound (which then is changed into its elemental form). An activity series can be used to determine whether a single replacement reaction will occur. The activity series lists elements in order from most reactive (most likely to be in a chemical compound) to least reactive (least likely to be in a chemical compound).

Redox reactions must be balanced with respect to the atoms in the reaction (as governed by the law of conservation of mass), and the charges must be balanced as well. Half-reactions are written that separate the reduction process from the oxidation process. Each half-reaction is then balanced with respect to atoms and charge by a set of rules (depending on whether the reaction occurs in acidic or basic solution), and the half-reactions are then added back together.

A voltaic (or galvanic) cell is a way of separating the oxidation and reduction half-reactions and allowing the ions to flow over a wire in order to capture the energy change as usable electricity. Ions flow from the anode (where oxidation occurs) to the cathode (where reduction occurs) over the wire. A salt bridge takes care of the buildup of charges; it allows ions to flow between the oxidation and reduction compartments.

Electrolysis is the use of electricity to cause a chemical reaction to occur. An electrolytic cell is one in which electricity is put into the cell in order to drive a redox reaction in the opposite direction than it would naturally occur.

Line notation is a shorthand method of writing the components of a cell. It includes the reactants and products of the oxidation and reduction half-reactions.

The potential energy difference (with the units of volts) of the electrons before and after the redox reaction can be measured in a voltaic cell using a voltmeter. A standard reduction potential table gives the potential difference between different reduction half-reactions if hydrogen is being oxidized. The standard reduction potentials can be used to determine the reduction potential of a cell at standard states (25°C, 1 atm, and 1 M solutions). The cell potential = (reduction potential of reduction half-reaction) − (reduction potential of the oxidation half-reaction).

Review

1. Explain the difference between reduction and oxidation. Why do they always have to occur simultaneously?

2. Explain the difference between a voltaic (or galvanic) cell and an electrolytic cell.

3. Explain what it means when a battery has "died."

4. Explain, in terms of voltaic cells and electrolytic cells, how rechargeable batteries work.

5. Determine the oxidation numbers for each of the following elements.

   a. NH_4^+

   b. NO_3^-

   c. NH_3

   d. HPO_4^{-2}

6. For each of the following reactions, determine what's being oxidized and what's being reduced. Also, indicate what is the oxidizing agent and what is the reducing agent.

   a. $V_2O_5 + 2 H_2 \rightarrow V_2O_3 + 2 H_2O$

   b. $CoS + NO_3^- \rightarrow Co^{+2} + NO + S_8$

7. For each of the following sets of reactants, use the activity series to determine whether the reaction will take place. If it will, write the products. If it will not, write "no reaction."

   a. $Mg + ZnCl_2 \rightarrow$

   b. $ZnCl_2 + Cu \rightarrow$

   c. $Mg + CuCl_2 \rightarrow$

8. Balance each of the following redox reactions in acid.

   a. $Zn + H^+ \rightarrow Zn^{+2} + H_2$

   b. $As_2O_3 + NO_3^- \rightarrow H_3AsO_4 + NO$

9. Balance each of the following redox reactions in base.

   a. $Al + MnO_4^- \rightarrow MnO_2 + Al(OH)_4^-$

   b. $CN^- + MnO_4^- \rightarrow CNO^- + MnO_2$

10. Write the line notation for the following reactions.

    a. Al^{+3} (aq) + Mg (s) $\rightarrow$ Al (s) + Mg^{+2} (aq)

    b. Ag^+ (aq) + Fe^{+2} (aq) $\rightarrow$ Ag (s) + Fe^{+3} (aq)

    c. Cu^{+2} (aq) + Fe (s) $\rightarrow$ Cu (s) + Fe^{+2} (aq)

11. Find the cell potential for each of the reactions in question 10.

Activity Series	
Li	Most reactive
K	
Ba	
Sr	
Ca	
Na	
Mg	
Al	
Mn	
Zn	
Cr	
Fe	
Cd	
Co	
Ni	
Sn	
Pb	
H	
Cu	
Hg	
Ag	
Pt	
Au	Least reactive

Polymers

Making Toys with Chemistry

IN THIS CHAPTER

- Hydrocarbons
- Organic functional groups
- Polymers

INTRODUCTORY ACTIVITY

What are your ideas about what a polymer is?

Make as many observations as you can on the polymer products that your teacher shows you. All of the products are made with polymers, yet they behave very differently. How can we explain this?

Are you surprised that any of these products are polymers?

to act as a product developer to create the bounciest ball.

Introduction

Plastics are everywhere—from your pencil to your bookbag to your water bottle, and just about anywhere else you can think of. Plastics are **polymers**—large molecules made of many small molecules joined together. But polymers don't compose just plastics; they are found in every living cell as well.

This chapter will introduce organic chemistry (carbon-based chemistry), naming and writing formulas (nomenclature) of organic molecules, how the structure and properties of these molecules relate, and how they connect to form large chains (polymers).

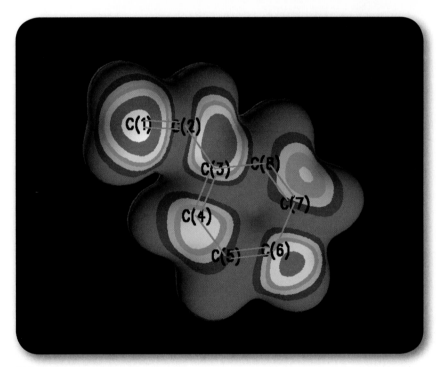

This is a computer drawing of an organic molecular model.

Polymers

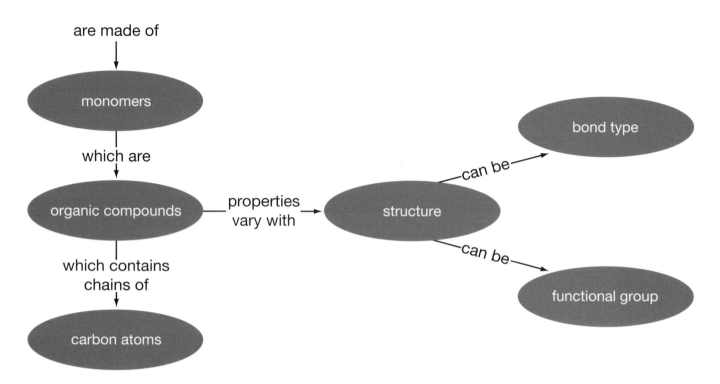

are made of

monomers

which are

organic compounds

which contains chains of

carbon atoms

properties vary with

structure

can be

bond type

can be

functional group

SECTION 11.1

Hydrocarbons

An **organic molecule** is one that contains carbon atoms bonded to carbon atoms. Carbon can bond to form long chains of itself. The simplest type of organic molecule is the **hydrocarbon**. It is composed of hydrogen and carbon only.

Hydrocarbons are nonpolar molecules that are not capable of hydrogen bonding, so the only intermolecular force they use is London dispersion forces (the weakest of the forces; see Section 5.5 for information on intermolecular forces). However, the larger the hydrocarbon, the stronger the London dispersion forces it has (because it has more electrons in the molecule). Therefore, as hydrocarbon molecules get larger and larger, their melting and boiling points increase.

Small hydrocarbons (such as methane) may be soluble in water, because they are small enough that they don't interfere greatly with the strong intermolecular forces of the water. Larger hydrocarbons, however, are not

Butter is a saturated hydrocarbon.

Go Online
Animated examples
http://webcom4.grtxle.com/
khk12Chemistry

soluble in water, because they do not have the capability to replace the dipole and hydrogen-bonding interactions between water molecules, and they are large enough that many of these water interactions would need to be broken in order for the hydrocarbon to dissolve.

Hydrocarbons can be grouped into three categories based on how they bond internally: alkane, alkene, or alkyne. **Nomenclature** is the set of rules that tells us how to name a molecule.

Alkanes

An **alkane** is a hydrocarbon that contains only single bonds between the carbons. Alkanes have the general formula C_nH_{2n+2}. They are also called **saturated hydrocarbons,** because they contain as many hydrogen atoms as is possible for that number of carbon atoms. Alkanes are named by counting the longest chain of carbon atoms and using the prefix for that number (see Table 11–1) with the suffix "-ane."

Table 11–1	Organic Prefixes
Number of carbon atoms in longest chain	**Prefix**
1	Meth-
2	Eth-
3	Prop-
4	But-
5	Pent-
6	Hex-
7	Hept-
8	Oct-
9	Non-
10	Dec-

Example 11.1A

Naming Alkanes

1. Give the name for the following alkane.

$$H-\overset{\displaystyle H}{\underset{\displaystyle H}{C}}-\overset{\displaystyle H}{\underset{\displaystyle H}{C}}-\overset{\displaystyle H}{\underset{\displaystyle H}{C}}-\overset{\displaystyle H}{\underset{\displaystyle H}{C}}-\overset{\displaystyle H}{\underset{\displaystyle H}{C}}-\overset{\displaystyle H}{\underset{\displaystyle H}{C}}-H$$

- Count the number of carbon atoms on the longest chain: 6.

- Hexane

2. Draw the structure for butane.

- Butane has four carbons. Because this is an "-ane," only single bonds are present and the carbons are saturated with hydrogens.

$$H-\overset{\displaystyle H}{\underset{\displaystyle H}{C}}-\overset{\displaystyle H}{\underset{\displaystyle H}{C}}-\overset{\displaystyle H}{\underset{\displaystyle H}{C}}-\overset{\displaystyle H}{\underset{\displaystyle H}{C}}-H$$

Alkenes

An **alkene** is a hydrocarbon that contains double bonds between carbon atoms. The general formula for an alkene is C_nH_{2n}. For a double bond to form between two carbons, the hydrocarbon must be unsaturated; there must be two carbons next to each other, and each has one fewer hydrogen atom than it can possibly hold. Alkenes are named by counting the longest carbon chain (that includes the double bond) and using the appropriate prefix (see Table 11–1) with the suffix "-ene." (The first three prefixes can use either "-ylene" or "-ene.")

Isomers

Sometimes there is more than one way to draw a structure with the same chemical formula. These structures are called **isomers**—more than one way to bond atoms in molecules with the same chemical formulas. Alkenes sometimes have more than one place where the double bond can be included in the molecule. We must indicate which specific isomer we're talking about. The way to do this is to number the longest chain of carbons (that includes the double bond), starting at the end closest to the double bond. The first carbon atom involved in the double bond is specified by putting that carbon's number before the alkene's name.

Saturn's moon Titan shows evidence of lakes and rivers similar to Earth's, but don't plan on jumping off the high dive there—first off, it's 179°C, the lakes are methane, and the clouds are ethane. This orange place is a giant factory of organic chemicals and has many times more hydrocarbons than we have here in our oil, coal, and natural gas reserves. Perhaps someday you will go there to study the dunes made of tholins, the complex molecules central to prebiotic chemistry.

Example 11.1B

Naming Alkenes

1. Draw the structure for 2-butene.

    • Butene contains four carbon atoms. The "-ene" indicates that there is a double bond. The "2" indicates that it begins with the number 2 carbon.

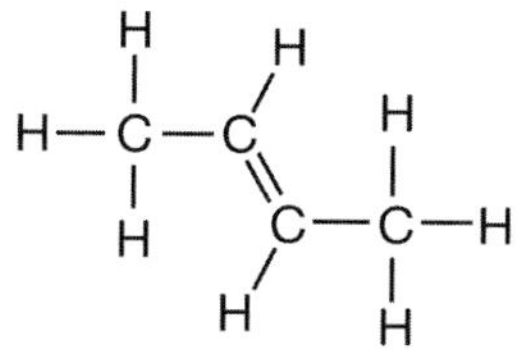

2. Name the following structure.

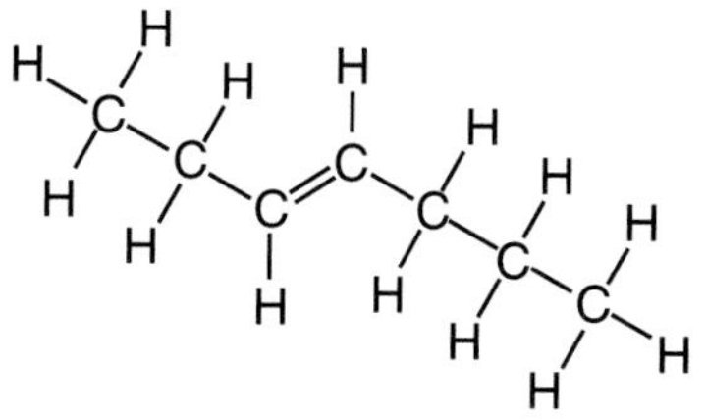

    • There are seven carbons, so hept- is the prefix; there is a double bond, so -ene is the suffix; the double bond is on carbon number 3 (counting from the side closest to the double bond).

    • *3-Heptene*

Alkynes

Alkynes are hydrocarbons with a triple bond between two carbon atoms. The general formula for an alkyne is C_nH_{2n-2}. For a triple bond to form between two carbons, the hydrocarbon must be unsaturated; there must be two carbon atoms right next to each other that both have two fewer hydrogen atoms than they can possibly hold. Again, count the longest chain of carbon atoms (that contains the triple bond), and use the appropriate prefix (Table 11–1) with the suffix -yne.

Alkynes can often have isomers; where exactly is the triple bond? Just as with the double bond in an alkene, count the longest carbon chain (that contains the triple bond) starting with the end closest to the triple bond. Use the number of the first carbon that is involved in the triple bond in the alkyne's name to specify the location of the triple bond.

Example 11.1C

Naming Alkynes

Give the name for the following structure.

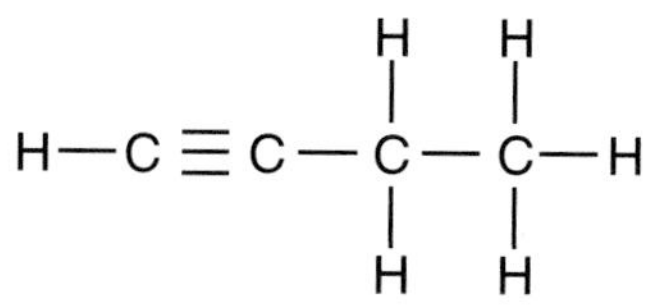

• There are four carbons, so but- is the prefix; there is a triple bond, so -yne is the suffix; the double bond starts on the first carbon (counting from the side closest to it).

• 1-Butyne

Alkene/alkyne isomers

It is possible that the same chemical formula could be drawn as an alkene with two double bonds or as an alkyne with one triple bond. You cannot tell the difference from the chemical formula, but the name would tell you specifically which chemical is being talked about.

Example 11.1D

Alkene and Alkyne Isomers

1. Give the chemical formula for each structure.

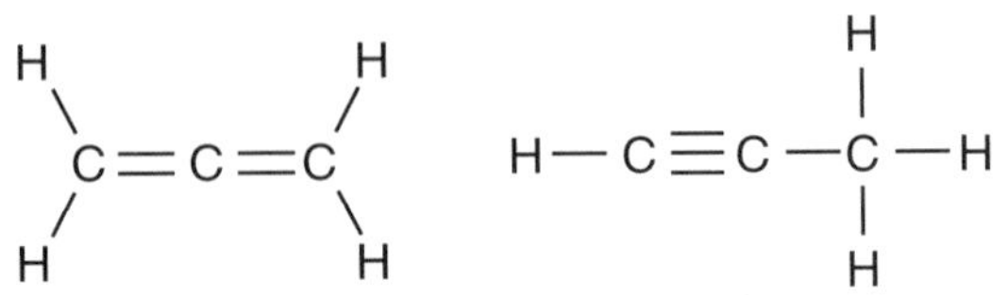

2. Give the name for each structure above.

- The first structure has three carbons, so prop- is the prefix; there are two double bonds, so the suffix is -diene (the "di" is added because there are two double bonds). The double bonds start on carbons 1 and 2.

- The formula for the first is C_3H_4. The formula for the second is also C_3H_4.

- 1,2-Propadiene

- Because the chemical formulas are the same although their actual structures are different, they are isomers. They will have different names even though their formulas are identical.

- The second structure has three carbons, so prop- is the prefix; there is a triple bond, so use -yne for the suffix; the triple bond begins on carbon 1.

- 1-Propyne

Saturation of hydrocarbons

Alkanes are called **saturated hydrocarbons** because they are saturated with (full of) hydrogens. They cannot possibly hold any more. Alkenes and alkynes are unsaturated, because they have multiple bonds that could hold more hydrogens. The more saturated a hydrocarbon is, the more easily it can stack to form intermolecular forces (see Figure 11–1). This is because *unsaturated* hydrocarbons have kinks or bends, because the multiple bonds don't let them get as close to one another to form intermolecular forces.

Saturated hydrocarbons are more likely to be solids with higher melting and boiling points than unsaturated hydrocarbons. For example, solid butter has more saturated fats (which are hydrocarbons) than cooking oil, which has more unsaturated fat.

Figure 11–1. Saturated and unsaturated hydrocarbons. The hydrocarbon on the left is saturated and can be stacked much more closely than the unsaturated hydrocarbon on the right.

Hydrocarbon side branches

A hydrocarbon is not always a straight chain of carbons—sometimes carbons form side branches off the main backbone. Side chains in hydrocarbons make them more bulky—they cannot get as close to each other as straight-line hydrocarbons. Therefore, they cannot form as many intermolecular forces with other molecules. This makes their melting and boiling points lower than those of straight-chain hydrocarbons of similar size (similar to the saturated versus unsaturated hydrocarbons). Branching also improves the automotive engine "octane rating" of a hydrocarbon since the more carbon atoms in the molecule, the more efficient the combustion reaction becomes.

Crude oil, extracted from the Earth to serve as a power source, is a hydrocarbon.

"In order to name a hydrocarbon with side branches, find the longest chain of carbons (even if it isn't written in a straight line). Use the length of the longest chain for the root of the name. Number the longest chain starting from the end closest to the first side chain (this will make sure that the side chains are on the lowest-numbered carbons possible). Count how many carbons are on each side chain, and use the prefix that is appropriate for that number. Write the side chain as the "carbon number-organic prefix." If there is more than one side chain, separate them by commas."

Example 11.1E

Hydrocarbon Side Branches

1. Draw the structure for 3-methylheptane.

   • "Hept-" means there are seven carbons (even if the chain is bent, it's still the longest chain you can find). The "3" indicates the side chain is on carbon 3. "Methyl" indicates the side chain has one carbon on it.

(continues)

Example 11.1E

Hydrocarbon Side Branches (*cont'd.*)

2. Name this compound, which is commonly called iso-octane or 100-octane.

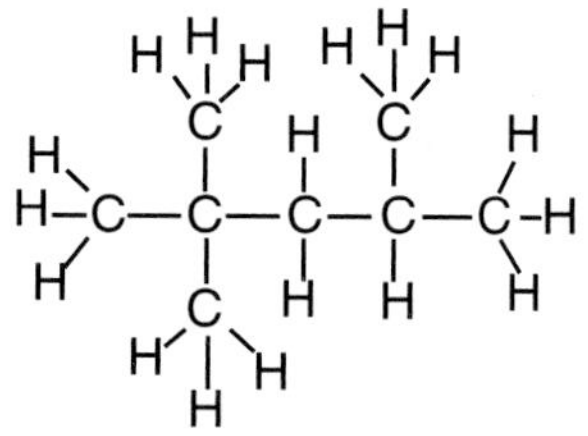

- The longest chain is five carbons long with single bonds, so use "pentane."

- There are three methyl side groups, so use "trimethyl."

- The methyl groups are located on carbon 2 (2 methyl groups) and carbon 4, so use "2,2,4."

- 2,2,4-Trimethylpentane

Go Online
Check your understanding
http://webcom4.grtxle.com/
khk12Chemistry

PRACTICE 11.1

Hydrocarbons

1. Name the following structures.

a.

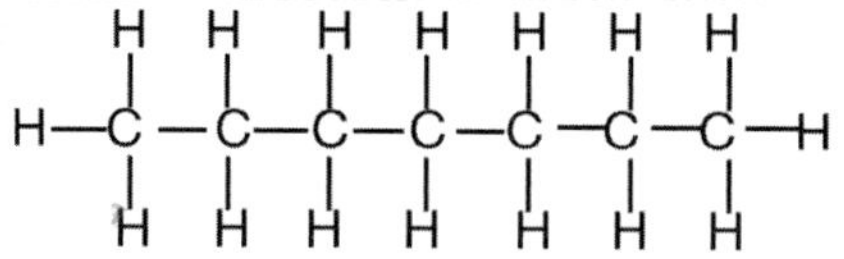

b.

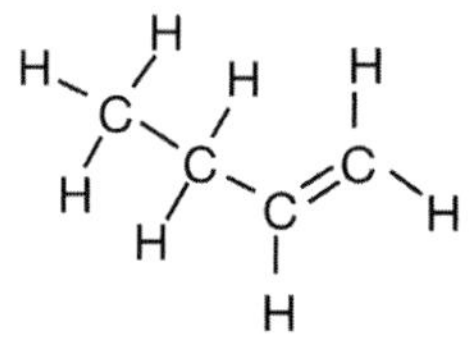

c. H—C≡C—H

d.

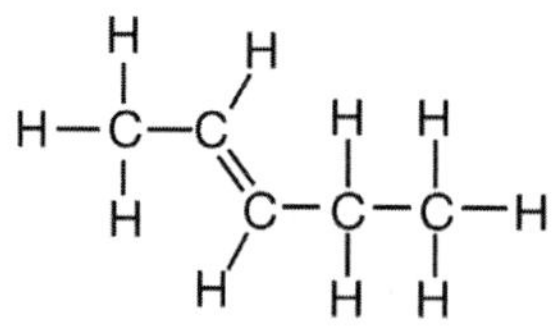

2. Draw the following structures.

a. Propane (the gas used in barbecue grills)

b. Pentane

c. 1-Butene

d. 2-Pentyne

Organic Functional Groups

Section 11.1 introduced the simplest hydrocarbons; they contained carbon and hydrogen only and had no side branching (groups of atoms sticking out the side of the chain of carbon). Many organic molecules contain **functional groups**—groups of atoms on the backbone of carbon and hydrogen that have functions which change the properties of the molecule.

Organic molecules can become very large and complex, with multiple functional groups on one molecule. The International Union of Pure and Applied Chemistry (IUPAC) develops rules that describe how to systematically name organic molecules so that each functional group and its location on the molecule are described. This allows a chemist to look at even a very complex compound's name and decipher the exact structure. We will work with only the simplest of these molecules in this chapter; if you take a course in Organic Chemistry, you will learn how to break down even the most complex-looking organic molecule name.

Each molecule has its systematic, IUPAC name. But sometimes a common name that was historically used is still used today. For example, "acetic" is often used in place of eth-based words for many compounds. Ethanoic acid is an IUPAC name, but the same molecule is often called acetic acid. Likewise, ethanoic anhydride (the IUPAC name) is often called acetic anhydride. This chapter will use the IUPAC systematic name, but if there is a common name for the molecule, both names will be given.

The International Union of Pure and Applied Chemistry (IUPAC) was formed in 1919 to foster worldwide communication in the chemical sciences. The standardization of weights, measures, names, and symbols is essential to science and to the smooth development and growth of international trade. For example, IUPAC recently provided data on methanol, which is timely information due to today's emphasis on cleaner fuels, in which methanol's use is expanding.

Haloalkanes

A **haloalkane** is when one or more of the hydrogens in an alkane (hydrocarbon with all single bonds) is replaced by a halogen atom (F, Cl, Br, or I). Haloalkanes produce polar molecules (unlike hydrocarbons). Therefore, they are able to form dipole–dipole intermolecular forces. This ability causes them to have higher melting and boiling points and increases their solubility in water, compared to hydrocarbons of similar size.

The basis of the name for a haloalkane is formed by naming the alkane. Count the carbon atoms in the longest chain so that the halogen atoms are on the lowest possible carbon number (start counting from the side closest to the halogen atom). The carbon number and halogen prefix (fluoro-, chloro-, bromo-, or iodo-) are indicated before the alkane name.

Go Online
Animated examples
http://webcom4.grtxle.com/
khk12Chemistry

Example 11.2A

Haloalkanes

Name the following structure.

$$H-\overset{\overset{\displaystyle H}{|}}{\underset{\underset{\displaystyle H}{|}}{C}}-\overset{\overset{\displaystyle Br}{|}}{\underset{\underset{\displaystyle H}{|}}{C}}-\overset{\overset{\displaystyle H}{|}}{\underset{\underset{\displaystyle H}{|}}{C}}-\overset{\overset{\displaystyle H}{|}}{\underset{\underset{\displaystyle H}{|}}{C}}-H$$

- There are four carbons, so "but-"; there are all single bonds, so "-ane"; there is a bromine atom on the second carbon, so "2-bromo."

- 2-Bromobutane

Alcohols

Alcohols are organic molecules that contain a hydroxyl group (–OH). Alcohols can form hydrogen bonds, like water, and many are therefore soluble in water (unlike many organic compounds). They have higher melting and boiling points than the hydrocarbons or haloalkanes of similar size, because of their increased ability to form strong intermolecular forces.

The –OH in an alcohol is not an ionic bond. The hydrogen is not acidic and does not dissociate from the oxygen when placed in water.

Beverage alcohol is a solution of ethanol, and rubbing alcohol is a solution of 2-propanol. Alcohols are toxic, including drinking alcohol. The body can tolerate small quantities of ethanol (other alcohols shouldn't be ingested at all), but if the levels in the body increase too much before it can be excreted, they can cause coma and death.

Alcohols are named by the longest chain of carbons (just as for hydrocarbons) with an -ol suffix. If the hydroxyl group is in the middle of the hydrocarbon chain, the carbons are numbered so that the hydroxyl group is on the lowest possible number carbon, and the number is included before the alcohol name.

Alcohols	
General Format	**Example**
$-O\diagdown_H$	$H-\overset{\overset{\displaystyle H}{|}}{\underset{\underset{\displaystyle H}{|}}{C}}-\overset{\overset{\displaystyle H}{|}}{\underset{\underset{\displaystyle H}{|}}{C}}-\overset{\overset{\displaystyle H}{|}}{\underset{\underset{\displaystyle H}{|}}{C}}-O\diagup^{H}$ 1-Propanol

Example 11.2B

Alcohols

Draw the structure for 2-butanol.

- The but- prefix means there are four carbons, the -ol suffix indicates an -OH group, and the 2 means that it's on the second carbon.

Ethers

Ethers are organic molecules that have an oxygen in the middle of a chain of carbons. Ethers are somewhat similar to alcohols in that they contain oxygen; however, the oxygen is surrounded by two carbons rather than by a carbon and a hydrogen, as in alcohols. This produces molecules with lower ability to form intermolecular forces (they cannot form hydrogen bonds); therefore, they do not have melting or boiling points as high as alcohols, and—except for the two smallest ethers—they are insoluble in water.

Ethers are named by counting the longest carbon chain on each side of the oxygen and then naming each of those chains separately, using organic prefixes with "ether" at the end.

Ethers	
General Format	**Example**
	Dimethyl ether

Example 11.2C

Ethers

Draw the structure for methyl ethyl ether.

- Methyl describes a 1-carbon side group, ethyl describes a 2-carbon side group, and ether means there is an oxygen bonded between the end carbons of each side group.

Amines

An **amine** is a functional group with a nitrogen and one to three saturated carbon atoms attached to it. (Remember, *saturated* means as many hydrogens bonded to it as possible.) Amines do have the ability to form hydrogen bonds with water, but the N–H bond is less polar than the O–H bond. Therefore, the N–H bond does not form as strong a hydrogen bond as the O–H bond. This means that amines are less soluble in water than alcohols of similar size. Also, their melting and boiling points are generally lower than those of the alcohols as well. Small amines generally smell bad (some are responsible for the smell of decaying organic material). The nitrogen on the amines can accept a hydrogen atom from water or in an acid–base reaction; therefore, amines typically act as Lewis bases (they donate electrons to a Lewis acid).

Amines are named by the carbon chains connected to the nitrogen atom with the suffix -amine.

Amines	
General Format	**Example**

Methyl ethylamine

Carbonyl-containing compounds

A **carbonyl** is a carbon that is double bonded to an oxygen atom. A carbonyl group is a polar functional group.

Carboxylic acids   A carboxylic acid is a compound that contains a carbonyl group in which the carbon is bonded on one side to a hydrogen or a carbon chain, and on the other side to a hydroxyl group (–OH). Together, this –COOH group is called a carboxyl group. The hydrogen of the hydroxyl group is acidic; it can be donated to water or in an acid–base reaction. Carboxylic acids are named by counting the carbon chain (including the carbon in the carbonyl), using the alkane name (for example, butane), but changing the suffix -ane to -oic acid (so, butanoic acid).

Aldehyde   An aldehyde is a compound that contains a carbonyl group in which the carbon is bonded on one side to a hydrogen and to a carbon chain on the other side. Aldehydes are named by counting the carbon chain (including the carbon in the carbonyl) and adding the suffix -al.

Many aldehydes produce pleasant smells; the smells of lemons, cinnamon, vanilla, cherries, and almonds are all caused by the aldehydes present. However, some have not-so-pleasant smells, such as formaldehyde (the preservative you might have encountered while dissecting in biology class).

Aldehyde	
General Format	Example
(structure: carbonyl group with C double-bonded to O and single-bonded to H)	(structure: H—C(=O)—H) Methanal (common name formaldehyde)

Ketones   A ketone has a carbonyl group in which the carbon is bonded to two other carbons. Ketones are named by counting the carbon chains on either side of the carbonyl (this time the carbonyl is *not* counted) and adding the ending word *ketone.*

Carboxylic Acids	
General Format	Example
(structure: carbonyl group C double-bonded to O and single-bonded to O—H)	(structure: H—C—C—C—C chain with final carbon double-bonded to O and single-bonded to O—H) Butanoic acid (also butyric acid, causes odor of rancid butter)

Anhydride   An anhydride is an organic molecule that contains two carbonyl groups with their carbon atoms separated by an oxygen atom. The other side of each of the carbonyl carbons is bonded to a carbon chain. Anhydrides are often symmetrical molecules—the carbon chains on each side of the carbonyls are identical. They are named by counting the carbon chain (including the carbonyl carbon) on one side of the oxygen atom in the middle (if both sides are identical, count just one of them), and using that prefix with -oic anhydride. If the anhydride is not symmetrical, it is called a *mixed anhydride,* and the name for each carbon chain (when counting, include the carbonyl carbon) is given followed by -oic anhydride.

Ketones

General Format	Example
Methyl ethyl ketone |

Anhydrides

General Format	Example
Ethanoic anhydride (commonly called acetic anhydride) |

Example 11.2D

Carboxylic Acid Compounds

1. Draw the structure for methanoic acid (also commonly called formic acid).

   - The meth- prefix indicates one carbon, and the -ic acid indicates a carbonyl group with an –OH on the other end. For carboxylic acids, the meth- includes the carbonyl carbon.

2. Draw the structure for propanal.

   - The prop- prefix indicates three carbons, and the -al suffix indicates the carbonyl carbon with a hydrogen on the other side. For aldehydes, propyl- includes the carbonyl carbon.

3. Draw the structure for methyl ethyl ketone.

   - Methyl indicates a one-carbon side chain, ethyl indicates a two-carbon side chain, and ketone shows there is a carbonyl in between the two side chains.

Aromatic compounds

An aromatic organic compound is a ring of six carbons that have alternating single and double bonds between them. The name *aromatic* comes from the fact that many of these compounds have odors. However, it is unwise to sniff these compounds, because they are often **carcinogens** (they cause cancer). Aromatic rings can be connected together, or they can have functional groups off to the side (such as a hydrocarbon side chain, a halogen, etc.). Aromatic compounds are generally insoluble in water. **Phenols** are aromatic rings with a hydroxyl group (–OH) on one of the carbons. Phenols have weak acid properties: the hydrogen in the hydroxyl group can be lost in an acid–base reaction. Figure 11–2 shows the structure of two common aromatic compounds, benzene and phenol.

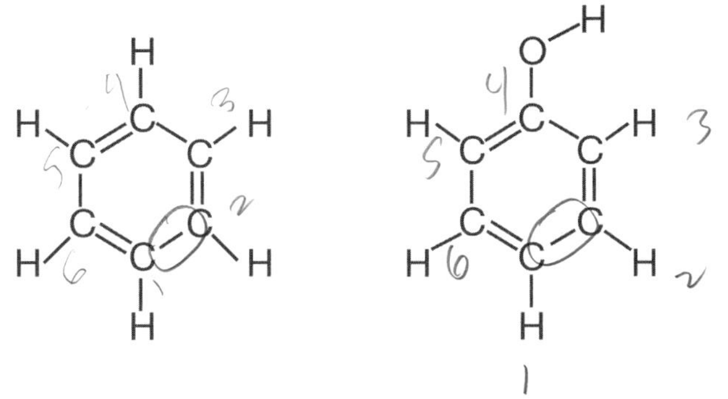

Figure 11–2. Aromatic rings.
On the left is the simplest aromatic ring, benzene; on the right is the simplest phenol.

LAB 11.2

Synthesis of an Organic Molecule: Aspirin

Purpose To synthesize aspirin

Background information The reaction you will use to synthesize aspirin is between salicylic acid and ethanoic anhydride (also called acetic anhydride). It produces aspirin and ethanoic acid (also called acetic acid—a solution of which is vinegar).

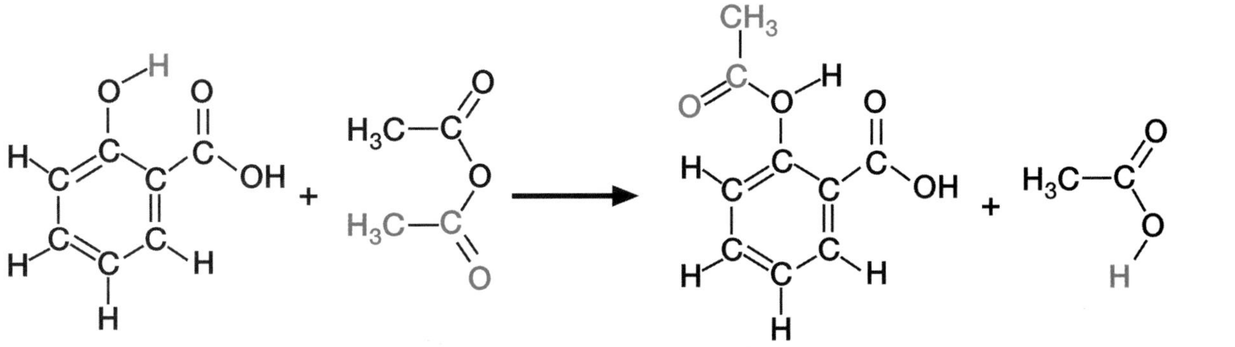

| Salicylic acid | Acetic anhydride | Acetyl salicylic acid (aspirin) | Acetic acid |

(continues)

LAB 11.2

Synthesis of an Organic Molecule: Aspirin (*cont'd.*)

Materials 250 mL flask, salicylic acid, cold water bath, filtration set-up (Büchner funnel and aspirator if available), balance, burette or pipette, and, in the fume hood: acetic anhydride, 85% phosphoric acid, and hot water bath

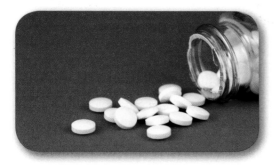

In the experiment, aspirin will be synthesized using salicyclic acid and ethanoic anhydride.

⚠ Safety Wear goggles, use caution with glassware (especially hot glassware), and report any spills or accidents to your teacher. The acetic anhydride and phosphoric acid can both cause serious burns—use them in the fume hood to minimize inhaling the vapors. Use caution with these chemicals—wear gloves in addition to your goggles! DO NOT ingest your final product—it is not purified!

Procedure

1. Weigh out 3.0 g of salicylic acid and place it in a 250 mL flask. Record exact mass in data table.

2. Perform the next four steps *in the fume hood!*

   a. Take your flask to the fume hood. Add 6.0 mL of acetic anhydride from the burette or volumetric or graduated pipette into your flask.

   b. Carefully add 5–10 drops of 85% phosphoric acid (which acts as a catalyst for this reaction). Swirl the flask.

   c. Heat the mixture for 10 minutes in a warm water bath (70°–80°C).

   d. After heating, cautiously add 20 drops of distilled water. This will destroy any remaining acetic anhydride that may be in the flask. Swirl the flask to make certain all of the anhydride is destroyed by the water.

3. You may now proceed at your lab table.

   a. Add 20 mL of distilled water and cool the solution in an ice bath. If you don't see crystals beginning to appear, you can scratch the side of the flask with the stir-rod to encourage crystal formation.

   b. Obtain a piece of filter paper and fold it into quarters (or use fluted filter paper). Write your name on it in pencil. Record the exact mass of the filter paper.

   c. Filter the solution from the crystals. Wash the crystals into the filter paper with 2–3 mL of cold water. Note in your observations any odor from this solution. The solution that filtered through is mostly water and can be poured down the drain.

4. Allow the crystals to dry overnight on the filter paper.

5. The next day, record the mass of the filter paper and the crystals.

Data/Observations

Mass of salicylic acid added _____

Mass of filter paper _____

Mass of filter paper and crystals _____

Describe any odor of the solution that was filtered away from the aspirin crystals.

Calculations

1. Write the balanced chemical formula equation from the structures drawn in the background information.

2. Use stoichiometry (see Section 6.5), the balanced chemical equation, and the mass of salicylic acid to find the theoretical mass of aspirin you could produce from this reaction.

3. Find the actual mass of the aspirin crystals produced using your lab data.

4. Find the percent yield with the theoretical mass of aspirin and the actual mass of aspirin you produced.

Synthesis of an Organic Molecule: Aspirin (*cont'd.*)

Discussion

1. Draw the structures for each reactant and product (from the figure above). For each of the structures, circle and identify each of the functional groups present (hydrocarbon side chain, halogen, hydroxyl, carbonyl, etc.).

2. For each of the reactants and products, identify which class of organic molecules it belongs to (alcohol, aldehyde, etc.).

3. The phosphoric acid in this lab was a catalyst—what does that mean? (See Section 2.8 for information on catalysts.)

4. The procedure says that water was added to destroy any remaining acetic anhydride in the flask. What does this tell you about which reactant was limiting and which was in excess? (See Section 6.6 for discussion on limiting reactants.)

5. Think about your answer from question 4 and the fact that you began your stoichiometry calculations with the mass of salicylic acid. Does it make sense? Why or why not?

6. What kind of properties could you test your crystals for to ensure that they are indeed aspirin?

7. How does the smell of the filtered solution add evidence that you did indeed produce aspirin?

Procedure adapted with permission from
http://chemistry.csustan.edu/.

Small-bladed (acicular) crystals growing on the walls of a glass container.

Go Online

Check your understanding
http://webcom4.grtxle.com/
khk12Chemistry

PRACTICE 11.2

Organic Functional Groups

1. Write the names for the following structures.

a. 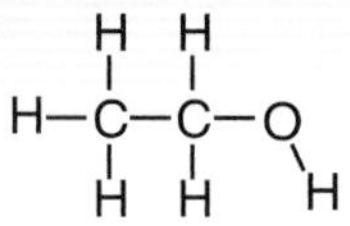
```
    H   H
    |   |
H — C — C — O
    |   |      \
    H   H       H
```

b.
```
    H   H   H   H   O
    |   |   |   |   ‖
H — C — C — C — C — C
    |   |   |   |      \
    H   H   H   H       O
                         \
                          H
```

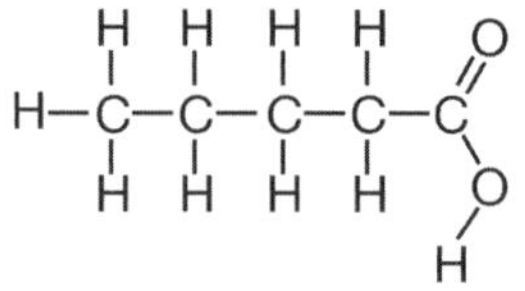

c.
```
            O
            ‖
      H     C     H
      |    / \    |
  H — C — C   C — C — H
      |   |   |   |
      H   H   H   H
      H         H
      (CH)        C
                 / \
                H   H
                    H
```

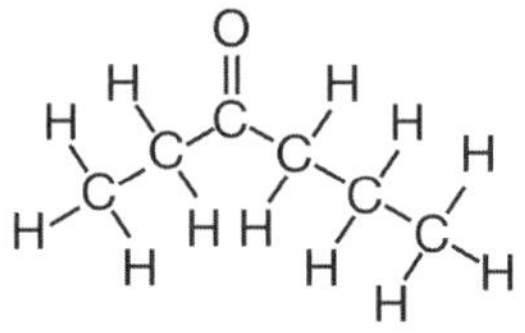

d. 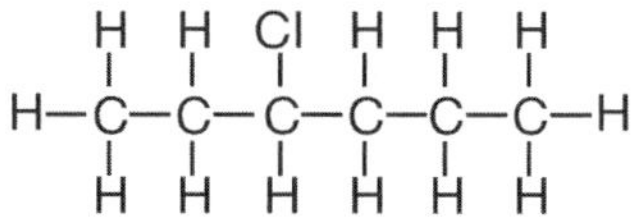
```
    H   H   Cl  H   H   H
    |   |   |   |   |   |
H — C — C — C — C — C — C — H
    |   |   |   |   |   |
    H   H   H   H   H   H
```

2. Draw the structure for rubbing alcohol: 2-propanol.

3. Diethyl ether was one of the earliest anesthetics. Draw its structure.

4. Dimethyl ketone (also commonly referred to as acetone) is in fingernail polish remover. Draw its structure.

5. Ethanoic acid (also commonly referred to as acetic acid) is in vinegar. Draw its structure.

SECTION 11.3

Polymers

Go Online
Topic: polymers
Go to: www.scilinks.org
Code: Chem1e398

SC/INKS
NSTA

Polymers are very large molecules built from chains or networks of smaller molecules—usually from 1000 to 50,000 molecules. Because polymers are very large molecules, they have some unique properties. Polymers can have functional groups in them just as regular organic molecules do.

The smaller molecules that make up a polymer are called **monomers**. Some polymers are made of the same monomer repeated over and over; some are made from a couple of monomers in alternating patterns, or in patterns of blocks of the same monomer. Other polymers are random combinations of various monomers.

Bakelite was one of the earliest synthetics (developed about 1907) that transformed the materials used in modern life. It is a polymeric plastic made from phenol and formaldehyde. Prized by collectors, you'll often see it at flea markets.

Thermoplastic versus thermoset polymers

There are two types of polymers: thermoplastic and thermoset. **Thermoplastic polymers** can be heated, molded into a shape, and then cooled. This process can be repeated over and over to make new shapes with the same piece of polymer. Polyethylene is a thermoplastic polymer. **Thermoset polymers** form cross-linkages (bonds between separate polymer chains that connect multiple chains together) when they are first heated and molded. Therefore, once they have formed these linkages and cooled, they cannot be reheated and reshaped—they are heat resistant. The handles on pots and pans for cooking are made of thermoset plastics.

Reactions forming polymers

Addition polymerization   One way to create a polymer is through an addition reaction. Addition polymerization reactions require an initiator—something to get the reaction started. Often, the initiator is a radical. A **radical** is an atom that has one free electron which is not involved in a

Natural rubber is produced from rubber trees.

bonding pair or a lone pair (see Chapter 5 for information on bonding and lone pairs). Radicals are highly chemically reactive because they are unstable, with one single electron and an incomplete valance shell. The reactive radicals bond quickly with any monomer with which they come in contact. When a radical reacts with a monomer, it becomes an **activated monomer,** which then reacts with another monomer to begin the chain. The reaction continues to build a chain until all the monomers are used or until the reaction is quenched by another chemical added to the reaction that stops it. Addition reactions need only a small amount of initiator, occur very rapidly, are usually exothermic, and produce very large polymers.

An example of an addition reaction uses the simplest alkene, ethylene (C_2H_4). The reaction between two ethylene molecules is shown in Figure 11–3. When this reaction occurs over and over again, it forms a long chain. The polymer is called *polyethylene.*

Addition polymerization can produce unwanted, uncontrolled results. For example, scientists knew that rubber was a polymer of isoprene; however, when they tried to synthesize rubber from isoprene in the lab, they got a sticky, useless mess instead of rubber. The isoprene monomers had been allowed to react in an uncontrolled environment which produced a mix of two arrangements of double bonds (called *cis* and *trans*). Natural rubber is produced in rubber trees, where an enzyme is present that controls the reaction and allows it to proceed in an orderly fashion, producing only the desired arrangement of double bond (*cis*). Scientists began using a catalyst in the laboratory trials and were able to produce usable rubber.

Side branching can also occur in radical addition polymerization, producing polymer chains that aren't all the same (or what the scientist was trying to produce).

Figure 11–3. Formation of polyethylene from ethylene molecules. The radical is symbolized by the Z.

Condensation polymerization Polymerization can also happen through **condensation reactions,** which are reactions that release another small molecule (such as water). Figure 11–4 shows an example of a condensation reaction. These reactions do not need an initiator, and they often produce smaller polymers. The released molecule must be removed throughout the process to keep it going (recall Le Chatelier's principle,

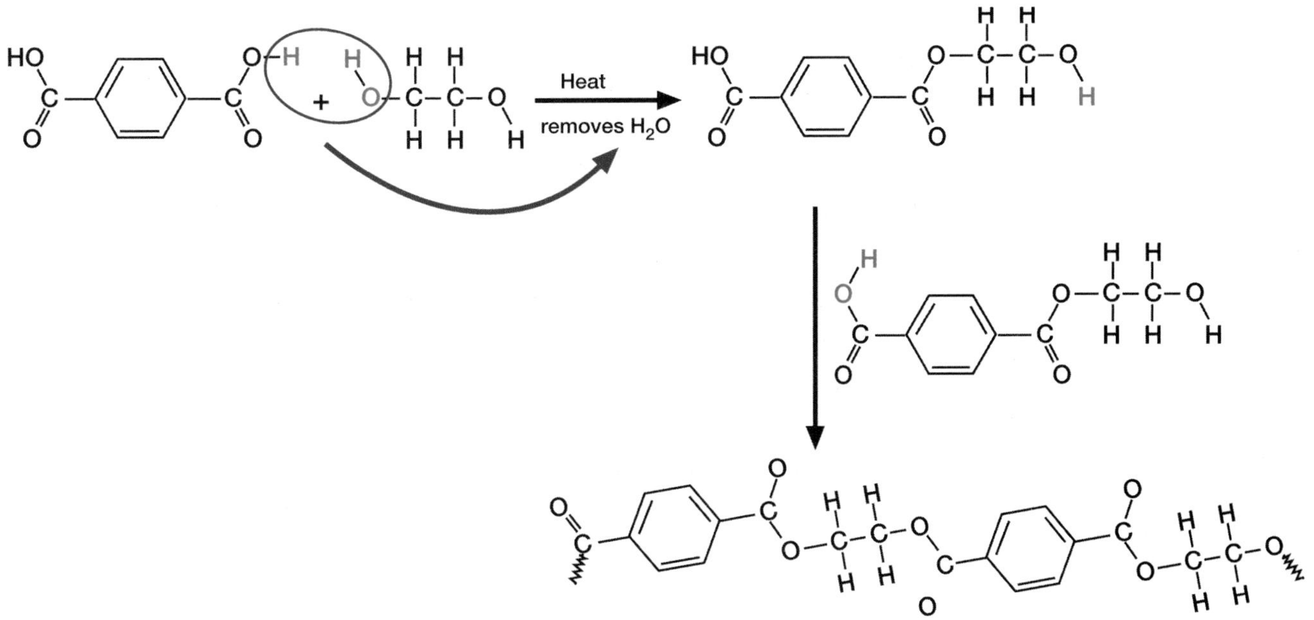

Figure 11–4. Formation of Dacron (a type of polyester). Each addition of another monomer releases a water molecule.

in Section 8.4: when a product is removed, more products are made). Condensation polymerization tends to form smaller chains than addition polymerization.

Condensation reactions can occur only at the location of the function group; therefore, they are less likely to form side chains. The monomers for condensation reactions must have a functional group on each side of the molecule, so that it can be reacted on both sides to form a chain.

Properties of polymers

The more interactions (intermolecular forces) there are between the polymer chains, the higher the melting and boiling points, and the more rigid the polymer. The properties of a polymer depend on the type of monomer, the size of the polymer, the amount of branching, and the strength of the intermolecular forces between the polymer chains.

Some polymers have side branching. Side branching affects the properties of a polymer similarly to how a compound's being saturated or unsaturated affects its properties (see Section 11.1). A polymer with significant side branching won't be able to stack closely to other polymer chains and form intermolecular forces. Therefore, polymers with significant side branching will have fewer attractions between separate chains, have lower melting and boiling points, and be softer, less rigid polymers.

Polyesters (formed from a condensation reaction) do not form side chains, and are therefore capable of being very close to one another. This allows the polymer chains to be spun into fibers, made into fabric, and used for clothing.

Plastic beads are made of polymers (very large molecules built from chains of smaller molecules).

Cross-linkages are covalent bonds (not intermolecular forces, but an actual chemical bond) between more than one polymer chain. Some polymers are liquids at room temperatures, but cross-linkages can be added that connect different polymer strands together. This makes them more gel-like or solid. Slime, the toy, is made by cross-linking a solution of polyvinyl alcohol polymers (which would be a liquid on their own).

Different polymers need different recycling methods, which accounts for the coding system (the triangle with a number inside it, found on the bottoms of recyclable plastic bottles). The plastics can then be sorted by number, and the process will group polymers together that can be recycled in the same manner.

Table 11–2, showing common polymers and their properties, is at the end of this chapter.

Polymers in biological settings

Polymers are found in more places than just plastics and rubber. Proteins are important polymers in the body; they are needed for nutrition. The monomers that make up the proteins in plants and animals, including humans, are called **amino acids.** There are 20 amino acids, and different combinations of these 20 make up all the various proteins. These amino acids form polymers through condensation reactions. DNA and RNA are also polymers formed from amino acids in our bodies—they tell the body how to build various proteins and structures that we need.

Observing Polymers

Purpose To observe polyvinyl alcohol fibers and film

Background information The solution of polyvinyl alcohol that you will be working with contains long polymer chains of polyvinyl alcohol. The chains will be dried by two methods. The first is by pulling it through dimethyl ketone (also known as acetone), which removes water from the threads. This works because the polymer is soluble in water but not in acetone; therefore, as it is "pulled" through the acetone it is in a solid form (not soluble). Acetone "dries" or removes water, resulting in a dry, solid thread of polyvinyl alcohol polymers. The second method is allowing a thin film of the solution to dry out overnight. The fibers and films will be observed dry and wet.

Materials 50 mL of 4% polyvinyl alcohol solution, 50 mL of acetone, 150 mL beaker, forceps or tweezers, stir-rod or plastic spoon, 30 cm × 30 cm piece of aluminum foil, aluminum pie pan

Safety Wear goggles. Acetone is very flammable—no open flames in lab when this is present. Avoid inhalation of acetone vapor.

Procedure

1. Pour about 50 mL of 4% polyvinyl alcohol solution into the 150 mL beaker (it should be about 2 cm deep).

2. Tip the beaker and pour (down the side of the beaker) about an equal depth of acetone so that it mixes as little as possible. Record observations of the contact area between the two layers.

3. Use the forceps or tweezers to reach in and grab hold of the interface layer between the two solutions. Slowly pull straight up out of the beaker.

4. Lay the strand on the aluminum foil.

5. Repeat the process several more times, as long as the reactants continue to produce the polymer.

6. Pour enough *fresh* 4% polyvinyl alcohol solution to cover the bottom of the aluminum pan with a thin film.

7. Allow the solution in the pan and the threads on the foil to dry overnight.

8. The next day, test the threads and a piece cut from the film in the pan for flexibility and stretchiness. Record observations.

9. Dip the thread in a container of water one time and repeat your observations about its flexibility and stretchiness. Do this with a piece of the film as well.

Observations

Discussion

1. Draw the structure for the dimethyl ketone (acetone).

2. The polyvinyl alcohol solution is 4% (W/V). If your teacher needed to make 500 mL of this solution for the lab today, how many grams of polyvinyl alcohol would be needed? (See Section 6.2 for discussion on concentrations of solutions.)

3. In this lab, you were given a solution with the polymer already formed. You dried the polymer in two manners. Did you perform a chemical reaction or a physical change?

4. Which solution, the polyvinyl alcohol or the acetone, is less dense? Give evidence to defend your answer.

5. Describe the polymer you used: is it the same monomer repeated, several monomers repeated in a pattern, or a random polymer?

6. The monomer that the polymer is formed from is ($-CH_2CHOH-$) where the hydroxyl group ($-OH$) is

(continues)

Observing Polymers (cont'd.)

connected to the second carbon atom, and each carbon atom has an open spot to bond to another monomer. Draw the structure for one monomer (leaving open each "end" to show where it would connect to other monomers). Draw the structure for three monomers in a row (leaving open each "end" to show where the rest of the polymer chain would be).

7. Describe the differences in flexibility and stretchiness of the dry polymer versus when it was dipped in water for a few seconds.

8. Can you think of a time when this type of difference in properties might be useful? What kind of product could be made out of a polymer like this? What kind of a polymer could *not* be made out of a polymer like this?

9. PVA is used in some hair gels and cosmetic facemask gels. Explain why this might be, based upon your observations in this lab.

Procedure adapted with permission from *Science in Our World: Chain Gang—The Chemistry of Polymers* by Terrific Science Press (*www.terrificscience.org*).

Go Online
Check your understanding
http://webcom4.grtxle.com/
khk12Chemistry

PRACTICE 11.3

Polymers

1. What's the difference between monomers and polymers?

2. What's the difference between thermoset and thermoplastic polymers? Give an example of each (not the same examples given in the text).

3. Explain the difference between addition polymerization and condensation polymerization. How do the polymers formed by these two processes differ?

4. How do the properties of a very large polymer differ from those of a very small polymer?

Dr. Daniel W. Fox of General Electric (GE) Company's Chemical Development Operation holds Lexan, GE's polycarbonate thermoplastic, developed in 1953. It is as clear as glass and nearly as tough as steel. Some uses include blender pitchers and helmets. You may have also seen Lexan on clear skateboards

FINAL CHAPTER PROJECT

Here is your your chance to use the chemistry you know to act as
a product developer to create the bounciest ball.

Bouncy ball contest

Purpose To formulate the highest-bouncing
ball possible

Background information White glue contains
polyvinyl acetate. Borax (used as a laundry cleaner)
contains sodium borate. When sodium borate dissolves, it dissociates to form borate anions (and
sodium cations). The borate anions form bridges to
connect the polyvinyl acetate polymers. This forms
a cross-linked polymer that can also form hydrogen
bonds between the polymer chains. The cross-linking and hydrogen bonding create a three-dimensional polymer that has open space for water. Filled
with water, the spaces and the polymer produce a
non-Newtonian fluid. This means that it acts somewhat like a liquid (it will flow and drip) and somewhat like a solid (it bounces and shatters).

Instructions Each lab group is a research team that
is trying to develop the bounciest product possible.
Your research group has been presented with the
following information:

- The bouncy product is currently being produced
  by dissolving 10 g of borax in 10 mL of water, then
  mixing 10 g of glue with 10 mL of water. The two
  solutions are then combined.

- The problem is that this produces a product that
  is too runny and milky, with too many byproducts,
  and it's not bouncy enough.

- Each research team has been given $15 to fund
  their research and produce the best bouncy ball
  possible.

- The costs the team will need to consider when
  planning and conducting their research are as
  follows:

  - 1 gram of glue = $0.10

  - 5.00 grams of borax = $0.15

  - Paper cup (to measure out or
    mix reactants) = $0.25

- Stir-rod = $0.10

- Rental of lab station = $1.00 per class period

- Rental of balance = $0.50 per class period

- Rental of graduated cylinder =
  $0.50 per class period

Each group must plan several experiments. The
experiments can be written into a flow chart with
various recipes (as shown below). Experiment 1
must differ from the original recipe in some manner. (Which variable will your group change first?)
Depending on the results, the team will then
move on to either Experiment 2A or 2B. The group
should continue to alter the recipe for a total of
three levels (as shown below) before they begin
experimenting on their own. Teams may continue
to add levels after level 3, keeping in mind their
research budget ($15). Teams don't need to do
every recipe they come up with. For example, if
2A improved upon the results from Experiment 1,
then it's the team's choice whether to continue on
from there or to go back and do 2B to see which is
the better at that level. Each group should make
educated judgment calls.

Your write-up must include:

- **Title**

- **Purpose**

- **Background information** (You may use some that
  is given above, but you should also include information you know about, or definitions of, monomers, polymers, cross-linked polymers, etc.)

- **Safety** (Some students may be allergic to
  borax—avoid inhalation and ingestion. Wear
  goggles. Report any spills or accidents to your
  teacher.)

- **Experimental flow chart** (Each experiment
  should give a new recipe, along with the cost for
  that experiment. The arrows between the different experiments should say "more bounce" or "less

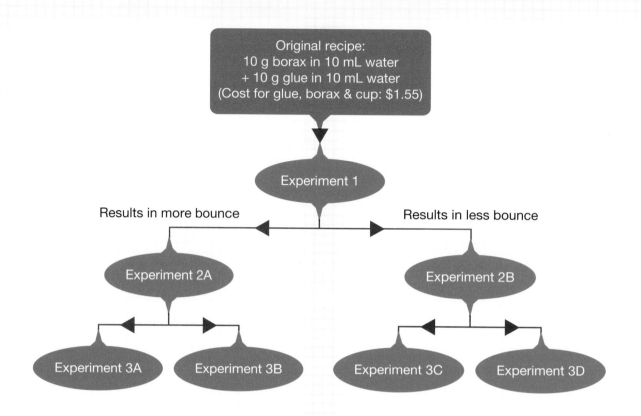

Original recipe:
10 g borax in 10 mL water
+ 10 g glue in 10 mL water
(Cost for glue, borax & cup: $1.55)

Experiment 1

Results in more bounce   Results in less bounce

Experiment 2A   Experiment 2B

Experiment 3A   Experiment 3B   Experiment 3C   Experiment 3D

bounce" to show which way you will move on the flow chart, based on your observations of the previous experiment.)

- **Balance sheet** Each group should show a beginning balance of $15, with deductions for major equipment rental and single items (lab space, balance, etc.). (Hint—You can use the same paper cup to measure out the borax and glue each time, but each separate experiment requires a new paper cup for mixing the two ingredients together.) Record each purchase you make from the "store" as you make it. You will need to bring this balance sheet with you each time you make a purchase to show the "storekeeper" that you do indeed have enough in your account to make the purchase. (NOTE—Fines will be imposed for groups that improperly account for time or that fail to clean up their research areas!) The balance sheet should show a table with three columns (see the example provided).

Description	Amount	Balance
Beginning balance		$15.00
Rental of lab space	−$1.00	$14.00

Once the required parts of the write-up are complete, you may begin your research in the lab and continue with the rest of the write-up. Include the experiment numbers that you actually performed from your flow chart, and observations on the product of each one.

- **Results** (Your final best recipe and your observations about its product's performance)

- **Conclusion** Restate the purpose. Give your overall evaluation of the performance of the best product you produced. What characteristic did each of the three ingredients (glue, borax, and water) add to the finished product (meaning, if you increased one of the ingredients, how did it affect the properties of the polymer)? How did placing a cost on lab materials change your approach to the problem? Your company now wants to produce a slimy material type of play substance made of polyvinyl alcohol, borax, and water. What would that recipe look like, as opposed to the one for your bouncy ball?

Activity adapted from Dow/NSTA Summer Workshop Lesson Plan, "Research and Development of a Polymer."

Chapter 11 Summary

Organic molecules contain carbon atoms bonded to other carbon atoms. The properties of an organic molecule, as with any molecule, are determined by the structure and types of intermolecular forces that the molecule can exhibit.

Hydrocarbons are the simplest organic molecules, containing hydrogen and carbon only. Hydrocarbons with only single bonds are alkanes; hydrocarbons with double bonds between carbon atoms are alkenes; and hydrocarbons with triple bonds between carbon atoms are alkynes.

Organic molecules can also have functional groups that change the properties of the compound. Functional groups include hydrocarbon side branches, halogens, hydroxyl groups, oxygen atoms, nitrogen-containing groups, carbonyls, and carboxylic acid groups. Organic molecules are grouped into classes depending on which functional groups they contain, such as alcohols, ethers, amines, carboxylic acids, ketones, aldehydes, and aromatic rings.

Nomenclature is the system of naming molecules. The International Union of Pure and Applied Chemistry (IUPAC) governs the rules of nomenclature for organic molecules. Hydrocarbons are named by counting the carbon atoms in the longest chain and adding the organic prefix for the number of carbon atoms with the suffix for the types of bonds in the hydrocarbon. Organic molecules with functional groups are named in such a way that the specific carbon containing the functional group is identified along with the functional group itself.

One polymer that is used to create polyester fabric, thread, and buttons is used for clothing such as shirts and ties.

Isomers are molecules that have the same chemical formula but are bonded differently. Isomers cannot be distinguished from one another using only their chemical formulas, but by using their systematic names they can be.

Polymers are large molecules formed from small molecules called monomers. Polymer properties depend on the structure and intermolecular forces of the monomers and the arrangement in which the monomers are connected. Some polymers are cross-linked, meaning that there are bonds connecting separate polymer chains together. Polymers can be formed through addition polymerization reactions, which require an initiator (usually a radical) and produce very large polymers, or through condensation reactions, which release a small molecule (often water) and produce smaller polymers.

1. Compare and contrast saturated and unsaturated hydrocarbons.

2. Why are functional groups called "functional" groups?

3. Compare and contrast addition and condensation polymerization.

4. How does adding a polar functional group affect a molecule's ability to form intermolecular forces? How does this affect the molecule's properties?

5. How does adding a nonpolar functional group affect a molecule's ability to form intermolecular forces? How does this affect the molecule's properties?

6. Explain how the size of a polymer affects the properties of the polymer.

7. Name the following structures.

   a. 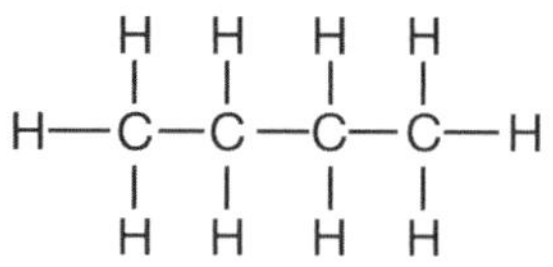
   b. 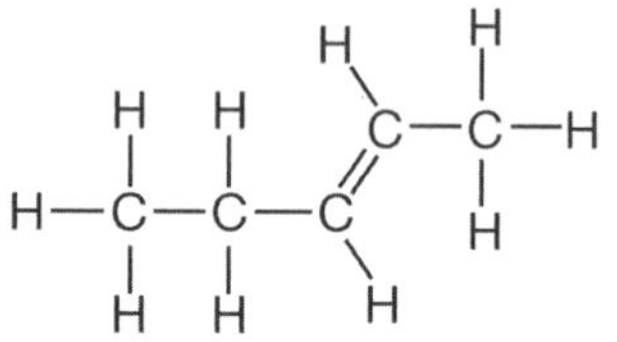
   c. 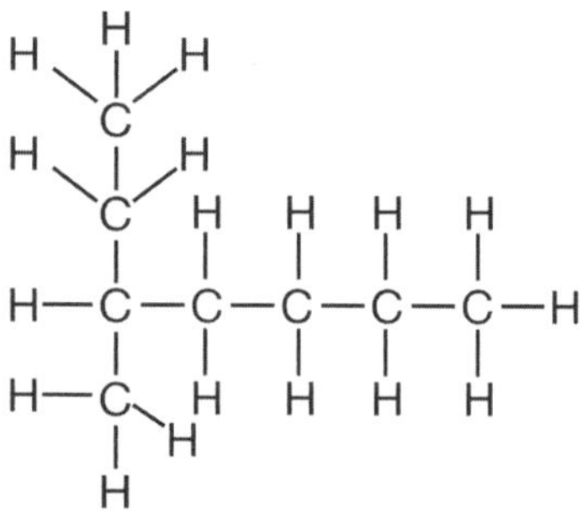
   d. 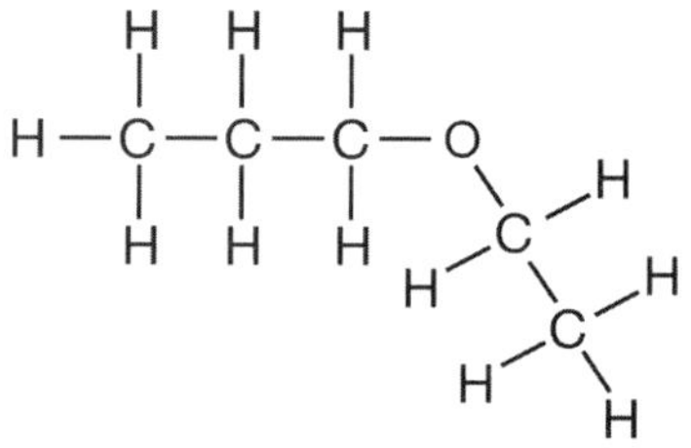
   e. 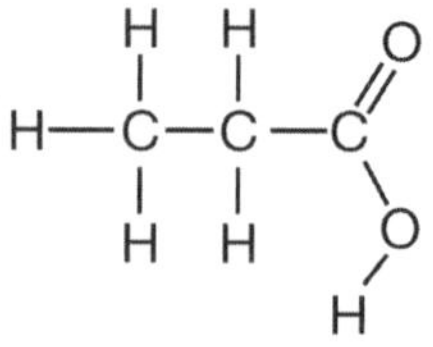
   f. 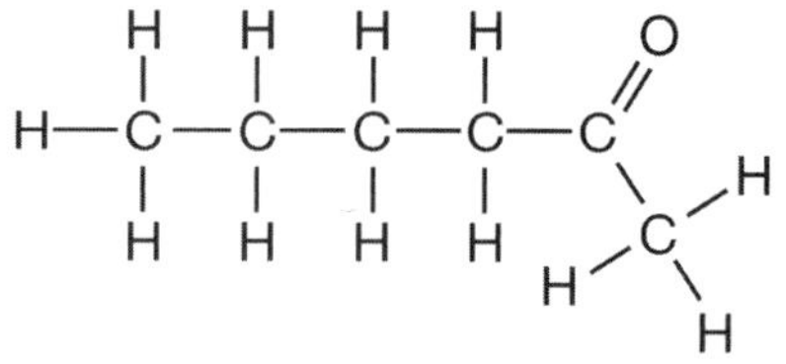
   g.

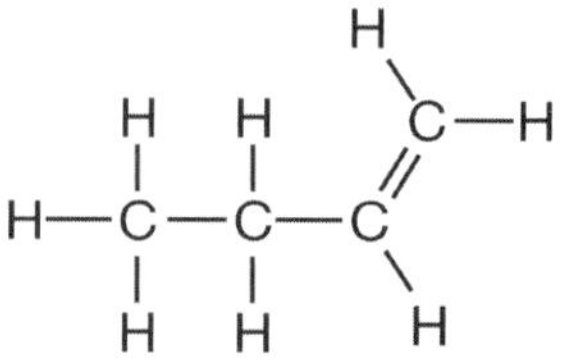

8. Draw the following structures.

   a. Ethane

   b. 2-Chloropropane

   c. 1,4-Pentadiene

   d. Methanol

   e. Methyl propyl ketone

9. Explain why addition polymerization produces different-sized polymers than condensation polymerization.

10. Explain how side branching can affect a polymer's properties.

11. Explain how addition polymerization can produce uncontrolled results and how addition polymerization can be controlled.

Name(s)	Formula	Monomer	Properties	Uses
Polyethylene, low density (LDPE)	$-(CH_2\text{-}CH_2)_n-$	Ethylene $CH_2=CH_2$	Soft, waxy solid	Film wrap, plastic bags
Polyethylene, high density (HDPE)	$-(CH_2\text{-}CH_2)_n-$	Ethylene $CH_2=CH_2$	Rigid, translucent solid	Electrical insulation, kayaks, bottles, toys
Polypropylene (PP); different grades	$-[CH_2\text{-}CH(CH_3)]_n-$	Propylene $CH_2=CHCH_3$	Soft, elastic solid *or* hard, strong solid	Similar to LDPE; carpet, upholstery
Poly(vinyl chloride) (PVC)	$-(CH_2\text{-}CHCl)_n-$	Vinyl chloride $CH_2=CHCl$	Strong, rigid solid	Pipes, siding, flooring
Poly(vinylidene chloride) (Saran A)	$-(CH_2\text{-}CCl_2)_n-$	Vinylidene chloride $CH_2=CCl_2$	Dense, high-melting solid	Seat covers, films
Polystyrene (PS)	$-[CH_2-CH(C_6H_5)]_n-$	Styrene $CH_2=CHC_6H_5$	Hard, rigid, clear solid; soluble in organic solvents	Toys, cabinets, packaging (foamed)
Polyacrylonitrile (PAN, Orlon, Acrilan)	$-(CH_2-CHCN)_n-$	Acrylonitrile $CH_2=CHCN$	High-melting solid; soluble in organic solvents	Rugs, blankets, clothing
Polytetrafluoroethylene (PTFE, Teflon)	$-(CF_2-CF_2)_n-$	Tetrafluoroethylene $CF_2=CF_2$	Resistant, smooth solid	Nonstick surfaces; electrical insulation
Poly(methyl methacrylate) (PMMA, Lucite, Plexiglas)	$-[CH_2-(CH_3)CO_2CH_3]_n-$	Methyl methacrylate $CH_2=C(CH_3)CO_2CH_3$	Hard, transparent solid	Lighting covers, signs, skylights
Poly(vinyl acetate) (PVAc)	$-(CH_2-CHOCOCH_3)_n-$	Vinyl acetate $CH_2=CHOCOCH_3$	Soft, sticky solid	Latex paints, adhesives
***cis*-Polyisoprene,** natural rubber	$-[CH_2-CH=C(CH_3)-CH_2]_n-$	Isoprene $CH_2=CH-C(CH_3)=CH_2$	Soft, sticky solid	Requires vulcanization for practical use
Polychloroprene, *(cis + trans)* (Neoprene)	$-[CH_2-CH=CCl-CH_2]_n-$	Chloroprene $CH_2=CH-CCl=CH_2$	Tough, rubbery solid	Synthetic rubber; oil resistant

Table 11-2   Common Polymers

Printed with permission from William Reusch, *http://www.cem.msu.edu/~reusch/VirtualText/polymers.htm.*

Nuclear Radiation
Chemistry Is Harmful and Helpful

IN THIS CHAPTER

- Nuclear reactions
- Nuclear radiation: Harmful or helpful?

INTRODUCTORY ACTIVITY

In what contexts have you heard about nuclear reactions, nuclear power generators, radioactivity, or radiation?

Do those contexts make you think positively or negatively, in general, about nuclear reactions and radioactivity?

Think about these questions, share your thoughts with a partner and then with the class.

to evaluate how nuclear waste is being handled.

Introduction

Most people have heard of nuclear reactions or radioactivity, but are unsure what, exactly, these terms mean. A **nuclear reaction** is one in which the nucleus of the atom is changed. **Radiation** is what is released during a nuclear reaction.

This chapter will introduce nuclear reactions, discuss the types of radiation produced, teach you how to write nuclear reaction equations, and discuss how these reactions are both harmful and helpful in our lives.

This is a 3-D visualization of a sea urchin generated using a high-resolution, computerized tomographic scanner system so that scientists can see inside of it. Neurosurgeons can use a specially developed system and operating table to scan a patient before and after surgery, so they can perform a precise surgery and minimize the need for after-surgery radiation treatments.

Nuclear Radiation

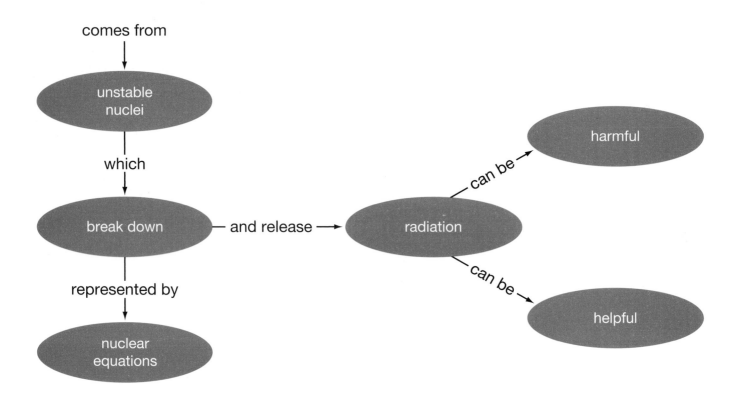

SECTION 12.1

Nuclear Reactions

Discovery of nuclear radioactivity

French scientist Henri Becquerel stumbled upon nuclear radioactivity in 1896. He had stored photographic plates in a drawer with some uranium while waiting for a sunny day to continue his experiments with the photographic material. Several days later, he saw that those photographic plates had been exposed, even though they had been in the drawer and had not been in sunlight. The uranium sample was radioactive—that's how the photographic plates were exposed. But it wasn't until Marie Curie asked Becquerel for help finding a topic for her doctoral research that the source of the radiation (the uranium) was determined.

What is nuclear radioactivity?

A **radioactive** element is one that changes the makeup of its nucleus spontaneously (on its own). That is, if an element changes the number of protons or neutrons contained in its atoms on its own (which is a nuclear reaction), it is radioactive.

If the number of protons in an atom's nucleus changes, the atom is now a different element—the number of protons defines the element's properties. So if the number of protons changes, then the element has changed, too. Remember that a chemical reaction cannot produce new elements—you used the law of conservation of mass to balance chemical equations so that the number of atoms of each element was the same on the reactants and on the products side. The atoms of the elements can be neither created nor destroyed in a chemical reaction. However, a nuclear reaction often does produce new elements that were not present before as the number of protons changes.

Radioactivity occurs when a nucleus in an atom is unstable—it releases some of its components to produce a more stable nucleus (see Figure 12–1). Whenever a change is made to a more stable structure, energy is released. Nuclear reactions release very large amounts of energy. For example, the radioactive decay of one gram of uranium-235 (uranium with a mass number of 235) produces 82,000,000 kJ of energy, whereas the burning of one gram of methane gas produces only 52 kJ of energy.

Some elements have several unstable, radioactive isotopes; others have only stable isotopes (see Section 4.2 for information on isotopes).

In 1898, Marie Curie discovered polonium and radium, working with her husband Pierre. She earned two Nobel prizes prior to her death from anemia, likely from exposure to radiation. When she worked with these substances, their dangers were not yet known.

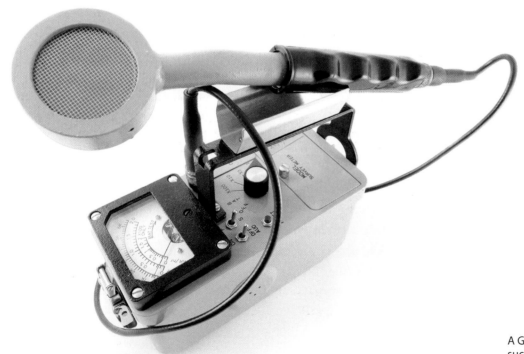

A Geiger counter detects radiation, such as alpha and beta radiation.

Types of radioactive decay

There are three types of radiation produced by nuclear reactions: alpha (α), beta (β), and gamma (γ).

Alpha particles are essentially the nuclei of helium atoms. They contain two protons, two neutrons, and no electrons, which is exactly what the nucleus of a helium atom contains. Because they have a total positive charge of +2 and no negative electrons, the overall charge will be +2. The nucleus has two protons and two neutrons, so the mass number will be 4. The symbol for an alpha particle is $^4_2\text{He}^{+2}$ (see Section 4.2 for information on writing element symbols). The alpha particles produced from radioactive decay deep underground take on electrons from their environment and make up much of the supply of helium on Earth.

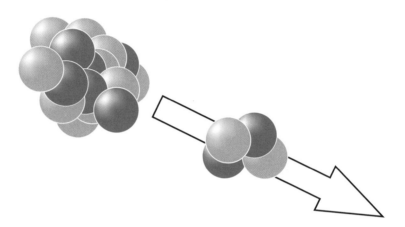

Figure 12–1. Alpha decay. Radioactive decay is when a nucleus releases some of its components—in this case, two protons and two neutrons. This released particle is an alpha particle.

A **beta particle** is a rapidly moving electron emitted from an atom when a neutron turns into a proton and an electron. The original neutron had a mass of 1 amu and a neutral charge. The new proton has a mass of 1 amu and a charge of +1. The new electron has a mass of 0 amu and a charge of –1. The new proton and new electron add up to the neutral charge and mass of 1 amu of the original neutron.

Because a beta particle (the emitted electron) has no protons or neutrons, its mass number is 0. The "atomic number" position in the element symbol is filled with "–1" in the beta particle symbol to aid in balancing nuclear reactions, but that's not really an atomic number—it allows the balancing of the new proton with the original number of protons. The beta particle symbol is $^0_{-1}e$.

Gamma radiation is electromagnetic radiation similar to light (see Section 4.6 for information on electromagnetic radiation). The frequency of gamma radiation is greater than 1×10^{20} Hz. Each photon in the stream

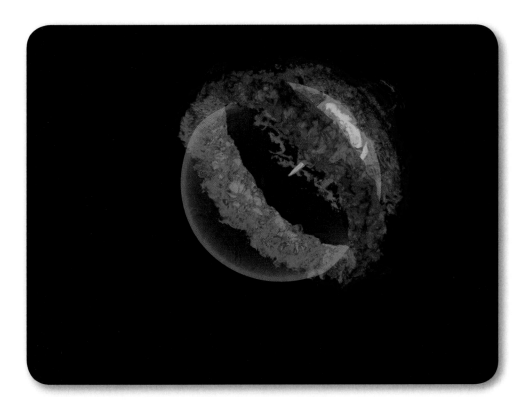

Nuclear reactions of carbon in the core of a white dwarf star.

of photons that make up gamma radiation is given off as the nucleus releases energy. Because gamma radiation is a form of electromagnetic energy, it has no charge and no mass.

Alpha particles are usually given off by heavier elements, beta radiation by lighter elements. When the alpha or beta particles are emitted from the nucleus, this emission is accompanied by a large change in energy (as mentioned above). Therefore, gamma radiation is often emitted with the ejection of an alpha or beta particle.

Nuclear reactions and equations

During a nuclear reaction, the original atoms emit radiation (alpha or beta particles, sometimes accompanied by gamma radiation) and are then left with a different nucleus. The product is called the **daughter nucleus**, and it is now a different element. Elements cannot be changed during a chemical reaction, only rearranged—therefore, whenever the nucleus of an atom is changed, it is a nuclear reaction.

By determining which type of radiation is given off during a nuclear change, you can find the identity of the daughter nucleus also, by writing a balanced nuclear equation. *The atomic numbers and mass numbers must balance in a nuclear equation.*

Containers and trucks should use hazard signs warning of their contents.

Example 12.1

Nuclear Equations

When radium-226 (atomic number 88) undergoes radioactive decay, it emits one alpha particle per radium atom. Identify the product of the reaction.

$$^{226}_{88}\text{Ra} \rightarrow {}^{4}_{2}\text{He}^{+2} + ?$$

- If radium loses two protons, then the daughter nucleus will have an atomic number of 86, which is radon.

- If the radium, with a mass number of 226, loses a total mass of 4, then the daughter nucleus will have a mass number of 222.

$$^{226}_{88}\text{Ra} \rightarrow {}^{4}_{2}\text{He}^{+2} + {}^{222}_{86}\text{Rn}$$

LAB 12.1

Determining Half-Life

Purpose To determine the half-life of an isotope by observing the decay over time

Materials 50 M&M "atoms" and a box or other container

! Safety Do not eat the M&Ms unless you are doing this activity outside the chemistry lab area, with fresh candy and equipment that is clean—your teacher will tell you if you are allowed to eat them!

Background information Each M&M represents an atom of a radioactive isotope. You will place them inside the covered box and shake the box. Each time the box is shaken equals one minute of time that the M&Ms are allowed to decay. An atom has decayed into the daughter nucleus when the M&M logo is facing up.

Procedure

1. Place 50 M&Ms in the box, with the logos facing down.

2. Cover the box with the lid.

3. Shake the box once, representing one minute of decay.

4. Open the box and remove any candies with the logo facing up; these atoms have undergone radioactive decay.

5. Repeat the process, removing any "atoms" that have "decayed" after each "minute." Keep going until you end up with one undecayed atom remaining.

Data table

Use the following table format and add as many time trials as necessary until you run out of isotopes.

Time (min)	Number of isotopes decayed in this minute	Number of isotopes remaining
0	N/A	50
1		

Results Create a graph with time on the x axis and number of isotopes remaining on the y axis. Draw a best-fit smooth curve through your data points. Use that curve (not your individual data points) to answer the questions below.

Discussion

1. Explain why the best-fit curve was drawn and used to determine the half-life, rather than using the data points or a connect-the-dots line.

Determining Half-Life (*cont'd.*)

2. Create a class histogram (see Lab 2.7, Discussion question 5). Describe the class results. Is there a clear mode? If not, suggest possible reasons.

3. Use your graph to determine how long it would take you to go

   a. From 40 atoms to 20 atoms.

   b. From 10 atoms to 5 atoms.

   c. From 24 atoms to 12 atoms.

   d. From 36 atoms to 18 atoms.

4. What did you notice about the time it took for you to halve your original atoms in the previous

question? Share your results with the class. Does everyone have similar results?

5. Define in your own words what you think "half-life" might mean in the context of radiation.

6. Was there any way to predict which "atom" would "decay" next? Were any "atoms" more likely to decay at any given moment than the others?

7. If you had begun with 100 "atoms," how long would it take to be left with only 50?

8. If you had begun with 100 "atoms," how long would it take to be left with only 25?

Half-lives

The **law of radioactive decay**, as determined by experimental measurement, shows that the relationship between the speed at which radiation is released is directly proportional to the number of radioactive nuclei present in a sample. However, each radioactive isotope decays at a different speed—some very quickly, and some over long periods of time. Radioactive half-lives (symbolized by $t_{1/2}$, the time it takes for half the radioactive nuclei in a sample to decay) are used to describe how quickly a specific isotope decays. The **half-life** of a radioactive element can be determined by measuring how many nuclei decay over a period of time. Some half-lives of common radioactive isotopes are given in Table 12–1.

Table 12–1 Half-Lives of Common Isotopes	
Isotope	Half-life
Tritium (hydrogen-3)	12.3 years
Carbon-14	5,730 years
Carbon-15	2.4 seconds
Potassium-40	1,260,000,000 years
Cobalt-60	5.26 years
Strontium-90	28.1 years
Iodine-131	8.05 days
Cesium-137	30.17 years
Radium-226	1,600 years
Uranium-235	710,000,000 years
Uranium-238	4,500,000,000 years
Fermium-244	0.0033 second
Plutonium-239	24,000 years

Some isotopes are calculated to take billions of years for half of the nuclei to decay—they release radiation extremely slowly—whereas others take only milliseconds.

The half-life of a radioactive isotope is an intensive property (see Section 3.2 for information on intensive properties). It doesn't matter how many atoms you begin with; it will take the same amount of time for half of them to undergo decay. For example, the half-life of iodine-131 is a little more than 8 days. This means that if you begin with 100 iodine-131 atoms, it would take 8 days for there to only be 50 left undecayed. Likewise, once those 50 atoms remain, it would take another 8 days for them to be reduced to half again (for there to be 25 undecayed atoms remaining).

There is no way to predict *which* radioactive nuclei will decay at any given moment—each has an equal chance of decaying at any moment. The half-life equation allows us to determine how many atoms are left after a number of half-life time periods given the original number of atoms.

$$y = a(1/2)^b$$

where a is the original number of atoms, b is the number of half-lives elapsed, and y is the number of atoms left after b half-lives.

The first test of a nuclear weapon in New Mexico, in 1945, resulted in these rocks called trinitite. The desert floor melted, creating a glass made of silica and feldspar.

Folding 1,000 paper cranes, they say, allows a true wish. Here, where the atom bomb fell in Nagasaki, Japan, there are many folded cranes and many wishes for peace. The bomb, used by the United States in 1945 to end the war with Japan, killed or injured 149,000 people.

PRACTICE 12.1

Nuclear Reactions

1. Explain how the three types of radiation are different.

2. How are the three types of radiation similar?

3. What is meant by "half-life"?

4. Which poses a bigger storage problem: an element with a short half-life or one with a long half-life? Why?

5. Which poses the greater danger to someone exposed for only a brief amount of time: an element with a short half-life or an element with a long half-life? Why?

6. Complete the following nuclear reactions.

   a. $^{3}_{1}\text{H} \rightarrow$ _____ $+ ^{3}_{2}\text{He}$

   b. $^{210}_{84}\text{Po} \rightarrow ^{206}_{82}\text{Pb} +$ _____

   c. _____ $\rightarrow ^{234}_{90}\text{Th} + ^{4}_{2}\text{He}$

   d. $^{234}_{90}\text{Th} \rightarrow$ _____ $+ ^{0}_{-1}\text{e}$

7. Draw the reaction in question #6a. Be sure to show all the protons, neutrons, and electrons in each atom and particle in the reaction, and make a key to your drawing to show the difference between each of the subatomic particles.

Go Online
Check your understanding
http://webcom4.grtxle.com/
khk12Chemistry

Nuclear Radiation: Harmful or Helpful?

Effects of radiation on the body

Radiation causes cancer   Nuclear radiation of all types can cause cancer in the body. Cancer results when DNA or the enzymes that carry out the DNA "orders" are damaged in such a way that they can no longer perform their duties correctly. This can result in cells that continue to multiply and grow without regulation—tumors. The level of damage to tissue is determined by the type of radiation, the amount of radiation absorbed, and the type of tissue that is exposed. In order to understand the effects of each type of radiation, the ability of the three types of radiation to penetrate matter must be understood.

Alpha particles are very heavy and strongly charged. When they hit any type of matter, they take on electrons from the matter and convert to helium particles, which then move off into the atmosphere. This means that alpha particles have very little ability to penetrate matter.

However, when alpha particles run into matter, they do so with enough energy that atoms could be bumped out of molecules. If this happens to DNA or the enzymes the DNA regulates, it could lead to cancer. Most often, the dead skin cells on the outer layer of our bodies would absorb the impact of this radiation, but if radiation is inhaled or ingested, it will interact with active cells in our body.

The fast-moving, small beta particles can penetrate about 1 cm into humans, which means they are more dangerous than alpha particles.

Gamma radiation can pass through not only human bodies but also the buildings that we live and work in. Gamma radiation can ionize molecules that it comes in contact with, destroying their ability to function correctly in our body. Lead or thick concrete can protect people from this type of radiation.

People working around radioactive material must be closely monitored to ensure that they are not being exposed to dangerously high levels. These workers wear badges made out of film that can be periodically checked to determine the level of exposure for that worker.

Radioactive elements replace other elements in the body   Another concern surrounding exposure to radioactive material is isotopes that can replace other elements used in the body, causing the molecules that use them to be unable to operate correctly.

A person's DNA can be damaged by radiation, and this damage can lead to mutations (and perhaps tumors). Astronauts can be exposed to radiation from solar flares, and their risk of cancer is higher than that of the average person.

A mushroom cloud formed by a nuclear explosion is a large mass of hot, low-density gasses near the base that surge upward, creating turbulence, forcing a column or stem in the center, and after spreading out at higher altitudes it becomes fallout.

Plutonium, which is often thought of as the most dangerous radioactive material, emits alpha radiation. As discussed above, plutonium can be handled without much shielding, because the alpha particles are not able to penetrate the skin. However, it is easily oxidized to a +4 charge (see Section 10.1 for information on oxidation). The Pu^{+4} ion has chemical properties very similar to those of the Fe^{+3} ion. This is cause for concern because the plutonium ion can replace the iron ion in the body, which could then cause radiation sickness or cancer.

Strontium-90, which is released in nuclear bomb fallout, settles to the ground as a very fine dust. It is chemically similar to calcium and can work its way through the environment and become incorporated into our bones in place of calcium. Once in our bones, it can emit radiation from inside our bodies.

Radiation in medicine   The ways in which radiation can cause cancer were discussed above. However, radiation is also used as a treatment for those with cancer. Radiation therapy is narrowly focused to destroy the cancerous cells (with isotopes such as cobalt-60). However, the radiation can also destroy any healthy cells that it encounters. Therefore, patients undergoing radiation therapy often become very ill and prone to infection as healthy cells in their body are destroyed along with the tumor cells. New research is producing better techniques for targeting the cancerous cells while minimizing damage to healthy cells. For example, boron neutron capture uses boron-10 isotopes, which are not radioactive. The boron-10

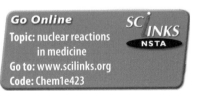

Go Online

Topic: nuclear reactions in medicine
Go to: www.scilinks.org
Code: Chem1e423

SCINKS
NSTA

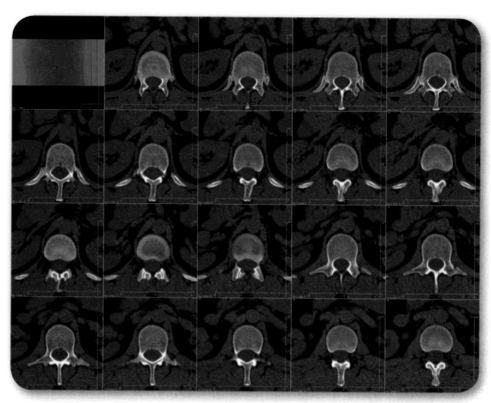

PET (positron-emission tomography) can scan a person's backbone in successive detail.

isotopes are absorbed into the tumor; the patient is then bombarded with neutrons for a very short period of time. This bombardment induces the boron-10 isotopes in the tumor to emit alpha particles, which destroy the tumor cells without penetrating through to healthy tissue.

Radiation is also used for imaging techniques. Various isotopes (such as technetium-99 and fluorine-18) can be injected into the body and absorbed by the specific part of the body the doctor needs to look at. Doctors use isotopes that are active, have short half-lives (meaning they will emit radiation for a shorter period of time), and emit gamma radiation. Alpha and beta particles would not make it out of the body before interacting with the matter—and the radiation *must* make it out of the body so that it can be detected by the imaging machine—so gamma radiating isotopes are used. PET (positron-emission tomography) scans are one such way to detect the radiation and provide an image of the tissue into which the isotopes were absorbed.

Other isotopes are used to monitor how the body metabolizes or moves fluids throughout itself. Iodine-131 is used to monitor how fast the thyroid takes up iodine. Sodium-24 is used to observe blood flow. Strontium-87 is used to determine bone growth.

Each of these medical uses for radiation isn't without its risk to healthy tissue in the body, but precautions are taken to minimize those risks and to ensure that the benefit of the procedure outweighs the risks.

Nuclear dating

Carbon-14 isotopes, which are made in the atmosphere when nitrogen is bombarded with neutrons from cosmic rays, work their way into living organisms by way of carbon dioxide from respiration of plants. Animals then ingest those plants, and the carbon-14 along with them. The carbon-14 isotopes leave living things via respiration, excretion, and by decaying to carbon-12 isotopes. All living things have a constant ratio of carbon-12 to carbon-14 isotopes (there are many, many more carbon-12 isotopes, compared to carbon-14). After an organism dies, it no longer removes the carbon-14 through respiration and excretion. The only way it can leave the organism is by radioactive decay, with a steady half-life. Therefore, by determining the ratio of carbon-12 to carbon-14 isotopes in dead organic material, we can determine how long the carbon-14 has been decaying. Therefore, we can determine how long ago a living organism died, using a method called carbon dating.

For items believed to be extremely old, an isotope with a longer half-life is needed to date the material. Therefore, uranium-238 (with a half-life of 4,500,000,000 years) and potassium-40 (with a half-life of 1,260,000,000 years) are used. For fairly recent material, hydrogen-3, with a half-life of 12.3 years, is used.

Carbon-14 isotopes can tell that this Tyrannosaurus Rex lived 68 to 65 million years ago.

Energy—fission versus fusion

Nuclear reactions are accompanied with large releases of energy. This fact has led to interest in harnessing that energy release to generate power. Nuclear power also has the added benefit of not adding carbon dioxide (a greenhouse gas) to the atmosphere. Two separate processes have been investigated: fission and fusion.

Fission is the breaking of a nucleus into multiple, smaller nuclei. Fission can occur on its own, in spontaneous nuclear fission, or by bombarding a heavy nucleus with neutrons, as in induced nuclear fission. Fission reactions are used to produce electricity in nuclear power plants. The isotopes used in these power plants include uranium-235, uranium-233, and plutonium-239. Fission, however, generates nuclear waste, which must then be isolated for long periods of time until it is no longer dangerous. This presents a serious societal problem: where to put all the nuclear waste. Have you heard the acronym "NIMBY"? It stands for "Not in my backyard." No one wants nuclear waste in their backyard—or even traveling past their backyard, for that matter.

Fusion is the process of joining two smaller nuclei into one larger one. Two hydrogen atoms can be fused into one helium atom. Fusion does not generate harmful nuclear waste, and the fuel can even be taken from seawater. However, fusion is difficult to achieve in real life. The nuclei must be hurled together at such high energies to cause fusion that it's difficult to achieve. However, human-made fusion on a large scale is still in its theoretical stage, and research is beginning to show promise.

Here is your chance to use the chemistry you know to evaluate current methods and future plans for handling nuclear waste.

Research and write about nuclear waste

Research information on how nuclear waste from nuclear power plants is currently being handled and stored. What precautions are taken to prevent leakage and contamination? Has leakage or contamination already occurred anywhere? What plans do governments have to change the way these materials are handled? What groups support these plans, and what groups oppose them? What are the arguments used by the proponents and opponents? What do you think is the best possible choice or decision?

Answer these questions in a three- to four-page paper, double spaced, with citations.

Radioactive atoms spontaneously change the composition of their nucleus, releasing alpha, beta, or gamma radiation. Alpha particles are two protons and two neutrons, beta particles are rapidly moving electrons, and gamma radiation is electromagnetic radiation similar to light. Nuclear chemical equations must be balanced by atomic numbers and mass numbers. Each radioactive isotope has a half-life, which is the time it takes for half of the atoms in the sample to radioactively decay. Half-lives vary from less than a second to billions of years.

Radiation can cause cancer or be used to destroy cancer in the body. Radiation can also be used for medical imaging, for dating materials, and as an energy source. Fission is the breaking up of a nucleus, which produces useful energy but also nuclear waste that must be contained. Fusion is the joining of two smaller nuclei into one large nucleus, which would—theoretically—result in a large release of energy. Fusion does not result in nuclear waste, but it takes larger amounts of energy input to achieve.

The desolate Soviet town of Chernobyl decayed after its evacuation due to the 1986 nuclear power plant disaster. Thousands of people relocated to escape radiation contamination. People are still not allowed in a certain zone. In addition to deaths in the explosion and due to radiation exposure while trying to contain the explosion, several thousand children and teens developed thyroid cancer, likely from the release of radioactive iodine. Thyroid cancer can be treated if caught early and monitored over one's life.

1. What is nuclear radiation?

2. How are alpha, beta, and gamma radiation similar?

3. How are the three types of radiation different?

4. Explain the difference between nuclear fission and fusion.

5. How are nuclear fission and fusion similar?

6. Iodine-131 has a half-life of 8.05 days. You begin with a sample of 120 atoms. How long will it take until only 15 atoms remain?

7. How many iodine-131 atoms would be left after 48.3 days (6 half-lives) if you began with 500?

8. Complete the following nuclear equations.

a. $^{238}_{92}U \rightarrow \underline{\quad} + ^{234}_{90}Th$

b. $^{131}_{53}I \rightarrow ^{0}_{-1}e + \underline{\quad}$

c. $\underline{\quad} \rightarrow ^{234}_{91}Pa + ^{0}_{-1}e$

d. $^{237}_{93}Np \rightarrow \underline{\quad} + ^{4}_{2}He$

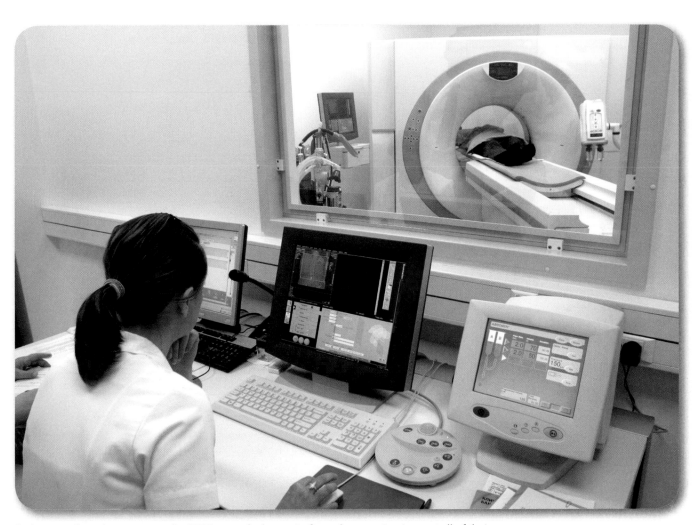

Patients undergoing tomography (PET) scans feel no pain from the examination, yet all of their internal structures can be visualized with amazing detail. Large X-ray images make up the scan, allowing doctors to diagnose internal problems, especially in the lungs and arteries.

Units and Measurement

Quantities Commonly Measured in Chemistry

Quantity	SI Unit	What is used to measure?
Mass—the amount of matter in a sample	Kilograms (kg)	Balance (not a "scale")
Volume—the amount of space an object takes up	Milliliter (mL)	Graduated cylinder
Temperature—related to the speed with which molecules move	Celsius (°C) or Kelvin (K)	Thermometer
Length	Meters (m)	Ruler, meter stick
Time	Seconds (s or sec)	Stopwatch, clock
Energy	Joule (J)	Measured indirectly

Unit Abbreviations

°C	degree Celsius (temperature)
cal	calorie (energy)
J	joule (energy)
K	kelvin (temperature, thermo-dynamic)
mm Hg	millimeters of mercury (pressure)
M	molarity (concentration)
Pa	pascal (pressure)
psi	pounds per square inch (pressure)
V	volt (electric potential difference)

Common Equivalents

1 ft	12 in
1 in	2.54 cm
1 min	60 s
1 hr	3600 s
1 quart	0.946 L
2 pints	1 quart
1 pound	454 g

Metric Prefixes

Prefix	Symbol	Equivalent	(Example)
giga-	G	1 giga = 1,000,000,000 base units	(1 G = 1,000,000,000 g)
mega-	M	1 mega = 1,000,000 base units	(1 M = 1,000,000 g)
kilo-	k	1 kilo = 1000 base units	(1 kg = (1000 g)
hecto-	h	1 hecto = 100 base units	(1 h = 100 g)
deka-	da	1 deka = 10 base units	(1 dag = 10 g)
deci-	d	1 deci = 0.1 base units	(1 dg = 0.1 g)
centi-	c	1 cent = 0.01 base units	(1 cg = 0.01 g)
milli-	m	1 milli = 0.001 base units	(1 mg = 0.001 g)
micro-	μ	1 micro = $1 \cdot 10^{-6}$ base units	(1 μg = $1 \cdot 10^{-6}$ g)
nano-	n	1 nano = $1 \cdot 10^{-9}$ base units	1 ng = ($1 \cdot 10^{-9}$ g)
pico-	p	1 pico = $1 \cdot 10^{-12}$ base units	(1 p = $1 \cdot 10^{-12}$ g)

Symbols	
Symbol	**Stands for**
α	helium nucleus (also $^4_2$He) emission from radioactive materials
β	electron (also $^0_{-1}e$) emission from radioactive materials
γ	high-energy photo emission from radioactive materials
Δ	change in a given quantity (e.g., ΔH for change in enthalpy)
c	speed of light in vacuum
C_p	specific heat capacity (at constant pressure)
D	density
E_a	activation energy
E^0	standard electrode potential
E^0_{cell}	standard potential of an electrochemical cell
H	enthalpy
ΔH^0	standard enthalpy of reaction
ΔH^0_f	standard molar enthalpy of formation
K_{eq}	equilibrium constantionization constant
K_{sp}	solubility-product constant disassociation constant enthalpy
m	mass
MM	molar mass
N_A	Avogadro's number
n	number of moles
P	pressure
pH	measure of acidity ($-\log[H_3O^+]$)
R	ideal gas law constant
T	temperature
V	volume
State symbols	
(aq)	substance is dissolved in water
(s)	substance in the solid state
(l)	substance in the liquid state
(g)	substance in the gaseous state

Common Polyatomic Ions

Acetate, CH_3COO^{-1} or $C_2H_3O_2^{-1}$	Hydroxide, OH^{-1}
Ammonium, NH_4^{+1}	Hypochlorite, ClO^{-1}
Bromate, BrO_3^{-1}	Iodate, IO_3^{-1}
Bromite, BrO_2^{-1}	Iodite, IO_2^{-1}
Carbonate, CO_3^{-2}	Nitrate, NO_3^{-1}
Chlorate, ClO_3^{-1}	Nitrite, NO_2^{-1}
Chlorite, ClO_2^{-1}	Oxalate, $C_2O_4^{-2}$
Chromate, CrO_4^{-2}	Perchlorate, ClO_4^{-1}
Cyanide, CN^{-1}	Permanganate, MnO_4^{-1}
Dichromate, $Cr_2O_7^{-2}$	Peroxide, O_2^{-2}
Dihydrogen phosphate, $H_2PO_4^{-1}$	Phosphate, PO_4^{-3}
Hydrogen carbonate or bicarbonate, HCO_3^{-1}	Phosphite, PO_3^{-3}
Hydrogen phosphate or biphosphate, HPO_4^{-2}	Silicate, SiO_3^{-1}
Hydrogen sulfate or bisulfate, HSO_4^{-1}	Sulfate, SO_4^{-2}
Hydronium, H_3O^+	Sulfite, SO_3^{-2}

Common Multivalent Metals and Their Charges

Type of metal		
Chromium	Cr^{2+}	Cr^{+3}
Cobalt	Co^{+2}	Co^{+3}
Copper	Cu^{+1}	Cu^{+2}
Iron	Fe^{+2}	Fe^{+3}
Lead	Pb^{+2}	Pb^{+4}
Manganese	Mn^{+2}	Mn^{+3}
Mercury	Hg_2^{+2}	Hg^{+2}
Tin	Sn^{+2}	Sn^{+4}

Diatomic Elements and Formulas**

Hydrogen	H_2
Oxygen	O_2
Fluorine	F_2
Bromine	Br_2
Iodine	I_2
Nitrogen	N_2
Chlorine	Cl_2

Their chemical symbols can be placed in a word to remember: **HOFBrINCl, pronounced "**Hoffbrinkle**."

Prefixes Used in Molecular Compounds

1. mono-
2. di-
3. tri-
4. tetra-
5. penta-
6. hexa-
7. hepta-
8. octa-
9. nona-
10. deca-

Organic Nomenclature Prefixes

Number of atoms	Prefix for carbon atoms in an organic molecule
1	Meth-
2	Eth-
3	Prop-
4	But-
5	Pent-
6	Hex-
7	Hept-
8	Oct-
9	Non-
10	Dec-

Solubility Rules

These anions	Form soluble compounds with these cations	Form insoluble compounds with these cations
NO_3^- nitrate	Most cations	No common cations
CH_3COO^- acetate	Most cations	Ag^+
Cl^- chloride	Most cations	$Ag^+, Pb^{2+}, Hg_2^{2+}, Tl^{+1}$
Br^- bromide	Most cations	$Ag^+, Pb^{2+}, Hg_2^{2+}, Tl^{+1}$
I^- iodide	Most cations	$Ag^+, Pb^{2+}, Hg_2^{2+}, Tl^{+1}$
SO_4^{2-} sulfate	Most cations	$Ba^{2+}, Sr^{2+}, Pb^{2+}, Ag^+, Ca^{2+}$
CrO_4^{2-} chromate	Most cations	$Ba^{2+}, Sr^{2+}, Pb^{2+}, Ag^+$
S^{2-} sulfide	NH_4^+, cations of column 1, cations of column 2	Most other cations
OH^- hydroxide	NH_4^+, cations of column 1, and Ba^{2+} and Sr^{2+}	Most other cations
CO_3^{2-} carbonate	NH_4^+, cations of column 1 except Li^+	Most other cations
PO_4^{3-} phosphate	NH_4^+, cations of column 1 except Li^+	Most other cations

Solubility Product Constants (25°C)

Salt	K_{sp}
Ag_2CO_3	8.4×10^{-12}
$AgCl$	1.8×10^{-10}
Ag_2CrO_4	1.1×10^{-12}
Ag_2S	1.1×10^{-49}
$AgBr$	5.4×10^{-13}
AgI	8.5×10^{-17}
$AlPO_4$	9.8×10^{-21}
$BaSO_4$	1.1×10^{-10}
$CaCO_3$	5.0×10^{-9}
$Ca(OH)_2$	4.7×10^{-7}
$Ca_3(PO_4)_2$	2.1×10^{-33}
$CaSO_4$	7.1×10^{-5}
CuS	1.3×10^{-36}
$FeCO_3$	3.1×10^{-11}

Solubility Product Constants (25°C) (cont'd.)

Salt	K_{sp}
$Fe(OH)_2$	4.9×10^{-17}
$Fe(OH)_3$	2.6×10^{-39}
FeS	1.6×10^{-19}
$MgCO_3$	6.8×10^{-6}
$Mg(OH)_2$	5.6×10^{-12}
$Mg_3(PO_4)_2$	9.9×10^{-25}
$MnCO_3$	2.2×10^{-11}
$Pb(OH)_2$	1.4×10^{-20}
PbS	9.0×10^{-29}
$PbSO_4$	1.8×10^{-8}
$SrSO_4$	3.4×10^{-7}
$ZnCO_3$	1.2×10^{-10}
ZnS	2.9×10^{-25}

Compound Solubility

In grams of solute that can be dissolved at these temperatures in 100 g of water.

Formula	0°C	20°C	60°C	100°C
$Al_2(SO_4)_3$	31.2	36.4	59.2	89.0
NH_4Cl	29.4	37.2	55.3	77.3
NH_4NO_3	118.0	192.0	421.0	871.0
$(NH_4)_2SO_4$	70.6	75.4	88.0	103.0
$BaCl_2 \cdot 2H_2O$	31.2	35.8	46.2	59.4
$Ba(OH)_2$	1.67	3.89	20.94	$101.40^{80°}$
$Ba(NO_3)_2$	4.95	9.02	20.4	34.4
$Ca(HCO_3)_2$	16.15	16.60	17.50	18.40
$Ca(OH)_2$	0.189	0.173	0.121	0.076
$CuCl_2$	68.6	73.0	96.5	120.0
$CuSO_4 \cdot 5H_2O$	23.1	32.0	61.8	114.0
$PbCl_2$	0.67	1.00	1.94	3.20
$Pb(NO_3)_2$	37.5	54.3	91.6	133.0
$LiCl$	69.2	83.5	98.4	128.0
Li_2SO_4	36.1	34.8	32.6	$30.9^{90°}$
$MgSO_4$	22.0	33.7	54.6	68.3
$HgCl_2$	3.63	6.57	16.3	61.3
KBr	53.6	65.3	85.5	104.0
$KClO_3$	3.3	7.3	23.8	56.3
KCl	28.0	34.2	45.8	56.3
K_2CrO_4	56.3	63.7	70.1	$74.5^{90°}$
KI	128.0	144.0	176.0	206.0
KNO_3	13.9	31.6	106.0	245.0
K_2SO_4	7.4	11.1	18.2	24.1
$AgC_2H_3O_2$	0.73	1.05	1.93	$2.59^{80°}$
$AgNO_3$	122.0	216.0	440.0	733.0
$NaC_2H_3O_2$	36.2	46.4	139.0	170.0
$NaClO_3$	79.6	95.9	137.0	204.0
$NaCl$	35.7	35.9	37.1	39.2
$NaNO_3$	73.0	87.6	122.0	180.0
$C_{12}H_{22}O_{11}$	179.2	203.9	287.3	487.2

Useful Constants

Equilibrium	
Atomic mass unit (amu)	$1.6605402 \times 10^{-27}$ kg
Avogadro's number (N_A)	6.022137×10^{23}/mol
Electron rest mass (m_e)	$9.1093897 \times 10^{-31}$ kg 5.4858×10^{-4} amu
Gas law constant, R, with atm pressure unit	$0.0821 \dfrac{L \times atm}{mole \times K}$
Gas law constant, R, with kPa pressure units	$8.31 \dfrac{L \times kPa}{mole \times K}$
Enthalpy of fusion of water (H_{fus})	80.87 cal/g
Enthalpy of vaporization of water (H_{vap})	547.2 cal/g
Volume of one mole of a gase at STP	22.41410 L/mol
Mass of a neutron	$1.6749286 \times 10^{-27}$ kg 1.008665 amu
Normal boiling point of water (T_b)	373.15 K = 100.0°C
Normal freezing point of water (T_f)	273.15 K = 0.00°C
Planck's constant (h)	6.626076×10^{-34} $J \times s$
Mass of a proton	$1.6726231 \times 10^{-27}$ kg 1.007276 amu
Specific heat capacity of *liquid water* (C_p)	1.00 cal/g°C
Specific heat capacity of *ice* (C_p)	0.51 cal/g°C
Specific heat capacity of *steam* (C_p)	0.48 cal/g°C
Speed of light in a vacuum (c)	$2.997924\ 58 \times 10^8$ m/s
Temperature of triple point of water	273.16 K = 0.01°C

Electrochemistry

Activity Series

Li	Most reactive
K	
Ba	
Sr	
Ca	
Na	
Mg	
Al	
Mn	
Zn	
Cr	
Fe	
Cd	
Co	
Ni	
Sn	
Pb	
H	
Cu	
Hg	
Ag	
Pt	Least reactive
Au	

Reduction

Reduction half-reaction	Standard reduction potential (volts)
$F_2\,(g) + 2\,e^{-1} \rightarrow 2\,F^{-1}$	2.87
$Co^{+3} + e^{-1} \rightarrow Co^{+2}$	1.82
$Au^{+3} + 3\,e^{-1} \rightarrow Au\,(s)$	1.50
$Cl_2\,(g) + 2\,e^{-} \rightarrow 2\,Cl^{-1}$	1.36
$O_2\,(g) + 4\,H^{+} \rightarrow 2\,H_2O\,(l)$	1.23
$Br_2\,(l) + 2\,e^{-1} \rightarrow 2\,Br^{-1}$	1.07
$2\,Hg^{+2} + 2\,e^{-1} \rightarrow Hg_2^{+2}$	0.92
$Hg^{+2} + 2\,e^{-1} \rightarrow Hg\,(l)$	0.85
$Ag^{+1} + e^{-1} \rightarrow Ag\,(s)$	0.80
$Hg_2^{+2} + 2\,e^{-1} \rightarrow 2\,Hg\,(l)$	0.79
$Fe^{+3} + e^{-1} \rightarrow Fe^{+2}$	0.77
$I_2\,(s) + 2\,e^{-1} \rightarrow 2\,I^{-1}$	0.53
$Cu^{+} + e^{-1} \rightarrow Cu\,(s)$	0.52
$Cu^{+2} + 2\,e^{-1} \rightarrow Cu\,(s)$	0.34
$Cu^{+2} + e^{-1} \rightarrow Cu^{+1}$	0.15
$Sn^{+4} + 2\,e^{-1} \rightarrow Sn^{+2}$	0.15
$S\,(s) + 2\,H^{+} + 2\,e^{-1} \rightarrow H_2S\,(g)$	0.14
$2\,H^{+} + 2\,e^{-1} \rightarrow H_2\,(g)$	0.00
$Pb^{+2} + 2\,e^{-1} \rightarrow Pb\,(s)$	−0.13
$Sn^{+2} + 2\,e^{-1} \rightarrow Sn(s)$	−0.14

Reduction

Reduction half-reaction	Standard reduction potential (volts)
$Ni^{+2} + 2\,e^{-1} \rightarrow Ni\,(s)$	−0.25
$Co^{+2} + 2\,e^{-1} \rightarrow Co\,(s)$	−0.28
$Tl^{+1} + e^{-1} \rightarrow Tl\,(s)$	−0.34
$Cd^{+2} + 2\,e^{-1} \rightarrow Cd\,(s)$	−0.40
$Cr^{+3} + e^{-1} \rightarrow Cr^{+2}$	−0.41
$Fe^{+2} + 2\,e^{-1} \rightarrow Fe\,(s)$	−0.44
$Cr^{+3} + 3\,e^{-1} \rightarrow Cr\,(s)$	−0.74
$Zn^{+2} + 2\,e^{-1} \rightarrow Zn\,(s)$	−0.76
$Mn^{+2} + 2\,e^{-1} \rightarrow Mn\,(s)$	−1.18
$Al^{+3} + 3\,e^{-1} \rightarrow Al\,(s)$	−1.66
$Be^{+2} + 2\,e^{-1} \rightarrow Be\,(s)$	−1.70
$Mg^{+2} + 2\,e^{-1} \rightarrow Mg\,(s)$	−2.37
$Na^{+1} + e^{-1} \rightarrow Na\,(s)$	−2.71
$Ca^{+2} + 2\,e^{-1} \rightarrow Ca\,(s)$	−2.87
$Sr^{+2} + 2\,e^{-1} \rightarrow Sr\,(s)$	−2.89
$Ba^{+2} + 2\,e^{-1} \rightarrow Ba\,(s)$	−2.90
$Rb^{+1} + e^{-1} \rightarrow Rb\,(s)$	−2.92
$K^{+1} + e^{-1} \rightarrow K\,(s)$	−2.92
$Cs^{+1} + e^{-1} \rightarrow Cs\,(s)$	−2.92
$Li^{+1} + e^{-1} \rightarrow Li\,(s)$	−3.05

Enthalpies of Formation (H_f) kJ/mole

Enthalpies of Formation (H_f) kJ/mole

Aluminum	
Al(s)	0
AlCl$_3$(s)	−704.2
Al$_2$O$_3$(s)	−1675.7

Barium	
BaCl$_2$(s)	−858.6
BaO(s)	−553.5
BaSO$_4$(s)	−1473.2

Beryllium	
Be(s)	0
Be(OH)$_2$	−902.5

Bromine	
Br(g)	111.9
Br$_2$(l)	0
Br$_2$(g)	−30.9
BrF$_3$(g)	−255.6

Calcium	
Ca(s)	0
Ca(g)	178.2
Ca^{+2}(g)	1925.9
CaC$_2$(s)	−59.8
CaCO$_3$(s; calcite)	−1206.9
CaCl$_2$(s)	−795.8
CaF$_2$(s)	−1219.6
CaH$_2$(s)	−186.2
CaO(s)	−635.1
CaS(s)	−482.4
Ca(OH)$_2$(s)	−986.1
Ca(OH)$_2$(aq)	−1002.8
CaSO$_4$(s)	−1434.1

Carbon	
C(s; graphite)	0
C(s; diamond)	1.9
C(g)	716.7
CCl$_4$(l)	−135.4
CCl$_4$(g)	−102.9
CHCl$_3$(l)	−134.5
CHCl$_3$(g)	−103.1
HgCl$_2$(s)	−224.3
HgO(s)	−90.8
CH$_4$(g; methane)	−74.81
C$_2$H$_2$(g; ethyne)	226.7
C$_2$H$_4$(g; ethene)	52.3
C$_2$H$_6$(g; ethane)	−84.7
C$_3$H$_8$(g; propane)	−103.8
C$_6$H$_6$(l; benzene)	49.0
CH$_3$OH(l; methanol)	−238.7
CH$_3$OH(g; methanol)	−200.7
C$_2$H$_5$OH(l; ethanol)	−277.7
C$_2$H$_5$OH(g; ethanol)	−235.1
CO(g)	−110.5
CO$_2$(g)	−393.5
CS$_2$(g)	117.36
COCl$_2$(g)	−218.8

Cesium	
Cs(s)	0
Cs^{+1}(g)	458.0
CsCl(s)	−443.0

Chlorine	
Cl(g)	121.7
Cl^{-1}(g)	−233.1
Cl$_2$(g)	0

Chromium	
Cr(s)	0
Cr$_2$O$_3$(s)	−1139.7
CrCl$_2$(s)	−556.5

Copper	
Cu(s)	0
CuO(s)	−157.3
CuCl$_2$(s)	−220.1

Fluorine	
F$_2$(g)	0
F(g)	79
F^{-1}(g)	−255.4
F^{-1}(aq)	−332.6

Hydrogen	
H$_2$(g)	0
H(g)	218
H^{+1}(g)	1536.2
H$_2$O(l)	−285.8
H$_2$O(g)	−241.8
H$_2$O$_2$(l)	−187.8

Iodine	
I$_2$(s)	0
I$_2$(g)	62.4
I(g)	106.8
I^{-1}(g)	−197.0
ICl(g)	17.78

Iron	
Fe(s)	0
FeO(s)	−272
Fe$_2$O$_3$ (s; hematite)	−824.2
Fe$_3$O$_4$(s; magnetite)	−1118.4
FeCl$_2$(s)	−341.8
FeCl$_3$(s)	−399.5
FeS$_2$(s; pyrite)	−178.2
Fe(CO)$_5$(l)	−774

Enthalpies of Formation (H_f) kJ/mole

Lead	
Pb(s)	0
$PbCl_2$(s)	−359.4
PbO(s)	−217.3
PbS(s)	−100.4

Lithium	
Li(s)	0
Li^{+1}(g)	685.8
LiOH(s)	−484.9
LiOH(aq)	−508.5
LiCl(s)	−408.7

Magnesium	
Mg(s)	0
$MgCl_2$(s)	−641.3
MgO(s)	−601.7
$Mg(OH)_2$(s)	−924.5
MgS(s)	−346

Mercury	
Hg(l)	0
HgCl2(s)	−224.3
HgO(s)	−90.8
HgS(s)	−58.2

Nickel	
Ni(s)	0
NiO(s)	−239.7
NiCl(s)	−305.3

Nitrogen	
N_2(g)	0
N(g)	472.7
NH_3(g)	−46.11
N_2H_4(l)	50.6
NH_4Cl(s)	−314.4
NH_4Cl(aq)	−299.7
NH_4NO_3(s)	−365.6
NH_4NO_3(aq)	−339.9
NO(g)	90.3
NO_2(g)	33.2
N_2O(g)	82.1
N_2O_4(g)	9.16
NOCl(g)	51.7

Oxygen	
O_2(g)	0
O(g)	249.17
O_3(g)	142.7

Phosphorus	
P(g)	314.6
PH_3(g)	5.4
PCl_3(g)	−287.0
P_4O_{10}(s)	−2984.0

Potassium	
K(s)	0
KCl(s)	−436.7
$KClO_3$(s)	−397.7
KI(s)	−327.9
KOH(s)	−424.8
KOH(aq)	−482.4

Silicon	
Si(s)	0
$SiBr_4$(l)	−457.3
SiC(s)	−65.3
$SiCl_4$(g)	−657
SiH_4(g)	34.3
SiF_4(g)	−1614.9
SiO_2(s; quartz)	−910.9

Silver	
Ag(s)	0
Ag_2O(s)	−31.1
AgCl(s)	−127.1
$AgNO_3$(s)	−124.4

Sodium	
Na(s)	0
Na(g)	107.3
Na^{+1}(g)	609.4
NaBr(s)	−361.1
NaCl(s)	−411.2
NaCl(g)	−176.65
NaCl(aq)	−407.3
NaOH(s)	−425.6
NaOH(aq)	−470.1
Na_2CO_3(s)	−1130.7
Na_2SO_4(aq)	−1387.1

Sulfur	
S(s; rhombic)	0
S(g)	278.8
S_2Cl_2(g)	−18.4
SF_6(g)	1209
SO_2(g)	−296.8
SO_3(g)	−395.7
$SOCl_2$(g)	−212.5

Tin	
Sn(s; white)	0
Sn(s; gray)	−2.09
$SnCl_4$(l)	−511.3
$SnCl_4$(g)	−471.5
SnO_2(g)	−580.7

Titanium	
Ti(s)	0
$TiCFl_4$(l)	−804.2
$TiCl_4$(g)	−763.2
TiO_2	−939.7

Zinc	
Zn(s)	0
$ZnCl_2$(s)	−415.1
ZnO(s)	−348.3
ZnS(s; sphalerite)	−205.98

Acids	
HBr(g)	−36.4
HCl(g)	−92.3
HCl(aq)	−167.2
HF(g)	−271.1
HF(aq)	−332.6
HNO_3(l)	−174.1
HNO_3(g)	−135.1
HNO_3(aq)	−207.0
H_3PO_4(s)	−1279.0
H_2S(g)	−20.6
H_2SO_4(l)	−814.0
H_2SO_4(aq)	−909.3

The Elements			
Name	Symbol	Atomic Number	Atomic Mass
Actinium	Ac	89	(227)
Aluminum	Al	13	26.08
Americium	Am	95	(243)
Antimony	Sb	51	121.8
Argon	Ar	18	39.95
Arsenic	As	33	74.92
Astatine	At	85	(210)
Barium	Ba	56	137.3
Berkelium	Bk	97	(247)
Beryllium	Be	4	9.01
Bismuth	Bi	83	209.0
Boron	B	5	10.81
Bromine	Br	35	79.90
Cadmium	Cd	48	112.4
Calcium	Ca	20	40.08
Californium	Cf	98	(251)
Carbon	C	6	12.01
Cerium	Ce	58	140.1
Cesium	Cs	55	132.9
Chlorine	Cl	17	35.45
Chromium	Cr	24	52.00
Cobalt	Co	27	58.93
Copper	Cu	29	63.55
Curium	Cm	96	(247)
Dysprosium	Dy	66	162.5
Einsteinium	Es	99	(252)
Erbium	Er	68	167.3
Europium	Eu	63	152.0
Fermium	Fm	100	(257)
Fluorine	F	9	19.00
Francium	Fr	87	(223)
Gadolinium	Gd	64	157.3
Gallium	Ga	31	69.72
Germanium	Ge	32	72.59

The Elements (*cont'd.*)			
Name	**Symbol**	**Atomic Number**	**Atomic Mass**
Gold	Au	79	197.0
Hafnium	Hf	72	178.5
Helium	He	2	4.00
Holmium	Ho	67	164.9
Hydrogen	H	1	1.01
Indium	In	49	114.8
Iodine	I	53	126.9
Iridium	Ir	77	192.2
Iron	Fe	26	55.85
Krypton	Kr	36	83.80
Lanthanum	La	57	138.9
Lawrencium	Lr	103	(260)
Lead	Pb	82	207.2
Lithium	Li	3	6.94
Lutetium	Lu	71	175.0
Magnesium	Mg	12	24.31
Manganese	Mn	25	54.94
Mendelevium	Md	101	(258)
Mercury	Hg	80	200.6
Molybdenum	Mo	42	95.94
Neodymium	Nd	60	144.2
Neon	Ne	10	20.18
Neptunium	Np	93	(237)
Nickel	Ni	28	58.70
Niobium	Nb	41	92.91
Nitrogen	N	7	14.01
Nobelium	No	102	(259)
Osmium	Os	76	190.2
Oxygen	O	8	16.00
Palladium	Pd	46	106.4
Phosphorus	P	15	30.97
Platinum	Pt	78	195.1
Plutonium	Pu	94	(244)
Polonium	Po	84	(209)
Potassium	K	19	39.10

(continues)

The Elements (*cont'd.*)			
Name	**Symbol**	**Atomic Number**	**Atomic Mass**
Praseodymium	Pr	59	140.9
Promethium	Pm	61	(145)
Protactinium	Pa	91	(231)
Radium	Ra	88	226.0
Radon	Rn	86	(222)
Rhenium	Re	75	186.2
Rhodium	Rh	45	102.9
Rubidium	Rb	37	85.47
Ruthenium	Ru	44	101.1
Samarium	Sm	62	150.4
Scandium	Sc	21	44.96
Selenium	Se	34	78.96
Silicon	Si	14	28.09
Silver	Ag	47	107.9
Sodium	Na	11	22.99
Strontium	Sr	38	87.62
Sulfur	S	16	32.06
Tantalum	Ta	73	180.9
Technetium	Tc	43	(98)
Tellurium	Te	52	127.6
Terbium	Tb	65	158.9
Thallium	Tl	81	204.4
Thorium	Th	90	232.0
Thulium	Tm	69	168.9
Tin	Sn	50	118.7
Titanium	Ti	22	47.90
Tungsten	W	74	183.9
Uranium	U	92	238.0
Vanadium	V	23	50.94
Xenon	Xe	54	131.3
Ytterbium	Yb	70	173.0
Yttrium	Y	39	88.91
Zinc	Zn	30	65.38
Zirconium	Zr	40	91.22

Name	Form/color	Common oxidation states	Density (g/cm^3)	Boiling Point (°C)	Melting point (°C)
Aluminum	Silver metal	3+	2.702	2467	660.37
Arsenic	Gray metalloid	3−, 3+, 5+	5.72714	613 (sublimes)	817 (28 atm)
Barium	Bluish white metal	2+	3.51	1640	725
Bromine	Red-brown liquid	1−, 1+, 3+, 5+, 7+	3.119	58.78	27.2
Calcium	Silver metal	2+	1.54	1484	839 ± 2
Carbon	Diamond	2+, 4+	3.51	3930	3500 (63.5 atm)
	Graphite	—	2.25	—	3652 (sublimes)
Chlorine	Green-yellow gas	1− 1+, 3+, 5+, 7+	3.214*	234.6	2100.98
Chromium	Gray metal	2+, 3+, 6+	7.2028	2672	1857 ± 20
Cobalt	Gray metal	2+, 3+	8.9	2870	1495
Copper	Red metal	1+, 2+	8.92	2567	1083.4 ± 0.2
Fluorine	Yellow gas	1−	1.69‡	2188.14	2219.62
Germanium	Gray metalloid	4+	5.32325	2830	937.4
Gold	Yellow metal	1+, 3+	19.31	2808±2	1064.43
Helium	Colorless gas	0	0.1785*	2268.9	2272.2 (26 atm)
Hydrogen	Colorless gas	1−, 1+	0.0899*	2252.8	2259.34
Iodine	Blue-black solid	1−, 1+, 3+, 5+ 7+	4.93	184.35	113.5
Iron	Silver metal	2+, 3+	7.86	2750	1535
Lead	Bluish white metal	2+, 4+	11.343716	1740	327.502
Lithium	Silver metal	1+	0.534	1342	180.54
Magnesium	Silver metal	2+	1.745	1107	648.8
Manganese	Gray-white metal	2+, 3+, 4+, 6+, 7+	7.20	1962	1244 ± 3
Mercury	Silver liquid metal	1+, 2+	13.5462	356.58	238.87
Neon	Colorless gas	0	0.9002*	2245.9	2248.67
Nickel	Silver metal	2+, 3+	8.90	2730	1455
Nitrogen	Colorless gas	3−, 3+, 5+	1.2506*	2195.8	2209.86
Oxygen	Colorless gas	2−	1.429*	2182.962	2218.4
Phosphorus	Yellow solid	3−, 3+, 5+	1.82	280	44.1
Platinum	Silver metal	2+, 4+	21.45	3827 ± 100	1772
Potassium	Silver metal	1+	0.86	760	63.25
Silicon	Gray metalloid	2+, 4+	2.33 ± 0.01	2355	1410
Silver	White metal	1+	10.5	2212	961.93
Sodium	Silver metal	1+	0.97	882.9	97.8
Strontium	Silver metal	2+	2.6	1384	769
Sulfur	Yellow solid	2−, 4+, 6+	1.96	444.674	119.0
Tin	White metal	2+, 4+	7.28	2260	231.88
Titanium	White metal	2+, 3+, 4+	4.5	3287	1660 ± 10
Uranium	Silver metal	3+, 4+, 6+	19.05 ± 0.0225	3818	1132.3 ± 0.8
Zinc	Blue-white metal	2+	7.14	907	419.58

*Densities of gases given in g/L at STP
†Densities obtained at 20°C unless otherwise noted (superscript)
‡ Density of fluorine given in g/L at 1 atm and 15°C

The Periodic Table

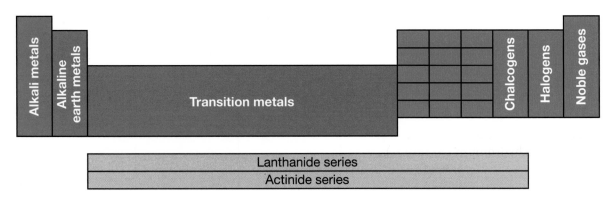

Group names on the periodic table

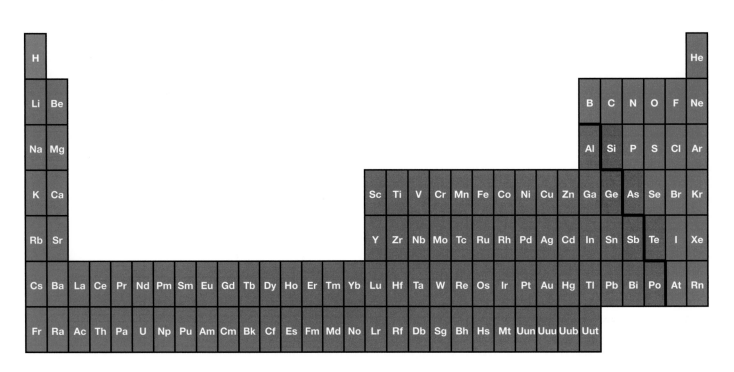

The periodic table

GLOSSARY

A

Accurate: Consistently within acceptable experimental error with respect to the accepted or expected value (see *precise*). (p. 10)

Acid, Arrhenius: A molecule that donates a hydrogen cation (H^+) to water to form a hydronium ion (H_3O^+). (p. 51)

Activation energy: Minimum energy that a molecular collision must have to produce a reaction. (p. 36)

Activity series: List of metals in order of reactivity. (p. 360)

Alpha particle: A helium nucleus—two protons and two neutrons. (p. 416)

Anhydride: The molecule that is left after the water has been evaporated from the starting hydrate. (p. 344)

Anode: The metal electrode at which oxidation occurs (see *cathode*). (p. 367)

Atmospheric pressure: The pressure caused by the gases in the atmosphere. (p. 96)

Atomic mass: The mass, in grams, of one mole of atoms (see *Avogadro's number*). (p. 102)

Aufbau principle: Electrons fill an element's orbitals in order of increasing energy. (p. 135)

Avogadro's number: The number of items in one mole: 6.02×10^{23}. (p. 100)

B

Base, Arrhenius: A molecule that forms the hydroxide ion (OH^-) when in water. (p. 54)

Beta particle: A high-energy electron that is emitted from the nucleus when a neutron turns into a proton and an electron during a nuclear reaction. (p. 416)

Bohr model: An atomic model in which protons and neutrons are in the center (nucleus), and in which the electrons are in concentric circles around the nucleus. (p. 126)

Bonding pair: A pair of electrons shared between two atoms to form a covalent bond. (p. 185)

C

Calorimetry: Laboratory technique to measure the energy change of the surroundings to determine the energy change (ΔH) of the system. (p. 261)

Catalyst: A molecule that speeds up a reaction without itself being used up in the reaction. (p. 71)

Cathode: The metal electrode at which reduction occurs (see *anode*). (p. 367)

Cation: A positively charged ion resulting from the loss of electrons. (p. 42)

Cell potential: The potential energy difference between an electron on the cathode side of a cell and the anode side of a cell. (p. 370)

Chemical equation: Description in words, chemical symbols, or drawings of the molecules reacting (reactants) and being produced (products) during a chemical reaction. (p. 59)

Chemical reaction: A change in which chemical bonds are formed and/or broken between atoms. (p. 59)

Chemistry: The study of matter and its interactions. (p. 5)

Chromatography: A technique for separating mixtures. (p. 330)

Collision theory: The theory that states that molecules need to collide with the correct orientation and minimum amount of energy to result in a chemical reaction. (p.68)

Colloid: A solution with particles that are large enough to scatter light. (p. 39)

Concentration: Ratio of solute to solvent or solute to solution. (p. 58)

Covalent bonding: Bonding in which electrons are shared between two atoms. (p. 165)

D

Density: The ratio of mass to volume. (p. 88)

Dependent variable: The variable that is measured or observed in an experiment (see *independent variable*). (p. 8)

Diffusion: The process of gas spreading out in a container or throughout space. (p. 98)

Dimensional analysis: Technique used to convert units by multiplying by equivalents. (p. 23)

Dipole–dipole interactions: Intermolecular force between two polar molecules. (p. 187)

Dissociation: Separation of an ionic compound into cation(s) and anion(s) when the compound is dissolved in water. (p. 208)

E

Effusion: Gas escaping through a tiny hole in its container. (p. 98)

Electrolysis: Using electricity to cause a reaction. (p. 373)

Electrolytes: Substances that conduct electricity when dissolved in water. (p. 167)

Electrolytic cell: An electrochemical cell to which external electricity is added to push a reaction in a non-spontaneous direction (compare to *galvanic cell* and *voltaic cell*). (p. 373)

Electron affinity: The energy change when an atom gains an electron. (p. 146)

Electronegativity: Attraction an atom has for the electrons it shares in a bond with another atom. (p. 183)

Electrons: Negatively charged particles found outside the nucleus of an atom. (p. 42)

Electrostatic attraction: Attraction between particles with opposite charges. (p. 172)

Element: An atom with a particular, distinctive number of protons; the elements are organized in the periodic table. (p. 38)

Empirical formula: The lowest whole-number ratio of atoms in a molecule is used as the subscripts in a chemical formula to show the relative number of each type of atom. (p. 339)

Endothermic reaction: A chemical reaction during which energy is transferred from the surroundings to the system (compare to *exothermic reaction*). (p. 255)

Enthalpy: Heat when pressure is held constant. (p. 256)

Enthalpy of formation: Total energy change when a new molecule is formed from other atoms and/or molecules. (p. 269)

Equilibrium: Condition in which the forward reaction rate is equal to the reverse reaction rate. (p. 287)

Equilibrium constant expression: Ratio of products to reactants, with balanced equation coefficients as their exponents, when a reversible reaction is at equilibrium. (p. 290)

Excitation: The phenomenon of energy being absorbed by an electron that then jumps to a higher energy level within the atom. (p. 151)

Exothermic reaction: A chemical reaction during which energy is transferred from the system to the surroundings (compare to *endothermic reaction*). (p. 255)

Extensive property: A characteristic that depends on the size of the sample (see *intensive property*). (p. 86)

F

Functional group: A group of atoms on the carbon backbone of an organic molecule that affects the properties of the molecule. (p. 389)

G

Galvanic cell: A cell that transforms chemical energy to electrical energy (see *voltaic cell*). (p. 366)

Gamma radiation: High-energy electromagnetic energy released during some nuclear reactions or decay processes. (p. 416)

Group (periodic table): A column in the periodic table; also known as a "family." (p. 141)

H

Half-life: The time it takes for half of the atoms in a sample to undergo nuclear decay. (p. 419)

Heat: Flow of energy from an object with more energy (more heat) to an object with less energy (less heat); the difference in temperatures drives this flow of energy. (p. 256)

Heat capacity: Amount of energy that a material can absorb before a noticeable change in temperature results. (p. 258)

Hess's law: The energy changes of stepwise reactions add up to the energy change of the overall reaction. (p. 275)

Heterogeneous mixture: A mixture of more than one substance in which there are visible, different parts. (p. 39)

Homogeneous mixture: A mixture of more than one substance that appears to be all one substance; also called a solution. (p. 39)

Hund's rule: When electrons are assigned to orbitals of equal energy, one electron at a time is added to the empty orbitals before the second electron is added. (p. 137)

Hydrate: A molecule with water molecules physically attached (see *anhydride*). (p. 344)

Hydration: The process of a solute being surrounded by water molecules, forming intermolecular forces with the water molecules, and dissolving. (p. 208)

Hydrogen bonding: The strongest intermolecular force; it is formed between a hydrogen typically bonded to a nitrogen, oxygen, or fluorine atom and another electronegative atom (often, but not always, nitrogen, oxygen, or fluorine). (p. 187)

Hydronium ion: H_3O^{+1} cation. (p. 51)

Hydroxide ion: OH^{-1} anion. (p. 54)

Hypothesis: An attempt to explain a natural behavior or phenomenon. (p. 9)

I

Independent variable: The variable being controlled, manipulated, or changed in an experiment, to determine the effect on the dependent variable(s). (p. 8)

Indicator: Liquid or paper substance that changes color at different pH values. (p. 56)

Intensive property: A characteristic that does not depend on the size of the sample (see *extensive property*). (p. 85)

Intermolecular forces: Physical connections between separate molecules. (p. 186)

Intramolecular forces: Chemical connections within a single molecule. (p. 186)

Ion: An atom with a charge resulting from the gain or loss of electrons. (p. 129)

Ionic bonding: Connection formed between a cation and an anion by electrostatic attraction. (p. 165)

Ionization energy: The energy required to remove the outermost electron of an atom. (p. 146)

Isomers: Molecules with the same chemical formulas but different chemical structures and properties. (p. 176)

Isotopes: Atoms of the same element (they have the same atomic number) but different numbers of neutrons and, therefore, different atomic masses. (p. 131)

K

Kinetic molecular theory (KMT): The theory that attempts to explain particle motion and behavior in the gas state. (p. 97)

Kinetics: The study of reaction rates. (p. 71)

L

Law: An attempt to describe or predict behavior; a law is often shown mathematically. (p. 11)

Law of conservation of mass: Mass will always be constant before, during, and after all physical and chemical changes. (p. 64)

Le Chatelier's principle: When a system at equilibrium is disturbed, it will readjust to reach equilibrium again. (p. 301)

Lewis dot structures: Pictures using the element symbol as the nucleus and dots around it as electrons to show bonding and lone pairs. (p. 170)

Limiting reactant: Reactant that runs out first in a reaction and causes it to stop. (p. 237)

London dispersion forces: Weakest intermolecular forces formed between two molecules with temporary or induced dipoles. (p. 186)

Lone pair: Pair of electrons not being shared in bonding. (p. 174)

M

Mass number: Total number of protons plus neutrons in the atomic nucleus. (p. 128)

Matter: Anything that has mass and takes up volume. (p. 5)

Metallic bonding: Bonding between metal atoms; the electrons are shared in a large pool. (p. 166)

Mole: A unit used to count very large groups of particles or molecules; for example, one mole of water contains 6.02×10^{23} molecules of water (see *Avogadro's number*). (p. 100)

Molecular formula: Chemical formula with the actual ratio of atoms represented by subscript numbers. (p. 340)

Molecular mass: Sum of the atomic masses for the atoms in a molecule; the mass, in grams, of one mole of molecules. (p. 102)

Monomers: The small molecules that form chains or networks called polymers. (p. 398)

Multivalent metal: A metal that can form more than one positive charge. (p. 45)

N

Neutralization reaction: A double replacement reaction between an acid and a base, producing a salt and water (see *single replacement reaction*). (p. 61)

Neutron: Neutral particle in the nucleus of an atom. (p. 126)

Nomenclature: The rules that govern the writing of chemical formulas and naming chemicals. (p. 41)

Nonpolar covalent bonding: A covalent bond in which the electrons are shared evenly between the atoms. (p. 165)

Nuclear reaction: A reaction in which the nucleus of an atom is changed. (p. 413)

Nucleus: The dense center of an atom; contains protons and neutrons. (p. 126)

O

Orbital: In modern atomic theory, the area of probability of finding an electron. (p. 135)

Organic molecule: A molecule that contains carbon atoms, often bonded to other carbon atoms. (p. 382)

Oxidation: The loss of electrons. (p. 355)

Oxidation number: The charge an atom would have if the electrons shared in a bond were assigned to the more electronegative atom in the bond. (p. 355)

P

Pauli exclusion principle: The assertion that, when two electrons share an orbital, they must have different spin values (for example, "up" and "down"). (p. 137)

Periodic table: The table that organizes the elements in rows (periods) and columns (groups or families). (p. 140)

Periodicity: The observation that properties vary in predictable patterns across a period or down a column in the periodic table. (p. 145)

pH scale: Scale from 0 to 14 that indicates the level of acidity of a sample; pH = $-\log [H_3O^+]$. (p. 58)

Physical change: A change in which chemical bonds are neither formed nor broken. (p. 93)

Polar covalent bonding: A bond in which electrons are shared unevenly; the more electronegative atom pulls the electrons closer to itself, creating a partial separation in charge. (p. 165)

Polyatomic ion: A group of atoms that are covalently bonded, that together have a charge. (p. 43)

Polymer: A very large molecule composed of multiple smaller components (monomers); numerous monomers form a polymer. (p. 381)

Precipitate: An insoluble compound formed out of a solution of two soluble compounds. (p. 223)

Precise: Consistently within acceptable experimental error (see *accurate*). (p. 10)

Prediction: A guess as to what will occur. (p. 9)

Pressure: Force of particles running into the walls of their container. (p. 95)

Proton: Positively charged particle in the nucleus of an atom; the number of protons determines the identity of the atom. (p. 125)

Pure substance: A substance in which every particle (either every atom, for an element, or every molecule) is the same. (p. 38)

R

Reaction quotient: The equilibrium constant expression used with current concentrations to determine whether a reaction is at equilibrium. (p. 298)

Redox reaction: Chemical reaction in which reduction and oxidation occur. (p. 353)

Reduction: The gaining of electrons. (p. 354)

Relaxation: The process whereby an electron releases energy and relaxes back to a lower energy level in the atom. (p. 152)

Representative elements: Elements in columns 1, 2, and 13–19 in the periodic table (IUPAC column classification); also called "main group elements." (p. 170)

Retention factor: The ratio of the distance a component of the sample travels to the distance the solvent travels. (p. 331)

Reversible reaction: A reaction that can proceed both forward and backward. (p. 286)

S

Saturated solution: A solution that is holding the maximum amount of solute for a specific temperature. (p. 210)

SI units: The International System of Units ("SI" comes from the French "Système International d'Unités"), based on the metric system. (p. 14)

Single replacement reaction: A reaction in which one element in a compound is replaced by a neutral element (see *neutralization reaction*). (p. 358)

Solute: A substance that is dissolved in a solution. (p. 190)

Solution: A homogeneous mixture. (p. 210)

Solvent: The liquid into which a substance is dissolved. (p. 190)

Standard reduction potential: The cell potential found when an element is placed in a voltaic cell with hydrogen. (p. 370)

Stoichiometry: Using the mole ratio of the balanced equation to calculate information about one species in the reaction, given information about another species in the reaction. (p. 227)

Supersaturated solution: A solution that is holding more than the maximum amount of solute that it should be able to hold at that temperature. (p. 211)

Surface tension: Resistance of a substance to spreading out. (p. 192)

Surroundings: Everything around the molecules that are reacting or changing. (p. 255)

Suspension: A mixture in which the solute particles are large enough to settle out over time. (p. 39)

System: The set of molecules reacting or changing. (p. 254)

T

Temperature: A physical property that is proportional to the average kinetic energy of the particles. (p. 97)

Theory: An explanation of how or why things happen. (p. 11)

Titration: A laboratory technique used to determine the concentration or amount of a substance through stoichiometry and a known amount of another substance that is reacted. (p. 230)

Tyndall effect: The scattering of light in a colloid. (p. 39)

Unsaturated solution: A solution that is holding less than the maximum amount of solute at that temperature. (p. 210)

Valence electrons: The electrons in an atom's outermost shell; these are involved in bonding. (p. 138)

Valence shell electron pair repulsion theory (VSEPR): The theory that explains the three-dimensional structure of a molecule on the basis of repulsion of the electrons that form bonds in the molecule. (p. 182)

Vapor pressure: The pressure caused by particles that have evaporated from a sample. (p. 240)

Viscosity: Resistance of a substance to flow or pour. (p. 190)

Voltaic cell: A cell that converts chemical energy to electrical energy (see *galvanic cell*). (p. 366)

INDEX

Page references followed by "f" denote figures, photographs, or illustrations; those followed by "t" denote tables.

A

Absolute zero, 108
Accuracy, 10, 445
Acid(s)
Arrhenius definition, 51–52, 445
characteristics of, 56–59, 57t
concentration, 58, 58t
as electrolytes, 220
naming, 52, 53
neutralization reaction, 61–62
nonoxygen, 52
oxyacid, 52
pH, 58–59
strength, 57–58, 58f, 58t, 216–218, 217f, 218f
writing formula, 52, 53
Acid inhibitor, 37
Acid rain, 310
Activated monomer, 400
Activation energy, 69–71, 70f, 445
Activity series, 359–361, 377t, 437t, 445
Addition polymerization, 399–400, 400f
Aerosol, 310
Airbag, 81–82, 81f, 82f, 114–115
Airplanes, effect of air density on, 90f
Air pollution, 309–310, 309f
-al (suffix), 392
Alcohol, 390–391
Aldehyde, 392–393
Algae, bioluminescent, 123
Alkane, 383
Alka-Seltzer® cannon, 36
Alkene, 384, 385
Alkyne, 385, 386
Allison, F. E., 32f
Alpha particles, 126, 126f, 416, 416f, 417, 422, 445
Amine, 392
-amine (suffix), 392
Amino acid(s), 402
Ammonia, 47, 54, 178f

Analysis
of chemical formula, 337–346
qualitative, 327
quantitative, 327
using chromatography, 330–337
using solubility, 320–330
Analytical balance, 100f
-ane (suffix), 383
Anhydride, 344, 345, 393, 394, 445
Anion(s)
definition, 129
formation, 146
hydration of, 207, 208f
in ionic bonding, 42, 165, 172
ion radius, 146
polyatomic, 178
Anode, 367, 367f, 445
Antacid, 37, 38f, 72
Aromatic compounds, 395
Aspirin, synthesis of, 395–397
-ate (suffix), 49, 52
Atmospheres (atm), 107
Atmospheric pressure, 96, 445
Atom(s)
atomic structure, 128–134
as building blocks of matter, 5
isotopes, 131
mass number, 128, 131
spectrum of, 154, 154f
Atomic mass
average, 131–134
definition, 102, 445
mass number, 128, 131, 133
table of, 440t–442t
Atomic mass unit (amu), 128
Atomic number
definition, 128
in periodic table, 140–142
table of, 440t–442t
Atomic orbital. See Orbital
Atomic radius, 144, 145–146, 183
Atomic theory
Bohr model, 126–127, 127f, 445
Dalton's, 124
modern, 127
plum pudding model, 125–126
Atomium, 177f
Aufbau principle, 135, 137, 445

Aurora, 174f
Autoionization of water, 220
Average atomic mass, 131–134
Avogadro's law, 108
Avogadro's number, 100, 445

B

Background information, gathering in lab design, 18
Bakelite, 399f
Balance, analytical, 100f
Balancing chemical equations, 64–66
Balloon, 89f
Barometer, 107
Barometric pressure, 107
Base(s)
amines, 392
Arrhenius definition, 54, 445
characteristics of, 56–59, 57t
concentration, 58
as electrolytes, 220
naming and writing, 54–55
neutralization reaction, 61–62
pH, 58–59
strength, 57–58, 219, 219f
Battery
car, 353f
cell potential, 370–371
concentration cell, 372, 373f
electrolytic cell, 373–374
gel, 364f
lead-acid, 353f
lithium-ion, 373f
making, 369–370
nonstandard cell, 371–372
overview, 354f
redox reactions, 353
research project, 375
voltaic cell, 366–367, 367f
Becquerel, Henri, 414
Benzene, 395, 395f
Berzelius, Jons Jakob, 48f
Beta particle, 416, 417, 422, 445
Bicarbonate soda, 77
Binary ionic compound
naming, 42–43
writing chemical formula, 48–49

Bioluminescence, 123, 130f, 155–156
Bleach, 353
Bohr, Niels, 126
Bohr's atomic model, 126–127, 127f, 445
Boiling, 84, 189
Boiling point, 84, 166, 189, 242, 264–265, 266, 443t
Boiling point elevation constant, 242
Bond angle, 182, 182f
Bonding pair, 445
Bonds and bonding
    characteristics of molecules by bond type, 166–167
    double, 175–176, 384, 385
    hydrogen bonding, 187–188, 188f, 447
    ionic, 165
    laboratory (Types of Bonds), 169
    between metals, 165–166
    between metals and nonmetals, 164–165
    between nonmetals, 165
    nonpolar covalent, 165, 448
    polar, 165, 184–185, 184f, 185f
    single, 173
    triple, 176, 385, 386
    types, 164–169
Boron, 423–424
Bouncy Ball Contest, 405–406
Boyle, Robert, 109f
Boyle's law, 109
Burning, as chemical change, 94
Butter, 383f, 386

C

Calorie (cal), 257
Calorimeter, 259f
Calorimetry, 261–263, 445
Cancer, 422, 422f
Cannon, Alka-Seltzer®, 36
Carbohydrates, use during exercise, 205
Carbon-14, 425, 425f
Carbonated beverage, 245–246
Carbon dating, 425
Carbon dioxide, as greenhouse gas, 311–312
Carbonyl, 392–394
Carboxylic acid, 392, 393, 394
Carcinogen, 395
Catalyst, 71, 304, 445
Cathode, 367, 367f, 445
Cathode ray, 125, 125f

Cation(s)
    definition, 42, 129, 445
    hydration of, 207, 208f
    in ionic bonding, 42, 165, 172
    ion radius, 147
    polyatomic, 178
CAT scan, 429f
Cell potential, 370–371, 445
CFCs (chlorofluorocarbons), effect on ozone, 310–311
Chadwick, James, 126
Chalcanthite, 361f
Changes in state, 263–269
Charge
    balancing in ionic structures, 172–173
    of common ions, 45f
    definition, 129
    multivalent metals, 45–46, 45t, 433t
Charles' law, 108–109
Chemical changes, in matter, 92–93, 94
Chemical engineer, 285
Chemical equation. *See* Equation, chemical
Chemical equilibrium. *See* Equilibrium
Chemical properties, 85
Chemical reaction. *See* Reaction, chemical
Chemical spill, 307f
Chemiluminescence, 155–156
Chemistry
    definition, 5, 445
    as experimental science, 6
    in industry, 282–315
Chernobyl, 428f
Chlorofluorocarbons (CFCs), effect on ozone, 310–311
Chromatography
    column, 332, 334–335
    definition, 445
    description of process, 330
    gas, 333, 333f
    liquid, 332–333
    paper, 330–332, 331f, 335–336
    thin layer, 332
Clean Air Act, 309
Clear (descriptive term), 14
Cloudy (descriptive term), 14
Coal, 307
Cobalt-60, 423
Coefficient, 64
Cold pack, 253–254, 254f, 278–279
Collision theory, 68–71, 287, 290, 445
Colloid, 39, 39f, 446

Colorless (descriptive term), 14
Colors, of visible light, 149
Column chromatography, 332, 334–335
Combined gas law, 109
Combustion reaction, 353
Composting, 305–306
Compound. *See also specific types*
    description, 38, 38t
    naming, 41–47
    solubility, 435t
Concentration
    of acids and bases, 58
    definition, 58, 446
    effect of changes in equilibrium, 301–302
    of electrolytes, 214
    in equilibrium constant expressions, 290–293
    molarity, 213
    percent, 212
    symbolic representation for, 290
Concentration cell, 372, 373f
Condensation, 84, 265
Condensation point, 84
Condensation reaction, 400–401, 401f
Constant, 8, 436t
Control setup, 8
Cooling curve, 266–267, 266f
Core electron, 138
Covalent bond
    definition, 165, 446
    double, 175–176
    geometry, 182
    nonpolar, 165, 448
    single, 173
    triple, 176
Covalent molecule
    formation of, 165
    isomers, 176–177, 177f
    laboratory (Covalent Molecules in 3D), 181
    Lewis structure for, 173–177
    properties of, 166
Curie, Marie, 414, 415f

D

Dacron, 401f
Dalton, John, 124–125
Dalton's atomic theory, 124
Data. *See also* Measurement
    accuracy, 10
    gathering techniques, 7–8
    precision, 9–11

Data (continued)
    qualitative, 14
    quantitative, 14
Data table, 19
Dating, nuclear, 425
Daughter nucleus, 417
Decimal places, number of, 16, 16f, 18
Dehydration, prevention with sports
    drinks, 205–206
Density
    of common elements, 443t
    of common materials, 89t
    definition, 88, 446
    effect of air density on airplanes,
      90f
    floating, 89
    graphs, 88
    laboratory for study of, 88
    layering, 88, 88f, 89
    problems, 90
    units, 88
Dependent variable, 8, 446
Deposition, 84
Desalination of water, 307–308
Detergents, 163, 168f
Diatomic element, 51, 51t, 433t
Diffusion, of gas, 98, 446
Dimensional analysis, 23–24, 446
Dipole, temporary, 186–187, 187f
Dipole-dipole interactions, 187, 389,
    446
Dissociation, 208, 446
Dissolving
    basis for process, 320–321
    effect of intermolecular forces on,
      190, 190f
    equilibrium, 322, 324
    ionic compounds in water, 207–
      208, 208f, 321
    as physical change in matter,
      94–95
    polar covalent molecule in water,
      209, 209f
    solubility product, 322–325
DNA, 402
Dobereiner, Johann, 140
Double bond, 175–176, 384, 385
Double replacement reaction, 61, 61f,
    223
Drying, as physical change, 94
Dynamic equilibrium, 288–289

E

Ecological stoichiometry, 246f
Effusion, of gas, 98, 446

Electricity
    conduction of, 166–167
    redox reaction and, 366
Electrode
    in cathode ray tube, 125
    in voltaic cell, 366–367, 367f
Electrolysis, 373, 446
Electrolyte(s)
    acids and bases, 220
    concentration, 214
    definition, 167, 446
    effect on solution properties,
      241–242, 244
    formation in water, 208
    loss in sweat, 206
    strong and weak, 208
    terminology, 209
Electrolytic cell, 373–374, 446
Electromagnetic radiation, 148, 148f, 149
Electron(s)
    beta particle, 416
    bonding pair, 445
    core, 138
    in covalent bonding, 165
    definition, 42, 446
    discovery of, 125
    energy levels, 126, 127, 135, 136f,
      142, 152–153, 153f
    excitation, 151–152, 152f
    ground state, 151–152
    in ionic bonding, 165
    in Lewis dot structures, 170–171
    lone pairs, 174, 182, 182f, 448
    mass of, 128
    in metallic bonding, 165, 166
    noble gas notation, 138, 142–143
    octet rule, 164, 179
    orbital diagrams, 137
    orbitals, 127, 135, 136f, 137, 448
    relaxation, 152, 152f, 153–154
    shielding of, 146
    spectrographic notation, 138
    spin, 137
    structure, 134–139
    subshells, 135, 136, 142
    valence, 138, 142, 165, 170, 170f,
      450
Electron affinity, 146–147, 446
Electron configuration
    methods of showing, 137–138
    periodic table and, 141–143, 142f
Electronegativity
    definition, 183, 446
    polar bonds, 184
    trend in periodic table, 183, 184f
Electrostatic attraction, 172, 446

Element(s)
    atomic mass, 102, 440t–442t
    definition, 38, 446
    diatomic, 51, 51t, 433t
    list of, 440t–442t
    nomenclature, 47
    properties of, 443t
    as pure substance, 38
    radioactive, 414–415, 422–423
    representative, 170, 449
    symbol, 41
Empirical formula, 339–340, 342–343,
    446
Employment, as chemist, 119, 174
Enceladus (Saturn moon), 189f
Endothermic, 254, 255, 303, 313, 446
End point, 230
-ene (suffix), 384
Energy
    absorption with endothermic
      process, 254, 255, 303
    activation energy, 69–71, 70f, 445
    calorimetry and, 261
    changes in state and, 263–267
    cooling curve and, 266–267, 266f
    electromagnetic radiation, 148
    electron affinity, 146–147
    enthalpy, 256–257
    heat, 256
    heat capacity, 258
    heating curve and, 265–266, 265f
    ionization, 144–145, 146, 165, 447
    kinetic, 69, 84, 240–241, 241f, 256
    nuclear power, 426
    potential, 370
    release with exothermic process,
      254, 255, 303–304
    thermal conductance, 166
    units of measurement, 257
Energy diagram, 152–153, 153f
Energy resources
    nonrenewable, 306–307
    renewable, 307
Enthalpy
    definition, 256–257, 446
    of formation (H_f), 269–270, 271,
      438t–439t, 446
    of fusion, 264, 266, 268–269
    Hess's law and, 275–277
    stoichiometry and, 272–273
    of vaporization, 264–265, 266
Enthalpy change
    during change in state, 264–265
    during chemical reaction,
      269–274
    in heat capacity calculations, 258

Environmental chemistry, 295
Environmental concerns
    air, 309–310
    citizen action on, 312
    energy resources, 306–307
    greenhouse gases and global
        warming, 311–312
    ozone, 310–311, 310f
    waste, 305–306
    water, 307–309
Environmental Protection Agency
    (EPA), 309
Enzyme, 71
Epsom salt, 344
Equation, chemical
    balancing, 64–66
    coefficients in, 64
    definition, 59, 445
    examples, 59
    parts of, 60
    writing, 60–61
Equation, nuclear, 417–418
Equilibrium
    definition, 287, 446
    determining existence of, 289,
        297–298
    dynamic, 288–289
    effect of catalyst, 304
    effect of changing concentration,
        301–302
    effect of changing temperature,
        303–304
    effect of changing volume/
        pressure, 302–303
    establishment of, 287–288, 287f
    importance in industry, 301
    laboratory procedure for studying
        changes in, 299–300
    Le Chatelier's principle, 301
    saturated solution, 322, 324–325
    thermal, 261
Equilibrium constant (K_{eq})
    description, 289
    lab procedure for determination
        of, 294–297
    meaning of, 292–293
    solubility (K_{sp}), 322
    solving equilibrium constant
        expression for, 291–292
    temperature dependence, 293
    units, 292
Equilibrium constant expression
    aqueous solutions and gases in, 290
    description, 290, 446
    pure liquids in, 291
    pure solids in, 291

Equilibrium constant expression
    (continued)
    for solubility, 322
    using in calculations, 291–292
    writing, 290
Error
    experimental, 9, 10
    relative, 15–16
Ethanol, 390
Ether, 391
Evaporation, 189, 194–195, 241
Excitation, 151–152, 152f, 446
Exothermic, 254, 255, 303–304, 313,
    446
Experiment. See also Scientific
    investigations
    designing your own labs, 18–23
    examples of simple, 5
    multiple trials, 9
    predictions and hypotheses, 8–9
    types, 7–8
    variables and constants, 6–7, 7f
Experimental error, 9, 10
Experimental setup, 8
Extensive property, 86, 446

F

Family (periodic table), 141
Faraday, Michael, 363f
Fatty acids, 163, 192f
Filler, in medicines, 39
Fingerprints, 327f
Firefly (lightning bug), 123, 130f
Fission, 426
Floating, 88f, 89
Fluorescence, 155
Food calorie (Cal), 257
Forensic chemistry, 319, 320f, 347
Formula
    analysis of, 337–346
    empirical, 339–340, 342–343
    hydrate, 344–346
    molecular, 340–341, 448
    writing chemical, 48–51, 48f
        binary ionic compounds,
            48–49
        diatomic element, 51, 51t
        molecular compounds, 50
        polyatomic compounds,
            49–50
Formula equation
    example, 59
    writing, 60–61
Formula mass, 102
Fossil fuels, 311

Freezing, 83–84, 84f, 264
Freezing point, 83, 243–244, 265, 266
Freezing point depression constant,
    244
Frequency, 148
Functional group(s)
    alcohol, 390–391
    aldehyde, 392–393
    amine, 392
    anhydride, 393, 394
    carbonyl, 392–394
    carboxyl, 392, 393, 394
    definition, 389, 446
    ether, 391
    haloalkane, 389–390
    ketone, 393, 394
    in polymers, 398
Fusion
    enthalpy of, 264, 266, 268–269
    nuclear, 426

G

Galvanic cell, 366–367, 367f, 446. See
    also Battery
Gamma radiation, 416–417, 422, 446
Gas(es)
    behavior, 95–99
        diffusion, 98
        effusion, 98
        ideal gas, 97
        kinetic molecular theory, 97
        pressure, 95–97
        real gas, 97–98
    ideal gas law, 229–230
    pressure, 108–110
    properties of, 83, 83f
    stoichiometry, 229–230
    vapor pressure, 240–241
Gas chromatography, 333, 333f
Gas laws, 105–113
    Avogadro's, 108
    Boyle's, 109
    Charles', 108–109
    choosing the appropriate law, 110
    combined, 109
    ideal, 110
    laboratory for study of, 105–106
    temperature units, 108
Gatorade, 205
Geiger, Hans, 126
Geiger counter, 415f
Geysers, 96f, 189f
Global warming, 312
Glowing objects, 123–124, 130f, 155f,
    157

Gold foil experiment, 126, 126f
Goldstein, Eugene, 125
Gram(s)
    converting between moles and,
        103–104
    converting moles, 227
Greenhouse gases, 311–312
Ground state, 151–152
Group (periodic table), 141, 141f, 447

H

Half-life, 418–420, 419t, 447
Half-reaction, 362, 370–371, 437t
Haloalkane, 389–390
Halogen, in haloalkanes, 389–390
H_2 blocker, 77
Heartburn, 37, 37f, 77
Heat
    definition, 256, 447
    enthalpy, 257
Heat capacity, 257–261, 447
Heating curve, 265–266, 265f
Helium, 89
Hertz, 148
Hess's law, 275–277, 447
Heterogeneous mixture, 39, 447
High-pressure liquid chromatography
    (HPLC), 332
Homogeneous mixture, 39, 447
Hot pack, 253–254, 254f, 278–279
Hund's rule, 137, 447
Hydrate, 344, 447
Hydrate formula, 344–346
Hydration
    definition, 208, 447
    of electrolyte, 208, 208f
    of non-electrolyte, 209, 209f
Hydro- (prefix), 52
Hydrocarbon(s)
    alkanes, 383
    alkenes, 384, 385
    alkynes, 385, 386
    definition, 382
    isomers, 384, 386
    properties, 382–383
    saturated, 383, 386, 387f
    side branches, 387–388
Hydrogen
    hydrogen-3 use in nuclear dating,
        425
    oxidation number, 356
Hydrogen bonding, 187–188, 188f, 447
Hydrologic cycle, 307
Hydronium ion (H_3O^+)
    autoionization of water, 220

Hydronium ion (H_3O^+) (continued)
    calculating pH from concentration
        of, 216–218
    definition, 51, 447
    formation of, 51–52, 52f
    pH scale, 58
    solving pH equation from
        concentration of, 218
Hydroxide ion (OH^-)
    autoionization of water, 220
    in bases, 54
    definition, 54, 447
    formation of, 219, 219f
    pH scale, 58
Hydroxyl group (-OH)
    in alcohols, 390
    in carboxylic acids, 392
    in phenols, 395
Hypothesis, 8–9, 447

I

-ic (suffix), 52
Ice, enthalpy of fusion of, 268–269
-ide (suffix), 42, 43, 46, 48
Ideal gas law, 110, 229–230
Incandescence, 155
Independent variable, 8, 447
Indicator, pH, 56, 59, 230–231, 447
Industrial smog, 310
Industry, chemistry in, 282–315
Intensive property
    definition, 85–86, 447
    density and molecular mass, 291
    half-life of radioactive isotope, 420
    standard reduction potential, 371
Intermolecular forces
    definition, 186, 447
    dipole-dipole interactions, 187,
        446
    effect on properties of a substance,
        188–195
    hydrogen bonding, 187–188, 188f,
        447
    London dispersion forces, 186–
        187, 448
International System of Measurement,
    14
International Union of Pure and
    Applied Chemistry (IUPAC), 389
Intramolecular force(s), 186, 447
Iodine-131, 420, 424
Ion(s)
    charges of common, 45f
    description, 42, 129, 447
    hydration of, 208, 208f

Ion(s) (continued)
    oxidation number, 355–356
        polyatomic, 43–44, 44t, 49–50,
            178–179, 432t, 448
Ionic bonding, 165, 447
Ionic compound(s)
    arrangement of ions in, 182–183,
        183f
    dissolution in water, 207–208,
        208f, 321
    formation of, 41–42, 165
    Lewis dot structures for, 171–173
    naming, 41–46
        binary, 42–43
        with multivalent metals,
            45–46, 45t
        polyatomic, 43–44, 44t
    oxidation number of ions in, 355
    properties of, 166–167
    solubility, 223
    writing formulas, 48–50
        binary compounds, 48–49
        polyatomic compounds,
            49–50
Ionization, 208
Ionization energy, 144–145, 146, 165,
    447
Ion radius, 147
Isomer
    alkene, 384, 386
    alkyne, 385, 386
    definition, 176, 384, 447
    drawing, 176–177, 177f
    naming, 177
Isoprene, 400
Isotope
    carbon, 425
    description, 131, 447
    mass, 131, 133
    radioactive, 415, 418–420, 419t
-ite (suffix), 49, 52

J

Jobs, in chemistry, 119, 174
Joules (J), 257
Julian, Percy, 167f

K

Kelvin (K), 108
Ketone, 393, 394
Kilocalorie (kcal), 257
Kilopascals (kPa), 107

Kinetic energy
    changes in matter state and, 84
    temperature relationship to, 69,
        240–241, 256
    vapor formation and, 240–241,
        241f
Kinetic molecular theory (KMT), 97,
    447
Kinetics, 71, 447

L

Lab design process
    background information, 18
    changing procedure, 20
    discussing results, 20
    example lab, 21–23
    identifying purpose, problem, or
        question, 18
    materials list, 19
    optimization, 20
    results, calculations, and data
        table, 19
    safety concerns, 19
    writing procedure, 19
Labs
    Acids and Bases, 56–57
    Activity Series, 359–360
    Analysis with Paper
        Chromatography, 335–336
    Analysis with Solubility, 328
    Average Atomic Mass, 131–132
    Calorimetry, 262–263
    Changes to Equilibrium, 299–300
    Chemical Changes, 92–93
    Column Chromatography,
        334–335
    Concentration of Solutions, 216
    Conservation of Matter, 63
    Covalent Molecules in 3D, 181
    Density, 87
    Determining Half-Life, 418–419
    Empirical Formulas, 342–343
    Enthalpy of a Reaction, 273–274
    Enthalpy of Fusion of Ice, 268–269
    Equilibrium Constants, 294–297
    Finding a Solubility Product,
        323–324
    Gas Laws, 105–106
    Intermolecular Forces and
        Evaporation, 194–195
    Introduction to Stoichiometry,
        225–226
    Light and Matter, 150–151
    Limiting Reactants, 236

Labs (continued)
    Making a Battery, 369–370
    Making a Periodic Table, 139–140
    Moles, 101
    The Most Absorbent Paper Towel,
        21–23
    Observing Polymers, 403–404
    Periodicity, 144–145
    Properties of Solutions, 239–240
    Solubility and Precipitation,
        221–222
    Solution Saturation and
        Temperature, 210
    Speeding Up a Reaction, 67
    Stoichiometry: Gravimetric,
        234–235
    Stoichiometry: Titration, 233–234
    Synthesis of an Organic Molecule:
        Aspirin, 395–397
    Taking Measurements, 17
    Taking Observations, 13
    Types of Bonds, 169
Lactic acid, 205
Landfill, 305, 306, 306f
Law, 11, 447
Law of conservation of mass/matter, 64
Layering, 88, 88f, 89
Le Chatelier's principle, 301, 372, 448
Lewis base, 392
Lewis dot structure (Lewis structure)
    for covalent compounds, 173–177
    definition, 170, 448
    electron placement, 170–171
    for ionic compounds, 171–173
    for polyatomic ions, 178–179
Light
    color, 149
    interaction with matter, 150–155
    photons, 149, 151–154
    production of, 155–156
    speed of, 148
    Tyndall effect, 39, 39f
    wave properties, 148
Limiting reactant, 236–238, 448
Line notation, 367–369
Liquid
    properties of, 83, 83f
    viscosity, 190
Liquid chromatography, 332–333
Litmus paper, 59
Logarithm (log), 217
London dispersion forces, 186–187,
    382, 448
Lone pairs, 174, 182, 182f, 448
Lovell, Jim, 123
Luminol, 123, 319, 322f

M

Manometer, 302f
Mars Climate Orbiter, 14–15, 15f
Mass
    atomic, 102, 131–134, 440t–442t,
        445
    conservation of, 64
    molecular, 102–104, 448
Mass number, 128, 131, 133, 448
Materials list, in lab design process, 19
Matter
    changes in
        chemical, 92–93, 94
        misconceptions concerning,
            94–95
        physical, 94
        state, 83–84, 84f, 263–269
    conservation of, 63, 64
    definition, 5, 38, 448
    interaction with light, 150–155
    properties
        chemical, 85
        extensive, 86
        intensive, 85–86
        physical, 85
    states of
        changes in states, 83–84, 84f,
            263–269
        properties of states, 82–83, 83f
    types, 38–40, 38f
        mixtures, 38–39
        pure substances, 38
Measurement
    choosing correct tool for, 15, 16f
    common equivalent, 24t, 430t
    converting units, 23–26
    decimal places in, 16, 16f, 18
    International System of
        Measurement, 14
    scientific notation, 30–31
    significant digits, 27–30
    uncertainty in, 15
Medicine, radiation in, 423
Medicines, as mixtures, 39
Melting, 83–84, 84f, 94, 189, 262–264
Melting point, 83, 166, 189, 265, 265f,
    443t
Mendeleev, Dimitri, 140
Metal(s)
    activity series, 359–361, 377t, 437t,
        445
    bonding between, 165–166
    bonding with nonmetals, 164–165
    multivalent, 45–46, 45t, 433t, 448
    in periodic table, 41–42, 41f
    properties of, 166

Metallic bonding, 166, 448
Metric system
    converting units, 25
    prefixes, 24t, 25, 430t
Micelle, 191, 191f
Millimeters of mercury (mm Hg), 107
Mixture
    description, 38–39, 38f
    heterogeneous, 39, 447
    homogeneous, 39, 447
Mobile phase, 330
Molarity
    calculating concentration in, 213
    converting between volume and
        moles, 228
    use in stoichiometry, 228, 229
Mole
    converting between grams and,
        103–104
    converting between number of
        particles and, 101
    converting grams, 227
    definition, 100, 448
    laboratory for study of, 101
    use in stoichiometry, 226–229
Molecular compound
    naming, 46–47, 46t, 433t
    writing chemical formula, 50
Molecular formula, 340–341, 448
Molecular mass
    converting between grams and
        moles, 103–104, 227
    definition, 102, 448
    finding, 102–103
    use in stoichiometry, 227–228, 229
Molecules
    counting, 100–104
    drawing, 170–180
    geometry of, 181–183
    polarity of, 183–186
    spaces between, 84, 84f
    spectrum of, 154f, 155
Mole ratio, in balanced chemical
    equation, 226–227
Monomer
    activated, 400
    definition, 398, 448
Multivalent metal, 45–46, 45t, 433t,
    448

N

Naming chemicals. *See* Nomenclature
Nanowire, 372f
NASA Mars Climate Orbiter, 14–15, 15f
Natural gas, 307

Neutralization reaction, 61–62, 448
Neutron(s)
    definition, 126
    discovery of, 126
    number of, 128, 131
Newlands, John A. R., 140
Noble gas notation, 138, 142–143
Nomenclature
    acids, 51–53
    alcohol, 390–391
    aldehyde, 392
    alkane, 383
    alkene, 384, 385
    alkyne, 385, 386
    anhydride, 393
    bases, 54–55
    carboxylic acids, 392, 394
    common name, 47, 389
    definition, 41, 383, 448
    elements, 47
    ether, 391
    haloalkane, 389–390
    hydrocarbon side branches, 387
    International Union of Pure and
        Applied Chemistry (IUPAC),
        389
    ionic compounds, 41–46
        binary, 42–43
        multivalent metals, 45–46, 45t
        polyatomic, 43–44, 44t
    ketone, 393
    molecular compounds, 46–47, 46t
    prefixes
        metric system, 24t, 25, 430t
        molecular compound, 46, 46t,
        433t
        organic compound, 383t, 433t
    subscripts, 41
Non-electrolyte, hydration of, 209,
    209f
Nonmetal(s)
    bonding between, 165
    bonding with metals, 164–165
    in molecular compounds, 46
    in periodic table, 41, 41f
Nonpolar covalent bond, 165, 448
Nuclear dating, 425
Nuclear power, 426
Nuclear radiation, 410–429
    definition, 413
    effects on body, 422–423
    energy, 426
    half-life, 418–420, 419t
    handling nuclear waste, 427
    nuclear dating, 425
    overview, 414f

Nuclear radiation (*continued*)
    radioactive decay, 416–417, 416f
    use in medicine, 423–424, 424f
Nuclear reaction
    definition, 413, 448
    equation, 417–418
    fission, 426
    fusion, 426
Nucleus
    daughter, 417
    definition, 126, 448
    discovery of, 126

O

Observations, 13, 14
Octane rating, 387
Octet rule
    definition, 164
    exceptions to, 179
-oic acid (suffix), 392
-oic anhydride (suffix), 393
Oil, 191
-ol (suffix), 390
Opaque (descriptive term), 14
Open system, 257
Optimization, of lab design, 20
Orbital, 127, 135, 136f, 137, 448
Orbital diagram, 137
Organic molecule
    aromatic, 395
    definition, 382, 448
    functional groups, 389–398
    hydrocarbons, 382–388
    prefixes, 383t, 433t
    synthesis of aspirin, 395–397
-ous (suffix), 52
Oxidation
    definition, 355, 448
    half-reaction, 362, 371
    state of common elements, 443t
Oxidation and reduction (redox)
    reaction
        balancing, 362–365
            in acidic solution, 362–363
            in basic solution, 364–365
            writing half-reactions, 362
        batteries, 353, 366–374
        definition, 353, 355, 448
        single replacement reactions,
            358–359, 359f, 360
Oxidation number, 355–357, 359
Oxidizing agent, 357
Oxyacid, 52
Oxygen, oxidation number of, 356
Ozone, 310–311, 310f

P

Paper chromatography, 330–332, 331f, 335–336
Paper cranes, 421f
Particulates, 310
Pauli exclusion principle, 137, 448
PCBs (polychlorinated biphenyls), 309
Percent composition, 337–339
Percent concentration, 212
Percent weight per volume, %(W/V), 212
Percent yield, 231
Period (periodic table), 141
Periodicity, 144–147, 448
Periodic table
  constructing, 139–140
  definition, 140, 448
  electron configuration and, 141–143, 142f
  electronegativity, 183, 184f
  history of development, 140
  organization of, 128, 140–141, 141f, 444
  periodicity, 145–147
  representative elements, 170, 449
  with valence electrons, 170f
Periodic trend, 145
PET (positron-emission tomography), 424, 424f
Petroleum, 307
PH
  calculating from concentration of hydronium, 216–218
  as logarithmic value, 217–218, 218f
  measuring, 59
Phenol, 395, 395f
Phenylalanine, 175f
PH indicator, 56, 230–231, 447
PH meter, 57, 59, 219f
Phosphorescence, 155
Photochemical smog, 310
Photons, 149, 151–154
PH paper, 59
PH scale, 58, 448
Physical change, 94, 448
Physical properties, 85
Pictograph, 201, 201f
Plastics, 381, 402, 402f
Plum pudding model, 125–126
Polar covalent bond, 165, 448
Polar covalent molecules
  definition, 165
  dissolution in water, 209, 209f

Polar covalent molecules (*continued*)
  as non-electrolytes, 209
  properties of, 166
Polarity
  of bonds, 184–185, 184f, 185f
  intermolecular forces, 186–188
  of molecules, 185–186, 185f
Polyatomic ion(s)
  definition, 43, 448
  in ionic compounds, 43–44, 49–50
  Lewis dot structures for, 178–179
  table of common, 44t, 432t
Polyatomic ion compound
  naming, 43–44
  writing chemical formula, 49–50
Polychlorinated biphenyls (PCBs), 309
Polyester, 401
Polyethylene, 399, 400, 400f
Polymer
  biological, 402
  Bouncy Ball Contest, 405–406
  cross-linkages, 402
  definition, 381, 398, 449
  formation
    addition polymerization, 399–400, 400f
    condensation polymerization, 400–401, 401f
  laboratory for observation of, 403–404
  plastics, 381, 402, 402f
  properties, 401–402
  side branching, 401
  table of common, 409t
  thermoplastic, 399
  thermoset, 399
Positron-emission tomography (PET), 424, 424f
Potassium-40, 425
Potential difference, 370
Potential energy, of electrons, 370
Pounds per square inch (psi), 107
Precipitate, 321f, 325, 325f, 326, 326f, 327, 449
Precipitation reaction, 221–222, 223, 224, 326
Precision, 9–11, 449
Prediction, 8–9, 449
Prefix
  metric system, 24t, 25, 430t
  molecular compound, 46, 46t, 433t
  organic, 383t, 433t
Pressure
  atmospheric, 96, 445
  barometric, 107
  changes in, 96–97

Pressure (*continued*)
  definition, 95, 449
  effect of changes on equilibrium, 302–303
  relationship to number of particles, 97, 108, 109–110
  relationship with temperature, 97, 108–110
  relationship with volume, 97, 109–110
  standard, 110
  units of, 107–108
Principal energy level, 135
Prism, 149
Problem, identifying in lab design, 18
Procedure
  changing lab, 20
  writing lab, 19
Product, in chemical equation, 60
Projects
  An endo- or exothermic reaction?, 313
  Battery research, 375
  Bouncy ball contest, 405–406
  Carbonated beverage, 245–246
  Different ways to make a gas in an airbag, 114–115
  Forensics writing project, 347
  Making a hot or cold pack, 278–279
  Making and evaluating soap, 196–197
  The most effective antacid, 72
  Research and write about nuclear waste, 427
  Writing about glowing things, 157
Proteins, 402
Proton(s)
  definition, 125, 449
  discovery of, 125
  mass of, 128
  number of, 128
Proton-pump inhibitor, 77
Pure substance, 38, 38f, 449
Purpose, identifying in lab design, 18

Q

Qualitative analysis, 327
Qualitative data, 14
Quantitative analysis, 327
Quantitative data, 14
Quantum mechanics, 127
Question, identifying in lab design, 18

R

Radiation. *See also* Nuclear radiation
 definition, 413
 electromagnetic, 148, 148f, 149
Radical, 399–400
Radioactive decay
 alpha particle, 126, 126f, 416, 416f,
  417, 422, 445
 beta particle, 416, 417, 422, 445
 gamma radiation, 416–417, 422,
  446
 half-life, 418–420, 419t, 447
 law of, 418
 nuclear dating, 425
Radioactive element, 414–415
Radioactivity
 description of, 414–415
 discovery of, 414
 types of decay, 416–417
Radius
 atomic, 144, 145–146, 183
 ion, 147
Rainbow, 149
Rate of reaction
 collision theory and, 287, 290
 effect of catalyst, 304
 reversible reaction, 287, 290
Reactant
 in chemical equation, 60
 collisions, 68–71
 excess, 237
 limiting, 236–238, 448
Reaction, chemical
 addition, 399–400, 400f
 balancing equations, 64–66
 catalysts, 71
 combustion, 353
 condensation, 400–401, 401f
 definition, 59, 445
 double replacement, 61, 61f, 223
 endothermic, 255, 303, 313
 enthalpy of chemical reaction,
  269–274
 exothermic, 255, 303–304, 313
 neutralization, 61–62, 62f, 448
 oxidation and reduction (redox),
  353, 358–366
 polymer forming, 399–401, 400f,
  401f
 precipitation, 221–222, 223, 224,
  326
 reversible, 286
 single replacement, 358–359, 359f,
  360, 449
 speed of, 67–71

Reaction, nuclear, 413, 417, 426, 448
Reaction coordinate diagram, 70f
Reaction quotient (*Q*), 298, 324–325,
 449
Real gas, 97–98
Recycling, 305, 402
Redox reaction. *See* Oxidation and
 reduction (redox) reaction
Reducing agent, 357
Reduction. *See also* Oxidation and
 reduction (redox) reaction
  definition, 354–355, 449
  half-reaction, 362, 370–371, 437t
Relaxation, 152, 152f, 153–154, 449
Representative elements, 170, 449
Research chemist, 119
Results
  data table for, 19
  discussion of, 20
Retention factor (R_f), 331–332, 449
Reversible reaction, 286, 449
RNA, 402
Rubber, 400, 400f
Rust, 353
Rutherford, Ernest, 126

S

Safety concerns, in lab design process,
 19
Salt bridge, 367, 367f
Salts, 163
Saturated hydrocarbons, 383, 386, 387f
Saturated solution, 322, 324–325, 449
Science
  description of, 5
  non-linearity of, 6
Scientific investigations
  community findings, 11
  data-gathering techniques, 7–8
  data precision and accuracy, 9–11
  designing your own labs, 18–123
  drawing conclusions, 11
  multiple trials, 9
  predictions and hypotheses, 8–9
  procedures, 9
  process overview, 6–7, 7f
  variables and constants, 6–7, 7f
Scientific notation, 30–31
Sea urchin, 413f
Significant digits
  performing calculations with,
   28–29
  rules for counting, 27–28
  rules for math, 29

Single bond, 173
Single replacement reactions, 358–359,
 359f, 360, 449
SI units, 14, 14t, 449
Smog, 310
Soap, 164f
 effect on solubility, 191, 191f
 effect on surface tension, 193–194
 experiments with, 162
 making and evaluating, 196–197
 as salts of fatty acids, 163, 192f
Sodium-24, 424
Sodium azide, in airbags, 82
Solid, properties of, 82–83, 83f
Solubility
 analysis with, 327–329
 bond type, influence of, 166
 of common compounds, 435t
 effect of intermolecular forces on,
  190, 190f
 effect of soap on, 191, 191f
 equilibrium, 322, 324
 ionic compounds, 223
 laboratory procedure, 221–222
 precipitation, 321f, 325, 325f, 326,
  326f, 327
 what substances dissolve in water,
  320–321
Solubility product, 322–325, 434t
Solubility rules, 221–222, 223, 249t,
 326, 434t
Solute, 190, 210, 449
Solution
 boiling point, 242
 definition, 210, 449
 freezing point, 243–244
 as homogeneous mixture, 39
 properties, 239–244
 saturated, 210, 322, 324–325, 449
 stoichiometry, 228
 supersaturated, 211, 449
 unsaturated, 210, 321, 324, 450
 vapor pressure, 240–241
Solvent, 190, 210, 449
Specific heat capacity (C_p), 258, 266
Spectral lines, 154, 154f
Spectrographic notation, 138
Spectrometer, 154
Spectrum, 154–155, 154f
Sports drink, 204–206, 207f
Standard reduction potential, 370, 371,
 437t, 449
Standard reduction potential table, 370
Standard temperature and pressure
 (STP), 110

States of matter
changes, 83–84, 84f, 263–269
properties, 82–83, 83f
Stationary phase, 330
Stoichiometric proportions, 236
Stoichiometry
carbonated beverage preparation,
245–246
combining molecular mass and
molarity in problems, 229
description, 227, 449
ecological, 246f
enthalpy and, 272–273
with gases, 229–230
laboratory procedures, 225–226,
233–236
with masses, 228
mole ratio in a balanced chemical
equation, 226–227
with moles, 227
with solutions, 228
titration, 230–231, 233–234
Stoichiometry point, 230
STP (standard temperature and
pressure), 110
Strong acid, 57–58, 58f
Strong base, 58
Strontium, 423, 424
Sublimation, 84
Subscript, 41
Subshells, 135, 136, 142
Supersaturated solution, 211, 449
Surface tension, 192–194, 192f, 449
Surroundings, 254–255, 449
Suspension, 39, 449
Sweat, 205–206, 255, 255f
Symbols
element, 41, 440t–442t
table of symbols, 431t
System, 254–255, 449

T

Temperature
definition, 97, 449
effect of changes on equilibrium,
303–304
effect on equilibrium constant,
293
effect on kinetic energy, 69, 240–
241, 256
effect on reaction speed, 69
kelvin scale, 108

Temperature (*continued*)
relationship with pressure, 97,
108–110
standard, 110
states of matter, relationship to, 83
Theory, 11, 449
Thermal conductance, 166
Thermal equilibrium, 261
Thermal image, 150f
Thermoplastic polymer, 399
Thermoset polymer, 399
Thin layer chromatography (TLC), 332
Thomson, J. J., 125
Titan (Saturn moon), 384f
Titration, 230–231, 233–234, 449
Tornado, 107f
Torr, 107
Trash, 305–306
Trials, multiple, 9
Triboluminescence, 156
Trinitite, 420f
Triple bond, 176, 385, 386
Tyndall effect, 39, 39f, 449
Tyrannosaurus rex, 425f

U

Ultraviolet light, absorption by ozone,
310–311
Units
abbreviations, 430t
common quantities, table of, 430t
converting, 23–26
density, 88
for measuring energy, 257
of pressure, 107–108
SI, 14, 14t, 449
volume, 25
Unsaturated hydrocarbons, 386, 387f
Unsaturated solution, 321, 324, 450
Uranium, 414, 425, 426

V

Vacuum tube, 125f
Valence electron, 138, 142, 165, 170,
450
Valence level, 164–165, 170
Valence shell electron pair repulsion
(VSEPR) theory, 182, 200t, 450
Van der Waals forces, 186. *See also*
Intermolecular forces

Vaporization, enthalpy of, 264–265,
266
Vapor pressure, 240–241, 450
Variable, 8, 446, 447
Venus, 110f
Viscosity, 190, 450
Volt, 370
Voltaic cell, 366–367, 367f, 450. *See
also* Battery
Volume
effect of changes on equilibrium,
302–303
relationship with pressure, 97,
109–110
units of, 25
VSEPR (valence shell electron pair
repulsion) theory, 182, 200t, 450

W

Waste production, 305–306
Water
acid dissociation in, 216–217, 217f
autoionization, 220
cooling curve of, 266–267, 266f
density of, 89
desalination, 307–308
dissolution of ionic compounds,
207–208, 208f, 321
dissolution of polar compounds,
209, 209f
electrolyte formation in, 208
heating curve of, 265–266, 265f
hydrologic cycle, 307
intermolecular forces of, 190, 191
polarity of, 167, 167f
pollution, 308–309
for rehydration, 206
surface tension, 192, 192f
tap, 39, 209
uses of, 308
Wavelength, 148
Wave properties, 148, 148f
Weak acid, 58, 58f
Weak base, 58

Y

-yne (suffix), 385

PHOTO CREDITS

Inc. Chapter 7 Page 250-251: © Alexander Gorbunov, 2010. Under license from Shutterstock, Inc.; Page 252, background: © Bruno Medley, 2010. Under license from Shutterstock, Inc.; Page 252, bottom: Shutterstock: Copyright (Stockbroker), 2008. Used under license from Shutterstock, Inc.; Page 255: Shutterstock: Copyright (Emmanuel R Lacoste), 2008. Used under license from Shutterstock, Inc.; Page 257: Shutterstock: Copyright (Laurence Gough), 2008. Used under license from Shutterstock, Inc.; Page 259: CHF Collections. Courtesy of the Chemical Heritage Foundation Collections, Philadelphia, PA.; Page 261: Shutterstock: Copyright (Photoroller), 2008. Used under license from Shutterstock, Inc.; Page 263: Shutterstock: Copyright (Vicente Barcelo Varona), 2008. Used under license from Shutterstock, Inc.; Page 264: Shutterstock: Copyright (Amra Pasic), 2008. Used under license from Shutterstock, Inc.; Page 269: Shutterstock: Copyright (Eugene Bochkarev) 2008. Used under license from Shutterstock, Inc.; Page 274: Shutterstock: Copyright (Laurence Gough), 2008. Used under license from Shutterstock, Inc.; Page 276: Photo courtesy of The Ohio State University Archives.; Page 278: Shutterstock: Copyright (Oliver Hoffmann), 2008. Used under license from Shutterstock, Inc. Chapter 8 Page 282-283: Shutterstock: Copyright (Jakub Niezabitowski), 2008. Used under license from Shutterstock, Inc.; Page 284, background: Shutterstock: Copyright (Charlie Bishop), 2008. Used under license from Shutterstock, Inc.; Page 284, bottom: Shutterstock: Copyright (Eugene Bochkarev), 2008. Used under license from Shutterstock, Inc.; Page 287: Shutterstock: Copyright (Orla), 2008. Used under license from Shutterstock, Inc.; Page 288: Courtesy of Actelion Pharmaceuticals, Ltd.; Page 293: Shutterstock: Copyright (Olivier Le Queinec), 2008. Used under license from Shutterstock, Inc.; Page 300: Shutterstock: Copyright (Sourav and Joyeeta Chowdhury), 2008. Used under license from Shutterstock, Inc.; Page 302: Shutterstock: Copyright (George_S), 2008. Used under license from Shutterstock, Inc.; Page 303: The credit line "Courtesy of Brookhaven National Laboratory" shall be included in the photo caption or as a separate photo credit adjacent to the image.; Page 306: Shutterstock: Copyright (Michael Zysman), 2008. Used under license from Shutterstock, Inc.; Page 307:: Shutterstock: Copyright (Dale A Stork), 2008. Used under license from Shutterstock, Inc.; Page 308: Shutterstock: Copyright (argus), 2008. Used under license from Shutterstock, Inc.; Page 309: Shutterstock: Copyright (Sai Yeung Chan), 2008. Used under license from Shutterstock, Inc.; Page 311: Shutterstock: Copyright (Dr. Morley Read), 2008. Used under license from Shutterstock, Inc.; Page 313: Shutterstock: Copyright (Laurence Gough), 2008. Used under license from Shutterstock, Inc. Chapter 9 Page 316-317: Shutterstock: Copyright (Bruce Rolff), 2008. Used under license from Shutterstock, Inc.; Page 318, background:: Shutterstock: Copyright (Katrina Brown), 2008. Used under license from Shutterstock, Inc.; Page 318, bottom: Shutterstock: Copyright (Yuri Arcurs), 2008. Used under license from Shutterstock, Inc.; Page 319: Shutterstock: Copyright (Kevin L Chesson), 2008. Used under license from Shutterstock, Inc.; Page 321, left: Steven Loy.; Page 321, right: Steven Loy.; Page 322: Shutterstock: Copyright (Kevin L Chesson), 2008. Used under license from Shutterstock, Inc.; Page 323: Shutterstock: Copyright (pgmstudio), 2008. Used under license from Shutterstock, Inc.; Page 324: Shutterstock: Copyright (Laurence Gough) 2008. Used under license from Shutterstock, Inc.; Page 325: Shutterstock: Copyright (Andrew Kerr), 2008. Used under license from Shutterstock, Inc.; Page 326: Steven Loy.; Page 327: Forensics and Investigative Technologies Division Federal Law Enforcement Training Center; Page 328: Shutterstock: Copyright (Laurence Gough), 2008. Used under license from Shutterstock, Inc.; Page 330: Shutterstock: Copyright (Kevin L Chesson), 2008. Used under license from Shutterstock, Inc.; Page 331: Shutterstock: Copyright (Stephen Sweet), 2008. Used under license from Shutterstock, Inc.; Page 332: Shutterstock: Copyright (William Attard McCarthy), 2008. Used under license from Shutterstock, Inc.; Page 333: CHF Collections. Courtesy of the Chemical Heritage Foundation Collections, Philadelphia, PA.; Page 335: Shutterstock: Copyright (RTimages), 2008. Used under license from Shutterstock, Inc.; Page 336: Shutterstock: Copyright (Dmitry Terentjev), 2008. Used under license from Shutterstock, Inc.; Page 340: Image courtesy of PAX-it software by MIS, Inc.; Page 341: Shutterstock: Copyright (Leah-Anne Thompson), 2008. Used under license from Shutterstock, Inc.; Page 343: Forensics and Investigative Technologies Division Federal Law Enforcement Training Center.; Page 344: Forensics and Investigative Technologies Division Federal Law Enforcement Training Center.; Page 346: Shutterstock: Copyright (Christopher King), 2008. Used under license from Shutterstock, Inc.; Page 347: Shutterstock: Copyright (Undergroundarts.co.uk), 2008. Used under license from Shutterstock, Inc.; Page 348: Shutter-

stock: Copyright (Elisanth), 2008. Used under license from Shutterstock, Inc.; Page 349: Shutterstock: Copyright (Dale A Stork), 2008. Used under license from Shutterstock, Inc. Chapter 10 Page 350-351: Shutterstock: Copyright (Peter Blottman), 2009. Used under license from Shutterstock, Inc.; Page 352, background: Shutterstock: Copyright (Gareth Trevor), 2008. Used under license from Shutterstock, Inc.; Page 352, bottom: Shutterstock: Copyright (Martin Fischer), 2008. Used under license from Shutterstock, Inc.; Page 353: Shutterstock: Copyright (Albert Lozano), 2008. Used under license from Shutterstock, Inc.; Page 359, left: Steven Loy; Page 359, right: Steven Loy.; Page 360: Shutterstock: Copyright (MWProductions), 2008. Used under license from Shutterstock, Inc.; Page 361: Shutterstock: Copyright (Shi Yali), 2008. Used under license from Shutterstock, Inc.; Page 363: CHF Collections. Courtesy of the Chemical Heritage Foundation Collections, Philadelphia, PA.; Page 364: Shutterstock: Copyright (Digicanon), 2008. Used under license from Shutterstock, Inc.; Page 368: CHF Collections. Courtesy of the Chemical Heritage Foundation Collections, Philadelphia, PA.; Page 369: Shutterstock: Copyright (Andrea Danti), 2008. Used under license from Shutterstock, Inc.; Page 372: Materials Research Society Science as Art Competition, and artist Fanny Beron.; Page 373: Shutterstock: Copyright (Chad McDermott), 2008. Used under license from Shutterstock, Inc.; Page 374: Shutterstock: Copyright (Ionescu Ilie Cristian), 2008. Used under license from Shutterstock, Inc.; Page 375: Shutterstock: Copyright (Daniel Padavona), 2008. Used under license from Shutterstock, Inc. Chapter 11 Page 378-379: Shutterstock: Copyright (CnApTaK), 2008. Used under license from Shutterstock, Inc.; Page 380, background: Shutterstock: Copyright: (YKh), 2008. Used under license from Shutterstock, Inc.; Page 380, bottom: Shutterstock: Copyright (Carsten Medom Madsen), 2008. Used under license from Shutterstock, Inc.; Page 381: Copyright Dr. Carl Aronson of Kettering University, Flint, Mich.; Page 383: Shutterstock: Copyright (Multiart), 2008. Used under license from Shutterstock, Inc.; Page 384: Courtesy NASA/JPL-Caltech.; Page 387: Shutterstock: Copyright (TebNad), 2008. Used under license from Shutterstock, Inc.; Page 392: Shutterstock: Copyright (MWProductions), 2008. Used under license from Shutterstock, Inc.; Page 396: Shutterstock: Copyright (Darren Hester), 2008. Used under license from Shutterstock, Inc.; Page 397: Shutterstock: Copyright (yurok), 2008. Used under license from Shutterstock, Inc.; Page 399: CHF Collections. Courtesy of the Chemical Heritage Foundation Collections, Philadelphia, PA.; Page 400: Shutterstock: Copyright (ZTS), 2008. Used under license from Shutterstock, Inc.; Page 402: Shutterstock: Copyright (Freerk Brouwer), 2008. Used under license from Shutterstock, Inc.; Page 403: Shutterstock: Copyright (ukrphoto), 2008. Used under license from Shutterstock, Inc.; Page 404: CHF Collections. Courtesy of the Chemical Heritage Foundation Collections, Philadelphia, PA.; Page 407: Shutterstock: Copyright (Kheng Guan Toh), 2008. Used under license from Shutterstock, Inc. Chapter 12 Page 410-411: Shutterstock: Copyright (Ant Clausen), 2008. Used under license from Shutterstock, Inc.; Page 412: Shutterstock: Copyright (Yannis Ntousiopoulos), 2008. Used under license from Shutterstock, Inc.; Page 413: Image Courtesy of DigiMorph.org; Page 415, top: Image Courtesy of The American Institute of Physics.; Page 415, bottom: Shutterstock: Copyright (Ilya Rabkin), 2008. Used under license from Shutterstock, Inc.; Page 417, top: Credit: Visualization Group of the DOE NNSA ASC / Alliance Center for Astrophysical Thermonuclear Flashes at the University of Chicago.; Page 417, bottom: Shutterstock: Copyright (Vannucci Roberto) 2008. Used under license from Shutterstock, Inc.; Page 418: Shutterstock: Copyright (Charles Taylor), 2008. Used under license from Shutterstock, Inc.; Page 420: Shutterstock: Copyright (Steve Shoup), 2008. Used under license from Shutterstock, Inc.; Page 421: Shutterstock: Copyright (Sam DCruz), 2008. Used under license from Shutterstock, Inc.; Page 422: Shutterstock: Copyright (Sai Yeung Chan), 2008. Used under license from Shutterstock, Inc.; Page 423: Shutterstock: Copyright (Michael Ransburg), 2008. Used under license from Shutterstock, Inc.; Page 424: Shutterstock: Copyright (Trutta55), 2008. Used under license from Shutterstock, Inc.; Page 425: Shutterstock: Copyright (Scott Sanders), 2008. Used under license from Shutterstock, Inc.; Page 426, top: Shutterstock: Copyright (Tatonka), 2008. Used under license from Shutterstock, Inc.; Page 426, bottom: Shutterstock: Copyright (gualtiero boffi), 2008. Used under license from Shutterstock, Inc.; Page 427: Shutterstock: Copyright (Daniel Mandik), 2008. Used under license from Shutterstock, Inc.; Page 428: Shutterstock: Copyright (Zholudov Serhij), 2008. Used under license from Shutterstock, Inc.; Page 429: Shutterstock: Copyright (PhotoCreate), 2008. Used under license from Shutterstock, Inc.